The story of intellectual
 disability

The Story of Intellectual Disability

The Story of Intellectual Disability

An Evolution of Meaning, Understanding, and Public Perception

edited by

Michael L. Wehmeyer, PhD

with contributions from

Ellis M. Craig, PhD

Dianne L. Ferguson, PhD

Philip M. Ferguson, PhD

Steven Noll, PhD

Robert L. Schalock, PhD

J. David Smith, PhD

Parnel Wickham, PhD

·P A U L·H·
BROOKES
PUBLISHING CO ®

Baltimore • London • Sydney

Paul H. Brookes Publishing Co.
Post Office Box 10624
Baltimore, Maryland 21285–0624

www.brookespublishing.com

Typeset by Apex CoVantage, LLC, Herndon, VA.
Manufactured in the United States of America by
Sheridan Books, Inc., Chelsea, Michigan.

All royalties from the sale of this book will be donated to the American Association on Intellectual and
Developmental Disabilities.

As applicable, photos are used by permission of the individuals pictured and/or their guardians/family, are used by
rightsholder permission, or are from the volume editor's private collection and/or in the public domain.

Permission to use the material in Figures 7.8 and 7.9 is gratefully acknowledged. The views or opinions expressed in
this book, and the context in which the images are used, do not necessarily reflect the views or policy of, nor imply
approval or endorsement by, the United States Holocaust Memorial Museum.

The graphic that appears at the beginning of each chapter ("The Idiot Fool" from Hans Holbein the Younger's
Danse Macabre, circa 1538), and also appears in Figure 4.1, is in the public domain and was retrieved from http://
commons.wikimedia.org/wiki/File:Holbein_Danse_Macabre_45.jpg

Library of Congress Cataloging-in-Publication Data

The story of intellectual disability : an evolution of meaning, understanding, and public perception / edited by
Michael L. Wehmeyer, Ph.D., University of Kansas, Lawrence.
    pages cm
  Includes bibliographical references and index.
  ISBN 978-1-55766-987-2
   1. People with mental disabilities—History.   2. Mental retardation—Social aspects—History.   I. Wehmeyer,
Michael L.

   HV3004.S85 2013
   362.3—dc23
                                                                                                    2013019452

British Library Cataloguing in Publication data are available from the British Library.

2017   2016   2015   2014   2013

10   9   8   7   6   5   4   3   2   1

Contents

About the Editor

Michael L. Wehmeyer, PhD, is professor of special education; director, Kansas University Center on Developmental Disabilities; and senior scientist, Beach Center on Disability, all at the University of Kansas. He has published 30 books and 290 scholarly articles and book chapters on topics related to self-determination, special education, intellectual disability, and eugenics. He is coauthor of the widely used textbook *Exceptional Lives: Special Education in Today's Schools*, published by Merrill/Prentice Hall, now in its seventh edition. His most recent book, coauthored with J. David Smith, is *Good Blood, Bad Blood: Science, Nature, and the Myth of the Kallikaks*, published by the American Association on Intellectual and Developmental Disabilities (AAIDD). Dr. Wehmeyer is past president (2010–2011) of the board of directors for and a fellow of AAIDD and co-editor of the AAIDD e-journal, *Inclusion*; a past president of the Council for Exceptional Children's Division on Career Development and Transition (DCDT); a fellow of the American Psychological Association (APA), Intellectual and Developmental Disabilities Division (Div. 33); a fellow and Vice President of the Americas of the International Association for the Scientific Study of Intellectual and Developmental Disabilities (IASSIDD); and former editor-in-chief of the journal *Remedial and Special Education*. He is a coauthor of the AAIDD *Supports Intensity Scale* and the 2010 AAIDD *Intellectual Disability: Terminology, Classification, and Systems of Supports* manual.

About the Contributors

Ellis M. (Pat) Craig, PhD, retired in 2003 after 36 years of service from the Texas Department of Mental Health and Mental Retardation. Dr. Craig currently consults as a psychologist for intellectual disability programs, conducting diagnostic assessments and behavior programming. In addition to authoring 22 book chapters and articles in professional journals, Dr. Craig has made presentations at numerous conferences. He has served as president of the AAIDD Psychology Division as well as president of state and regional AAIDD chapters and is a coauthor of the AAIDD *Supports Intensity Scale*.

Dianne L. Ferguson, PhD, is professor and director of program improvement and accreditation at Chapman University. She brings expertise and experience in the areas of school reform, inclusive practices, teacher education, families, and disability studies. She is experienced at preparing teachers and designing systems and approaches that support and sustain ongoing school improvement efforts that are inclusive of very diverse groups of children, youth, and their families. As a parent of a young man with significant disabilities, she has worked with families, schools, and service systems. She is currently on the board of a nonprofit organization that provides self-directed support services to adults with disabilities in Eugene, Oregon. Dr. Ferguson has taught classes and provided consultation for general and special educators in Canada, Iceland (as a Fulbright Scholar), Finland, Norway, Sweden, Denmark (also as a Fulbright Scholar), New Zealand, and India as well as in numerous states in the United States. Her areas of interest and expertise include issues and strategies for school inclusion for students with disabilities, family experience and the relationships between school personnel and families, administrator and teacher support for licensure and professional development and collaboration, and use of interpretivist research methods in education. She has served as a college administrator and consultant on higher education reform, teacher education reform, licensure reform, and ongoing assessment of teacher quality. Dr. Ferguson has published widely, is the author or co-editor of seven books, and serves as an associate editor or on the editorial board of four professional journals.

Philip M. Ferguson, PhD, is a professor in the College of Educational Studies at Chapman University in Orange, California. In addition to the history of disability, his research is focused on family/professional interactions and support policy, social policy, and qualitative research methods in disability studies and education. In addition to numerous articles, book chapters, and monographs, Dr. Ferguson's publications include *Abandoned to Their Fate: Social Policy and Practice Toward Severely Disabled Persons, 1820–1920*—a book and accompanying video on the history of individuals with intellectual disability and their families.

Steven Noll, PhD, is senior lecturer in the Department of History at the University of Florida, where he teaches American history, Florida history, and the history of disability. He is currently working on a history of the 1977 disability rights protests, tentatively titled *Nothing About Us Without Us*. He is also the author of *Feeble-Minded in Our Midst: Institutions for the Mentally Retarded in the South, 1900–1940* (1995) and co-editor (with James Trent) of *Mental Retardation in America: A Historical Reader* (2004).

Robert L. Schalock, PhD, is professor emeritus at Hastings College (Nebraska), where he chaired the Psychology Department and directed the Cognitive Behavior Lab from 1967 to 2000. Since 1972, his work has focused on the development and evaluation of community-based programs for people with disabilities and the key role that the concept of quality of life plays in the planning and delivering of individualized services and supports. Dr. Schalock has published widely in the areas of personal and program outcomes, the supports paradigm, adaptive behavior, clinical judgment, and quality of life. He is a past president (1997–1998) and fellow of the American Association on Intellectual and Developmental Disabilities (AAIDD) and chaired the AAIDD Terminology and Classification committee that issued its most recent manual on diagnosis, classification, and systems of supports. He is also coauthor of the *AAIDD Supports Intensity Scale* and the *Diagnostic Adaptive Behavior Scale*. Dr. Schalock is a frequent speaker at national and international conferences and has assisted a number of countries in their efforts to develop community-based programs for people with intellectual and closely related developmental disabilities within the context of the supports paradigm, the quality-of-life construct, and outcomes-based evaluation.

J. David Smith, EdD, is professor emeritus at the University of North Carolina at Greensboro. He also teaches graduate courses at the University of Richmond. He earned both baccalaureate and master of science degrees from Virginia Commonwealth University, and he was awarded a second master's degree and doctorate from Teachers College, Columbia University. His professional experience includes work as a special education teacher, school counselor, licensed professional counselor, professor, department chair, dean, and provost. Nearing 100 published articles, Dr. Smith regularly contributes to the literature on special education, human services, and public policy in scholarly and professional journals. He is the author or partnering author of 15 books.

Parnel Wickham, PhD, is professor of special education at Dowling College, Oakdale, New York. Her research interests include the history of intellectual disability, particularly in early New England. She has spent her entire career in the field of special education, first as founder and director of the Center for Handicapped Children, Inc., in Buffalo, New York, and then as education director of the Syracuse (NY) Developmental Center.

Preface

$\mathcal{T}$n 2005, leaders in the American Association on Intellectual and Developmental Disabilities (AAIDD) began discussions about the need for a more current history of intellectual disability. Existing texts were by then more than two decades old and had long been out of print. Given the explosion of knowledge about intellectual disability in the previous three decades, however, the feasibility of creating a single volume that did justice to most topics seemed daunting, to say the least. Take, for example, research in the eugenics era. A quick scan of *Books in Print* identified more than 50 texts on eugenics, almost all of which focused on the eugenics movement and people with intellectual disability, published since the late 1980s. A comprehensive history of just that 30-year span alone would fill multiple volumes.

The question as to what unique contribution such a volume might make was also raised, considering that there are a number of excellent scholarly texts on the history of intellectual disability available, authored and edited by distinguished historians. Professor James Trent's *Inventing the Feeble Mind: A History of Mental Retardation in the United States* (1994) and Professors Steven Noll and James Trent's edited volume *Mental Retardation in America: A Historical Record* (2004) are examples of the availability of rigorous historical treatments of aspects of intellectual disability. Source documents related to disability history are also now widely available online from sources such as the Disability History Museum (http://www.disabilitymuseum.org), which also called into question the need for a straight history.

What appealed to us, as authors, more as we discussed options was the idea of a volume that provided an informal history of what is now referred to as intellectual disability (our thanks to James Trent for leading us in this direction). *Informal* has more meanings than one might surmise, and a number of them apply to our efforts. Informal refers to something that is not formal; without formality or ceremony; casual. Our efforts with this text have been to keep the tone informal and casual; to provide a look at intellectual disability through stories, cases, anecdotes, images, and through scholarly interpretation but not to give a formal history that attempts to document every important point in the construct's history. *Informal* also refers to something that is not done in the customary way, or something that is unofficial or irregular. Again, our approach, particularly in the Modern Times chapters, where the amount of information can quickly overwhelm a reader (or writer), is irregular in that we didn't intend to review every important point or to discuss every important person. In fact, to the extent possible, we avoided the "history as a litany of great people" narrative that is so easy to fall into when writing about intellectual disability.

In general, we were really interested in questions about how the intellectual disability construct was understood and defined across time, how that affected the lives of people experiencing intellectual disability and the supports available to them, and what the lives of people with intellectual disability were like during different eras. This provided a more manageable task; for one, we did not have to document exhaustively every major event in the history of intellectual disability. Furthermore, we could bring in the voices and perspectives of people with intellectual disability and their families along with those of professionals and examine how intellectual disability was depicted in cultural artifacts.

That is the intent and structure of *The Story of Intellectual Disability*. As noted, the impetus for this text began with conversations within AAIDD, the oldest professional association in the field of intellectual disability. AAIDD publishes three journals, one of which, *Intellectual and Developmental Disabilities* (*IDD*, formerly *Mental Retardation*), focuses on issues often associated with the history of intellectual disability and how the construct is understood. The royalties from this text go to AAIDD, and in cases in which an essay that has appeared in *IDD* that informs our attempts to examine the understanding of the construct, we have included the essay or article in its entirety. Finally, it should also be noted that in attempting to write about how a construct such as intellectual disability has been understood throughout history, it is almost impossible to do so without using the language particular to the particular era. Terms referring to people with intellectual disability—ranging from *idiot* to *feebleminded* to *moron* that today are highly offensive—were at the time clinical terms, widely accepted. The terms used also help in understanding how people thought about individuals with disabilities at that time. As such, we have opted to use the terms appropriate or applicable to the particular era, and we trust the reader will understand the need so to do.

REFERENCES

Trent, J. W. (1994). Inventing the feeble mind: A history of mental retardation in the United States. Berkeley: University of California Press.

Noll, S., & Trent, J.W. (2004). Mental retardation in America: A historical reader. New York: New York University Press.

Hank Bersani, Jr., shortly after his AAIDD Presidential Speech (wearing the AAIDD Presidential Medal) with his friend and pioneering self-advocate, Bernard Carabello.

This book is dedicated to the memory of our friend and colleague, Henry "Hank" Bersani, Jr. Hank was originally a coauthor on this text, but his untimely passing deprived us not only of his warm, generous presence but also of his insight into the self-advocacy movement. Hank's 1996 book, *New Voices: Self-Advocacy by People with Disabilities*, co-edited with Gunnar Dybwad, was a milestone in recognizing the importance of the self-advocacy movement. Like many of us, Hank was concerned that people entering the field today would not understand the history of the disability movement or the devastating toll that institutionalization and segregation took on the lives of far too many people with intellectual disability. It is our hope that this text provides the context that will enable professionals and other stakeholders to understand where we have been and to avoid repeating the errors of the past. To the degree that this is achieved, we will have gone a long way toward honoring our friend, colleague, mentor, and moral compass.

1

Introduction to the
Intellectual Disability Construct

Robert L. Schalock

This text explores how the construct we now refer to as *intellectual disability* has been understood throughout history and how those understandings influenced how people with intellectual and developmental disabilities were treated. This first chapter provides the reader with a discussion of how that construct is understood currently, so as to set the stage for comparison with understandings emphasized in subsequent chapters.

*T*hroughout the historical eras discussed in this text, readers will find reference to five critical issues that have often vexed both people with intellectual disability and the societies in which they lived: 1) what to call the phenomenon, 2) how to explain the phenomenon, 3) how to define the phenomenon and determine who is a member of the class, 4) how to classify people so defined and identified, and 5) how to establish public policy that aligns societal values with services and supports for such people. The purpose of this chapter is to provide contemporary answers to each of these five issues.

Throughout the chapter I use the term *intellectual disability*, even though historically and even as of 2013 other terms are used to denote people who experience significant limitations in intellectual functioning and adaptive behavior and whose condition originates during the developmental period or before cultural norms of adulthood are reached. As discussed more fully in Parmenter (2004); Schalock et al. (2007); Schroeder, Gertz, and Velazquez (2002); and Wehmeyer et al. (2008), the term *intellectual disability* is increasingly being used internationally because it reflects the changed construct of disability; aligns better with current professional practices that focus on functional behaviors and contextual factors; provides a logical basis for individualized supports provision because of its basis in a social-ecological framework; is less offensive to people with the disability; and is more consistent with international terminology, including journal titles, published research, and organization names.

NAMING THE PHENOMENON: THE LANGUAGE OF THOUGHT AND MENTAL MODELS

Naming involves attaching a specific term to something or someone. Naming is a powerful process that carries many messages about perceived value and human relationships (Luckasson & Reeve, 2001) and is the prerequisite for defining and ultimately classifying people who are members of the class (Simeonsson, Granlund, & Bjorck-Akesson, 2006). The terminology used to refer to people with intellectual disability has varied significantly across the three eras discussed in this text: prehistory and ancient times, the Middle Ages, and modern times. Even in 2013 there is considerable variation in terminology, both nationally and internationally. As discussed in more detail in Brown (2007), Brown and Radford (2007), and Schalock (2011), these terms include *mental deficiency, mental handicap, mental subnormality, developmental disability* (especially in Canada), and *learning disabilities* (especially in the United Kingdom). The language of thought and one's mental model can influence the term that is used.

Language of Thought

Terminology cannot be separated from the language of thought. In that regard, Pinker noted, "Language is a window into human nature, exposing deep and universal features of our thoughts and feelings" (2007, p. 148). As Pinker also discussed, a "language of thought" (p. 81) includes 1) a cast of basic concepts (e.g., event, state, thing, path, place, property, manner), 2) a set of relationships that enmesh these concepts with one another (e.g., acting, going, being, having), 3) a taxonomy of entities (e.g., human vs. nonhuman, animate vs. inanimate, object vs. stuff, individual vs. collective, flexible vs. rigid), 4) a system of spatial concepts to define places and paths (e.g., the meaning of on, at, in, to, and under), 5) a family of causal relationships (e.g., causing, letting, enabling, preventing, impeding, encouraging), and 6) the concept of a goal and the distinction between means and ends. These six aspects of thought have influenced not only terminology but also the issues discussed in subsequent sections of this chapter: how the phenomenon has been explained and defined, how people defined by this have been classified, and what has been expected of them as reflected in public policy. In addition, each of these language-of-thought elements has been the basis for, and reinforcement of, one's mental model.

Mental Models

Mental models are deeply ingrained assumptions, generalizations, and images people use to understand the world (Senge, 2006). Throughout the history of intellectual disability in the Western world, a number of mental models have negatively affected the terminology used, the explanation and definition of the phenomenon proposed, the classification system used, and the policies and practices implemented. Chief among these are models of disablement that focus on personal *defectology* rather than on human potential and the ameliorating effects of environmental factors and an overemphasis on control, power, health, safety, defectology, and categorization as opposed to an emphasis on social inclusion, self-determination, personal development, community inclusion, and the provision of individualized supports (Schalock, Verdugo, Bonham, Fantova, & van Loon, 2008).

EXPLAINING THE PHENOMENON

As readers of the subsequent chapters will learn, explanations of the phenomenon of intellectual disability have varied throughout history, from those rooted in deification to those rooted in defectology. As of 2013, intellectual disability is characterized by significant limitations in intellectual functioning and adaptive behavior that manifest during an individual's developmental period. Intellectual disability is also a multidimensional state of human functioning. Understanding these two key concepts—the construct of disability and the multidimensionality of human functioning—is essential for explaining the phenomenon and also for providing a framework to understand and explain its etiology.

The Construct of Disability

The construct of intellectual disability belongs within the general construct of disability, which focuses on the expression of limitations in individual functioning within a social context and represents a substantial disadvantage to the individual. Disability has its genesis in a health condition that gives rise to impairments in body functions and structures, activity limitations, and participation restrictions within the context of personal and environmental factors (Luckasson et al., 2002; World Health Organization [WHO], 2001).

The current construct of disability has emerged since the early 1990s due primarily to an increased understanding of the process of disablement and its amelioration. Major factors in this evolution include 1) the research on the social construction of illness and the extensive impact that societal attitudes, roles, and policies have on the ways that individuals experience health disorders (Aronowitz, 1998); 2) the blurring of the historical distinction between biological and social causes of disability (Institute of Medicine, 1991); and 3) the recognition of the multidimensionality of human functioning (Buntinx, 2006; Luckasson et al., 2002; Wehmeyer et al., 2008; WHO, 2001). Because of these factors, the concept of disability has evolved from a person-centered trait or characteristic (often referred to as a *deficit*) to a human phenomenon, with its genesis in organic and social factors. These organic and social factors give rise to functional limitations that reflect an inability or constraint in both personal functioning and performing roles and tasks that are expected of an individual within a social environment (Bach, 2007; DePloy & Gilson, 2004; Hahn & Hegamin, 2001; Nagi, 1991; Oliver, 1996; Rioux, 1997; Schalock, 2004).

This social-ecological conception of disability is reflected well in current publications of both the American Association on Intellectual and Developmental Disabilities (AAIDD) and WHO. In the 2002 AAIDD manual (Luckasson et al., 2002), *disability* is defined as the expression of limitations in individual functioning within a social context and represents a substantial disadvantage to the individual. Similarly, in WHO's *International Classification of Functioning, Disability and Health* (*ICF*; 2001), disability is described as having its genesis in a health condition (disorder or disease) that gives rise to impairments in body functions and structures, activity limitations, and participation restrictions within the context of personal and environmental factors.

The importance of this evolutionary change in the construct of disability is that intellectual disability is no longer considered entirely an absolute, invariant trait of the person (DeKraai, 2002; Devlieger, Rusch, & Pfeiffer, 2003; Switzky & Greenspan, 2006). Rather, this social-ecological construct of intellectual disability exemplifies the interaction between the person and his or her environment; focuses on the role that individualized supports can play in enhancing individual functioning; and allows for the pursuit and understanding of disability identity, whose principles include self-worth, subjective well-being, pride, common cause, policy alternatives, and engagement in political action (Powers, Dinerstein, & Holmes, 2005; Putnam, 2005; Schalock, 2004; Vehmas, 2004).

Multidimensionality of Human Functioning

As proposed by WHO (2001), *human functioning* is an umbrella term for all life activities and encompasses body structures and functions, personal activities, and participation. Because all dimensions of human functioning and influencing factors are important to fully understand a person with intellectual disability, the current conceptual framework of human functioning emphasizes its multidimensional nature and the key role played by individualized supports. This conceptual model of human functioning, which is shown in Figure 1.1 and discussed more fully in Schalock et al. (2010) and Wehmeyer et al. (2008), includes the following five dimensions.

1. *Intellectual abilities:* Intelligence is a general, mental capability. It includes reasoning, planning, solving problems, thinking abstractly, comprehending complex ideas, learning quickly, and learning from experience (Gottfredson, 1997; Neisser, Boodo, Bouchard, & Boykin, 1996).

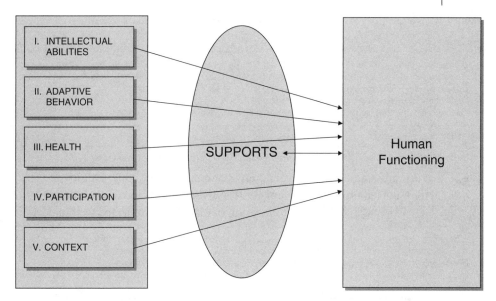

Figure 1.1. Conceptual framework of human functioning.
(From Schalock, R.L., Borthwick-Duffy, S.A., Bradley, V.J., Buntinx, W.H.E., Coulter, D.L., Craig, E.M., . . . Yeager, M.H. [2010]. *Intellectual disability: Definition, classification, and systems of supports* [11th ed., p. 14]. Washington, DC: American Association on Intellectual and Developmental Disabilities; reprinted by permission.)

2. *Adaptive behavior:* Adaptive behavior is the collection of conceptual, social, and practical skills that have been learned and are performed by people in their everyday lives (Schalock et al., 2010).

3. *Health:* Health is a state of complete physical, mental, and social well-being (WHO, 1993).

4. *Participation:* Participation is the performance of people in actual activities in social life domains and is related to the functioning of the individual in society. It refers to roles and interactions in the areas of home living, work, education, leisure, spirituality, and cultural activities (Wehmeyer et al., 2008).

5. *Context:* Context describes the interrelated conditions within which people live their everyday lives. It includes environmental and personal factors that represent the complete background of an individual's life (WHO, 2001, p. 10). Environmental factors make up the physical, social, and attitudinal environment in which people live and conduct their lives. Personal factors are characteristics of the person, such as gender, race, age, motivation, lifestyle, habits, upbringing, coping styles, social background, educational level, past and current experiences, character style, and individual psychological assets. Any or all of these characteristics may play a role in the manifestation of a disability (Schalock et al., 2010; WHO, 2001).

The Etiology of Intellectual Disability

Increasingly, the etiology of intellectual disability is conceptualized as a multifactorial construct composed of four categories of risk factors that interact across time, including across the life of the individual and across generations from parent to child. This

Table 1.1. Exemplary prenatal, perinatal, and postnatal risk factors in intellectual disability

Prenatal
• Biomedical: chromosomal disorders, metabolic disorders, transplacental infections (e.g., rubella, herpes, HIV), exposure to toxins or teratogens (e.g., alcohol, lead, mercury), undernutrition (e.g., maternal iodine deficiency)   • Social: poverty, maternal malnutrition, domestic violence, lack of prenatal care   • Behavioral: parental drug use, parental immaturity   • Educational: parental disability without supports, lack of educational opportunities

Perinatal
• Biomedical: prematurity, birth injury, hypoxia, neonatal disorders, rhesus incompatibility   • Social: lack of access to birth care   • Behavioral: parental rejection of caretaking, parental abandonment of child   • Educational: lack of medical referral for intervention services at discharge

Postnatal
• Biomedical: traumatic brain injury, malnutrition, degenerative or seizure disorders, toxins   • Social: lack of adequate stimulation, family poverty, chronic illness, institutionalization   • Behavioral: child abuse or neglect, domestic violence, difficult child behaviors   • Educational: delayed diagnosis, inadequate early intervention, inadequate special education services, inadequate family support

multifactorial understanding of etiology is replacing the historical approach that divided etiology of intellectual disability (previously referred to as *mental retardation*) into two broad types: those due to biological origin and those due to psychosocial disadvantage. The multifactorial approach to etiology expands the list of causal factors in two directions: types of factors and timing of factors (Schalock et al., 2010). In reference to types of factors, there are four categories of risk factors.

1. *Biomedical*: Biomedical factors are related to biologic processes, such as genetic disorders or nutrition, maternal illness, or parental age.

2. *Social*: Social factors are related to social and family factors, such as poverty, maternal malnutrition, stimulation, and adult responsiveness.

3. *Behavioral*: Behavioral factors relate to potentially causal behaviors, such as dangerous (injurious) activities or material substance abuse.

4. *Educational*: Educational factors relate to the availability of educational supports that promote mental development and the development of adaptive skills.

In reference to timing, the occurrence of causal factors can take place prenatally, perinatally, or postnatally. Table 1.1, which is based on the work of Emerson, Fujiura, and Hatton (2007); Schalock et al. (2010); and Walker et al. (2007), summarizes key risk factors from each of these three perspectives.

DEFINING THE CLASS

Defining involves explaining as precisely as possible the name or term of something. As stated by Felce, "The clarity of definition is clearly necessary to science" (2006, p. xiii). The definition should establish the boundaries of the term and separate who or what is included within the term from whom or what is outside the term. The importance of an operational definition is that it establishes meaning, helps meet the basic human drive for understanding, and affects a person's social and legal status (Greenspan & Switzky, 2006; Schalock et al., 2007).

As discussed later in this section, there is an important distinction between an operational and constitutive definition of intellectual disability. Before discussing the distinction, however, a little history is useful to establish a context. Historically, four approaches have been used to identify the class of people with intellectual disability: social, clinical, intellectual, and dual criterion (Schalock, 2006).

- *Social criterion*: Initially, people with intellectual disability were defined or identified because they failed to adapt socially to their environment. Because an emphasis on intelligence and the role of intelligent people in society came later, the oldest historical approach was to focus on social behavior and the natural behavioral prototype (Greenspan, 2003).

- *Clinical criterion*: With the rise of the medical model, the focus for defining the class shifted to one's symptom complex and clinical syndrome. This approach did not negate the social criterion, but gradually there was a shift toward the role of organicity, heredity, pathology, and need for segregation (Devlieger et al., 2003).

- *Intellectual criterion*: With the emergence of intelligence as a viable construct to explain the class and the rise of the intellectual testing movement, the criterion for defining the class shifted to intellectual functioning as measured by an IQ test. This emphasis led to the emergence of IQ-based statistical norms as a way to define the class and classify individuals within it (Devlieger, 2003).

- *Dual criterion*: The first attempt to use both intellectual and social criteria to define the class was found in the 1959 American Association on Mental Deficiency (AAMD) manual (Heber, 1959), which defined intellectual disability (then referred to as *mental retardation*) as referring to subaverage general intellectual functioning that originates during the developmental period and is associated with impairments in maturation, learning, and social adjustments. In the 1961 AAMD manual (Heber, 1961), maturation, learning, and social adjustments were folded into a single, largely undefined new term, *adaptive behavior*. The dual-criterion approach has also included age of onset as an accompanying element.

Operational Definition of Intellectual Disability   An operational definition focuses on the operations with which a construct (e.g., intellectual disability) can be observed and measured. An operational definition of intellectual disability includes three key aspects: 1) the actual definition and the assumptions underlying it, 2) the construct's boundaries, and 3) the use of the statistical concept of standard error of measurement (SEM) to establish a statistical confidence interval within which the individual's true score falls.

Definition and Assumptions   Based on a review of the international literature (Schalock, 2011), the most commonly referenced operational definition of intellectual disability is that promulgated by the American Association on Intellectual and Developmental Disabilities (AAIDD; formerly American Association on Mental

Retardation; American Association on Mental Deficiency). According to this operational definition in Schalock et al., "intellectual disability is characterized by significant limitations both in intellectual functioning and in adaptive behavior as expressed in conceptual, social, and practical adaptive skills. This disability originates before age 18." (2010, p. 1)

Assumptions are an explicit part of a definition because they clarify the context from which the definition arises and indicate how the definition must be applied. Thus, the definition of intellectual disability cannot stand alone. The following five assumptions are essential to the application of the previously stated operational definition: 1) limitations in functioning must be considered within the context of community environments typical of the individual's age peers and culture; 2) valid assessment considers cultural and linguistic diversity as well as differences in communication, sensory, motor, and behavioral factors; 3) within an individual, limitations often coexist with strengths; 4) an important purpose of describing limitations is to develop a profile of needed supports; and 5) with appropriate personalized supports over a sustained period, the life functioning of the person with intellectual disability generally will improve (Schalock et al., 2010, p. 1).

The Construct's Boundaries   Cutoff scores that establish the construct's boundaries are used to identify (i.e., diagnose) a person who falls within the class. Based on the presented operational definition of intellectual disability, the *identification* of intellectual disability is based on three criteria: significant limitations in intellectual functioning; significant limitations in adaptive behavior, as expressed in cognitive, social, and practical adaptive skills; and age of onset prior to age 18. Each of the first two criteria (significant limitations in intellectual functioning and adaptive behavior) is *defined* in terms of cutoff scores and *interpreted* in reference to a statistical confidence interval (Schalock et al., 2010).

- The *significant limitations in intellectual functioning* criterion for a diagnosis of intellectual disability is an IQ score that is approximately 2 standard deviations below the mean, considering the SEM for the specific instruments used and the instruments' strengths and limitations.

- The *significant limitations in adaptive behavior* criterion for a diagnosis of intellectual disability is performance that is approximately 2 standard deviations below the mean of either 1) one of the three types of adaptive behavior—conceptual, social, or practical—or 2) an overall score on a standardized measure of conceptual, social, and practical skills. As with the intellectual functioning criterion, the assessment instrument's SEM must be considered when interpreting the individual's obtained score.

Standard Error of Measurement and Confidence Interval   The results of any psychometric assessment must be evaluated in terms of the accuracy of the instrument being used. Obtained scores are subject to variability as a function of a number of potential sources of error, including variations in test performance, examiner's behavior, cooperation of the test taker, and other personal and environmental factors. The term *standard error of measurement,* which varies by test, subgroup, and age group, is used to quantify this variability and provide the basis for establishing a statistical confidence interval around the obtained score within which the individual's true score falls. From the properties of the normal curve, a range of statistical confidence can be established with parameters of at least one SEM (66% probability) or parameters of two SEM (95% probability).

Constitutive Definition of Intellectual Disability

Although the operational criteria (based on the operational definition of intellectual disability) for diagnosis have been generally consistent since the early 1950s (Schalock et al., 2007), the construct underlying the term *intellectual disability* (and, thus, the constitutive definition of intellectual disability) has changed significantly due to the impact of the social-ecological model of disability. In this model, intellectual disability is understood as a multidimensional state of human functioning in relation to environmental demands.

A constitutive definition of intellectual disability can also be used to define the construct in relation to other constructs and thus helps to better explain the theoretical underpinnings of the construct of intellectual disability. For example, Wehmeyer et al. (2008) discussed the significant differences between the construct that underlies the term *intellectual disability* and the construct underlying the term *mental retardation*. The major difference is with regard to where the disability resides: the former construct (mental retardation) viewed the disability as a defect within the individual, whereas the current construct (intellectual disability) views the disability as the fit between the individual's capacities and the context within which the individual is to function. The term *mental retardation* referred to a condition that is internal to the individual (e.g., slowness of mind); *intellectual disability* refers to a state of functioning, not a condition. Both constructions, however, see the condition (as in mental retardation) or the state of functioning (as in intellectual disability) as best defined in terms of limitations in typical human functioning.

Thus, a constitutive definition of intellectual disability defines the phenomenon in terms of limitations in human functioning, implies an understanding of disability consistent with an ecological and multidimensional perspective, and emphasizes the significant role that individualized supports play in improving human functioning. The advantages to a constitutive definition of intellectual disability are that it recognizes the vast biological and social complexities associated with intellectual disability (Baumeister, 2006; Switzky & Greenspan, 2006), captures the essential characteristics of a person with this disability (Simeonsson et al., 2006), establishes an ecological framework for supports provision (Thompson et al., 2009), and provides a solid conceptual basis to differentiate among people with other cognitive and developmental disabilities (Thompson & Wehmeyer, 2008).

CLASSIFYING MEMBERS OF THE CLASS: THE EMERGENCE OF MULTIDIMENSIONAL CLASSIFICATION SYSTEMS

All classification systems have as their fundamental purpose the provision of an organized scheme for the categorization of various kinds of observations. Classification systems are used typically for four purposes: funding, research, services and supports, and communication about selected characteristics of individuals and their environments.

Table 1.2. Exemplary components of a multidimensional classification system

Dimension	Exemplary measures	Classification scheme
Intellectual abilities	Individually administered IQ tests	IQ ranges or levels
Adaptive behavior	Adaptive behavior scales	Adaptive behavior levels
Health	Health and wellness inventories	Health status
	Mental health measures	Mental health status
	Etiologic assessment	Risk factors
		Etiology groupings
Participation	Community integration scales	Degree of community integration
	Community involvement scales	Degree of community involvement
	Measures of social relationships	Level of social interactions
	Measures of home life	Level of in-home activities
Context	Environmental assessments (physical, social, attitudinal)	Environmental status
	Personal assessments (motivation, coping styles, learning styles, lifestyles)	Personal status
Supports	Support need scales	Level of needed support
	Functional behavior assessment	Pattern of needed supports

Three classification systems most frequently used internationally are currently in the field of intellectual disability: *International Classification of Diseases* (*ICD-9-CM*; Medicode, 1998), *International Classification of Diseases* (*ICD-10;* WHO, 1993), and the *Diagnostic and Statistical Manual of Mental Disorders, Fourth Edition, Text Revision* (*DSM-IV-TR*; American Psychiatric Association, 2000). In each system, mental retardation (the term *intellectual disability* is not used, though at the time this chapter was written revisions of the *ICD* and *DSM* were underway that will include changes in terms used) is coded primarily on the basis of full-scale IQ scores.

As the field of intellectual disability moves increasingly to an ecological focus and a supports paradigm, a number of policies and practices have emerged that require a broader, multidimensional approach to classification than does the unidimensional (i.e., IQ-based) approach used by the three systems referenced previously. These changes relate to 1) grouping for reimbursement or funding on the basis of some combination and weighting of levels of assessed support need, level of adaptive behavior, health status, or contextual factors such as residential platform and geographical location; 2) research methods that focus on multidimensional predictors of human functioning or desired personal outcomes; and 3) individualized services and supports based on the pattern and intensity of assessed support needs across the five dimensions of human functioning (intellectual functioning, adaptive behavior, health, participation, and context). As a result of these changes in policies and practices, multidimensional classification frameworks are emerging that reflect the multidimensionality of human functioning, as is shown in Figure 1.1. One such framework, which is consistent with both the AAIDD system (Schalock et el., 2010) and the ICF model (WHO, 2001) is shown in Table 1.2. Although exemplary measures are referenced in the table, it is beyond the scope of this chapter to list specific assessment instruments or scales.

ESTABLISHING PUBLIC POLICY

As of 2013, international disability policy regarding people with intellectual disability is premised on a number of core concepts and principles that are 1) person referenced—such as inclusion, self-determination, empowerment, individualized and relevant supports, productivity and contribution, and family integrity and unity—and 2) service-delivery referenced—such as antidiscrimination, coordination and collaboration, and accountability (Brown & Percy, 2007; Montreal Declaration, 2004; Salamanca Statement, 1994; Shogren et al., 2009). These concepts and principles have resulted in significant changes in service-delivery policies and practices and a significant effort to conceptualize and measure important life domains. In reference to the former, policies and practices have been enacted internationally that provide education, community living and employment opportunities, technological supports and assistive technology, person-centered planning, and a framework to assess person- and family-referenced valued outcomes. In reference to the latter, the concepts and principles mentioned previously have been operationalized in the following eight universally recognized life domains (United Nations, 2006):

1. Rights (access and privacy)

2. Participation

3. Autonomy, independence, and choice

4. Physical well-being

5. Material well-being (work and employment)

6. Inclusion, accessibility, and participation

7. Emotional well-being (freedom from exploitation, violence, and abuse)

8. Personal development (education and rehabilitation)

Although there is considerable variability across countries, the net effect of these concepts, principles, and related changes has been the development of an array of services and supports for people with intellectual disability and an increasing focus on measuring public policy outcomes.

Array of Services and Supports

As is discussed more fully by Emerson et al. (2007) and Mercier, Saxena, Lecomte, Cumbrera, and Harnois (2008), people with disabilities, including people with intellectual disability, are provided with an array of educational, residential, occupational, and support services. Although the availability and composition vary across countries, the general parameters of this array include the following:

- Educational opportunities vary, from highly segregated classrooms to resource rooms to schools providing full inclusion for students with intellectual disability.

- Residential options vary, from large, congregate living facilities and nursing homes to group homes to supported community living private residences. It should be noted, however, that across the globe, only a small proportion of people with intellectual disability live in residential settings; most reside with their families (Emerson et al., 2007).

- Occupational (i.e., vocational, work) opportunities vary from day activity centers to sheltered workshops to general work skills and vocational preparation to integrated employment.

- Support services include leisure activities, transportation, assistive technology, rights and advocacy support, and nutritional assistance.

The concept of supports is being applied to people with intellectual disability in different ways. For some, the supports orientation has brought together (generally within an individualized support plan) the related practices of person-centered planning; personal growth and development opportunities; community inclusion; self-determination; empowerment; the application of positive psychology; and the application of a systems of supports that includes policies and practices, incentives, cognitive supports (i.e., assistive technology), prosthetics, skills and knowledge, environmental accommodations, and professional services (Shogren, Wehmeyer, Buchanan, & Lopez, 2006; Thompson et al., 2009). For others, a quality of life framework has been integrated into an individualized planning process so as to align supports provision within the quality of life framework and thus focus on the potentially effective role that individualized supports play in the enhancement of quality-of-life–related personal outcomes (van Loon, 2008). Yet for others, supports are provided through a community-based rehabilitation model, which consists of small programs implemented through the combined efforts of those with disabilities, their families, and the community, using indigenous supports (McConkey & O'Toole, 1995). According to Emerson et al. (2007) this model remains the centerpiece of international development strategies.

Measuring Public Policy Outcomes

Public policy outcomes can be used for multiple purposes, including analyzing the impact of specific public policies, monitoring the effectiveness and efficiency of services and supports, providing a basis for quality improvement and performance enhancement, meeting the increasing need for accountability, and helping establish the parameters of best practices. Although just appearing in the field of intellectual disability, public and social policy outcomes are being assessed in three broad areas: personal, family, and societal. The framework used to measure these outcomes is based on the delineation of valued life domains and the assessment of core indicators associated with each life domain. Table 1.3 summarizes exemplary outcome domains, including relevant published literature.

CONCLUSION

Language of thought and mental models not only explain the past and present—they also frame the future. In that regard, three contextual factors will affect how professionals and policy makers address the construct of intellectual disability in the future. The first is the increasingly recognized distinction between an *operational* definition of intellectual disability that is used to establish membership in the class from a *constitutive* definition of intellectual disability that includes an ecological construct of

Table 1.3. Public policy outcome measures: Domains and referent group

Person-referenced outcome domains*			
Rights	Personal development	Self-determination	Physical well-being
Inclusion	Emotional well-being	Material well-being	Participation

Family-referenced outcome domains**		
Family interaction	Emotional well-being	Personal development
Parenting	Physical well-being	Financial well-being
Community/civic involvement	Disability-related supports	

Societal-referenced outcomes***		
Socioeconomic position	Health	Subjective well-being

*Based on the work of Alverson, Bayliss, Naranjo, Yamamoto, and Unruh (2006); Bradley and Moseley (2007); Gardner and Caran (2005); and Schalock and Verdugo (2002).

**From Aznar and Castanon (2005); Isaacs et al. (2007); and Summers et al. (2005).

***Based on the work of Arthaud-Day, Rode, Mooney, and Near (2005); Emerson, Graham, and Hatton (2006); and Emerson and Hatton (2008).

disability and a supports paradigm that focuses on the assessment of a person's support needs and the mainstream provision of a system of supports that enhance human functioning. The second contextual factor is the emergence of a transdisciplinary approach to research that jointly involves researchers and practitioners. Such an approach results in both scientific (understanding) and social (application) effects and allows the field to better integrate principles and methods into public policy, program practices, and program standards (Walter, Helgenberger, Wiek, & Scholz, 2007). This approach to research also incorporates a more functional perspective of intellectual disability based on a multidimensional model of etiology and the principles of human potential, positive psychology, and self-determination (Emerson et al., 2007; Schalock, Bonham, & Verdugo, 2008; Shogren et al., 2006; Wehmeyer et al., 2008).

The third contextual factor is the better understanding of the role of assessment in intellectual disability. As discussed more fully in Schalock et al. (2010) and Schalock and Luckasson (2005), an assessment framework needs to meet three criteria: the assessment tools and processes should match the purpose for the assessment, the assessment findings should be as valid as possible, and the results should be both useful and purposefully applied. Furthermore, such an assessment framework needs to align data from assessment instruments and strategies to the three clinical functions of diagnosis, classification, and planning supports and would entail the following:

- Intellectual disability is diagnosed by using assessment information obtained from standardized and individually administered instruments that assess intellectual functioning and adaptive behavior and by documenting the age of onset. If the three criteria for a diagnosis of intellectual disability are met, the diagnosis may be applied to achieve several focused purposes, including but not limited to establishing the presence of the disability in an individual and confirming an individual's eligibility for services, benefits, and legal protections.

- Multiple classification systems are used to group or classify individuals with intellectual disability (or the individuals themselves) for several purposes, such as conducting research, providing service reimbursement or funding, developing services and supports, and communicating about selected characteristics. As shown in Table 1.2, a multidimensional classification system is based on the assessment of intellectual functioning, adaptive behavior, health, participation, context, and the pattern or intensity of needed supports. The particular classification system selected should be consistent with a specific purpose and used to benefit members of the group.

• Planning supports should integrate assessment information obtained from standardized and informal measures of individual support needs, person-centered planning information, and other input from knowledgeable informants.

These three contextual factors will help resolve emerging epistemological issues. Chief among these are those related to the construct of disability, how intellectual disability fits within the general construct of disability, and the relationship of intellectual disability to other developmental disabilities (Brown & Percy, 2007; Finlay & Lyons, 2005; Schalock & Luckasson, 2005; Switzky & Greenspan, 2006); the social construction of intellectual disability (Rapley, 2004); the ethical analysis of the concept of disability (Vehmas, 2004); whether the elements of the intellectual disability construct and the construct itself is relevant internationally due to the cultural relativity of the constructs of intellectual functioning and adaptive behavior (Emerson et al., 2007); and whether the functionalist-objectivist paradigm of intellectual disability can be reconciled with the interpretative-subjective paradigm of intellectual disability (Switzky & Greenspan, 2006).

In conclusion, the resolution of these epistemological issues will be facilitated by a meaningful distinction between an operational and constitutive definition of intellectual disability, the employment of a transdisciplinary approach to research, and a clear understanding of the role of assessment in the three clinical functions of diagnosis, classification, and planning supports. In addition, their resolution will be facilitated by a better understanding of the multidimensionality of human functioning, an expanding understanding of the etiology of intellectual disability and the risk factors involved in the manifestation of intellectual disability, and a general international movement toward the recognition of the legal and human rights of individuals with intellectual disability and their inclusion into the mainstream of life.

REFERENCES

Alverson, C.Y., Bayliss, C., Naranjo, J.M., Yamamoto, S.H., & Unruh, D. (2006). *Methods of conducting post-school outcomes follow-up studies: A review of the literature.* Eugene: University of Oregon, National Post-School Outcomes Center.

American Psychiatric Association. (2000). *Diagnostic and statistical manual of mental disorders* (4th ed., text rev.). Washington, DC: Author.

Aronowitz, R.A. (1998). *Making sense of illness: Science, society, and disease.* Cambridge, United Kingdom: Cambridge University Press.

Arthaud-Day, M.E., Rode, J.C., Mooney, C.H., & Near, J.P. (2005). The subjective well-being construct: A test of its convergent, discriminate, and factorial validity. *Social Indicators Research, 74,* 445–476.

Aznar, A.S., & Castanon, D.G. (2005). Quality of life from the point of view of Latin American families: A participative research study. *Journal of Intellectual Disability Research, 49*(10), 784–788.

Bach, M. (2007). Changing perspectives on developmental disabilities. In I. Brown & M. Percy

(Eds.), *A comprehensive guide to intellectual and developmental disabilities* (pp. 35–44). Baltimore, MD: Paul H. Brookes Publishing Co.

Baumeister, A.A. (2006). Mental retardation: Confusing sentiment with science. In H.N. Switzky & S. Greenspan (Eds.), *What is mental retardation? Ideas for an evolving disability in the 21st century* (Rev. ed., pp. 95–126). Washington, DC: American Association on Mental Retardation.

Bradley, V.J., & Moseley, C. (2007). National core indicators: Ten years of collaborative performance measurement. *Intellectual and Developmental Disabilities, 45*(5), 354–358.

Brown, I. (2007). What is meant by intellectual and developmental disabilities? In I. Brown & M. Percy (Eds.), *A comprehensive guide to intellectual and developmental disabilities* (pp. 3–15). Baltimore, MD: Paul H. Brookes Publishing Co.

Brown, I., & Percy, M. (Eds.). (2007). *A comprehensive guide to intellectual and developmental disabilities.* Baltimore, MD: Paul H. Brookes Publishing Co.

Brown, I., & Radford, J.P. (2007). Historical overview of intellectual and developmental disabilities. In I. Brown & M. Percy (Eds.), *A comprehensive guide to intellectual and developmental disabilities* (pp. 17–34). Baltimore, MD: Paul H. Brookes Publishing Co.

Buntinx, W.H.E. (2006). The relationship between WHO-ICF and the AAMR 2002 system. In H. Switzky & S. Greenspan (Eds.), *What is mental retardation? Ideas for an evolving disability in the 21st century* (Rev. ed., pp. 303–323). Washington, DC: American Association on Mental Retardation.

DeKraai, M. (2002). In the beginning: The first hundred years (1850 to 1950). In R.L. Schalock (Ed.), *Out of darkness and into the light: Nebraska's experience with mental retardation* (pp. 103–122). Washington, DC: American Association on Mental Retardation.

DePloy, E., & Gilson, S.F. (2004). *Rethinking disability: Principles for professional and social change.* Belmont, CA: Thomson Brooks/Cole.

Devlieger, J.P. (2003). From "idiots" to "person with mental retardation": Defining differences in an effort to dissolve it. In J.P. Devlieger, R. Rusch, & D. Pfeiffer (Eds.), *Rethinking disability: The emergence of new definitions, concepts, and communities* (pp. 169–188.) Antwerp, Belgium: Garant.

Devlieger, J.P., Rusch, F., & Pfeiffer, D. (Eds.). (2003). *Rethinking disability: The emergence of new definition, concepts, and communities.* Antwerp, Belgium: Garant.

Emerson, E., Fujiura, G.T., & Hatton, C. (2007). International perspectives. In S.L. Odom, R.H. Horner, M.E. Snell, & J. Blacher (Eds.), *Handbook of developmental disabilities* (pp. 593–613). New York, NY: Guilford Press.

Emerson, E., Graham, H., & Hatton, C. (2006). The measurement of poverty and socio-economic position in research involving people with intellectual disability. In L.M. Glidden (Ed.), *International review of research in mental retardation* (pp. 77–108). New York, NY: Academic Press.

Emerson, E., & Hatton, C. (2008). Self-reported well-being of women and men with intellectual disabilities in England. *American Journal on Mental Retardation, 113*(2), 143–155.

Felce, D. (2006). What is mental retardation? In H.N. Switzky & S. Greenspan (Eds.), *What is mental retardation? Ideas for an evolving disability in the 21st century* (Rev. ed., pp. xiii–xiv). Washington, DC: American Association on Mental Retardation.

Finlay, W.M.L., & Lyons, E. (2005). Rejecting the label: A social constructionist analysis. *Mental Retardation, 43*(2), 120–134.

Gardner, J.F., & Caran, D. (2005). Attainment of personal outcomes by people with developmental disabilities. *Mental Retardation, 43*(3), 157–174.

Gottfredson, L.S. (1997). Mainstream science on intelligence: An editorial with 52 signatories, history, and bibliography. *Intelligence, 24*(1), 13–23.

Greenspan, S. (2003). Mental retardation: Some issues for concern. In H.N. Switzky & S. Greenspan (Eds.), *What is mental retardation? Ideas for an evolving disability* (pp. 64–74) [E-Book]. Washington, DC: American Association on Mental Retardation. Retrieved from http://www.disabilitybooksonline.com

Greenspan, S., & Switzky, H.N. (2006). Forty-four years of AAMR manuals. In H.N. Switzky & S. Greenspan (Eds.), *What is mental retardation? Ideas for an evolving disability in the 21st century* (Rev. ed., pp. 3–28). Washington, DC: American Association on Mental Retardation.

Hahn, H., & Hegamin, A.P. (2001). Assessing scientific meaning of disability. *Journal of Disability Policy Studies, 12,* 114–121.

Heber, R. (1959). A manual on terminology and classification in mental retardation [Monograph suppl.]. *American Journal of Mental Deficiency, 64*(2).

Heber, R. (1961). *A manual on terminology and classification on mental retardation* (2nd ed.) [Monograph suppl.]. Washington, DC: American Association on Mental Deficiency.

Institute of Medicine. (1991). *Disability in America: Towards a national agenda for prevention.* Washington, DC: National Academy Press.

Isaacs, B.J., Brown, I., Brown, R., Baum, N., Meyerscough, T., Neikerg, S. . . . Wang, M. (2007). The international family quality of life project: Goals and description of a survey tool. *Journal of Policy and Practice in Intellectual Disabilities, 4*(3), 177–185.

Luckasson, R., Borthwick-Duffy, S., Buntinx, W.H.E., Coulter, D.L., Craig, E.M., Reeve, A., . . . Tasse, M.J. (2002). *Mental retardation: Definition, classification, and systems of supports* (10th ed.). Washington, DC: American Association on Mental Retardation.

Luckasson, R., & Reeve, A. (2001). Naming, defining, and classifying in mental retardation. *Mental Retardation, 39*(1), 47–52.

McConkey, R., & O'Toole, B. (1995). Towards the new millennium. In B. O'Toole & R. McConkey (Eds.), *Innovations in developing countries for people with disabilities* (pp. 3–14). Lancashire, United Kingdom: Lisieux Hall.

Medicode. (1998). *International classification of diseases* (9th rev.): *Clinical modification* (6th ed.). Salt Lake City, UT: Author.

Mercier, C., Saxena, S., Lecomte, J., Cumbrera, M.G., & Harnois, G. (2008). WHO ATLAS in global resources for persons with intellectual disabilities 2007: Key findings relevant to low- and middle-income countries. *Journal of Policy and Practices in Intellectual Disabilities, 5*(2), 81–88.

Montreal Declaration. (2004, December 8–10). *Montreal declaration on intellectual disability.* Montreal, Canada: PAHO/WHO Conference.

Nagi, S.Z. (1991). Disability concepts revisited: Implications for prevention. In A.M. Pope & A.R. Tarlov (Eds.), *Disability in America: Towards a national agenda for prevention* (pp. 309–327). Washington, DC: National Academy Press.

Neisser, U., Boodo, G., Bouchard, T.J., & Boykin, A.W. (1996). Intelligence: Knowns and unknowns. *American Psychologist, 51*(2), 77–101.

Oliver, M. (1996). *Understanding disability from theory to practice.* Basingstoke Hampshire, United Kingdom: Palgrave Macmillan.

Parmenter, T.R. (2004). Contributions of IASSID to the scientific study of intellectual disability: The past, the present, and the future. *Journal of Policy and Practice in Intellectual Disabilities, 1*(2), 71–78.

Pinker, S. (2007). *The stuff of thought: Language as a window into human nature.* New York, NY: Viking Penguin.

Powers, L., Dinerstein, R., & Holmes, S. (2005). Self-advocacy, self-determination, social freedom, and opportunity. In K.C. Lakin & A. Turnbull (Eds.), *National goals and research for people with intellectual and developmental disabilities* (pp. 257–287). Washington, DC: American Association on Mental Retardation.

Putnam, M. (2005). Conceptualizing disability: Developing a framework for political disability identity. *Journal of Disability Policy Studies, 16*(3), 188–198.

Rapley, M. (2004). *The social construction of intellectual disability.* Cambridge, United Kingdom: Cambridge University Press.

Rioux, M.H. (1997). Disability: The place of judgment in a world of fact. *Journal of Intellectual Disability Research, 41*(2), 102–111.

Salamanca Statement. (1994). *Salamanca statement and framework for action in special needs education.* Salamanca, Spain: University of Salamanca–Department of Psychology.

Schalock, R.L. (2004). The emerging disability paradigm and its implications for policy and practice. *Journal of Disability Policy Studies, 14*(4), 204–215.

Schalock, R.L. (2006). Scientific and judgmental issues involved in defining mental retardation. In H.N. Switzky & S. Greenspan (Eds.), *What is mental retardation? Ideas for an evolving disability in the 21st century* (Rev. ed., pp. 231–245). Washington, DC: American Association on Mental Retardation.

Schalock, R.L. (2011). International perspectives on intellectual disability. In K.D. Keith (Ed.), *Cross-cultural psychology: A contemporary reader* (pp. 312–328). New York, NY: Blackwell.

Schalock, R.L., Bonham, G.S., & Verdugo, M.A. (2008). The conceptualization and measurement of quality of life: Implications for program planning and evaluation in the field of intellectual disabilities. *Evaluation and Program Planning, 31*(2), 181–190.

Schalock, R.L., Borthwick-Duffy, S.A., Bradley, V.J., Buntinx, W.H.E., Coulter, D.L., Craig, E.M. . . . Yeager, M. (2010). *Intellectual disability: Definition, classification, and systems of supports* (11th ed.). Washington, DC: American Association on Intellectual and Developmental Disabilities.

Schalock, R.L., & Luckasson, R. (2005). AAMR's definition, classification, and systems of supports and its relation to international trends and issues in the field of intellectual disabilities. *Journal of Policy and Practice in Intellectual Disability*, *1*(3), 136–146.

Schalock, R.L., Luckasson, R., Shogren, K., Borthwick-Duffy, S., Bradley, V., Buntinx, W.H.E. . . . Yeager, M. (2007). The renaming of *mental retardation*: Understanding the change to the term *intellectual disability*. *Intellectual and Developmental Disabilities*, *45*, 116–124.

Schalock, R.L., & Verdugo, M.A. (2002). *Handbook on quality of life for human services practitioners*. Washington, DC: American Association on Mental Retardation.

Schalock, R.L., Verdugo, M.A., Bonham, G.S., Fantova, F., & van Loon, J. (2008). Enhancing personal outcomes: Organizational strategies, guidelines, and examples. *Journal of Policy and Practice in Intellectual Disabilities*, *5*(4), 276–285.

Schroeder, S.R., Gertz, G., & Velazquez, F. (2002). *Final project report: Usage of the term "mental retardation": Language, image and public education*. Lawrence: Kansas University Center on Developmental Disabilities.

Senge, P.M. (2006). *The fifth discipline: The art and practice of the learning organization* (Rev. ed.). New York, NY: Doubleday.

Shogren, K.A., Bradley, V.J., Gomez, S.C., Yeager, M.H., Schalock, R.L., Borthwick-Duffy, S. . . . Wehmeyer, M. (2009). Public policy and the enhancement of desired public policy outcomes for persons with intellectual disability. *Intellectual and Developmental Disabilities, 47*(4), 307–319.

Shogren, K. A., Wehmeyer, M. L., Buchanan, C.L., & Lopez, S.J. (2006). The application of positive psychology and self-determination to research in intellectual disability: A content analysis of 30 years of literature. *Research & Practice for Persons With Severe Disabilities*, *31*(4), 338–345.

Simeonsson, R.J., Granlund, M., & Bjorck-Akesson, E. (2006). The concept and classification of mental retardation. In H.N. Switzky & S. Greenspan (Eds.), *What is mental retardation? Ideas for an evolving disability in the 21st century* (Rev. ed., pp. 247–266). Washington, DC: American Association on Mental Retardation.

Summers, J.A., Poston, D.J., Turnbull, A.P., Marquis, J., Hoffman, L., Mannan, H. . . . Wang, M. (2005). Conceptualizing and measuring family quality of life. *Journal of Intellectual Disabilities Research*, *49*(10), 777–783.

Switzky, H.N. & Greenspan, S. (2006). Summary and conclusion: Can so many diverse ideas be integrated? Multiparadigmatic models of understanding mental retardation in the 21st century. In H.N. Switzky & S. Greenspan (Eds.), *What is mental retardation: Ideas for an evolving disability in the 21st century* (Rev. ed., pp. 341–358). Washington, DC: American Association on Mental Retardation.

Thompson, J.R., Bradley, V., Buntinx, W.H.E., Schalock, R.L. Shogren, K.A., Snell, M., . . . Yeager, M. (2009). Conceptualizing supports and support needs. *Intellectual and Developmental Disabilities*, *47*(2), 135–146.

Thompson, J.R., & Wehmeyer, M.L. (2008). Historical and legal issues in developmental disabilities. In H. P. Parette & G.R. Peterson-Karlan (Eds.), *Research-based practices in developmental disabilities* (2nd ed., pp. 13–42). Austin, TX: PRO-ED.

United Nations. (2006). *Convention on the rights of persons with disabilities*. Retrieved from http://www.un.org/disabilities/convention

van Loon, J. (2008). Aligning quality of life domains and indicators to support intensity scale data. In *Supports intensity scale companion guide: A resource for SIS users* (pp. 80–87). Washington, DC: American Association on Intellectual and Developmental Disabilities.

Vehmas, S. (2004). Ethical analysis of the concept of disability. *Mental Retardation*, *42*(3), 209–222.

Walker, S.P., Wachs, T.D., Gardner, J.M., Losoff, B., Wasserman, G.A., Pollitt, E. . . . Carter, J.A. (2007). Child development: Risk factors for adverse outcomes in developing countries. *Lancet*, *369*, 145–157.

Walter, A.I., Helgenberger, S., Wiek, A., & Scholz, R. W. (2007). Measuring societal effects of transdisciplinary research projects: Design and application of an evaluation model. *Evaluation and Program Planning*, *30*(4), 325–338.

Wehmeyer, M.L., Buntinx, W.H.E., Coulter, D.L., Lachapelle, Y., Luckasson, R.A., Verdugo, M. A. . . . Yeager, M. (2008). The intellectual disability construct and its relation to human functioning. *Intellectual and Developmental Disabilities*, *46*(4), 311–318.

World Health Organization. (1993). *International statistical classification of diseases and related health problems* (10th ed.). Geneva, Switzerland: Author.

World Health Organization. (2001). *International classification of functioning, disability and health (ICF)*. Geneva, Switzerland: Author.

2

At the Dawn of Civilization

*Intellectual Disability in Prehistory
and Ancient Times (9000 BCE to 500 CE)*

Ellis M. Craig

Although little is known about how prehistoric and ancient people understood intellectual disability or, really, whether it was even recognized in light of the context of developing humanity, it stands to reason that there were people with intellectual disability within these early societies. This chapter examines the evidence pertaining to descriptions of disability during pre- and early civilization societies. These were prescientific societies and conceptualizations of disability and intellectual disability were rooted in religious beliefs and superstition. Nevertheless, even the limited information available suggests that people with intellectual and developmental disabilities and their families were subject to discrimination and lived difficult lives.

*T*he presentation of the history of the intellectual disability construct begins 9,000 years before the common era (BCE) in a fertile river valley in what is considered to be the start of civilization. The first people arrived in what came to be known as Mesopotamia about this time. They developed primitive villages along the swamps near where the Tigris and Euphrates rivers entered the Persian Gulf (today's Iraq). Although the land was generally inhospitable, the early inhabitants survived in small villages, usually in hilly areas, because a wider variety of food options were available in such locations. Others, however, settled along the rivers and produced sufficient crops by irrigating the land. This original group of farmers was known as Sumerians and the region as Sumer. The area was later called Mesopotamia by the Greeks, as *mesopotamia* meant "between the rivers" in Greek.

What was particularly remarkable about this settlement is that most of the human population at the time were living as nomads. This settlement is considered the birth of civilization (Hyslop, Jones, & Thompson, 1987). Among other contributions, it was the first to develop irrigated agriculture on a larger scale.

By 7000 BCE, the Sumerians had built large cities along the banks of the rivers. They were so successful in agriculture that they were able to turn their attention to other skills, including trading, art, and religion. A government and military were established. They invented the first form of writing (cuneiform script) in approximately 3100 BCE, thus beginning recorded history. They pursued astronomy and developed a calendar to aid them in their agricultural pursuits. They also began responding to injury in ways that moved beyond what amounts to first aid. Important to the history of disability, treatment for physical and mental impairments began to be provided by two groups of people: the empirical practitioner and the shaman, or medicine man. Neolithic man, probably with some historical precedents, believed firmly in animism; that is, the existence of spirits that could do evil. Thus, if someone were to become ill, he or she would call upon the shaman to exorcise the evil spirits. The shaman, in turn, relied heavily on magic or special rituals, including provisions for such defensive mechanisms as fetishes (objects with magical powers), amulets (protective objects against black magic), and talismans (good luck objects). More formal treatment also existed; medical practitioners applied such techniques as massages, baths, extractions, vegetable drugs, and bloodletting. They also engaged in trepanation (i.e., removing small circular sections of cranial bone from the top of the skull), potentially to expel demons from people with mental disorders and epilepsy. The pieces of removed cranial bones (called rondelles) were taken from the living, strung on necklaces, and worn as amulets (Scheerenberger, 1983, p. 4).

Furthermore, with the shift from hunter-gatherer societies to the agrarian communities of the Sumerians, diseases such as measles, which are known to be associated with intellectual impairments if left untreated, were more easily spread.

PRECIVILIZATION

The history of intellectual disability does not, of course, begin with the establishment of civilization. The existence of intellectual disability is presumed from the time *Homo sapiens* evolved 200,000 years ago, marking the emergence of modern humans. There is no record of people with intellectual disability from precivilization eras for a variety of reasons. It is probable that in hunter-gatherer societies, infants with more serious forms of intellectual impairment simply did not survive birth or early infancy. Children with orthopedic impairments that limited their capacity to keep up the nomadic requirements of earlier humans were, probably, subject to infanticide, a practice that continued through the establishment of civilization.

That said, there is evidence of compassion associated with disability, even as early as 50,000 years ago. Perhaps the best documented instance of which was the discovery in the early 1950s of the remains of several Neanderthal people near the village of Shanidar, in northern Iraq. Although he possessed exaggerated cranial features by today's standards, in all other physical aspects Neanderthals man were quite like modern humans. Neanderthals are

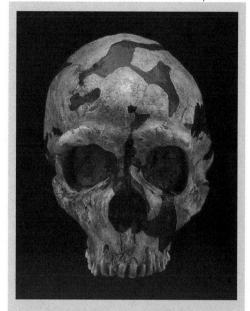

Figure 2.1. Image of Shanidar 1, skull, front view. (From Gordon, J. [2012]. *Shanidar skull*. Retrieved from http://commons.wikimedia.org/wiki/File:Shanidar_skull .jpg)

also not a direct ancestor of *Homo sapiens*. Nevertheless, they showed extreme compassion for their neighbors, as is illustrated by Shanidar I, the first remains to be discovered. Shanidar I, a male, had experienced some form of a blow to his head, damaging the orbital of his right eye and possibly resulting in blindness and impairments to his right arm and leg, resulting in, at best, a limp (Trinkaus & Zimmerman, 1982) (see Figure 2.1). Yet, despite the likelihood of traumatic brain injury and obvious physical limitations, Shanidar lived until the ripe old age—for a Neanderthal—of between 35 and 45 years, a feat that would not be accomplishable without the support of his family and peers.

It is important to note that in an agrarian society, people with intellectual disability and limited support needs would not have been identified as having a disability but would have been contributing members of their communities. In a trend repeated over history, the movement from agrarian to industrial societies introduced complexities that made successful functioning difficult for a wider array of people, including, presumably, people with intellectual disability who had limited support needs.

MESOPOTAMIA AND BABYLONIA

By 3000 BCE, there were more than a half million people in Sumer, most living in cities. Until 2800 BCE, the country was ruled by councils of elders; however, invasions by enemies had become frequent, and a single leader was appointed during these periods to direct the army. Over time these military leaders began governing all aspects of community life, essentially becoming kings. This system continued, with each king appointing a successor. Nevertheless, laws and a judicial system were established.

Social classes developed over time, and three distinct classes were identified: the aristocracy, a middle class, and slaves.

In the early years, Sumerians who became ill used spiritual remedies, primarily exorcists who would attempt to expel the demons causing the disease. Later, however, trained physicians used treatments based on compounds of natural ingredients. The golden age of Mesopotamia extended from 1700 to 560 BCE. Mesopotamian society, which was developed by the Sumerians and Semites, was creative, producing a complex oral and written language and inventing such mechanical devices as the wheel, the pulley, the screw, the wedge, and the inclined plane. Politically, it was a theocratic democracy that relied heavily upon a slavery-based economy. Disease and mental disability were viewed, if considered at all, as a punishment by God or a possession by evil spirits or the devil.

The Sumerian civilization began to unravel as various city-states within Sumer warred with each other. The Babylonian culture began to dominate the region. It absorbed much of the Sumerian culture, except for the language. The problem with the Sumerian language was that it is not linked to any other language, and thus was in the process of dying out as an active language (Nissen, 1988). Continued development of writing was based on the Babylonian Akkadian language. A direct outcome of the writing system was the development of a formal system of education. The schools were known as *edubbas*, or tablet houses. Their primary purpose was to train scribes for the necessary economic and administrative activities of agriculture and government. Most of the male students came from the wealthier class; no such education was available to the middle class and certainly not to the slaves. Kramer (1963) observes that only a single woman was documented as a scribe, and thus it is likely that the schools consisted of males only. The professors in these schools compiled the oldest known dictionaries for educating the students in the written language. The course of study began in early childhood and continued to adulthood.

In the end, one can really only speculate about the lives of people with intellectual disability in these early societies, and, as a theme that will be repeated throughout this book, most of what is known about the lives of people with intellectual disability come from observations about poverty and the poor (and slaves) during this era. Because there were frequent wars, the need for manpower was always great. Many of the poor did menial jobs and were drafted into canal building or into the army. Many of the less fortunate were reduced to begging or left to fend for themselves. People with severe intellectual impairments, often with concomitant medical issues, probably did not live long, given the absence of medical treatment, and people with less extensive cognitive impairments were probably not even noticed and were absorbed into the underclasses and the poor.

EGYPT

The world's second great civilization began along the banks of the Nile River in approximately 5200 BCE. Nomadic people began agricultural production in the silt deposited during the annual flooding of the river. A number of the Sumerian practices were adopted by these early Egyptians, including irrigation. In addition, systematic plowing, planting, and harvesting practices developed. Groups of rural villages along the Nile were eventually organized into provinces, and by 3000 BCE, Lower Egypt, to the north, where the Nile empties into the Mediterranean Sea and Upper Egypt, to the south, but upriver, were consolidated into a single state (Oakes & Gahlin, 2003).

The Egyptian pharaohs claimed mystical powers and believed that they would join the gods after death. Most Egyptians believed that immortality in an afterlife would occur as long as the body was preserved intact. Thus, the great tombs and pyramids were built to protect the bodies of the royalty through eternity. Of course, the ancient Egyptians did not understand the function of the brain, believing that the heart was the location of thinking and emotion. In fact, during the embalming process, the brain was removed and discarded as waste while the heart was left intact inside the body (Oakes & Gahlin, 2003).

Many of the grandeurs of Egypt remain and illustrate a culture of extreme ability and an artistry and craftsmanship that has rarely been exceeded. Yet, for the majority of people, life in Egypt was hard. The peasants who produced the crops were taxed heavily to support royalty and government officials. Taxation was in the form of agricultural products, and whatever was left had to feed the peasant for the year. In addition, the peasants were required to participate as soldiers in wars and in building the giant royal tombs. In fact, there was an annual requirement of 3 months labor by all adult males for building projects during the time that the Nile was flooded and agricultural activity slowed. A person with intellectual disability and limited support needs was likely able to contribute in such occupations and projects, as was anyone who was poor. It was, however, probably quite a difficult life in terms of physical demands. Oakes and Gahlin (2003) described an analysis of skeletal remains of likely workers discovered in a tomb as showing signs of arthritis, joint injuries, and a shorter lifespan than the more privileged of the time.

The Egyptians treated their children well, and there was little evidence of infanticide in the culture. There are oblique references to intellectual disability in a document called the *Papyrus of Thebes*, dated around 1500 BCE. The suggestion from this papyrus is that Egyptians conceived of mental and physical disabilities in much the same way. It is of note that Egyptian royalty apparently gave much respect to *little people* (e.g., people with dwarfism). They often attained important positions in the court. For example, the little person Seneb oversaw the royal wardrobe (see Figure 2.2). More than one cemetery devoted to little people and their families has been

Figure 2.2.   Picture of the tomb of Seneb and his wife. (From Bodsworth, J. [2007]. *Seneb and wife statue.* Retrieved from http://commons.wikimedia.org/wiki/File:Seneb_and_wife_statue .jpg)

discovered. Thus, it would appear that Egyptians were not prejudicial about people with physical disabilities. Dersin (1997) noted that being a musician was one of the few occupations available for people who were blind. An excavated carved image also illustrates an apparently honored man with a withered leg that was possibly the result of polio. However, it was also suggested that those who could not work might become beggars.

As in other great civilizations, the priests were the primary scientists, especially in astronomy. They also directed the worship of approximately 2,000 gods. However, the temples were not places of worship for congregations. Only the priests were usually allowed inside, to carry out designated rituals, but votive offerings might be made at a temple. For example, at the Temple of Satet in the Egyptian city of Elephantine, many figures of children were found, suggesting that the shrine may have attracted women hoping to give birth or seeking blessings for a newborn. It was also posited that the very form of particular deities was apotropaic (i.e., to ward off harm). For example, there is "the protective goddess of childbirth, Taweret, who is portrayed as a hippopotamus with additional characteristics of a crocodile and a lion. The idea was that such a potentially threatening combination would keep harm away from mother and child" (Oakes & Gahlin, 2003, p. 269). There is a similar story about the deity Horus, whose eyes were gouged out, but his eyesight was eventually restored. Thus, the Eye of Horus came to symbolize healing. Another example was the god Bes, whose gargoyle-like looks were thought to repel evil spirits. He was particularly associated with protection during childbirth and the early childhood years.

It is not surprising that there was widespread belief in spiritual causes of disease or disability. The cause could range from an angry deity to an evil demon, or even the ghost of a dead relative. Magic rituals to cure the ailment were offered by priests and other respected members of the community. The rituals usually involved recitation of a particular spell, based on the source of the problem. Even if more direct treatments were given in the form of internally or externally applied substances, rituals and spells were considered necessary. However, Dersin (1997) observed that typical salves and poultices were often intentionally made from distasteful ingredients, such as excrement, for the purpose of making the body repugnant to the disease or demon. Lack of basic hygiene was an endemic problem and likely led to many otherwise preventable diseases that most likely resulted in intellectual disability. Oakes and Gahlin (2003) suggest that the Egyptians accepted some illnesses as incurable and made no attempts to use the beginning of more mainstream medical training, which was available at the temples.

Magic rituals were especially invoked to ensure trouble-free pregnancies and births. Spells calling on the assistance of the goddess Hathor during the birth process were accompanied by music, singing, and dancing. Following the birth, the mother and child were separated from the outside world for a period of 14 days. At the end of the period, there was a ritual cleansing of the baby and the eating of a honey cake, considered necessary to keep the demons at bay. The use of spells was considered necessary to prevent infant illnesses, and mothers continued to nurse their children for at least three years. Nevertheless, mortality rates were extremely high, with estimates that only 50% of children reached age 5.

Beginning during the era of the Middle Kingdom (2000 BCE) the Egyptians conquered neighboring lands, particularly Nubia to the south. In turn, an Asiatic tribe called the Hykos conquered Egypt and ruled it from 1720 to 1580 BCE. After this, the Egyptians maintained some control over the Near East and were able to repel most invaders until Alexander's conquest centuries later (332 BCE).

PALESTINE

In the Early Canaanite or early Bronze Age (3150–2200 BCE), population in this region began to increase, primarily in city-states. These new inhabitants were Semitic speaking and likely came from Arabia. After initially prospering, the region suffered a severe drought and waves of invaders, reducing the area to bare subsistence. Palestine had both the fortune and the misfortune to lie midway between Egypt and Mesopotamia. This location brought trade, but it also brought war. Although it had few rivers, there was sufficient rain for productive agriculture. Furthermore, wells and a system of canals allowed the population to thrive.

The Canaanites were a very religious, polytheistic people. One of their sayings was, "Fools say to themselves, 'There is no God'" (Grant, 1997, p. 21). The religion, especially the primary deity El, had a major influence on Jewish practices. Since El was considered a charitable god, the Canaanite kings emphasized the importance of showing such behavior toward the underprivileged. Nevertheless, sacrifice of a firstborn son or daughter was considered the surest way of appeasing the deities in troubled times. Grant observed that the Jewish religion inherited much from that of the Canaanites, including a belief in a compassionate and merciful god who the people were to emulate.

GREECE

The history of Greece spans from the Heroic Age, roughly 1300 to 1100 BCE (immortalized by Homer, who, it should be noted, was blind), to a time of relative stagnation in the development of Greek culture and thought (1100 to 800 BCE), to the Archaic Period (800 to 480 BCE), to the Classical Period (roughly the fifth to the fourth centuries BCE), to the Hellenistic Period, lasting from the death of Alexander the Great in 323 BCE to the annexation of Greece by Rome in 146 BCE. One of the signature features of Greek culture throughout this time was an emphasis on physical robustness, strength, and beauty.

This emphasis is evident in Classical-era city-states such as Sparta. The Spartan army was the city-state's main source of power and pride. Every male was trained for war and was subject to military service from age 20 to age 60. The process of preparing men for war began at birth. A ruthless eugenics required that every child not only survive the father's right to infanticide but also be approved by a state council of inspectors. Any child who appeared deformed or defective in any way was thrown from a cliff on Mt. Taygetus. An essential part of child rearing was to toughen the child through exposure and physical stress. Selection of mates likewise emphasized eugenics. People considered the health and physical attributes of potential mates, and it was deemed absurd to mate with someone "who might be foolish, infirm, or diseased" (Durant, 1939, p. 82).

It seems obvious that a person with a more severe intellectual disability would have not been able to survive in Sparta, even if the intellectual impairment was not obvious at birth. A person with intellectual disability who needed minimal support and had a strong body, on the other hand, may have adapted well to this extreme culture.

Another city-state, Athens, was significant in emphasizing, at least during its formative and golden years, a democratic system of government, individual freedom, enterprise, and thought. Although children were highly prized and cherished, Athens, like other city-states, practiced infanticide. The nature and degree of this practice varied considerably over the years. In the beginning and during the golden years, infanticide was primarily limited to the weak or deformed. However, the practice varied from that of the Spartans. Newly born infants were placed in a large, earthen jar, which was placed by a temple in the event that someone might wish to adopt the child.

As Athens grew in affluence and its social values changed, infanticide became a common practice. By the third century BCE, most baby girls were automatically destroyed; only one family in a hundred had more than one girl. The lower classes killed so many of their children that the death rate exceeded the birth rate. "The whole of Greece," wrote Polybius in 150 BCE, "has been subject to a low birth rate and a general decrease of the population owing to which cities have become deserted and the land has ceased to yield fruit" (Scheerenberger, 1983, p. 13).

Most people with an intellectual disability were not conceptualized as such and existed, in all likelihood, among the poor and slaves. Slaves were an important element in the economy. Plato condemned the enslavement of Greeks but accepted it for others on the basis that some people have "unprivileged minds" (Durant, 1939, p. 180). He also recommended "exposure of all feeble children, and those born of base or elderly parents" (p. 287). As noted previously, it was legal for an Athenian father to expose (i.e., commit infanticide by exposing to the elements) a newborn child who was weak or deformed. This practice was also seen as a legitimate form of population control. However, at least in Athens, once a child was accepted into the family, it could not legally be exposed.

Boys were educated by private tutors; thus, poor children were not likely to receive an education. Females were educated in the home and received little training that was oriented toward mental development. As in Sparta, physical fitness was highly prized but there was less rigid training in Athens.

Despite being described as not particularly altruistic, wealthy Athenians were presumably generous in philanthropy, especially for the poor, people with disabilities, and the elderly. Durant (1939), however, quoted Thucydides as saying, "Men are more anxious to be called clever than honest, and suspect honesty of simplicity" (p. 295). In the same vein, Durant wrote, "The Athenians are too brilliant to be good, and scorn stupidity more than they abominate vice" (p. 297).

The rise of rational medicine was one of Greece's greatest contributions to the world. Its leading figure was Hippocrates, who was said to have liberated medicine from both philosophy and religion. He originated the doctrine of *humors*, which posits that the body is composed of blood, phlegm, yellow bile, and black bile. Perfect health requires that these elements be proportional and mingled. This theory was still influential in the 19th century.

One of the areas of disability about which Hippocrates wrote was epilepsy. Typical of most Greeks, Hippocrates believed that health involved the balance or the harmonious relationship of basic body substances, in this case, the four humors. Each of these substances had a specific location: in the heart, liver, spleen, and brain, respectively. Medical authors of subsequent years would relate mental illness and occasionally intellectual disability to the lack of balance due to "sluggish" black bile.

There are numerous references to people having limited intellectual functioning in Greek literature, although these references refer to a generic sense of incapacity and not any real understanding of intellectual impairment. In *Choephoroe,* Electra influences Orestes as "she pours into his simple mind the thought that he must kill their mother" (Durant, 1939, p. 389); Oedipus was exposed, but rescued by a shepherd; *The Trojan Women* includes the line, "Dance like an idiot in the wind" (Durant, 1939, p. 409). In describing his ideal society, Plato wrote,

> At twenty all are to be given physical, mental, and moral tests. Those that fail will become the economic classes of our state—businessmen, workingmen, farmers; . . . The survivors of the first test will receive ten further years of education and training. At thirty they will be tested again. Those that fail will become soldiers; . . .Those that pass the second test will now (and none before) take up for five years the study of the "divine philosophy" . . . At thirty-five, the survivors, with all the theory in their heads, will be flung into the practical world . . . At fifty such of them as are still alive shall become, without election, members of the guardian or ruling class. (Durant, 1939, p. 521)

According to Grant (1991), Plato also took the position that governmental rules should be implemented by force, if necessary, because reasoning is not the "natural inclination" of most people. Berkson (2004) argued that neither Plato nor Aristotle developed any explicit description of intellectual disability. They certainly recognized the variation in intelligence between people and provided views about rational thinking that could be considered the basis of the modern concept of intellectual disability. Although Plato discussed "ignorance," Berkson suggested that Plato's definition did not discriminate between simple naiveté, lack of opportunity, and lack of thinking ability. Another point raised by Berkson is that the Greeks did not view disability as a trait of the individual. One has a disability only if unable to function in society. This is consistent with a view that adaptive behavior is more important than intelligence in defining the construct of intellectual disability.

Durant (1939) claimed that Aristotle's *History of Animals* was the most influential scientific product of classical Greek civilization. It had a strong impact on physicians for centuries afterwards. His approach to classification of observations provided an underlying structure for later science.

ROME

Ancient Rome spanned a period of approximately 1300 years, from 800 BCE until the successful invasions of Germanic tribes in 476 BCE. Early in the Republic, Roman traditions mirrored those described in Greece. Families were patriarchal units, where the father held the power of life, death, and sale into bondage or slavery. The power of the Roman father over the lives of his children has no parallel in any other society. He could kill them, mutilate them, or sell them. Children were, in essence, property. Healing and medicine remained primarily a matter of herbs, magic, and prayer. The few physicians in Rome at the time, and well into the future, were primarily from Greece.

By the first century BCE, however, circumstances altered. By this time, Rome had become an empire, but was torn by a century of strife and civil war. Slavery and massive poverty resulted in children being viewed as liabilities instead of assets. Childbirth rates dropped significantly and infanticide became even more prevalent. Unwanted infants were placed at the base of *Columna Lactaria*, located in the produce market, *Forum Holitorium*. Apparently intended as a public charity where poor parents could bring their children for milk, the *Columna Lactaria* also became a location for child abandonment.

One of the few direct observations about a child with intellectual disability was offered by Roman Emperor Nero's mentor and friend, Lucius Annaeus Seneca (5 BCE–65 CE), one of Rome's greatest Stoic philosophers and lawyers. In a letter to a friend he wrote the following:

> You know that Herpaste, my wife's fool, was left on my hands as a hereditary charge, for I have a natural aversion to these monsters; and if I have a mind to laugh at a fool, I need not seek him far, I can laugh at myself. This fool has suddenly lost her sight. I am telling you a strange but true story. She is not aware that she is blind and constantly urges her keeper to take her out because she says my house is dark. (Scheerenberger, 1983, p. 17)

Vespasian (69–79 CE) established the first system of state education in classical antiquity, opened schools of medicine, and fostered the development of hospitals. Both men and women were encouraged to become physicians, and many were appointed to treat the poor at state expense. Although magic and superstition still reigned as primary medical treatment modalities—especially among the poor, which included the bulk of Roman society at any time—many specialties were developed, including urology, gynecology, obstetrics, ophthalmology, and dentistry.

As a result, knowledge about the anatomy and function of human systems began to emerge. Scientist and philosopher Galen of Pergamon (138–201 CE) created cerebral and spinal lesions to trace nerve pathways, accurately described the cranial bones, identified a neurological cause of aphasia, and ascertained that damage to one side of the brain would be manifest in bodily disorders on the opposite side. Galen, considered to be the father of experimental neurology, established the link between the brain and intelligence or cognitive functioning.

Aurelius Cornelius Celsus used the term *imbecillus* in *De Medicina,* an encyclopedia written in approximately 47 BCE. *De Medicina* encapsulates knowledge from ancient Greece and was used during the Middle Ages. *Imbecillus* denoted a general weakness or any form of debility. While Celsus was a competent writer, his attitudes toward the people with mental impairments were quite negative. He emphasized—for almost any minor infraction—the *fright hypothesis*, which in one form or another would be practiced until well into the 20th century. This consisted of torturing a person through food deprivation, chaining, or other means, until the person learned or remembered something. This was among a number of essentially punitive, and obviously ineffective, treatments that began to be implemented (Scheerenberger, 1983).

By the fourth century CE, however, state-mandated Christianity was beginning to exert its influence on Roman values and beliefs. Edicts against infanticide and the selling of children into slavery were issued by a series of Roman emperors, from

Constantine (in 315 and 321 CE) to Valentinian III (451 CE). In 314 CE, the Council of Ancyra decreed that a woman who killed her offspring should not be permitted to enter a church for the rest of her life. The Council of Nicaea (325 CE) decreed that in each Christian village a hostelry for the sick, poor, and vagrant should be established. Some of these became asylums for children. The Council of Vaison (442 CE) provided that an abandoned child should find sanctuary in a church for 10 days and that its parents must be found (Scheerenberger, 1983).

CONCLUSIONS

This book attempts to understand how the construct of intellectual disability was understood, how people with intellectual disability were treated and what their daily lives were like, and to "hear" from the voices of people with intellectual disability from that era. One can only speculate about these issues for people with intellectual disability in prehistory and antiquity. Very little direct information is available about people with intellectual disability, or any common individual, for that matter, during these earlier times. Historical anecdotes provide the bulk of the source material, and even those are limited.

Berkson (2004) has provided the most current and most extensive summary of the history of intellectual disability in prehistory, and his article is provided as Figure 2.3. Until the Common Era, cognitive and behavioral functioning were not associated with brain and neural functioning. Until Celsus used the term *imbecillus* as a medical term during the first century CE, there was no term to reflect the state of functioning of intellectual disability. It is incorrect, however, to associate the terms in antiquity, such as *imbecillus* and *idios,* with their commonly understood antecedents *imbecile* (or *imbecility*) and *idiot* (or *idiocy*). *Imbecillus* simply meant weak or feeble, ineffective; *idios* meant a private person, someone who was different. The Greek word *fatuity,* now known primarily for its adjectival form, *fatuous,* meant witless, but more in a sense of foolishness or silliness. If, as was suggested in the first chapter, naming is a prerequisite for defining and classifying people who are members of a class, then it would remain for peoples in the Middle Ages to name the state of functioning called intellectual disability.

To understand how intellectual disability was understood in any era, it is necessary to understand how intelligence was understood in that era. Cognition and neural functioning were not concepts understood in prehistory and antiquity. There was, however, as Privateer (2006) has noted, a tradition of intelligence in antiquity; "the Greeks produced three notions of intelligence: intelligence as a divine, absolute entity, . . . intelligence as a divine gift, given to humans, and intelligence personified, with the divine nature of intelligence incarnated as sophos, sophists, or Sophia; the clever, wise or highly knowledgeable person" (p. 23). Intelligence, as Privateer emphasizes, was associated with the divine, a notion that was to remain intact until John Locke and others challenged it in the late 16th century. It is not a stretch of the imagination to think that in prehistory and antiquity, when intelligence was seen as divinely granted and physical beauty was revered, people who might be considered neither intelligent nor physically attractive, more or less manifesting clear intellectual and physical impairments, were not highly valued.

MENTAL RETARDATION VOLUME 42, NUMBER 3: 195–208 | JUNE 2004

Intellectual and Physical Disabilities in Prehistory and Early Civilization

Gershon Berkson

Abstract
This paper is focused on three basic questions: The first concerns when specific disabilities first appeared during human evolution. The second question has to do with causes of disabilities. The third question concerns social responses to people with disabilities. Discussions on each of the issues are presented.

A great deal has been learned in the last 40 years since Kanner (1964) wrote his 2-page history of the dawn of concepts of mental retardation. By the early 1980s, Grmek (1983, e.g., p. 118) mentioned certain syndromes of mental retardation in his general review of illness in ancient Western civilization, and Scheerenberger (1983, pp. 3–16) was able to include the outlines of the current picture, primarily from secondary sources. Goodey (1995, 2001) has covered concepts of mental retardation from classical Greece through the 19th century. In the following article I attempt to bring the literature up to date through a review of what is known about the earliest history of general intellectual disabilities and relevant physical disabilities, primarily from the fields of paleopathology and ancient history.

This review is dominated by three central questions: What disorders were present in prehistoric populations and when did they appear? What were the causes of diseases, and what did these causes tell us about the societies in which these conditions occurred? Third, what was the social status of people with disabilities? I deal with the first two questions in the third and fourth sections of this paper, with a review of relevant paleopathological (archaeological) material. The fifth section also includes evidence from the field of ancient history.

The time spanned in this review is from prior to the evolution of human beings through classical Greece (about 2,500 years before the present, B.P.). This end point was chosen because it represents the dawn of the concepts underlying the formal definition of the modern concept of mental retardation.

Although it is likely that disabilities occurred and that they were recognized in ancient Asia or sub Saharan Africa (the area south of the Sahara Desert), I was able to find few relevant references about them for those regions (see Miles, 1997, and Savithri, 1987, for exceptions). Therefore, the material covered in this article deals mainly with Europe and the Americas. Also neglected in this review is coverage of mental illness because inclusion of that field would expand the last section of this paper unduly. For those interested in the history of mental illness, that aspect of the literature is covered in a monograph by Roccatagliata (1986) and for classical Greece, by Dodds (1963, chapters 3 and 4). The review by Dodds covers only chronic diseases. A good general review of acute diseases and their medical treatment is available in several general histories of medicine (e.g., A. Lloyd & Petrucelli, 1987).

The main points emphasized in this article include, first, the idea that individuals with mental and physical disabilities have been members of society since the emergence of Homo sapiens and probably well before that. Second, the increase and concentration of human populations and the development of agrarian societies brought with them an increase of certain diseases and the appearance of new disabilities. Third, nonhuman primate societies and human groups vary in their response to individuals with serious disabilities. Depending on

MENTAL RETARDATION   VOLUME 42, NUMBER 3: 195–208 | JUNE 2004

Early history of disabilities   G. Berkson

physical environmental factors and, particularly, on age and cultural factors, people with disabilities may be adulated, cared for, ignored, or rejected. Extended families probably provided compensatory care.

Most of the work in this field has been published in the last 30 years. However, for mental retardation workers, special mention should be made of Warkany's (1959) article on the history of teratology and Edgerton's (1968) cross-cultural survey of mental retardation in modern nonindustrialized societies. Warkany reviewed the history of thinking about malformations back to about 4,000 B.P. The earliest ideas were that malformations could predict the future. The author also covered reviews about causes, including the ideas that mental impressions on the mother and sexual congress with animals or with demons could produce malformations. It contrasts these ancient ideas with the modern science of teratology.

Edgerton's (1968) article provides a conceptual basis for understanding the cross-cultural literature in paleopathology. Archaeologists often use anthropological data to complement their observations on ancient societies. Edgerton's conclusions were highly tentative because the anthropological literature on social aspects of disability in nonindustrial societies was (and still is) meager and highly dispersed. However, in his review, he was able to challenge what he perceived as conventional views of the social status of people with disabilities. He denied that people with severe mental retardation are universally killed, that mild mental retardation is not noticed, that it is not stigmatized, and that it is not a problem for the societies involved. Instead, he emphasized that inter- and intracultural variation is characteristic of the social status of people with mental retardation and disabilities. This variation is partly accounted for by environmental stress, but cultural variations are other important determinants.

There are several recent general introductions to archaeological study of diseases and disabilities (i.e., paleopathology). Brief texts, articles in general encyclopedias, and textbook chapters provide very general introductions. For instance, Mays' (1998) text, Renfrew and Bahn's (2000) advanced introductory text, and one by Larsen (1997) provide general overviews. Especially useful for delving deeper into the field is a compendium of all known syndromes with references to specific articles (Aufderheide & Rodriguez-Martin, 1998). Also useful for this purpose are computerized databases (e.g.,

PubMed, which at the time of this writing, lists about 1,250 abstracts under the keyword *paleopathology*). There are not many general reviews of the history of disabilities; that is, after the emergence of civilization. However, Garland (1995) provided an extensive coverage of physical disabilities in ancient Greece and, to some extent, Rome.

More recent sources that might be of particular interest to mental retardation researchers are sections of recent chapters by Berkson (1993) and Braddock and Parish (2001). These researchers emphasize the complex nature of the responses to people with disabilities that have characterized society early in our evolutionary history. These complexities will be dealt with in more detail below.

Data Sources

The study of disability in prehistory and ancient history includes data from physical and cultural sources. The physical measures include mainly studies of abnormalities of bone (e.g., fractures, osteoarthritis, and specific malformations) and teeth (e.g., hypoplasias and developmental measures). Hair is sometimes also available for studies of effects of toxicity. Cultural data include "grave goods" (i.e, objects that are buried with skeletons), art objects depicting disabilities, and ancient written descriptions of disability. Less direct, but widely used, descriptions of epidemiology and anthropology in modern populations complement these more direct data. In general, my main interest in this article is in intellectual disabilities. Physical disabilities may or may not help to understand the emergence of our concepts of intellectual disabilities and are brought out when there are no data on intellectual disabilities or when they are clearly applicable to the main point being explicated.

General sources on methods include contributed chapters to Katzenberg and Saunders' edited volume (2000), in which the authors strongly emphasized methodology; chapters in a text on human osteology by White and Folkens (2000); and a volume on data standards by Buikstra and Ubelaker (1994) that provides excellent photos of bone and tooth abnormalities. The photos are accompanied by explanatory text and applications.

It will come as no surprise to readers to learn that archaeological data about ancient populations are hard to come by, and interpretation of those data often is also difficult. At least as important, bias in sampling of skeletons in burials is very com-

(continued)

Figure 2.3. *(continued)*

MENTAL RETARDATION   VOLUME 42, NUMBER 3: 195–208 | JUNE 2004
Early history of disabilities   G. Berkson

mon. In many ancient societies, not everyone was buried after death, and usually the bones only of adults and privileged people may be available (Papadopoulos, 2000, summarized the complex literature on this subject). In numerous societies, burial of many individuals in the same grave was the common practice, and in those cases, bones and teeth from different individuals may become lost; therefore, separate identification of specific skeletons is difficult.

Another source of bias is *taphonomy*, the natural destruction of biological tissue. One relevant taphonomic factor is the chemical nature of the soil. For instance, acidic soil destroys biological material very rapidly. Another problem is that all or parts of skeletons may disappear due to the action of animals.

These factors militate against reliable and valid estimates of prevalence in a population, not only because the instances of disabilities are probably underestimated, but also because population estimates of the group as a whole are difficult. These and several other sources of error make the science of paleopathology difficult (see Goodman, 1993, Stewart, 1969, and discussion below).

The characteristics of graves, sculptural, and figurative depictions (e.g., Anadiotis, 2000), and written products are the data used to assess the occurrence and social and cultural response to disabilities. Writing developed only 5,500 B.P. and known writings about disabilities did not appear before 4,400 years ago in the Middle East.

Moreover, although morbidity and mortality are higher in children than in adults, not only in modern underdeveloped countries, but also in archaeological material (Goodman & Armelagos, 1989), estimates of age in children are crude. This is especially important when one is interested in rates of development, so the difficulty of assessing age works against any precise estimates of rates of development in any individual. Age in children is usually determined through measures of the length of the long bones of the body (i.e., radius, ulna, tibia, and fibula). More stable than this indirect measure of height is an estimate of the eruption of the teeth. Even this best estimate of age is sometimes problematic in children with developmental delays, however, because the various anatomical measures of age are themselves delayed by the disorganization of growth that is common in people with mental retardation (Brothwell, 1960). It may be possible to correct somewhat for this problem by

the assessment of Harris lines (radio opaque lines that are formed in long bones during periods in which physical growth was disrupted). Nevertheless, the precision of physical and behavioral growth rate estimates that is currently possible may never be feasible in archaeological material. Despite these problems with age estimates, it has been possible to develop some data on morbidity over development during the childhood years (e.g., Goodman & Armelagos, 1989).

Perhaps most important, it seems in principle impossible to assess mental retardation directly from archaeological material. As I hope to make clear below, syndromes that include mental retardation as one defining characteristic (e.g., Down syndrome) might ultimately become the subject of serious study. However, because mental retardation is defined by behavior and we do not have samples of behavior from physical archaeological material, there are real limitations to the study of mental retardation from biological data. In particular, instances of mild mental retardation might not be detectable. On the other hand, pictorial and verbal references to disabilities are also part of the archaeological record, and it is from these depictions that the main history of mental retardation in antiquity ultimately will be written. The story for ancient Greece has been sharpened significantly by the work of Garland (1995), Goodey (1992, 1995, 1999, 2001), and Edwards (1996, 1997), but almost all other of the great civilizations need more integrative attention. Therefore, real barriers to development of a picture of disabilities in ancient times are apparent. Nevertheless, much is known, and I now turn to a summary of answers to the three major questions cited at the beginning of this paper.

First Appearance of Disabilities

"It has long been known on the basis of skeletal pathology that man has suffered disease and pain throughout his biological history" (Goldstein, 1969, p. 286). This general statement certainly applies to a variety of conditions, including disabling bone fractures and malformations in nonhuman primates, prehuman hominids, and early Homo sapiens. Nevertheless, finding examples of severely disabling conditions is remarkable, not only because of the general difficulties of archaeological work cited above, but also because of the generally low prevalence of severe disabilities and a higher mortality rate of individuals who suffer from them.

MENTAL RETARDATION   VOLUME 42, NUMBER 3: 195–208 | JUNE 2004

Early history of disabilities   G. Berkson

Nevertheless, many examples do exist. Schultz (1956) provided a detailed listing of the occurrence and frequency of diseases, parasites, fractures, osteoarthritis, and teratological conditions found in natural populations of monkeys and apes. Many instances of these conditions were relatively minor, but certainly some of the fractures must have been severely disabling, at least in the period that they were healing. Modern behavioral studies have supported the view that at least some monkeys and apes can survive with severe injuries. Perhaps the most famous of these are the individuals who are members of free-ranging Japanese monkey groups and who have thalidomide-like malformations (Furuya, 1966; Nakamichi, Fujii, & Koyama, 1982). Also, Berkson's (1977) experimental studies of macaque monkeys in natural, free-ranging, and laboratory groups is another example (see below for a more complete description of these studies).

There are fewer data for proto-human hominids. In a popular article Bower (1994) referred to a 400,000-year-old cranium found by Jean-Jacques Hublin that seemed to have an abnormality of fetal origin limiting head and limb movement. Better known are analyses of some Neanderthal skeletons. Neanderthals overlapped with Homo sapiens in Europe from about 100,000 to 30,000 years ago, when Neanderthal became extinct. Straus and Cave (1957) showed that the traditional picture of Neanderthal man as having a bent posture was incorrect because that posture was due to osteoarthritis in an elderly specimen. Osteoarthritis was common in ancient populations and is still prevalent today (e.g., Jurmain, 1990).

Another major find is in a family of Neanderthals, found by Solecki (1957) and first described in detail in a series of papers by Stewart (e.g., Stewart, 1958). Several members of the family had major defects. One of them, a 40-year old man (Shanidar I), had suffered injuries in childhood that left his left eye probably blind and his right arm paralyzed. Crubezy and Trinkaus (1992) believe that this individual suffered from vertebral and appendicular degenerative joint lesions that were independent of those defects described by Solecki (1957) and Stewart (1958). This Shanidar Neanderthal has generated much discussion about social care of individuals with disabilities, which will be reviewed below.

Homo sapiens appeared about 150,000 years ago, and the picture of disabilities in the first hundred thousand years does not change in important ways beyond the kinds of disabilities seen in monkeys, apes, and Neanderthal. Between 60,000 and 40,000 years ago, instances of artistic expression emerged (Marschack, 1996). Then, 10,000 years ago, in the Middle East and Europe, life patterns of humans changed from a nomadic hunter–gatherer economy to a settled agrarian life style. These changes began to occur later in Asia and still later in the Western hemisphere. Population levels and life expectancy increased, urbanization began, and writing, technology, and the arts flowered. With these important changes, evidence for conditions associated with mental retardation became more definite. Many of the conditions to be discussed probably existed before 10,000 B.P.; however, as yet, there is no relevant evidence because of the factors that have been listed above (i.e., low incidence, generally high mortality, and difficulty of obtaining any data).

In the period following the shift from hunter–gatherer to agrarian-based societies, instances of conditions associated with mental retardation are found. For example, the measles virus became epidemic, probably because measles requires significant population concentrations to become established. Warkany (1959), and more recently Pangas (2000), summarized the recognition of birth malformations by the Assyro-Babylonian culture of 2,800 B.P. The records indicate that people in this culture believed that these malformations at birth were divine portents of things to come and used these malformations for predicting the future.

Blindness is most frequently mentioned in the writings from the Middle East, perhaps because eye problems were so frequent there. Although mental retardation was not described explicitly prior to about 2,000 B.P., it is likely that cases of at least mild mental retardation have always been part of human history. Almost 2,000 years before the formal concept of mental retardation began emerging, mention of other disabilities in adults was part of law. The Hammurabi Code (about 3,700 B.P.) includes epilepsy (Pritchard, 1958, p. 167). Even before that (about 10,000 B.P.), a person with achondroplastic dwarfism was documented (Frayer, Macchaiarelli, & Mussi, 1988).

In addition to some of these conditions that *sometimes* are associated with mental retardation, there are others that *usually* imply mental disability (i.e., there are skeletal conditions and depictions of physical syndromes constituting evidence that the person also had mental retardation). One of these

(continued)

Figure 2.3. *(continued)*

MENTAL RETARDATION   VOLUME 42, NUMBER 3: 195–208 | JUNE 2004
Early history of disabilities   G. Berkson

conditions is Down syndrome. Aufderheide and Rodriguez-Martin (1998) described separate reports of two cases, one from Saxon England (about 1200 B.P.) and one in Austria (2,350 B.P.) (see also Brothwell, 1960). Diamandopoulos, Rakatsanis, and Diamantopoulos (1997) presented photographs of a figurine that they believed to be a depiction of a child with features similar to Down syndrome. This figurine was discovered in central Greece and was apparently from the Neolithic period (8,500 to 5,000 B.P.)

Aufderheide and Rodriguez (1998) also summarized the literature presenting skeletal instances of hydrocephaly, microcephaly, and anencephaly; but they found no literature on the paleopathology of cretinism. Richards and Anton (1991) not only presented a case of hydrocephaly from 1,500 to 4,500 B.P., but also reviewed the literature and defined the cranial characteristics. In Australia prior to the arrival of Europeans (about 230 B.P.), there was a case of meningocoele, a condition that is often associated with mental retardation (Webb & Thorne, 1985).

There are many instances of disabilities that are not associated with mental deficit. The most prominent of these are achondroplastic dwarfs, who attained high social position during the early dynasties of ancient Egypt. The most famous of these are Seneb (VIth Dynasty) and Khemhotpe (Jeffreys & Tait, 2000; Sullivan, 2001)

Some of these conditions definitely are associated with genetic abnormalities. Thus, recent advances in molecular biology promise to help answer the question of the origin of these disorders. However, DNA analysis has not yet been applied broadly to the study of the paleopathology of chronic disabilities (Stone, 2000, p. 354 ff.), and a fuller picture of the origin of the genetic disorders awaits such study.

Overall, the answer to the question of when disabilities became evident depends on the disorder. Healed fractures and osteoarthritis probably are part of our evolutionary heritage as far back as nonhuman primates. Conditions associated with mental retardation probably existed well before the shift from hunter–gatherer economies to agrarian-based societies. Nonetheless, rare evidence from skeletal remains, written records, and artistic depictions have been demonstrated only from times after populations increased and societies became more complex.

What caused disabilities, and what did these conditions tell us about the ancient societies? The answer to this question combines what is known from modern epidemiology of diseases together with archaeology of societies. Some studies show the way in which societies change as reflected in the patterns of disability at different times (e.g., Nerlich, Rohrbach, & Zink, 2002). However, the main questions studied have to do with (a) the influence of the transition from hunter–gatherer societies to sedentary, agrarian life and (b) the relative prevalence of certain disorders at different ages and from different social classes.

A major movement within paleopathology during the last 30 years has been a consideration of the influence of the shift from hunter–gatherer to agrarian societies. Beginning about 30 B.P., two principles became apparent and were manifested in a 1982 conference on paleopathology at the origins of agriculture (Cohen & Armelagos, 1984) One of these was the increasing use of multiple measures in the same study. The second was the understanding that indicators of health *decline* when agriculture first develops.

In the last 20 years, these two principles have been elaborated and their developments summarized in a 2002 conference (e.g., Armelagos & Brown, 2002; Goodman & Martin, 2002). Regression analyses have produced general health indices, perhaps partly because some conditions have generalized effects (Steckel, Sciulli, & Rose, 2002). Also, when a society is exposed to one deficiency condition, it is also subject to others (Goodman, 1998; Goodman & Armelagos, 1989). Regression analyses, which are based on substantial variability between societies (McCaa, 2002; Steckel, Sciulli, & Rose, 2002), have also allowed testing of the relationship between certain environmental variables and fertility or a general health index. For instance, climate or agriculture may not be a significant predictor of health, whereas urbanization may be more highly correlated with it.

Beyond general indices, there has also been interest recently on more specific correlations. Nutritional deprivations show up in various ways in bone material. Familiar examples include rickets (lack of Vitamin D) and scurvy (Vitamin C). However, perhaps the most intensively studied group of conditions in paleopathological research are those associated with the various anemias. Because recent epidemiological research (e.g., Hurtado, Claussen, & Scott, 1999) suggests that anemia is a risk factor for mental retardation independent of several other

MENTAL RETARDATION   VOLUME 42, NUMBER 3: 195–208 | JUNE 2004

Early history of disabilities   G. Berkson

likely correlated factors, these conditions producing anemia are relevant to the topic of this paper. One of the reasons that anemias are the subject of paleopathological studies is that their effects on the skeleton are obvious and a defining property of the conditions. In the archaeological material, anemia (whether produced by food deprivation, a high parasite load, or other diseases such as malaria) is accompanied by porotic hyperostosis (perhaps with cribria orbitalia). A spongy appearance of the bone of the cranium in frontal and parietal areas, perhaps with similar defects in the eye sockets, characterizes these conditions.

The paleopathological study of nutritional deprivations has been done in the context of the question of the effects of the shift from hunter–gatherer economies to sedentary agrarian existence. The basic question is whether this shift was beneficial. The overall answer to this question is a mixed one. Exemplifying this are two papers on the effects of the transition from a hunter–gatherer society to a sedentary agrarian culture. In the first paper Goodman (1998) summarized research at Dickson Mounds, Illinois. He examined pathology of bones and estimated age of death from skeletons of individuals who had lived during the Woodland (hunter–gatherer–nomadic) period through the Middle Mississippian (sedentary) culture. One might expect that life became easier through that transition. However, the evidence showed the opposite. The agrarian sample not only died at a younger age, but also had a higher rate of fractures and osteoporosis (which probably reflected increased work loads), increased enamel hypoplasias, increased bone infections, and increased porotic hyperostosis, reflecting dietary deficiency conditions. Thus, at least at first, it appears that agrarian culture, which depended largely on maize, was not particularly beneficial.

On the other hand, Hodges (1987) studied a sample from Oaxaca, Mexico, who engaged in either nonintensive or intensive agriculture and showed no health effects, perhaps because both groups continued to maintain a balanced diet by hunting and gathering.

Related studies are concerned with social class. Social class in some societies can be defined archaeologically from, for instance, differential location of graves and the quality of the objects (grave goods) buried in the grave with the person. Goodman (1998) summarized a study by Swartstedt that showed a clear difference in tooth defects from graves of ancient landowners and from indentured

slaves from a caste-like society. In his own study, Goodman failed to find a significant relationship between measures of social status and health at Dickson Mounds, perhaps because of a small sample; because social status was defined differently in that society; or, more interestingly, because the society at Dickson Mounds was egalitarian, at least with respect to dietary factors.

There are at least some data indicating that dietary factors were one cause of disease in ancient societies and that disease patterns were one indication of the organization of societies. The general approach of analyzing causes of disease and what they tell us about the organization of society is still very much at the beginning stages but so far is promising.

Social Status and Attitudes Toward People With Disabilities

Historically, attitudes toward people with disabilities have been ambivalent, ranging between positive responses (adulation, caretaking) and negative ones (rejection). This ambivalence is reflected in Edgerton's (1968) review, which is summarized above, and also recognized in animals in the classical statement by Charles Darwin (1871/1952):

> That animals sometimes are far from feeling sympathy is too certain; for they will expel a wounded animal from the herd, or gore or worry it to death. This is almost the blackest fact in natural history, unless, indeed, the explanation, which has been suggested, is true, that their instinct or reason leads them to expel an injured companion, lest beasts of prey including man, should be tempted to follow the troop. . . . Many animals, however, sympathize with each other's distress or danger. This is the case with birds. Captain Stanbury found on salt lake in Utah an old and completely blind pelican that was very fat, and must have been well fed for a long time by his companions. Mr. Blyth, as he informs me, saw Indian crows feeding two or three of their companions, which were blind. (pp. 306–307)

As indicated before, modern studies of macaque monkeys have shown tolerance and caregiving of group members who have severe disabilities. The most extensive of these is a series of studies I did on visually impaired members of groups in three habitats. The first was a natural group on an Island in the Gulf of Siam, which was completely dry during part of the year and contained a large monitor lizard that might have been a predator of baby monkeys. A second group was studied on another island off Puerto Rico that had no predators. This group was fed artificial food, and water was plentiful, but, as a result, the island was very crowded. The third

(continued)

Figure 2.3. *(continued)*

MENTAL RETARDATION   VOLUME 42, NUMBER 3: 195–208 | JUNE 2004

Early history of disabilities   G. Berkson

group was housed in group cages in a laboratory. The results were clear. In the natural habitat, the animals with disabilities were given compensatory care when they were babies, but they disappeared at 7 months of age. On the free-ranging island, the disabled animals were given compensatory care by the mother and other members of the group when they were babies but gradually became socially peripheral, although they stayed with their groups for 3 years until they became adults. In the laboratory, it was difficult to tell the difference between the impaired animals and controls. One impaired male even became the dominant male of the group when he was an adult. This study clearly shows variation in treatment of individuals with disabilities and the importance of the environment and of age as determinants, at least in these animals (Berkson, 1970, 1973, 1977).

Of course, there are no direct observations of social response toward individuals with disabilities among protohuman hominids. However, there is an interesting and instructive controversy about them. In the initial papers on the Shanidar I find (see above), nothing was said about social response toward him. However, in later, more popular publications (e.g., Trinkaus, 1983), investigators speculated that the survival of the Shanidar I individual with all of his disabilities must have meant that this Neanderthal was cared for by his group for an extended period.

The issue is met at two levels. One is whether the existence of a severe disability implies that others took care of that individual (see DeGusta, 2002, for a recent example). The second is whether such extended care implies that Neanderthal was capable of feeling compassion.

Dettwyler (1991) dealt primarily with the second of these levels. She presented three case histories of people with severe disabilities, the most recent from 7,500 B.P. and offered five assumptions underlying inferences of compassion: (a) The majority of a population's members are productive most of the time, (b) individuals who do not show skeletal evidence of impairments are not disabled, (c) a person with physical impairment is necessarily nonproductive, (d) survival of disabled individuals is indicative of compassion, and (e) caring for and facilitating the survival of a disabled individual is always the compassionate thing to do. She challenged the necessity of each of these assumptions in turn and concluded that whether or not an individual was "handicapped" cannot be determined

from archaeological evidence alone. In other words, she appropriately regards such speculation about mental faculties of prehistoric hominids and man as questionable, at best.

Clear evidence about how people with disabilities were thought about and how they were treated only began to be evident from artistic depictions and writing about 4,500 years ago. In dynastic Egypt at that time, achondroplastic dwarfs were functioning members and even honored members of society. Other people with disabilities may also have been protected, whereas still others who had contagious diseases, such as leprosy and tuberculosis, were separated from society (Jeffreys & Tait, 2000).

The Old Testament, which was put together from several sources 2,700 B.P., focuses on two attitudes. One of these, which has been emphasized recently in the literature (e.g., Olyan, 1998; Stiker, 1999, pp. 25–27), deals with one aspect of cultic practice that proscribed sacrifices by individuals with a disability (Leviticus, 21,16; Samuel II, V, 8). This was one aspect of the more general instruction against sacrificing an animal with any blemish. Whether this requirement reflects a general prejudice against disability is questionable. More likely its restriction is limited to the cultic practice of sacrifices to God. For instance, blind and lame priests could partake in the eating of the sacrificed animal. That negative attitudes existed at the time is probable also because the Old Testament further states in several places a commandment that "you shall not insult the deaf, or place a stumbling block before the blind" (Leviticus 19:14; Deuteronomy 27: 18). That is, one might infer an informal negative attitude from this prominent positive statement; but, most important, these statements also reflect the protective ethic of the time in formal statements.

The New Testament, written about 2,000 years ago, reflects two ideas:

As he passed by, he saw a man blind from his birth. And his disciples asked him, "Rabbi, who sinned, this man or his parents, that he was born blind." Jesus answered: "It was not that he sinned or his parents, but that the works of God are manifest in him. . . . As he said this, he spat on the ground and made clay of the spittle, and anointed the man's eyes with the clay, saying to him "Go wash in the pool of Siloam." . . . So he went and washed and came back seeing. (John, 9)

The first idea represented is that the sources of disabilities are not sin but represent natural phenomena, which are a manifestation of God's works. The second idea is that miraculous cures are pos-

MENTAL RETARDATION   VOLUME 42, NUMBER 3: 195–208 | JUNE 2004
Early history of disabilities   G. Berkson

sible, thus expressing the possibility that disabilities might be eliminated (at least through divine intervention).

The Quran, written about 1,400 years ago, likewise fostered a protective tradition. As part of a section assuring the support of orphans, the following is included: "And do not give away your property which Allah has made for you a support to the weak of understanding, and maintain them out of it, and clothe them and speak to them words of honest advice" (Surah IV; Verse 5).

Thus, all of the basic sources of modern Western religions imply the existence of negative attitudes but universally espouse an ethic that intends to protect people with disabilities. On the other hand, no such positive ethic is evident in classical Greece and Rome. The literature about attitudes toward people with physical disabilities from Greece and Rome is fairly extensive. In general, people with physical disabilities were mocked. However, some who had visual impairments might have been regarded as having special talents as poets and seers and were treated like shamans, and lame individuals were apparently economically relatively successful. Ancient Greece even had laws that provided small welfare payments to people with disabilities, especially if their disabilities had been the result of wounds in wars. However, overall, they were cared for by their families or were economically marginal and otherwise socially neglected or rejected (see Garland, 1995, for a much fuller treatment of attitudes toward physical disabilities in this period).

Perhaps the first mention of mental slowness is in Roccatagliata's (1986) general review of psychiatry in ancient times. In one paragraph (p. 85), he briefly suggested what he thought was the idea that an implication of the philosophy of Thales of Miletus (2,700 years B.P) provided. Roccatagliata's view was that Thales believed that brain physiology involved a range in its wetness, which in turn determines the difference between mental retardation and mental illness. Roccatagliata thought that an excessively moist brain might result in mental retardation, while excessive dryness would produce mental illness. Not only would this hypothesis include the observation that mental retardation and mental illness are different, but it might have been the first verbal depiction of mental retardation. However, because it is generally believed that Thales left no writings (Barnes, 1982; Freeman, 1959) and that all we know about him comes from Aristotle's works, written about 200 years after Thales

lived, this reference may reflect Roccatagliata's views more than those of Thales. Thus, locating the initial concept of mental retardation as originating with Thales probably is Roccatagliata's error.

Goodey (1995) described slow and fast mental states as underlying the concept of mental retardation and attributes the first statement of this idea to Empedocles and 100 years later to the Hippocratic writings, especially in *On Regimen* (see below). More definite are general statements made by Plato and his student Aristotle. They had not yet formed the explicit descriptions of intellectual disability that we have today, but their views about cognition may have provided the basis for the later development of the modern concept of mental retardation. Stainton (2001) did provide two quotations about "brutishness" from Aristotle's *Nichomachean Ethics* that might be construed as including mental retardation. However, Aristotle's examples of brutishness (*Nichomachean Ethics*, 1048b, 25–30) seem to refer to mental illness or characteristic of the minds of people from other cultures rather than mental retardation. Likewise, Aristotle's discussion of natural slaves does not mention people with intellectual disabilities (*Vide Supra Politics*, Book I, Chapter 4, 1054b; see also Goodey, 1999).

Perhaps Plato comes closest in his definition of simple "ignorance." However, the Greek for his concept is generally translated as "taking things at face value." With this concept, Plato does not differentiate between naiveté, lack of opportunity to learn, and lack of ability to think (or, indeed, the effects of congenital deafness).

Therefore, it seems that although general concepts in Plato and Aristotle may form the basis for later concepts of intellectual disability, neither of these philosophers provided a definite description of the concept of mental retardation as we know it today. Goodey (1992) put it most explicitly: "There is in fact no candidate in Plato—or, incidentally, in Aristotle—that measures up to the modern notion of a single unitary and purely human intelligence on a hierarchical scale" (p. 29). On the other hand, it is clear from their writings that Plato and Aristotle both valued honest rational thinking as the defining characteristic of the best in humanity. By implication, they saw individuals who were not wise (i.e., rational and/or moral) as lower in value. Therefore, it can fairly be said that they started a general way of thinking about intellectual ability and, thus, disabilities (see Goodey, 1999, and Stainton, 2001, for fuller accounts of this position).

(continued)

Figure 2.3. *(continued)*

MENTAL RETARDATION   VOLUME 42, NUMBER 3: 195–208 | JUNE 2004

Early history of disabilities   G. Berkson

Looking beyond Plato and Aristotle, one might think that there was a naming of specific types of intellectual disability in the corpus of writings attributed to Hippocrates and his followers (G. Lloyd, 1978). One possibility might be in *The Sacred Disease*, a description of epilepsy, which not only attacks the concept of the special divine source of the condition but also attempts to describe its locus in the body, with the Hippocratic account of its physiological mechanism. This part of the Hippocratic writings locates the source of madness in an excessive moisture of the brain and asserts that the brain, rather than the diaphragm or the heart, is the interpreter of consciousness and comprehension:

And by this same organ [the brain] we become mad and delirious, and fears and terrors assail us, some by night, and some by day, and dreams and untimely wanderings, and cares that are not suitable, and ignorance of present circumstances, desuetude, and unskillfulness. All these things we endure from the brain, when it is not healthy, but is more hot, more cold, more moist, or more dry than natural. (Adams, 1939, p. 358)

Although the authors of the Hippocratic writings attempt to explain the mechanism of the loss of consciousness and of the temporary loss of memory after an attack, there is no real mention of the chronic general intellectual disability that sometimes is a correlate of epilepsy. In *The Seed* and *The Nature of the Child*, the Hippocratic treatises on embryology, there is passing reference to malformations (e.g., G. Lloyd, 1978, p. 323), but, again, there is no reference to mental retardation or its specific levels and forms. In *On Regimen* there is a description of slow and fast mental states (see Goodey, 1995, above), but this seems to be a description of temporary rather than chronic traits.

More generally, Garland (1995), in his extensive monograph on attitudes to physical disability, included some questionable instances of severe intellectual disability in Greece and indicated that there is no information on mild intellectual disability. Except for some stories from Herodotus and photos of sculptural depictions of individuals from Roman culture in Egypt that he labeled as "cretins," he did not present any instances of mental retardation from the literature of Greece. However, his detailed account makes it clear that the situation is quite different with respect to attitudes in late Republican and Imperial ancient Rome when explicit references became clear (Garland, 1995, p. 34).

Why is it that explicit descriptions of general intellectual disability are so rare, whereas blindness, epilepsy, achondroplastic dwarfism, malformations, and other mental and physical disabilities are clearly referred to and described? Perhaps the generally high mortality rate of people with severe and profound mental retardation eliminated them from consideration. Perhaps the fact that one can depict intellectual disability only verbally and not through pictures or sculptures might limit their being mentioned. Maybe, for the few people who could write, intellectual disabilities were recognized but not regarded as important enough to mention.

One major possibility is that intellectual disability had not yet been distinguished from mental illness. However, a more interesting possibility also seems likely. Edwards (1997), in an article on physical disabilities in ancient Greece, made the case that the Greek concept of disabilities is somewhat different from the view that she believes is characteristic of modern Western culture. She proposed the view that "disability" for the Greeks was not an inherent characteristic of the individual. Instead, the idea was that a person might be regarded as deviant if they were "unable" to function in society. One might apply this concept to intellectual disability. If a person was supported by his or her family, could perform simple jobs, or was a slave, he or she would not be regarded as unable, and therefore no special mention would be called for.

There is one final hypothesis that may clarify the few cases that are detectable at birth. They might have been killed. Infanticide has occurred throughout civilized human history for population control, for sexual determination (favoring males), and against disabilities. Although some writers assume that infanticide against neonatally evident disabilities characterized ancient treatment of babies, the existence of severe disabilities in the archaeological and historical record demonstrates that infanticide for cases of disability was not practiced universally (e.g., see Scheerenberger, 1983). Plato and Aristotle espoused some selection against defects. In the *Republic*, which is Plato's statement of an ideal society, he espoused communal rearing of children, with the proviso that "the children of inferior parents, or any child of the others that is born defective, they'll hide in a secret and unknown place" (Republic, V, 460c, cited in Cooper, 1997, p. 1088). In his *Politics*, Aristotle expressed the view that there should be

a law that no deformed child shall live, but that on the ground of an excess in the number of children. If the established customs of the state forbid this (for in our state population has a limit), no child is to be exposed, but when couples have children in

MENTAL RETARDATION   VOLUME 42, NUMBER 3: 195–208 | JUNE 2004
Early history of disabilities   G. Berkson

excess, let abortion be procured before sense and life have begun. (*Politics*, VII, Chapter 16, 1335b cited in McKeon, 1941, p. 1301)

Thus, Aristotle tied infanticide against deformities to population control. Although infanticide has existed throughout known human history, and perhaps was common in certain societies, it was apparently used for general population control and for sexual selection in favor of males. Whether selection against disabilities that were evident at birth was related to these other reasons is not clear. However, it is known that when it was employed in ancient Greece, its practice was sporadic or evidence is lacking (see Edwards, 1996, for a fuller discussion). In any case, even when it occurred, killing of individuals with disabilities was limited to the neonatal period. Thereafter, rejection or adulation was more common, depending on the disability and the culture.

To conclude this review, a brief statement should also be made about treatments. Although spiritual treatments were in common use in antiquity, medical procedures were also widely employed. Herbs for healing and anesthesia were used. Various forms of surgery were applied. For instance, surgery for removal of cataracts, cauterization of wounds, and suturing wounds were all known in various parts of the world (Haeger, 1988). According to Padula and Friedmann (1987), the oldest surgical procedure, amputation of a limb, was conducted 43,000 years ago, and sophisticated ligature procedures with it were carried out at least 3,500 years ago. The oldest and best studied cranial surgery is trephination. This procedure, at least 7,000 years old, consists of drilling holes in the skull. The procedure was used in various places in Europe as well as Peru and perhaps Chile in the Western hemisphere (Gerszten, Gerszten, & Allison, 1998; Marino & Gonzales-Portillo, 2000; Piek, Lidke, Terberger, von Smekal, & Gaab, 1999). In one survey, at least 5% of skulls and at least a few of the patients survived the surgery. The reason for doing this operation is still obscure, but release of spirits and release of pressure from edema are the main hypotheses.

In addition to surgery, prosthetic devices of various kinds were used. Artificial limbs are known from at least 3,500 years ago and considering that amputation was practiced much earlier, were probably invented before then. In addition, in India of 3,000 years ago, the use of artificial eyes, artificial

teeth, as well as artificial legs was recorded (Fliegel & Feuer, 1966)

Thus, as far back in history as we know, attitudes toward people with intellectual and physical disabilities have depended on the values of the culture in which they live, with perhaps a bias in favor of young children after the neonatal period. In general also, informal attitudes have been generally more negative than those espoused in public documents and through medical treatment.

Conclusions

Although the science of paleopathology began almost 150 years ago, the general picture about chronic intellectual and physical disabilities in antiquity was not yet clear when Kanner wrote his history of mental retardation 40 years ago. However, since that time, increasing activity in this branch of archaeology as well as in the study of ancient history has brought the picture into focus. In this survey I have attempted to bring up to date this active field. In the next generation, advances in technology undoubtedly will bring with them further significant insights

Chronic illnesses, such as osteoarthritis, healed fractures, and heavy parasite loads, have probably been part of human evolution since before the development of the hominids. The long-term consequences of some communicable diseases and genetic disorders also may have been with us for a very long time. However, the difficulty of existence and early childhood vulnerability, together with low population levels that separated small populations of people, must have limited the emergence of the communicable diseases that result in chronic disabilities.

Increasing population concentration that ultimately came from the development of a sedentary and agrarian lifestyle allowed the transmission of the bacteria and viruses that are associated with disabilities, including mental retardation. Also, at least temporarily, certain specific nutritional deficiencies associated with high parasite loads and a more limited range of diet also caused some cases. It is at this time also that evidence for certain genetic disorders appeared, perhaps associated with low mortality and inbreeding of populations.

Depictions of physical disabilities and mental illness began in sculptures and written material about 4,500 years ago. These included primarily epilepsy, blindness, lameness, and mental illness.

(continued)

Figure 2.3.   *(continued)*

MENTAL RETARDATION   VOLUME 42, NUMBER 3: 195–208 | JUNE 2004

Early history of disabilities   G. Berkson

However, notably, although mental retardation un-doubtedly existed and although variation in con-cepts of intelligence was recognized in the writings of Plato and Aristotle, the concept of mental retar-dation was apparently not made explicit either in formal or informal writings prior to the Imperial Rome.

Why there was such a lag in the emergence of the concept of mental retardation is not clear. Per-haps evidence for mental retardation has not yet appeared. The concept may have been in common use, but may not have been thought to be worth mentioning in formal philosophical or medical writ-ings. Finally, mental retardation may not have been differentiated from mental illness until later in his-tory. In any case, it remains to be determined how the concept of a general intellectual deficit emerged after Classical Greece.

Neglect and rejection of individuals with chronic disabilities have characterized social life since before the evolution of Homo sapiens. At the same time, social responses that compensate for dis-abilities of group members also are common, espe-cially if the person with disabilities is a young mem-ber of the family. In some cultures, older blind or mentally ill people were thought to have special skills or powers of forethought and were treated with honor. When they were competent at tasks needed in the society, these individuals also may have overcome negative views and may have achieved high social status.

Although it has been common to believe that in antiquity babies with disabilities were killed at birth, this has been brought into question recently. In fact, the data are sparse, and proponents of the old interpretation did not consider infanticide for other reasons. Older individuals with disabilities were not killed and were sometimes honored. Med-ical treatment was common, and a variety of pros-thetic devices were in use.

Therefore, it is probable that mental retarda-tion has existed for a very long time, but there has been no evidence for it prior to the emergence of settled agrarian life. Moreover, the modern concept of mental retardation had not emerged in Western civilization until well after the recognition of other disabilities. These conclusions must be guarded, however, because aside from excellent studies of the thought of major Classical Greek philosophers, the literature on concepts about disabilities prior to a couple of hundred years ago is very sparse. Studies of mental retardation and other disabilities in pre-

history and in the great civilizations of Sumer, As-syria, Egypt, ancient Greece, Rome, Islam, early Eu-rope (Jewish and Christian), India, and China each would be helpful, if done by researchers equipped to do it.

When these studies are conducted, it is prob-able that investigators will find that the emergence of our modern concept of mental retardation has been slow indeed. As we have seen from the several classification systems that have come out in the past 50 years, the process of refinement of our percep-tions has continued.

References

Anadiotis, G. (2000). Genetic defects as recorded in the pottery of the Moche culture of Peru. *Clinical Genetics, 57,* 347–348.

Armelagos, G. J., & Brown, P. J. (2002). The body as evidence; the body of evidence. In R. H. Steckel & J. C. Rose (Eds.), *The backbone of history: Health and nutrition in the Western hemi-sphere* (pp. 593–602). Cambridge: Cambridge University Press.

Aufderheide, A. C., & Rodriguez-Martin, C. (1998). *The Cambridge encyclopedia of human paleopathology* (p. 478). Cambridge: Cambridge University Press.

Barnes, J. (1982). *The PreSocratic philosophers.* Lon-don: Routledge & Kegan Paul.

Berkson, G. (1970). Defective infants in a feral monkey group. *Folia Primatologia, 12,* 284–289.

Berkson, G. (1973). Social responses to abnormal infant monkeys. *American Journal of Physical Anthropology, 38,* 583–586.

Berkson, G. (1977). The social ecology of defects in primates. In S. Chevalier-Skolnikoff & F. Poirier (Eds.), *Primate biosocial development* (pp. 189–204). New York: Garland.

Berkson, G. (1993). *Children with handicaps: A re-view of behavioral research* (pp. 5–7). Hillsdale, NJ: Erlbaum.

Braddock, D. L., & Parish, S. (2001). An institu-tional history of disability. In G. L. Albrecht, K. D. Seelman, & M. Bury (Eds.), *Handbook of disability studies* (pp. 13–17). Thousand Oaks: Sage.

Brothwell, D. R. (1960). A possible case of mon-golism in a Saxon population. *Annals of Human Genetics, 24,* 141–150.

Buikstra, J. E., & Ubelaker, D. H. (Eds.). (1994). *Standards for data collection from human skeletal*

MENTAL RETARDATION   VOLUME 42, NUMBER 3: 195–208 | JUNE 2004

Early history of disabilities   G. Berkson

remains. Fayetteville: Arkansas Archaeological Survey #44.

Cohen, M. N., & Armelagos, G. J. (1984). *Paleopathology at the origins of agriculture.* New York: Academic Press.

Cooper, J. M. (Ed.). (1997). *Plato: Complete works.* Indianapolis: Hackett.

Crubezy, E., & Trinkaus, E. (1992). Shanidar 1: A case of hyperostotic disease (DISH) in the middle Paleolithic. *American Journal of Physical Anthropology, 89,* 411–420.

Darwin, C. (1871/1952). *The descent of man* (Part I, Chapter IV, pp. 306–307). Chicago: Encyclopedia Britannica.

DeGusta, D. (2002). Comparative skeletal pathology and the case for conspecific care in the middle Pleistocene hominids. *Journal of Archaeological Science, 29,* 1435–1438.

Dettwyler, K. A. (1991). Can paleopathology provide evidence for "compassion"? *American Journal of Physical Anthropology, 84,* 375–384.

Diamondopoulos, A. A., Rakatsantis, K. G., & Diamontopoulos, N. (1997). A Neolithic case of Down syndrome. *Journal of the History of the Neurosciences, 6,* 86–89.

Dodds, E. R. (1963). *The Greeks and the irrational.* Berkeley: University of California Press.

Edgerton, R. B. (1968). Mental retardation in non-Western societies: Toward a cross-cultural perspective on incompetence. In H. C. Haywood (Ed.), *Social-cultural aspects of mental retardation* (pp. 523–560). New York: Appleton-Century-Crofts.

Edwards, M. L. (1996). The cultural context of deformity in the Ancient Greek World: "Let there be a law that no deformed child shall be reared." *The Ancient History Bulletin, 10,* 79–92.

Edwards, M. L. (1997). Constructions of physical disability in the ancient Greek World. In D. Mitchell & S. Snyder (Eds.), *Discourses of disability: The body and physical differences in the humanities* (pp. 35–50). Ann Arbor: University of Michigan.

Fliegel, O., & Feuer, S. G. (1966). Prostheses. *Archives of Physical Medicine and Rehabilitation, 47,* 275–285.

Frayer, D. W., Macchaiarelli, R., & Mussi, M. (1988). A case of chrondrodystrophic dwarfism in the Italian late Upper Paleolithic. *American Journal of Physical Anthropology, 75,* 549–565.

Freeman, K. (1959). *The pre-Socratic philosophers.* Cambridge: Harvard University.

Furuya, Y. (1966). On the malformation occurred in the Gagyusan troop of wild Japanese monkeys. *Primates, 7,* 488–492.

Garland, R. (1995). *The eye of the beholder: Deformity and disability in the Graeco-Roman world.* Ithaca: Cornell University Press.

Gerszten, P. C., Gerszten, E., & Allison, M. J. (1998). Diseases of the skull in pre-Columbian South American mummies. *Neurosurgery, 42,* 1145–1151.

Goodey, C. F. (1992). Mental disabilities and human values in Plato's late dialogues. *Archiv fur Geschichte der Philosophie, 74,* 26–42.

Goodey, C. F. (1995). Mental retardation. In G. Gerrios & R. Porter (Eds.), *A history of clinical psychiatry: The origins and history of psychiatric disorders* (pp. 239–250). New York: New York University Press.

Goodey, C. F. (1999). Politics, nature, and necessity: Were Aristotle's slaves feeble minded? *Political Theory, 27,* 203–224.

Goodey, C. F. (2001). What is developmental disability? The origin and nature of our conceptual models. *Journal on Developmental Disabilities, 8,* 16–32.

Goodman, A. H. (1993). On the interpretation of health from skeletal remains. *Current Anthropology, 34,* 281–288.

Goodman, A. (1998). The biological consequences of inequality in antiquity. In A. H. Goodman & Leatherman, T. L. (Eds.), *Building a new biocultural synthesis* (pp. 147–169). Ann Arbor: University of Michigan.

Goodman, A. H., & Armelagos, G. J. (1989). Infant and childhood morbidity and mortality risks in archaeological populations. *World Archaeology, 21,* 225–243.

Goodman, A. H., & Martin, D. L. (2002). Reconstructing health profiles from skeletal remains. In R. H. Steckel & J. C. Rose (Eds.), *The backbone of history: Health and nutrition in the Western hemisphere* (pp. 11–60). Cambridge: Cambridge University Press.

Grmek, M. D. (1983). *Les maladies a l-aube de la civilisation occidentale.* Paris: Payot.

Haeger, K. (1988). *The illustrated history of surgery* (pp. 9–47). New York: Bell.

Hodges, D. C. (1987). Health and agricultural intensification in the prehistoric valley of Oaxa-

(continued)

Figure 2.3. *(continued)*

MENTAL RETARDATION   VOLUME 42, NUMBER 3: 195–208 | JUNE 2004
Early history of disabilities   G. Berkson

ca, Mexico. *American Journal of Physical Anthropology, 73,* 323–332.

Hurtado, E. K., Claussen, A. H., & Scott, K. G. (1999). Early childhood anemia and mild or moderate mental retardation. *American Journal of Clinical Nutrition, 69,* 115–119.

Jeffreys, D., & Tait, J. (2000). Disability, madness, and social exclusion in dynastic Egypt. In J. Humphrey (Ed.), *Madness, disability and social exclusion: The archaeology and anthropology of "difference"* (pp. 87–95). London: Routledge.

Jurmain, R. (1990). Paleoepidemiology of a central California prehistoric population from Ca-Ala-329: Degenerative disease. *American Journal of Physical Anthropology, 83,* 83–94.

Kanner, L. (1964). *A history of the care and study of the mentally retarded.* Springfield, IL: Thomas.

Katzenberg, M. A., & Saunders, S. R. (2000). *Biological anthropology of the human skeleton* (pp. 215–302). New York: Wiley-Liss.

Larsen, C. S. (1997). *Bioarchaeology: Interpreting behavior from the human skeleton.* Cambridge: Cambridge University Press.

Lloyd, G. E. R. (Ed.). (1978/1983). *Hippocratic writings.* Haamondsworth: Penguin.

Lloyd, A. S., & Petrucelli, R. J., II. (Eds.). (1987). *Medicine: An illustrated history.* New York: Adams.

Marino, R., Jr., & Gonzales-Portillo, M. (2000). Preconquest Peruvian neurosurgeons: A study of Inca and pre-Columbian trephination and the art of medicine in ancient Peru. *Neurosurgery, 47,* 940–950.

Marschack, A. (1996). A middle paleolithic symbolic composition for the Golan Heights: The earliest known depictive image. *Current Anthropology, 37,* 357–365.

Mays, S. (1998). *The archeology of human bones.* London: Routledge.

McCaa, R. (2002). Paleodemography of the Americas. In R. H. Steckel & J. C. Rose (Eds.), *The backbone of history: Health and nutrition in the Western hemisphere* (pp. 94–124). Cambridge: Cambridge University Press.

McKeon, R. (Ed). (1941). *The basic works of Aristotle.* New York: Random House.

Miles, M. (1997). Disabled learners in South Asia: Lessons from the past for educational exporters. *International Journal of Disability, Development, and Education, 44,* 97–104.

Nakamichi, M., Fujii, H., & Koyama, T. (1982). *Behavioral development of a malformed male juvenile in a free-ranging Japanese monkey* (Macaca fusucata) *group.* Paper presented at the International Psychological Society, Atlanta.

Nerlich, A. G., Rohrbach, H., & Zink, A. (2002). Paleopathology of ancient mummies and skeletons. Investigations on the occurrence and frequency of specific diseases during various time periods in the necropolis of Thebes-West (Abstract). *Pathologe, 23,* 379–385.

Olyan, S. M. (1998). "Anyone blind or lame shall not enter the house": On the interpretation of Second Samuel 5:8b. *Catholic Biblical Quarterly, 60,* 218–227.

Padula, P. A., & Friedmann, L. W. (1987). Acquired amputation and prostheses before the sixteenth century. *Angiology, 38,* 133–141.

Pangas, J. C. (2000). Birth malformations in Babylon and Assyria. *American Journal of Medical Genetics, 91,* 318–321.

Papadopoulos, J. K. (2000). Skeletons in wells: Toward the archaeology of social exclusion in the ancient Greek world. In J. Humphrey (Ed.), *Madness, disability and social exclusion: The archaeology and anthropology of "difference"* (pp. 96–118). London: Routledge.

Piek, J., Lidke, G., Terberger, T., von Smekal, U., & Gaab, M. R. (1999). Stone age skull surgery in Mecklenburg-Vorpommern: A systematic study. *Neurosurgery, 45,* 147–151.

Pritchard, J. B. (1958). *The ancient near east: An anthology of texts and pictures* (Vol. 1). Princeton: Princeton University Press.

Renfrew, C., & Bahn, P. (2000). *Archaeology: Theories, methods and practice* (3rd ed., pp. 438–450). London: Thames & Hudson.

Richards, G. D., & Anton, S. C. (1991). Craniofacial configuration and postcranial development of a hydrocephalic child (ca. 2500 B.C.–500 A.D.): With a review of cases and comment on diagnostic criteria. *American Journal of Physical Anthropology, 85,* 185–200.

Roccatagliata, G. (1986). *A history of ancient psychiatry.* New York: Greenwood Press.

Savithri, S. R. (1987). Speech pathology in ancient India. *Journal of Communication Disorders, 20,* 437–445.

Scheerenberger, R. (1983). *A history of mental retardation.* Baltimore: Brookes.

Schultz, A. H. (1956). The occurrence and frequency of pathological and teratological conditions and of twinning among non-human primates. *Primatologia, 1,* 965–1014.

MENTAL RETARDATION   VOLUME 42, NUMBER 3: 195–208 | JUNE 2004

Early history of disabilities   G. Berkson

Solecki, R. S. (1957). Shanidar cave. *Scientific American, 197,* 58–64.

Stainton, T. (2001). Reason and value: The thought of Plato and Aristotle and the construction of intellectual disability. *Mental Retardation, 39,* 452–460.

Steckel, R. H., Sciulli, P. W., & Rose, J. C. (2002). A health index from skeletal remains. In R. H. Steckel & J. C. Rose (Eds.), *The backbone of history: Health and nutrition in the Western hemisphere* (pp. 61–93). Cambridge: Cambridge University Press.

Stewart, T. D. (1958). The restored Shanidar I skull. *Annual Report of the Smithsonian Institution.*

Stewart, T. D. (1969). The effects of pathology on skeletal populations. *American Journal of Physical Anthropology, 30,* 443–450.

Stiker, H-J. (1999). *A history of disability.* Ann Arbor: University of Michigan Press.

Stone, A. C. (2000). Ancient DNA from skeletal remains. In M. A. Katzenberg & S. R. Saunders (Eds.), *Biological anthropology of the human skeleton* (pp. 351–371). New York: Wiley-Liss.

Straus, W. L., Jr., & Cave, A. J. E., III. (1957). Pathology and the posture of Neanderthal man. *Quarterly Review of Biology, 32,* 348–363.

Sullivan, R. (2001). Deformity—A modern Western prejudice with ancient origins. *Proceedings of the Royal College of Physicians of Edinborough, 31,* 262–266.

Trinkaus, E. (1983). *The Shanidar Neanderthals.* New York: Academic Press.

Warkany, J. (1959). Congenital malformations in the past. *Journal of Chronic Diseases, 10,* 84–96.

Webb, S. G., & Thorne, A. G. (1985). A congenital meningocoele in prehistoric Australia. *American Journal of Physical Anthropology, 68,* 525–533.

White, T. D., & Folkens, P. A. (2000). *Human osteology* (2nd ed.). San Diego: Academic Press.

Received 4/28/03, first decision 6/26/03, accepted 6/15/03.

Editor-in-charge: Steven J. Taylor

I thank Lawrence Keeley and Sloan Williams who introduced me to archaeology by permitting me to sit in on their classes. Thanks also to C. F. Goodey, Christopher Keys, Tim Stainton, and Sloan Williams for comments on the manuscript.

Author:

Gershon Berkson, PhD, Professor Emeritus, Department of Psychology (MC 285), University of Illinois at Chicago, Behavior Sciences Building, 1007 W. Harrison, Chicago, IL 60607. E-mail: gberkson@uic.edu

There is a sequence of life circumstances established in antiquity with regard to people with intellectual disability that is to be repeated throughout history and which reflects the circumstances and conditions of the time as much as the capacity of the person. In prehistory and into the earliest times in antiquity, people with intellectual disability were likely unnoticed if their level of impairment required minimal support. In early hunter-gatherer and agrarian societies, people with intellectual disability with limited support needs likely functioned as the rest of society. Clearly, the presence of any physical impairment stigmatized people, although there is evidence of humane treatment of people with physical disabilities, at least in early agrarian societies.

For children with the most severe intellectual impairments, for whom concomitant physical and sensory impairments would have been common, the story was very different. In the earliest societies, these infants would simply have died, often as not unable to adjust to the rigors of life and succumbing to medical issues because of the lack of medical treatments. Over time, this benign neglect or natural outcome became more systematized. Although people with intellectual disability who had minimal support needs likely continued to go unnoticed in Greek and Roman societies, albeit because they were likely slaves and members of the lowest classes, infants who were clearly impaired were subject to increasingly brutal treatment, from infanticide to mutilation.

The movement from rural, agrarian, or nomadic societies to larger cities created almost dichotomous outcomes for people with intellectual disability. The increased complexity of life and society would have increased the visibility of a person's limitations and difficulties because the person had greater difficulty adjusting to the demands of the context. This often resulted in the introduction of structured "services" for society's most vulnerable, such as the Roman *Columna Lactaria*, but also increased the vulnerability of people to ridicule and discrimination. People with intellectual disability with limited support needs were probably unnoticed in ancient hunter-gatherer and agrarian societies and later in city-based civilizations, such as Greece and Rome, although it was probably as slaves and lower class members during these later periods.

The role of religion in understanding disability, in all its complexity and contradictions, was first introduced during the Palestinian era and again in newly Christianized Rome. Across religious traditions and time, disability has often been equated with negative aspects of religious belief or performance: the personification of the devil or similar evil entities, faithlessness and disbelief or a test of one's faith, or punishment for sinful behavior on the part of either the parents or the person. Various illustrations are available across religious traditions: people are made to see, hear, or walk because their sins are forgiven; a person experiences disability because of his or her past life; "cripples" are made to walk because they have faith; disability is a test of the endurance of the believer; the faithless are "blind to the truth," "epileptics" are cured as demons are cast out. The teachings of virtually all religious traditions emphasize tolerance and compassion for people who are poor, ill, or disabled, but issues of understanding disability as a function of demonic possession or sin still persist and color how disability is understood and how supports are provided.

The family unit as a central component of disability and disability supports also begins to emerge in these early times. It is likely that any person with intellectual disability who lived a full life during prehistory and antiquity did so because of family support. Greek and Roman patriarchal family units and societal understandings of childhood and children became important to the fates of children with disabilities in these periods, often, unfortunately, in a negative way.

REFERENCES

Berkshon, G. (2004). Intellectual and physical disabilities in prehistory and early civilization. *Mental Retardation, 42*(3), 195–208. Washington, DC: American Association on Intellectual and Developmental Disabilities.

Dersin, D. (Ed.). (1997). *On the banks of the Nile.* Richmond, VA: Time-Life Books.

Durant, W. (1939). *Our oriental heritage.* New York, NY: Simon and Schuster.

Grant, M. (1991). *The founders of the western world: A history of Greece and Rome.* New York, NY: Charles Scribner's Sons.

Grant, M. (1997). *The history of ancient Israel.* London, United Kingdom: Orion Books.

Hyslop, S.G., Jones, R., & Thompson, D. S. (Eds.). (1987). *The age of god-kings*. Alexandria, VA: Time-Life Books.

Kramer, S.N. (1963). *The Sumerians*. Chicago, IL: University of Chicago Press.

Nissen, H.J. (1988). *The early history of the ancient Near East: 9000–2000 B.C.* (E. Lutzeier & K. J. Northcott, Trans.). Chicago, IL: The University of Chicago Press.

Oakes, L., & Gahlin, L. (2003). *Ancient Egypt*. New York, NY: Barnes & Noble.

Privateer, P. M. (2006). *Inventing intelligence: A social history of smart*. Malden, MA: Blackwell.

Scheerenberger, R.C. (1983). *A history of mental retardation*. Baltimore, MD: Paul H. Brookes Publishing Co.

Trinkaus, E., & Zimmerman, M. R. (1982). Trauma among the Shanidar Neandertals. *American Journal of Physical Anthropology, 57*(1), 61–76.

3

Poverty and the Emergence of Charity

Intellectual Disability in the Middle Ages (500 CE to 1500 CE)

Parnel Wickham

The Middle Ages provide few clues to explain the situation that was called idiocy, and there is no evidence of the lived experience during the period. The construct of intelligence was unknown and prescientific medicine took little interest in mental problems. Nevertheless, evidence of idiocy appears in rudimentary laws and emerging systems of classification. Indications of idiocy in the Middle Ages can also be inferred from concepts of childhood and approaches to children, in religious concepts and practices, and in the role of natural fools employed in the courts of the aristocracy.

*H*istorians date the Middle Ages from approximately 300 to 1500 CE, a period extending from the fall of the Roman Empire to the early modern era (Cantor, 1993). This period covers a wide expanse of time and ranges over a vast geographical region. Nevertheless, the term *Middle Ages* usually refers to the period that gave rise to Western Europe, the continent and the islands including England. This discussion of the concept of idiocy in the Middle Ages will focus primarily on developments in Europe.

Most historical accounts of the Middle Ages focus on the various struggles of powerful and not-so-powerful rulers to conquer by war, intrigue, politics, or economics their neighboring and, eventually, more distant territories. They are stories of rulers, sometimes gifted and mighty, sometimes weak and deeply flawed, whose aims were to dominate others and avoid submission. These stories, some of which appear in the accounts of firsthand witnesses, provide important insights into the origins of Western Europe and its culture. In most cases, however, they fail to offer much useful information about the ordinary people who lived throughout the Middle Ages, and if there is little known about the ordinary people, there is even less known about people who had mental problems, and more particularly, what we now call intellectual disability.

It is important to understand that the contemporary construct of intellectual disability has little to do with the problems that people in the Middle Ages might have experienced. In general, the concept of intelligence was unknown at that time (Privateer, 2006), and conditions analogous to intellectual disability were not a problem in the Middle Ages unless a person was unable to care for him- or herself, unable to earn a living, or unable to contribute to a household or community. In short, people with any kind of difficulty who could not provide for themselves were generally grouped among the poor and were treated accordingly. This is not to say that there were no people with something like intellectual disability among the aristocratic and ruling classes, for surely there were. Wolfensberger (2011) provided an analysis of how royalty dealt with the increased presence of family members with disabilities; that essay is provided as Figure 3.1. With sufficient resources, any disability might be managed and tolerated, if the individual was not banished. As a result, disability as a problem was not apparent in the Middle Ages unless it was accompanied by poverty. It is within the lower classes—those who had trouble finding sufficient food and who were threatened by injuries and overwhelmed by disease—that the vulnerability that accrued from additional disability might become a serious burden.

The study of the construct of idiocy in the Middle Ages is therefore largely a study of poverty and the approaches to ameliorate it, of laws developed to address some of the problems that arose from the acquisition and management of property, and of laws concerning criminals, most of whom would have belonged to the lower classes. That medieval society was aware of difference, social as well as intellectual, is evident in their construction of the court fool, who appears subsequently in this history of intellectual disability. In contrast, unlike Late Modern Times (see Chapter 6), the medical community had little interest in mental disability and especially in the condition they called idiocy, probably because it was thought to be hopelessly incurable and lifelong. Nevertheless, physicians, were aware of the problem. Two brief accounts of mental disability distinguished idiocy from insanity. One of these was written by Isidore of Seville (c. 560–636 CE), who became Bishop in 599 and wrote

INTELLECTUAL AND DEVELOPMENTAL DISABILITIES   VOLUME 49, NUMBER 1: 46–49 | FEBRUARY 2011

Perspectives

Idiocy and Madness in Princely European Families

Wolf Wolfensberger

DOI: 10.1352/1934-9556-49.1.46

Woods (1906) is the (rare) authoritative source on madness and idiocy in noble families in Europe, including some of the ruling houses. Midelfort (1995) wrote more specifically on families of the high nobility in Germany ca. 1490–1610. A weakness of both books is that they were more concerned with mental abnormality per se than with whether the abnormality was an intellectual one from birth or early age or a true "madness." This problem is particularly strong in Wood, who was very sloppy in his terminology, and in adducing evidence for one of these conditions versus the other. He contended that 35 of his 671 "subjects" were imbecilic.

These two sources (Woods and Midelfort) are full of factual details: names, places, dates, relationships, actions taken in individual instances, etc., but there is very little interpretation. Midelfort (1995) covered his material very selectively. Scores of pages were devoted to a single case, while hundreds of potential other cases were given minimal mention. It seems that there is a goldmine of unworked material.

This article is an effort to come up with what appear to be some reasonable interpretations, especially in light of Social Role Valorization (SRV) theory (Wolfensberger, 1991, 1998, 2000; Wolfensberger & Thomas, 2007).

How nobles treated their mentally afflicted family members varied widely. Much was at stake: who would rule, and who would inherit estates. Some families quietly removed their mentally afflicted relatives from any public role, for example, by sending them off to lonely castles, putting them into monasteries, imprisoning them in miserable dungeons, or outright murdering them. Others sought cures, sometimes of heroic form and at great expense, involving whatever physicians were then famous. Yet others accepted the person's affliction and tried to "work around it" via special helpers and

special provisions. These might include preventing the person from taking the public office the person ordinarily would have taken, but not preventing the person from a public and honored role at court.

From a Social Role Valorization perspective, the most successful solution was the role worked out for the imbecilic King Carlos II of Spain (who lived from 1661–1700 and reigned from 1665–1700), and there was a very good reason why this happened in Spain and at that time.

For centuries in the late medieval and post-medieval period, the Spanish royal court was in the habit of adopting many handicapped, dependent, or orphaned children, including some of the lowest birth and of low intelligence. Many of these children were literally raised at the court, and hence were called *niños palaciegos* (i.e., children of the palace). Many children thusly adopted were taken in upon the pleading of their desperate parents who wanted a better life for them. The Spanish royal court during the 16th and 17th centuries created a role identity for its bodily deformed and mentally impaired people that was called *hombres de placer* (i.e., people who please or who give others pleasure). These replaced what at other courts would have been court fools. Thus, many of the *niños palaciegos* were accorded the role of *hombre de placer* and were sometimes even called (in the singular) *gentel hombre de placer* (Tietze-Conrat, 1957), that is, genteel.

For hundreds of years, well into the 18th century, the Spanish court at any one time swarmed with scores of handicapped, malformed, and/or mentally impaired *hombres de placer*. The palace records of King Philip IV (1605–1665) recorded 110 by name and scores more without name. A whole wing of the royal palace, the Escorial, was allotted to them. Wherever there were members of the royal family, they were accompanied ("attended") by *hombres de placer*, and "attending" was one of their functions. Some were playmates of the royal

---

Figure 3.1.   "Idiocy and Madness in Princely European Families."
(From Wolfensberger, W. [2011]. Idiocy and madness in princely European families. *Intellectual and Developmental Disabilities, 49*[1], 46–49. Washington, DC: American Association on Intellectual and Developmental Disabilities; reprinted by permission.)

(continued)

Figure 3.1. *(continued)*

INTELLECTUAL AND DEVELOPMENTAL DISABILITIES
VOLUME 49, NUMBER 1: 46–49 | FEBRUARY 2011

Perspective: Idiocy and madness in princely European families
W. Wolfensberger

children, some served as grooms of the court's hunting dogs, some were ladies-in-waiting to the princesses. Others were not able to play any practical functions and might do no more than lend their well-attired, dignified, instructing, and sanctifying presence to the king, queen, or other members of the royal family, especially on public occasions. Their presence was seen as instructive insofar as they stood for reality and truth, in contrast to the duplicity and pretense that was often affected at court; and it was seen as sanctifying via their innocence, and by bringing others to service to the lowly. King Philip IV is said to have gone nowhere without his *hombres de placer* (Tietze-Conrat, 1957, p. 691). When the Spanish royal family dined, it was more likely to do so in the company of *hombres de placer* than of courtiers (Clair, 1968).

In 1568, King Philip II (ruled 1556–1598) appointed as his court painter one Juan Fernandez de Navarrete who had the surname El Mudo, because he was a deaf-mute man. When this man died in 1579, he was buried with great honors, and the prominent Spanish writer Lope de Vega composed his tomb inscription to the effect that even though he was mute, his works still spoke after his death (Kamen, 1997; Werner, 1932, p. 96).

Similarly, Prince Carignano (1628–1709) was a deaf-mute, but he had learned to communicate in writing and seemed to have had a good deal of sense. He was an officer in the Spanish army, participated in several military campaigns, and served as vice regent and governor of various principalities (Werner, 1932).

Thus, over the centuries, all of Spain had become used to seeing handicapped people in valued court roles. And so, when the only surviving child of King Philip IV of Spain and his second wife, the crown prince Carlos, was definitely of impaired intellect, and feeble health, he nevertheless assumed the throne as Carlos II in 1665, at age 4, and surprised everybody by living to the age of 39. Generations of familiarity with impaired people in valued roles is bound to have played a role in the Spanish nobility letting a person of very low intelligence rule as king for 35 years. In most other countries, his accession would have been prevented by legal or illegal means, and maybe even by murder. Indeed, we can contrast the Spanish practice of accepting the mentally impaired heir as the legitimate king, and crowning him Carlos II, with the British practice as late as into the 20th century of hiding away their handicapped heirs to the throne and other members of the royal house in institutions and announcing that they had died.

The evidence of Carlos' severe mental impairment includes information such as the following. He had been so feeble as a child that no attempts were made to educate him for fear that this would overtax him. He reportedly did not talk until he was 4 years old. During his lifetime, others did the work of state for him. He was described as "bewitched"— history often referred to him as "Charles the Bewitched" (*Encyclopedia Britannica*) or *El Hechizado*— "enchanted," as having "a feeble mind," and being "empty-headed," even as he was also said to have had a childlike innocence and piety. His conversation was said to match that of a 6-year-old child, and he spent only about a quarter hour per day on affairs of state and the rest in childish games with his charming and spirited first wife, such as picking strawberries and counting and recounting them endlessly or running back and forth through the palace. She died after reporting secretly to her family that the king was impotent, and he was, in fact, the last of his branch of the family.

The Spanish example greatly impressed other European courts. For instance, the other courts largely discontinued the practice of dressing court fools in traditional fool costumes, and instead they began to vest them in expensive tailor-made clothes of the highest quality, comparable to the clothes of nobles and court officials in Spain.

As to the situation in German lands, many retarded or insane German rulers were deposed by their relatives. One can be amazed at the large number of insane German princes during the Renaissance, but one can also infer from this that there was much more madness in German houses of nobility than one would have guessed even from Woods' (1906) extensive classic book. The amazing thing is how some princely houses managed to rule while having madness in their families for generations. One of Woods' conclusions was that both the good and bad genes in European royal houses had come from a small number of royal families who then widely intermarried.

Excessive intake of alcohol seemed to have played a big role in the instability of German princes. Perhaps wine was too easily accessible to them and its use little censored. Also, Protestant princes no longer had the consolations of the Catholic practices of confession and penance.

One of the few interpretive nuggets that came out of Midelfort was the interesting observation that

INTELLECTUAL AND DEVELOPMENTAL DISABILITIES VOLUME 49, NUMBER 1: 46–49 | FEBRUARY 2011
Perspective: Idiocy and madness in princely European families W. Wolfensberger

the nobles of the Renaissance era became more merciful toward their mentally afflicted members, and more respectful, in contrast to the brutality that often preceded it. Perhaps the Spanish influence played a role here. Previous to the Renaissance era (ca. 1490–1610), mad princes were commonly murdered or "disappeared."

There is very little on mental retardation by Midelfort. Three exceptions are Duke Philip I of Mecklenburg (1514–1557), who had suffered an early head wound in 1534; Friedrich, prince of Saxony (1504–1539); and Duke Johann III (1490–1539) of the line of Jülich-Cleves on the lower Rhine, who was nicknamed "The Simple" and was said to have "little brain." (His great-grandfather, Johannes II [1458–1521], was nicknamed "the baby-maker" [*proletarius*] because by age 31, he had begotten 63 children out of wedlock.) More equivocal was the situation of Duke Albrecht Friedrich of Prussia (1553–1618), who may have been mentally disordered rather than mentally retarded (von Kühn-Steinhausen, 1958). Another prince of an earlier line of dukes of Jülich-Berg, Duke Johann Wilhelm (died 1609), was also called "feeble-minded" (by the historian von Kühn-Steinhausen, 1958, p. 13).

It seems to me that there are good reasons why it is more difficult to (a) identify mental retardation in noble households than among other people and (b) distinguish it from mental disorder.

1. As explained in Social Role Valorization teaching, when people are of noble status, greater allowance is made for their deviant behavior to begin with (this is true for other kinds of valued people as well), so that the behaviors of madness and those of low intelligence easily got mixed up.

Mentally retarded members of noble houses were often indulged, and as a result they learned all sorts of bad behaviors. For instance, unrestricted consumption of wine often covered up the sources of their bad behaviors. And a temper tantrum by a disturbed child and a retarded one can look pretty much alike. Therefore, it also became more difficult to distinguish between low intelligence and mental disturbance. In fact, bad behaviors often looked more disturbed than retarded.

2. The evidence suggested to Midelfort that noble families found the behavior of their unintelligent members more challenging than the symptoms of their mentally disturbed ones.

Among the nobility (especially ruling houses), low intelligence is much more stigmatizing than

mental disorder, but with the means available to the nobility, it was easier to cover up the signs of low intelligence, if they desired to do so. For example, all sorts of things could be done to enhance the personal appearance of persons of low intelligence and to support their normal behaviors via the use of tutors, governors, competent companions, etc.

3. Signs of mental abnormality were easier to interpret as idiosyncrasies or illnesses, thereby reducing their stigma. Earlier scholars had often declared their theoretical loyalties by referring to mad people either in legal, medical, or vernacular terms. The abnormalities of princes were often interpreted as either madnesses or illnesses (Midelfort, 1995, p. 46). Sometimes, two domains overlapped, as in *furor* or melancholia, or *schwermütig* ("heavy-minded"), *nicht richtig* ("not right"), or *unsinnig* ("irrational"). There are a great many vernacular German terms for mental disorder.

Also, many princes whom we would consider insane were not so thought of in their day; rather, they were seen as reckless, untrustworthy, idiosyncratic, etc. (Midelfort, 1995).

The above speculations suggest that more attention should be paid to how social class impacts today on the behavior (in the sense of comportment, conduct, and manners) of mentally retarded persons. At one time, researchers seemed to have given a lot more attention to this, but in recent decades, this attention seems to have faded—though members of societally devalued and powerless classes are always more likely to be made the subjects of research than the wealthy and mighty, as one is likely to learn in the more advanced teaching of Social Role Valorization (Wolfensberger, 1998, 2000). One place to look at the comportment of mentally retarded persons of higher classes is in private residential schools and in affluent public school districts. One could hypothesize that the growing crudeness in society today is more expressed among the lower classes than the upper—one more good argument for belonging to the latter.

References

Clair, C. (1968). *Human curiosities*. New York: Abelard Schuman.

Kamen, H. (1997). *Philip of Spain*. New Haven: Yale University Press.

Midelfort, H. C. E. (1995). *Mad princes of Renaissance Germany*. Charlottesville: University Press of Virginia.

Figure 3.1. *(continued)*

INTELLECTUAL AND DEVELOPMENTAL DISABILITIES   VOLUME 49, NUMBER 1: 46–49 | FEBRUARY 2011

Perspective: Idiocy and madness in princely European families   W. Wolfensberger

Tietze-Conrat, E. (1957). *Dwarfs and jesters in art* (E. Osborn, trans.). London: Phaidon. (Distributed by Garden City Books, NY)

Von Kühn-Steinhausen, H. (1958). *Johann Wilhelm: Kurfürst von der Pfalz: Herzog von Jülich-Berg (1658-1716)*. Düsseldorf, Germany: Michael Triltsch Verlag.

Werner, H. (1932). *Geschichte des Taubstummenproblems bis ins 17. Jahrhundert*. Jena, Germany: Gustav Fischer.

Wolfensberger, W. (1991). *A brief introduction to Social Role Valorization as a high-order concept for structuring human services*. Syracuse: Training Institute for Human Service Planning, Leadership & Change Agentry, Syracuse University.

Wolfensberger, W. (1998). *A brief introduction to Social Role Valorization: A high-order concept for addressing the plight of societally devalued people, and for structuring human services* (3rd ed.). Syracuse: Training Institute for Human Service Planning, Leadership & Change Agentry, Syracuse University.

Wolfensberger, W. (2000). A brief overview of Social Role Valorization. *Mental Retardation, 38,* 105–123.

Wolfensberger, W., & Thomas, S. (2007). *PASSING: A tool for analyzing service quality according to Social Role Valorization criteria. Ratings manual* (3rd rev. ed.). Syracuse: Training Institute for Human Service Planning, Leadership & Change Agentry, Syracuse University.

Woods, F. A. (1906). *Mental and moral heredity in royalty: A statistical study in history and psychology.* New York: Henry Holt & Co.

Author:

Wolf Wolfensberger, PhD, Emeritus Professor, Syracuse University Training Institute for Human Service Planning, Leadership & Change Agentry, 518 James St., Ste. B3, Syracuse, NY 13203. (Phone: 315-473-2978, Fax: 315-473-2963)

prolifically on topics as various as theology, medicine, and educational reform. As the leader of the church in Spain, Isidore consolidated the church's power in the face of barbarian threats and the uncertainties of the age that spanned the classical period and the Middle Ages, and he is recognized for his efforts to develop schools to train monks throughout the region. His major work, *Libor Etymologiarium*, consists of an encyclopedia with 22 topics ranging from grammar to God, agriculture, and a brief chapter on medicine. In a section called "Differentiarum," Isidore explains the differences among mental conditions such as *dementia, delirium,* and *amentia,* a condition that might be analogous to intellectual disability. Sharpe (1964) summarized Isidore's writings on the topic: "*Dementia* can be distinguished from *amentia,* only because the former is temporary or develops over a period of time, while the latter is permanent" (p. 33). In a later footnote, Sharpe wrote that

> mental deficiency is briefly mentioned (XC. 79) by Isidore: "Demented, *demens,* means the same thing as "mindless," *amens,* that is, without a mind, or indicates that such have diminished mental power. Foolish, *desipiens,* in that they begin to understand less than is their wont. (p. 58)

A firm believer in *humoral* theories, which relied on physiological explanations rather than superstition, Isidore recommended a balanced approach to treatment for mental diseases, although he thought all of them to be chronic and incurable.

Moses Maimonides (1138–1204; see Figure 3.2) was another religious scholar and brilliant intellect—a Spaniard by birth, distinguished and revered as a Jewish leader, experienced as a medical doctor—who wrote in a different era of the Middle Ages and in another part of the world, Egypt, where he practiced medicine and served as rabbi. One of Maimonides's many remarkable achievements included publication of the *Mishneh Torah,* or Code of Law, in which he provided a legal definition of insanity with a brief reference to what might be thought of as intellectual disability:

The insane person [*shoteh*] is unacceptable as a witness by biblical law, because he is not subject to the commandments. By *shoteh* is to be understood not only one who walks around naked, breaks things and throws stones, but anyone whose mind has

Figure 3.2. Moses Maimonides.
(Illustration from Brockhaus and Efron Encyclopedic Dictionary, 1890–1907). (Image retrieved from unknown artist [Public domain] via Wikimedia Commons; http://commons.wikimedia.org/wiki/File:Brockhaus_and_Efron_Jewish_Encyclopedia_e10_513-0.jpg)

become disturbed so that his thinking is consistently confused in some domain although with respect to other matters he speaks to the point and asks pertinent questions, his evidence is nevertheless inadmissible and he is included among the insane.

The intellectually deficient who cannot recognize contradictions and are unable to comprehend things as ordinary people do and those who are extremely agitated and frantic are classed with the insane. Discretionary power is vested in the judge in this matter, as it is impossible to lay down detailed rules on this subject. (Kranzler, 1993, pp. 50–51)

Classifying the "intellectually deficient" with the "insane," Maimonides did not develop the topic further. There is no insight about how he might have approached the problem or if he actually did so in his practice. The great rabbi's theories of insanity lead to a broader discussion of legal applications concerning mental disability in the Middle Ages.

Jurisprudence during the Middle Ages consisted of a fragmentation of laws and decisions handed down by reigning kings in the various regions of continental Europe. Providing a modicum of a legal system was a legacy of civil law derived from the Roman Empire that permeated continental Europe. By the 1400s, the influence of the church helped revitalize Roman law to unify Europe's laws and their applications. Whatever legal actions were taken concerning people called idiots during this period reflected the heritage of Roman civil law, except in England, which developed a unique approach to legal matters, from the High Middle Ages and specifically under Henry the II, who in the mid-1100s instituted a system of common law. Whereas Roman law consisted of a written code that guided jurists in their legal decisions, common law developed through a combination of legislation acts, judicial decisions, trials by jury, and the Kings' decrees (Cantor, 1993). Because English common law took a more nuanced and naturalistic approach to idiocy than did Roman civil law, it is often cited in the history of idiocy during the Middle Ages.

English common law referred to mental disability in two important contexts: The first concerned the culpability of individuals with mental disability who were accused of criminal behavior, and the second was the disposition of property of people thought to be mentally incapable of managing their affairs. Although issues of criminal intent arose in the ancients' discussion, Henry de Bracton (c. 1210–1268) is often cited for introducing the concept of *mens rea,* or criminal intent, as it specifically concerned offenders with mental disabilities. Individuals who lacked the ability to reason sufficiently were to be exonerated when brought before criminal courts because they lacked civil status, similar to animals that lacked the ability to reason altogether. Evoking a common myth that associated mental disability with the wild nature of people isolated in the forest, Bracton recommended that criteria be adopted that compared the competence of individuals with that of wild beasts. More a philosophical principle than law, Bracton's concepts provide the basis for determination regarding culpability as it concerns mental disability (Clarke, 1975).

According to Neugebauer (1996), idiocy was addressed directly in English common law in the second half of the 1300s in matters of inheritance and the management of property, issues that were foremost in the lives of medieval property owners and a society concerned with stability and the conservancy of wealth. Although, traditionally, family members had made decisions regarding the property of people with mental disabilities (Clarke, 1975), eventually it became necessary for legal methods to resolve disputes. The first legal document concerning mental disability and the problem of property, *Prerogativa Regis,* distinguished between "natural fools" or "idiots" and people called "*non compos mentis*":

> The king shall have the custody of the lands of natural fools taking the profits of them without waste or destruction and shall find them their necessaries. . . . And after the death of such idiots he shall render it to the right heirs, so that such idiots shall not alien nor their heirs . . . be disinherited. (Neugebauer, 1996, p. 25)

Neugebauer (1996) explained that the term *idiot* was derived from a prior legal definition:

> Idiot is he that is a fool natural from his birth and know not how to account or number 20 pence, nor cannot name his father or mother, nor of what age himself is, or such like easy and common matters; so that it appears he has no manner of understanding or reason, nor government of himself, what is for his profit or disprofit. (p. 25)

By this definition, an idiot was determined to be permanently disabled from birth and incompetent in terms of what might be considered ordinary matters, such as counting, reading, and understanding simple matters, all of which were necessary in the management of property.

An individual thought to be *non compos mentis*, in contrast, was considered temporarily impaired with a difficulty that appeared later in life and that might disappear at intervals or altogether. The implications of the differences between these two mental states was important as far as property was concerned, for the idiot's property reverted to the King due to the presumption that the individual would never gain competence, while those with other mental problems retained their property due to the possibility that they might eventually recover and have use of it. Nevertheless, reports of an individual's acquiring idiocy later in life appear in the records. Two examples are found of men who were "of sound mind" in their youth, but for unknown reasons, becoming idiotic, perhaps through injuries to the head, required guardians for their people and their properties (Turner, 2010a, p. 88). A report of another individual thought to be an idiot in mid-1300s England follows:

> John de Heton appeared and was examined and found to be an idiot and incapable of ruling himself. . . . From his birth . . . until he was 24 years of age, he was in good sense and quite sane; and since then till to-day he has been continuously an idiot, insensible to his surroundings . . . , having a fancy in his head, whereby he remains unconscious of his own personality . . . and paying no heed to anything at all. He enjoys no lucid intervals. (Turner, 2010a, pp. 93–94)

Few doubt that the crown's representatives frequently erred on the side of idiocy rather than on *non compos mentis* when deciding cases of mental disability because such a decision benefitted the coffers of the King. For example, in 1351 the guardian of Robert di Vylers, "an idiot," was to provide for Robert and his children from the proceeds of his estate. If the guardian reneged, he could be both fined and replaced (Turner, 2010b, p. 25). In approximately 1396, considerable controversy arose concerning the disposition of the property of a man named Richard, "an idiot from birth," whose complicated estate aroused so much antipathy that his guardian "abducted and removed him [Richard] to some place unknown, so that the jurors know not whether he is alive or dead" (Turner, 2010b, p. 34). In another case, recorded in 1399, considerable confusion arose when it was found that Joan Spencer, an *"idiota,"* had squandered most of her estate, including "a tenement with 2 cellars . . . 2 shops in Fish Street Hill . . . a brewhouse, now called 'le Sterre', with certain shops adjoining" as a result of poor management by her guardians, John and Parnel Katerington, a problem that came to the attention of both the king and the mayor of London (Turner, 2010b, pp. 29–30). Alice Dungate, another property owner of farmland and of three shops, and identified as *"fatua et idiota,"* also came under the wardship of the king, despite previous arrangements with local authorities (Turner, 2010b, p. 31). Turner writes that family members who left wills with explicit directions regarding incompetent dependents could avoid some of the loss of income and the control of property to authorities, be it either the king or local boroughs.

Inquisitions, held by a jury and presided over by a local official, determined the extent of an individual's mental competence. An often-cited example of an examination provides insight into the kinds of questions that were asked and the decisions that were made, at least as it concerned one woman, Emma de Beston, from Cambridgeshire, who was brought before the court of inquisitors in 1383:

> The said Emma, being caused to appear before them, was asked whence she came and said that she did not know. Being asked in what town she was, she said that she was in

Ely. Being asked how many days there were in the week, she said seven but could not name them. Being asked how many husbands she had had in her time she said three, giving the name of one only and not knowing the names of the others. Being asked whether she had ever had issue by them, she said that she had a husband with a son, but did not know his name. Being asked how many shillings there were in forty pence, she said she did not know. Being asked whether she would rather have twenty silver groats than forty pence, she said they were of the same value. They examined her in all other ways which they thought best and found that she was not of sound mind, having neither sense nor memory nor sufficient intelligence to manage herself, her lands or her goods. As appeared by inspection she had the face and countenance of an idiot. (Neugebauer, 1996, p. 29)

Once declared an idiot, Emma was assigned a guardian who reported to the king. Others, however, were appointed guardians who were responsible to a borough rather than the king, in an arrangement that predated *Prerogativa Regis*. Traditionally, family members had been authorized to provide guardianship for dependents who were incapacitated in one way or another. Many urban jurisdictions formalized the procedure, ostensibly to assure that the appointed guardians were acting responsibly in the interests of their wards, although in those cases the income from the dependent's property reverted to the borough rather than to the king, a procedure that generated considerable dispute between the Crown and local authorities.

If court records are any indication, unscrupulous or incompetent guardians were commonplace. For example, in 1286 the guardianship of "Peter de Seyvill, a *freneticus idiota*" was assigned to his brother-in-law, John de Dychton, who failed to deliver the necessary documents regarding his duties, despite the revenues they promised him. Because John himself was thought incompetent, he lost the position of guardian to another relative of Peter's (Turner, 2010a, pp. 86–87). The author suggested that the difficulties people thought to be idiots had with reading others' emotions contributed to their problems with guardians. She described the situation of Maud Marlecomb, "a complete idiot," whose guardian "coldly and cleverly cheated her out of all her property," unbeknown to her (Turner, 2010a, pp. 91–92).

The possibilities of idiocy occurring within a variety of childhood disabilities and diseases, whether specifically mentioned or not, is discussed next. According to Clarke (1975), idiocy (or *fatui naturales*, as it was often called) could be found in many different contexts:

References to *fatui naturales* are brief and are not to be taken straightforwardly as meaning mental defect in the modern restricted sense. In addition to simple stupidity, the class is likely to have included numerous cases of congenital deafness, poor vision (not then corrigible), speech defects, spasticity and other physical handicaps, some epilepsies and some schizophrenic withdrawals and other eccentricities. Singly or in combination these would preclude adequate social learning and participation; even when there was real intelligence in the middle, it would have little chance to unfold. (p. 64)

Clues to the construction of intellectual disability are found in historical interpretations of childhood in the Middle Ages. Modern historians describe childhood as a construct, much as they think of intellectual disability as a construct (MacLehose, 2008). Isidore of Seville and others of the era anticipated contemporary stage theory when they analyzed childhood in terms of ages: infancy (*infantia*), marked by helpless dependency, lasted until the age of seven; childhood (*pueritia*) followed, from the ages of 7 to 14, when children were able to express themselves and distinguish between good and evil; and adolescence (*adolescentia*) occurred between the ages of 14 and 28. The status of childhood absolved young people from the responsibilities of adulthood, including religious rites and marriage, and, at least in England, they were protected by common law (Orme, 2001).

Despite often-cited contrary views, medieval parents demonstrated great fondness and love for their children and accommodated them with food, clothing, and furniture to suit their needs. The concept of childlike innocence dates to the Middle Ages, when children were valued as God-given trusts, although conversely, the religious context presented them as so "pathetic, weak, and foolish, they scarcely differ from beasts" (Shahar, 1990). By the 13th century, schools for boys became established with specialized curriculum through the monasteries. In short, children comprised a special segment of medieval culture; they were not thought of as miniature adults, and their parents experienced attachments and emotional responses to their children's joys and sorrows. Until adolescence, most children remained at home with their families; as they grew older, many boys and girls alike left home to work or to study (Orme, 2001). Most schooling outside of the home occurred in monasteries, where most likely only the more capable children progressed in their studies. Medieval schools would not have been a place where children with disabilities of any kind, and especially mental disabilities, would have been welcome.

The birth process threatened many infants as well as their mothers. If they survived, they were soon baptized, a Christian practice that became essential in Christian families with the advocacy of Augustine of Hippo (d. 430). The sacrament of baptism (and subsequent arguments made against infant baptism) were concerned with the infant's ability to reason and therefor to believe. To both believers and heretics, "the infant was depicted as entirely ignorant of faith, the sacraments, penance, salvation, and his own culpability in Adam's sin" (MacLehose, 2008, p. 59). Infants were, in short, incapable of reason and belief, unable to learn, foolish, and irresponsible, albeit worthy recipients of God's grace—characteristics that were also often attached to idiocy. Until 1300, it was common for parents to produce many children, although few survived childhood. Wealthy families in the early and High Middle Ages may have included up to half a dozen living children at a time, but by the later Middle Ages, they may have seen only two or three children survive. In poor families, fewer than two children may have survived at any time, although children of farming peasants may have been more fortunate. By 1350, however, when the population was decimated by the Black Death, nearly a quarter of all children died. The numbers improved again after 1500 (Orme, 2001). The death of a parent in a poor family, usually the father, often resulted in passing children into the care of a guardian or relative, although Orme claimed that such arrangements were not typical.

Infanticide, while not common, was practiced by parents who may have been burdened with an unwanted or unplanned pregnancy, by twins, or by an infant with deformities. "Some babies survived for only an hour or two, not through their own frailty but that of their parents. Killed when born, they were the victims of terror, shame, indifference, or mental illness" (Orme, 2001, p. 95). People of the Middle Ages abhorred the practice, and punishment could be severe. Abandonment was another option used by desperate parents to rid themselves of an unwanted child. Foundlings were taken in by private families, by hospitals, or by religious organizations. The numbers of abandoned children grew throughout the Middle Ages, along with the number of hospitals dedicated to their care.

Children's behavior was shaped at an early age by instruction and discipline. Christian children were expected to submit to their father's authority, much as Christian men submitted to the authority of their king and God. Instruction in manners and etiquette assured a respectful demeanor. Disrespect earned gentle but firm discipline. Corporal punishment, especially among wealthy families, was not only tolerated but encouraged by the church. Despite general perceptions of parents' harsh treatment of their children, most cared and nurtured their children as best they could. They understood the importance of play, adequate food, and sleep. They comforted their little ones when they cried, and they sought help—usually from religious symbols and saints or other supernatural sources—when they became ill or injured, and they were aware of the importance of affection and social interactions with their children. Shahar (1990) described one family who tried many approaches to teach the child to talk ("some useful, some ridiculous"; p. 93), including imploring a saint's intervention.

There are no numbers to document disability of any kind, but we can be sure they were significant. Medieval children became ill and often succumbed to a variety of diseases, infections, fevers, rashes, and tumors. They suffered from deafness, visual impairments, palsies, and paralyses, as evidenced in the records kept at the shrines where parents sought aid for their children (Shahar, 1990). Sexual and physical abuse was a noted problem (Orme, 2001). Many medieval children were seriously hurt or died from falls, fires, smothering, wandering and getting lost, fights, poisons from plants and objects containing lead, and attacks by animals. Inbreeding also contributed to births of children with mental disabilities (Clarke, 1975). Fatalistic attitudes failed to correct the parental carelessness that contributed to children's death and disabilities. According to Shahar (1990), despite the love parents felt for their children,

> medieval people were not, apparently, endowed with imagination about factors which might cause accidents and did not learn from experience; they were, on the one hand, governed by their instincts and were relatively fatalistic, on the other. (p. 143)

Clearly, many children suffered as a result of their caregivers' negligence. As a result, despite the absence of data, many young survivors of serious illness and injuries undoubtedly acquired mental disabilities, including the problems we associate with intellectual disability.

Children who lived in impoverished conditions faced many more difficulties. The Middle Ages is noted for the persistence of poverty throughout the population, urban and rural, as a result of economic stresses, wars, disease, accidents and injuries, famines, and natural and personal disasters. Poverty represented more than material deprivation: it signified humiliation and disgrace and, in Mollat's (1986) words, the situation of poverty "encompass[ed] the frustrated, the misfit, the antisocial, and the marginal" (p. 5). With the caveat that population data concerning the poor in the Middle Ages are incomplete and ambiguous at best, and often absent altogether, estimates of the proportion of poor within the larger population, derived at the earliest from the roles of those exempt from paying taxes in the 1300s, run from small percentages in certain regions to more than half in others. Within communities the poor were usually known, recognized as members of certain families and social groups. Among these were people referred to as *"idiotus, imbecillis, simplex"* (Mollat, 1986, p. 3), terms analogous to the concept of intellectual disability. Life for the poor was dismal. They lacked clothing and food; lived in the barest shelters if they were not taken in by charities, and were susceptible to disease, malnutrition, injury, and poisoning. Poor, healthy children as well as those who were ill and disabled fared even worse. When food and clothing were scarce, even young children were turned out to beg or to work, either alone or with parents, and even begging could be perilous, for the poor were subject to brutality and viciousness that was spared the wealthy. In Norwich, a boy named Robert, deformed from infancy, begged at houses

> while getting about on his knees with a pair of small crutches. He was cured at the shrine of St William in 1156. A mad girl of Lincoln lived from the charity of the wives of the city, presumably going from house to house, before she was cured at the tomb of St Hugh . . . soon after 1200. At Orpington (Kent), a crippled boy took up his station at the church door, waiting for alms. (Orme, 2001, p. 90)

In such circumstances, some parents may have intentionally injured their children in order to arouse sympathy and attract alms.

Christian principles provided the motivation for church authorities in both the East and the West to open their doors to the poor. Such a demonstration of charity to the poor served the church as well as the poor, for the benefactors gained God's grace with their service, and in the process, the difference between the giver and the recipient became more distinct. According to the principles of Saint Benedict, in the late ninth century, both the poor and their benefactors served God, whereby the poor provided objects in need of beneficence and the charitable helped to relieve their need. With growing populations of poor, some monasteries responded by devoting their care to certain groups, such as the "feeble-minded, lepers, [the] blind" (Mollat, 1986, p. 27). Throughout the Middle Ages, the concept of poverty depended on the pauper's ability and willingness to work: "His worthiness to receive aid from others depended on whether he was unfit for work, unable to find work, or unwilling to engage in work" (Mollat, p. 295), characteristics that helped define the competence of paupers with disabilities for centuries to come. Further development in assistance for the poor took place with the founding of hospitals, from as early as 1100. The mendicant orders, such as the order of Saint Francis, were particularly devoted to the care of the poor, and by the 13th century, collaborations of bishops and monks, laymen and their confraternities, kings and princes founded a proliferation of small and large hospitals. Not all monasteries, hospitals, or hostels welcomed people who were mentally ill and even avoided people thought to be idiots. More commonly these people found their way to asylums for the poor or were confined in jails. By the late 15th century, the exponential growth in the numbers of the poor throughout Europe, the result of famine, disease—including the plague—continuous wars, natural disasters, rising prices, low wages, and a myriad of other factors came together to increase exponentially the numbers of the poor. With the increase came considerable social unrest, anger among the poor, and riots that were to usher in the early modern period.

Issues of childhood disability in impoverished circumstances arose in other contexts as well. Orme (2001) cited a story of so-called green children who grew up in the East Anglian wilds on their own, in the year 1200, approximately. A boy and a girl, they lacked language and cried constantly. Taken into a nearby home, the boy languished and eventually died while the girl recovered, thrived, and eventually married. While narrators repeated their story with awe and wonder, recall the later accounts of the "Wild Boy of Aveyron" (Lane, 1976) and wonder, first if the tale has any truth to it and, if so, if the children were abandoned by their parents because they were disabled or deformed. Children born with or acquiring disabilities were not typical in the Middle Ages. Indeed, they were unusual enough to be objects of wonder. Furthermore, the presence of children with severe disabilities often raised questions of parentage, moral degeneration within families, a mother's vision or behavior during pregnancy, or supernatural occurrences, including astrological events, that produced monstrosities.

For some medieval parents, the pre-Christian myth of changelings accounted for the presence of disability or disfigurement within some superstitious families with newborns. According to lore, Satan's designees paid a surreptitious visit to some unsuspecting parents, made off with a healthy newborn and left in its place one that was impaired. Prescribed rituals intended to reverse the deed and bring the original baby back, including the baby's exposure to the elements, rough handling, and abusive practices, usually brought about the infant's death, a consequence that was probably not altogether unintended (Shahar, 1990).

In rare circumstances, children were sold into slavery, sometimes into the courts of the aristocracy where they served as fools (Alexandre-Biden & Lett, 1999). Orme (2001) described one child from the Isle of Wight as a "monster of nature . . . who was shown to the queen, who had him led around with her for the admiration of beholders" (p. 97). Orme explained further:

> Some of the fools employed in noble households in the later middle ages are likely to have been children or young people, disabled in understanding or small in size. Making them fools is distasteful by modern standards, but contemporaries may have thought that they were giving them roles in which they could earn a living. (p. 97)

Although fools had served as slaves in the Roman Empire, the earliest evidence of court fools is found in 12th century documents (Welsford, 1961). The occupation of court fool provided both natural and artificial fools with a home, food, and some degree of security in their employment, as long as they pleased their lords and the latter's positions were secure. Natural fools represented those individuals who were thought to be simple from birth, unable to learn or work in any occupation that required even a modicum of skill, and equally important, they were socially inept. The brunt of jokes and teasing, they served at the whim of their masters, who one day might treat them as pets and another day banish them altogether. Some individuals, unable to look after themselves, were assigned wardens who tended to them. Artificial fools, in contrast, were skilled actors who were also socially adept. Artificial fools acted the part of the natural in court plays and served as a foil in games of humor and jest. Both natural and artificial fools became scapegoats for whatever misfortunes the court encountered. Sometimes a fine line distinguished one from the other: It could be difficult to ascertain if a court fool was truly incompetent or simply acting the part; similarly, some natural fools were gifted with peculiar skills for music, mimicry, and dancing (Welsford, 1961).

Examples of many such fools abound in the records of English, French, and German courts. By the 14th century, it was generally acknowledged that natural fools were recipients of charity who served at the pleasure of the court, while artificial fools were paid for their services. Similar distinctions were made between fools and idiots: the fool might be employable while the idiot was not (Southworth, 1998). According to Southworth (1998), the distinctions between the two have never been clear: "The confusion between clever and innocent fools on the one hand, and between 'idiots' and wise naturals on the other, has bedeviled most writing on the subject of fools" (Southworth, 1998, p. 163). Nevertheless, employment as the court fool could be very risky because it depended entirely on the king's own security; if the king should be deposed, the fool was also cast out. By the early 16th century, fools were no longer in fashion in the courts of England and France (Welsford, 1961).

CONCLUSION

In closing, it is important to remember the words of Clarke (1975):

> One conclusion which is certain is that at no point in the Middle Ages will one generalisation serve to describe all the formulations and treatment of mental [disability] which were being employed; nor . . . is it very helpful to try to discern a thread of progress towards a supposed enlightenment in terms of empirical scientific method as applied to mental [disability]. (p. 70)

Indeed, significant changes in thinking about and approaches to address the problems associated with mental disability had to wait until the early modern era.

REFERENCES

Alexandre-Biden, D., & Lett, D. (1999). *Children in the Middle Ages: Fifth-fifteenth centuries.* Notre Dame, IN: University of Notre Dame Press.

Cantor, N.F. (1993). *The civilization of the Middle Ages.* New York, NY: Harper Collins.

Clarke, B. (1975). *Mental disorder in earlier Britain.* Cardiff, United Kingdom: University of Wales Press.

Kranzler, H.N. (1993). Maimonides' concept of mental illness and mental health. In R. Rosner & S.S. Kotek (Eds.), *Moses Maimonides: Physician, scientist, and philosopher* (pp. 49–57). Northvale, NJ: J. Aronson.

Lane, H.L. (1976). *The wild boy of Aveyron.* Cambridge, MA: Harvard University Press.

MacLehose, W.F. (2008). *"A tender age": Cultural anxieties over the child in the twelfth and thirteenth centuries.* New York, NY: Columbia University Press.

Mollat, M. (1986). *The poor in the Middle Ages: An essay in social history* (A. Goldhammer, Trans.). New York, NY: Yale University Press.

Neugebauer, R. (1996). Mental handicap in medieval and early modern Europe: Criteria, measurement and care. In D. Wright & A. Digby (Eds.), *From idiocy to mental deficiency: Historical perspectives on people with learning disabilities* (pp. 22–43). London, United Kingdom: Routledge.

Orme, N. (2001). *Medieval children.* New Haven, CT: Yale University Press.

Privateer, P.M. (2006). *Inventing intelligence: A social history of smart.* Oxford, UK: Blackwell.

Shahar, S. (1990). *Childhood in the Middle Ages.* London, United Kingdom: Routledge.

Sharpe, W.D. (1964). Isidore of Seville: The medical writings. *Transactions of the American Philosophical Society, 54*(2), 1–75.

Southworth, J. (1998). *Fools and jesters at the English court.* Thrupp, Gloucestershire: Sutton.

Turner, W.J. (2010a). Silent testimony: Emotional displays and lapses in memory as indicators of mental instability in medieval English investigations. In W.J. Turner (Ed.), *Madness in medieval law and custom* (pp. 81–95). Leiden, Netherlands: Brill.

Turner, W.J. (2010b). Town and country: A comparison of the mentally disabled in late medieval English common law and chartered boroughs. In W.J. Turner (Ed.), *Madness in medieval law and custom* (pp. 17–38). Leiden, Netherlands: Brill.

Welsford, E. (1961). *The fool: His social and literary history.* London, England: Faber and Faber.

Wolfensberger, W. (2011). Idiocy and madness in princely European families. *Intellectual and Developmental Disabilities, 49*(1), 46–49. Washington, DC: American Association on Intellectual and Developmental Disabilities.

4

Idiocy and Early Modern Law

Intellectual Disability in Early Modern Times (1500 CE to 1799 CE)

Parnel Wickham

How did early modern Europeans and their colonists in the years from 1500 to 1799 think about and respond to people they called idiots, natural fools, simple-minded, and other related colloquial terms? Like the Middle Ages, the situation of idiocy was found among the poorer classes and beneficiaries of public and private charity, in the laws and their applications, and more abstractly in the writings of physicians and philosophers. With few individuals identified during this period, there is no way to be sure about the lived experience of idiocy. Indeed, the absence of idiocy from the historical record suggests an early modern social environment marked by idiocy's invisibility and neglect.

*E*ssentially a modern concept, intellectual disability is a construct that is ultimately concerned with the degree to which certain people deviate from culturally accepted norms in terms of biology, behavior, and intelligence. Modern, too, are the arguments made by scholars who maintain that those components of intellectual disability, as well as the standards to assess them, represent values-based, culturally laden constructs. Many of the ideas related to intellectual disability, which were introduced in the late Middle Ages, emerged in the early modern period, with the condition often called "idiocy," used in reference in early modern Europe to people who were thought to be substantively different in terms of social, vocational, religious, and behavioral competence. With the articulation of the construct of idiocy, a movement toward identification took root. The effects of such identification are not benign; on the contrary, in early modern Europe and the contemporary West, people thought to be incompetent typically have been construed as inferior, and whether the term was *intellectual disability* or *idiocy*, they have often experienced discrimination. Separation followed by isolation has often led to maltreatment, and it is the source of this maltreatment for which many people look to previous eras to determine its causes, with the hope that future generations might avoid the conditions that have led to such maltreatment.

As in previous eras, indications of idiocy in early modern Europe emerged in certain medical and philosophical texts, in legal documents, and in artistic expressions where idiocy was defined by poverty, incompetence, and dependence. These documents are important not because they disclose much about the lived experience of idiocy but, on the contrary, because they represent idiocy in the abstract, where ideas apparently took precedence over individuals; indeed, idiocy in early modern Europe is notable for its absence rather than its presence.

IDIOCY AND THE PROBLEM OF POVERTY

Changing social and economic conditions marked the transition from the Middle Ages to early modern times. The 16th century (1500–1599), a period of continuous wars, brought price inflation in agricultural products and manufacturing, along with declining or stable wages that contributed to food shortages and famines, which weakened individuals' resistance to disease and increased the incidence of epidemics. Geremek (1994) explained that the economic expansion and modernization of the 16th century led to growing disparity between rich and poor, accompanied by declining standards of living for most people, who suffered considerably, particularly in those regions where the feudal system remained intact.

Rates of poverty increased from Europe's late medieval period into the 16th and 17th centuries, when one-fifth of the population was poor, with higher proportions of poverty in rural areas (Geremek, 1994). Traditionally, most people who had impairments or who were otherwise incapacitated were cared for by family members or friends, but with no one to help, they would have been turned out into the streets. Jutte (1994) reported that in the early modern period, 10%–25% of recipients of outdoor relief were sick, and the causes of illness among more than half of the poor were disability related or due to old age. In studies of two European cities, 2%–12% of recipients were considered "insane," an ambiguous condition defined in part by an inability to work. According to Jutte, "These halfwits were often forced to wander from place to place, surviving on what little food and money they received by begging in the streets" (Jutte, 1994, p. 24). Others may have been cared for by neighbors if not by family members, while large numbers of less fortunate individuals crowded into public or religious shelters.

From the 14th century onward, beginning with Bethlem Hospital and similar efforts, public hospitals were created to shelter the poor, care for the sick, and provide housing for travelers. Some had specialized populations, such as people who were blind, abandoned children, widows, and the amorphous category of the "mad," which included idiots as well as lunatics. Idiots were rarely distinguished from the mad in early modern Europe, particularly among the poor, for there was little need. Due to the stereotypes related to madness, the public discriminated between two types: people seen as fearfully demonic and people viewed as pathetically deformed, although usually they were all housed together. Other medieval European cities converted monasteries or built new asylums to house people with mental impairments—including people who were seen as insane, mad, or idiotic. Only people too poor to survive without aid, with no friends or family to help, and without the capacity to work would have been incarcerated in these hospitals, which, at the opening of the early modern era, numbered close to 10,000 (Jutte, 1994).

Increasingly, however, attitudes toward the poor shifted toward coercion, confinement, and correction for behavior that was presumed to be purposively reprehensible, an extension of the worthy poor concepts introduced in the late Middle Ages. Failure to find work, interpreted as idleness, further imperiled the plight of the poor. The proliferation of indoor relief was accompanied by bans on begging; in many cities, begging was outlawed and alms giving was prohibited. Indeed, fear and disgust were primary motivations for containing the poor, and no less the mad, for they represented threats to the social order, to personal safety, and to moral standards (Jutte, 1994). The earliest hospitals for people with mental impairments grew out of these shelters for the poor. England's Bethlem Hospital, mentioned in the previous section, was originally established in the 1300s as a Catholic priory but later became a hospital for the insane. Bethlem initially served as a repository for poor social misfits of various kinds, but by the 1600s, when overcrowding became a problem, admissions criteria became stricter and idiots already admitted were discharged. In 1624, when the hospital exceeded its capacity for 25 patients, a governor's report disclosed "eleven patients 'not fitt to bee kepte'; three of them were variously described as merely 'Idiot', 'simple' or 'something idle headed' and were to be removed" (Andrews, Briggs, Porter, Tucker, & Waddington, 1997, p. 326). However, the records of the Williamsburg Hospital, the first mental hospital in America, reveal a significant difference: Whereas Bethlem was never intended for idiots, the Williamsburg Hospital explicitly included idiots from the day it opened its doors (Wickham, 2006). Nevertheless, Williamsburg was quite different from other hospitals in this regard, for in general, hospitals intended for the mentally ill usually barred idiots.

As the divide between rich and poor widened, disdain for the poor deepened. The institutionalization of charity through religious channels served to stabilize the relationship between the charitable and their beneficiaries, thus reinforcing opposing roles of *haves* and *have nots*. By the end of the 16th century, particularly in Italy, the numbers of impoverished alms seekers had grown exponentially, crowding public spaces and threatening community trust and safety. Religious institutions as well as town and city officials proposed methods to control both the presence of alms seekers and the giving of alms. Issues related to poverty and its control fueled the controversies between Catholic and Protestant reformers. Authorities in Rome attempted to manage an influx of poor people with a perusal of public documents to expose possible fakeries of disability, including physical impairments, epilepsy, and mental disorders (Pestilli, 2007). Other approaches involved incarceration in poorhouses, and still others promoted work requirements for the poor, and forcibly returning the poor to their places of origin (Geremek, 1994).

In cities with Protestant populations, where disciplined work habits earned spiritual and economic benefits, distinctions were drawn between people who were thought to be capable of work and those who were not. Altogether, people incapable of working consisted of between 5% and 10% of the total population, a fairly stable figure into the 18th century (Jutte, 1994). Throughout the larger cities of Europe, with capitalist economies, workhouses were erected to get the poor off the streets and to compel their labor. In mid-1550's London, a new poorhouse with an imposed work program was established at Bridewell. Within a few years of its opening, the institution had degenerated into a sordid mix of the poor: the sick, disabled, infirm, the elderly, former soldiers, thieves, beggars, and derelicts of every kind (Geremek, 1994). The coercive nature of the emerging laws relating to the poor and the dismal aspects of housing combined with the vast numbers of people who cycled in and out reinforced the public's attitude toward the poor as not only socially inferior but also morally corrupt. As the number of England's workhouses grew, some were taken over by manufacturing concerns with the intent to make them economically profitable. Similar models of workhouses based on the values of the Protestant work ethic also emerged on the continent throughout the 16th and 17th centuries (Geremek, 1994). As they became increasingly oriented toward production, it seems likely that those inmates least likely to contribute, including idiots, were excluded altogether.

It is tempting to look at the early modern era's burgeoning industry of hospitals, poorhouses, and workhouses for insights into later systems of congregate care for idiots. However, idiocy is barely distinguished from other conditions suffered by the poor, who were largely undifferentiated from each other. If traces of idiocy can be found it is because they consisted of one small segment of a large population of poor people or because they were excluded altogether from early institutions selective as to their inhabitants. As hospitals converted to asylums for the insane, idiots were discharged; as workhouses evolved, idiots were excluded. In sum, there is little about idiocy in the history of the early modern era's approaches to indoor relief to suggest that entire institutions might eventually be devoted solely to their care, although provisions for the poor generally were minimal at best and dreadful at worst, particularly in congregate settings.

IDIOCY AND EARLY MODERN LAW

Legal approaches to idiocy offer additional insights into the ways people in the early modern period thought about the condition. More important, court records sometimes identified people who may have been idiots with information about the individuals and the disposition of their cases. First, a little background: By the end of the Middle Ages, legal systems on both the continent and in England consisted of civil codes derived from ancient Rome, Church canon, and local customs, all subject to the feudal systems that governed the lives of inhabitants socially, economically, and culturally. In criminal cases, most of early modern Europe applied the reasoning of the Roman jurist Justinian (c. 482–565) in determining the extent of a defendant's state of mind at the time a crime was committed: Was the defendant aware of what he or she had done and was the crime intended? Catholic canon law distinguished among three disturbed states of mind: 1) A state of ignorance, 2) an inability to control urges, and 3) a failure to reason. All three implied an absence of valued human qualities, or, put differently, the presence of attributes more animal-like than human (Midelfort, 1999). Without the freedom to act, an individual could not be said to sin. By the early 1500s, it was generally accepted throughout continental Europe, and especially in France, Spain, Italy, and Germany, that the insane lacked the will and the power to plan crimes, while idiots lacked the ability to understand the circumstances (Midelfort, 1999).

Although laws concerning the disposition of mentally disabled criminals were long established, and their implementation varied from region to region throughout this period, most scholars agree that specific cases were handled informally within communities where people were well acquainted with one another. Such a case was reported in Massachusetts in 1647, where Michael Smith was apprehended for voting illegally:

> It is ordered, that the fine of Mighill Smith for his putting in of three beans at once for one mans election, it being done in simplicity, & he being pore & of an harmles dispostion, it is ordered his fine is suspended till further order from the General Corte. (Shurtleff, 1853, p. 189)

Despite rudimentary methods to determine idiocy, most courts would have found them unnecessary; casual observations were enough to establish Smith's difficulties.

England's laws reflected the continental legal heritage but also asserted the authority of the king and his court in the lives of his subjects. Into the 17th century, the king of England claimed the right to decide both criminal and civil legal matters. The king's power was evident in the 13th century legal document *Perogativa Regis*, noted in the previous chapter which required different approaches for handling the property of people deemed mentally impaired: Where *non compos mentis* was concerned, the estates remained intact in case the individuals should recover and need resources; the estates of *fatuorum naturalium*, however, reverted to the king, ostensibly for the idiots' use, because there was no expectation the idiot would recover. In 1540, the various laws were formalized into a new statute that created the Court of Wards and Liveries to oversee dispositions regarding people with mental impairments and their guardians and to manage their related fiscal affairs (Neugebauer, 1987; Walker, 1968).

Throughout the early modern period, naturalistic methods to evaluate the mental ability of presumed idiots involved informal, practical tests of memory and understanding, demeanor and behavior, literacy and numeracy. Once idiocy was established, the care of that person was transferred to a private individual who, prior to

1540, purchased the rights from the king, and the care of the person's property was leased to a guardian who obtained rights to the returns of rentals. Although the laws of 1540 altered the fiscal arrangements, subsequent statutes were enacted throughout the early modern period regarding the legal status, monetary arrangements, and duties of the wards. Thus, *Perogativa Regis* and its various iterations set in motion the Crown's responsibilities for people with mental impairments across social classes, both idiots and lunatics, which are still evident in English law today (Neugebauer, 1987).

One example of the Crown's authority concerned the first person identified as an idiot in the English colony of Virginia, reported in a conflict regarding the care and property of a man named Benomi Buck, who was identified as an idiot. In 1637, Benomi Buck's caregivers, the Ambrose Harmars, lacking sufficient funds, petitioned the Crown for reimbursement from the guardian of his estate, Richard Kemp, who withheld the funds for his personal use. Although the court ruled in favor of Buck's caregivers, the governor of Virginia repudiated the Crown's decision and interceded on behalf of Kemp, who continued to appropriate Buck's estate for his own use. It would not have been unusual for local magistrates in outlying regions, especially one so distant from the king's court, to overrule the king for their own gain; thus, Virginia's authorities may have been concerned more for their own authority than for the care of an idiot. It took Buck's caregivers several trips to London to resolve the problem to their satisfaction. Buck died in 1639 in his early twenties, still under the care of the Harmars (Neugebauer, 1987).

IDIOCY AND EARLY MODERN MEDICINE

If jurists in Rome consulted the first comprehensive text of legal medicine, which was published serially in Rome beginning in 1621 by the physician Paulus Zacchias (1584–1659), they would have found advice for classifying, ranking, and ruling on cases that involved mental disability and issues of mental competence. In his method of classification, Zacchias systematically named and described levels based on various limitations of thinking and learning. Three levels are somewhat analogous to intellectual disability; others suggest the debilities associated with severe illness and old age. Zacchias began with an explanation of several types of fools, arguing against his predecessors' systems, such as Girolamo Cardano's, as too simplistic. Where Cardano (1501–1576) claimed that fools were either "witless" or they did "not reason correctly from things which they have recognized" (Cranefield & Federn, 1970, p. 7), Zacchias promoted a more complex, ranked system that he called "the Ignorant, Foolish, Stupid, Forgetful, and Bereft of Memory" (Cranefield & Federn, 1970, p. 6). The ignorant, who Zacchias also called "obtuse," were unable to learn like others from a rudimentary education; their judgment was comparable to that of a 14-year-old child. It would not be accurate to call these people fools, Zacchias claimed. Instead, he suggested that they were more likely "simpletons or people of a coarse grain or gross mind; in addition we call them slow, dolts, buffoons, clowns . . . and . . . blocks, etc." (Cranefield & Federn, 1970, p. 7). Such individuals, while they possessed good memories, often lacked courage. "To say it in a word, where an effort of the intellect is needed, they perform everything slowly and without measure, and not at the proper occasion or time. On the other hand, they excel in an exquisite memory of things"

(Cranefield & Federn, 1970, p. 8). In any event, they were not to be confused with those who were called crazed or insane.

All types of foolishness, according to Zacchias, depended on degrees of coldness in the brain. Thus, people with a higher grade of intellect had only moderate degrees of cooling, whereas people with more limited intellect were subject to colder brains. Ultimately, Zacchias concluded that there was no reason to prevent the highest grades of fools from testifying in court cases. Likewise, they should be permitted to marry and to make their wills, and they should be allowed to participate in religious rites. Nevertheless, they should be barred from church and public offices, and denied access to feudal estates. In criminal cases where intent was debated, Zacchias contended that such fools should be exonerated, as were children age 14 and younger, unless deceit and malice were evident, in which case the criminals should be punished, as were adults (Cranefield & Federn, 1970).

Zacchias referred to the second grade as fools not only lazy and slow, but their ability to reason was "below the condition of human nature" (Cranefield & Federn, 1970, p. 10). Barely able to speak, they progressed little beyond that of a 7-year-old child who preferred to play with toys. Lacking both memory and intellect, they learned little. According to Cranefield & Federn, 1970, "they are thought to be incapable of anything and can not be instructed in anything save some trifles, for they have very little intellect and are also devoid of memory" (p. 11) because their brains were cold and they lacked the necessary spirits. The third degree of fool Zacchias called "stupid and mindless, and metaphorically stones" (Cranefield & Federn, 1970, p. 11), for they had no memory and learned nothing at all. The latter two groups of fools should not be allowed to participate in civil activities and, like small children, should be exonerated of all crimes. Whether or not individuals in these two categories should marry or execute wills Zacchias left up to jurists, who, he claimed, could easily discern a fool's competence. With minor exceptions, other physicians agreed that conditions such as idiocy were not diseases; there was no possibility of improvement, and, consequently, there was no need for medical treatment. Their mention of the problem served merely to illustrate the varieties of human difficulties and to contrast hopeless affliction with illnesses that might respond to medical treatment.

Medical texts of two Swiss physicians, Paracelsus (1493–1541) and Felix Platter (1536–1614), referred to abnormalities of the mind, something analogous to intellectual disability but perhaps more broadly conceived as mental problems. Although they were both among the first medical men to consider mental disabilities, they approached their work from different vantage points. Paracelsus, the iconoclast, autodidact, inveterate outsider, attempted to explain human matters within a broad sweep of spirituality, while Platter, the more conventional physician, focused on the practical aspects of medicine and its application to mankind. Neither man thought of idiocy as a disease, and neither proposed cures. Both maintained God's presence in the affliction, but there the similarities end.

On the Begetting of Fools, published in 1567 by Paracelsus, adopted a philosophical approach to try to explain how God could create in his image "a fool, a simpleton, a stupid and ignorant one" (Cranefield & Federn, 1967, p. 57). Whereas all people embodied base animal nature as a result of original sin, most avoided degeneration by using the reason with which they were born. Fools, lacking the instruments of reason, were ruled primarily by animal nature. Even prosperous, socially prominent parents might give birth to fools, who were burdened by not only inherent sinfulness but also bore signs of the inferior work of *vulcani*, personifications of natural forces. Nevertheless, fools were not devoid of divine grace: "They have within them a light which shines through their fools' head" (Cranefield & Federn, 1967, p. 69), a light that remains at death, when the fool's spirit rises into heaven. Ultimately, however, Paracelsus concluded that "there is no disease, [for fools] are incurable, have no stones nor herbs whereby they might become intelligent" (Cranefield & Federn, 1967, p. 57) for even Christ was unable to heal them: " about medicine . . . there is nothing to say" (Cranefield & Federn, 1967, p. 59).

Felix Platter's references to problems relating to idiocy appeared sporadically throughout his important text, *Golden Practice of Physick*, originally published as *Praxeos Medicae* in 1656. Of particular interest was Platter's innovative attempt to systematize the kinds, the causes, and the cures of mental problems. Throughout, Platter wove references to various behaviors, physical characteristics, and cognitive processes that evoked concepts that were often indistinguishable among idiocy, lunacy, and the mental problems associated with aging, such as, for example, "a weakness of the minde" or "a dullness of the Minde" which could affect both those who were ill and those who were well (Platter, 1664, p. 1). One specific type he called "a slowness of wit," which referred not only to children but to certain elderly adults as well:

> Some want Wit, when they scarcely learn to speak; and they apprehend Learning, and other Arts with difficulty . . . sometimes they are void of Judgment, . . . and this may be called *Imprudence*. . . . For the most part the Memory is weakened when they hardly retain those this things which they have apprehended and learned; and its called *Oblivion*. (Platter, 1664, p. 1)

Among the many possible causes for such problems, Platter ventured that some were inherited from parents, "the ingenious and industrious" as well as the "drones." Other causes included physical malformations or injuries to the brain, especially when associated with excessive moisture or extreme dryness. If such a weakness was inherited or occurred through malformation or injury to the brain, or if the brain was too moist or too dry, Platter concluded the condition was incurable. Nevertheless, in some situations there was a possibility that with use—though not too much—the problems might be mitigated.

Foolishness, according to Platter, represented another aspect of mental disability that was sometimes evident in "old Folks" and children who "do not easily obey, are blockish so that oftentimes they learne not to speak, much less to perform other Duties, in which any industry is required" (Platter, 1664, p. 26). Others may have special gifts, yet they behave in ridiculous ways. In addition to the causes listed previously, Platter attributed some of these difficulties to the presence of the devil, although this was more typical with problems such as madness and melancholy. In such cases he recommended religious interventions, while he concluded that foolishness "may happen from an *evil Distemper of the Brain*, the which notwithstanding seeing it cannot be rightly explained, nor corrected, is no further to be enquired into" (Platter, 1664, p. 35).

Thomas Willis (1621–1675), English physician, represents a gradual shift in the ways people with mental disability were perceived by the 17th-century medical community. Although perceptions varied by geographic location, social customs, and religion, the views of Willis, who was a well-educated, conservative Anglican, were influential due to his highly respected publications on anatomy, the bourgeoning field of neurology, and his professional positions as physician and teacher. Early in his career, Willis agreed with his compatriots that certain cases of mental illness could be attributed to supernatural causes and ameliorated only by exorcism; however, as he grew older his position shifted from a philosophical orientation to one that was more naturalistic, derived in part from his experience as a physician and anatomist and from the emerging climate of early scientific thought. As a result, Willis was grounded in the religious and philosophical past, while he represented the firsthand experiences that more closely corresponded with later scientific approaches. Increasingly, he relied on anatomical studies and bedside observations while he argued for a theoretical view of human nature, whereby mankind comprised two kinds of souls: the inferior animal soul, which was physical in nature, and the superior rational soul, which having no physical properties, was immortal; furthermore, he relied on Galen's explanation of animal spirits to understand the function of the nervous system (Cranefield, 1961). For Willis, stupidity and foolishness represented defects of the rational soul and the animal spirits. These defects could be found in head size, shape, and formation. In some cases it was the substance of the brain that was defective: it could be too warm, too cold, too dry, or too moist, or sometimes the brain's consistency was too dense or too loose, a situation that prevented the animal spirits from flowing easily. Both conditions could be acquired from parents with impairments of the rational soul or animal spirits, or through injury or disease. Willis delineated between the two conditions in the following way:

> Those who are affected with [Foolishness] apprehend simple things well and quick enough, and keep them fast in Memory, but for want of Judgement, ill compound or divie Notions, and far worse infer one thing from another: Moreover, by fooling, and doing, and speaking a great many things unhappily or ridiculously, they move Laughter in the standers by: On the contrary, those that are stupid by reason of the defects of the Imagination, Memory, and Judgement, neither apprehend well, nor nimbly, nor argue well: Moreover, they do not behave themselves as the former . . . but blockishly and unseamly, and as it were, like Apes, and consequently the simplicity of these is more. (Willis, 1692/1977, p. 499)

Willis continued with his description of the many kinds of stupidity:

> Some Persons are accounted unfit as to the comprehension of all things, others only as to some: Some being wholly unfit for Learning, and the liberal Sciences, are apt enough to mechanical Arts: Others . . . can be taught only those things that regard eating and drinking, and the common way of living, others being mere Dolts, scarce understand any thing at all, or do any thing with Knowledge. (Willis, 1692/1977, p. 499)

The prognosis for stupidity depended on the age of onset and the cause: The longer it continued, the less likely the condition would improve. Even if not curable, however, most people could be treated with the combined efforts of a teacher and a physician who must diligently teach them the same things over and over again in order to activate the animal spirits. Other therapies were also recommended–bloodletting, trepanning, light diet and fresh air, various chemical compounds, coffee, chocolate, and small amounts of ale and beer (Willis, 1692/1977).

Despite the ambiguity surrounding the many terms and situations Willis described, and his generally negative assessment of all things having to do with mental impairment, one can look to his recommendation for educational therapies provided by teachers in tandem with physicians as one of the more hopeful signs for people thought to have a mental disability. In all other aspects, however, Willis was not much different from other physicians of the period who found little reason for medical intervention. They might describe a great variety of conditions that suggested deviations from the typical, and they thought about these conditions in different ways, but they did not concern themselves with individuals who might have been called idiots or with idiocy as such, because there was no expectation that people who were thought to be idiots would respond to their treatments.

IDIOCY AND THE PHILOSOPHERS

The work of John Locke (1632–1704), English scholar noted for his contributions to psychology, economics, political science, and religion, introduced the concept of empiricism to understand the workings of the mind. Locke's theories helped bridge the natural philosophy of early modern Europe with the rational approaches of the Enlightenment. According to Locke, humans were born without innate ideas, their mind blank until they gained direct experience with their environment by way of their sense organs. The operation of the mind actively converted those initial mental representations into more complex thoughts. Thus, humans possessed unique consciousness and mental operations that set them apart from animals.

How far apart were humans and animals? Locke tried to answer this with a comparison between the minds of "brutes" and the minds of humans in a series of operations that he called discerning, comparing, composition, and abstraction. In all these mental activities, brutes fell short. As for brutes' capacity for abstractions, Locke wrote that

> the power of *Abstracting* is not at all in them; and that the having of general *Ideas*, is that which puts a perfect distinction betwixt Man and Brutes; and is an Excellency which the Faculties of Brutes do by no means attain to. For it is evident, we observe no foot-steps in them, of making use of general signs for universal *Ideas*; from which we have reason to imagine, that they have not the faculty of abstracting, or making general *Ideas*, since they have no use of Words, or any other general Signs. (Locke, 1979, pp. 159–160)

Locke made the argument that the ability to think abstractly was a uniquely human quality, made evident with the use of language. He went on to explain the concept further, using idiocy rather than brutes for imagery:

> How far *Idiots* are concerned in the want or weakness of any, or all of the foregoing Faculties, an exact observation of their several ways of faltering, would no doubt discover. . . . Those who cannot distinguish, compare, and abstract, would hardly be able to

understand, and make use of Language, or judge, or reason to any tolerable degree: but only a little, and imperfectly, about things present, and very familiar to their Senses. . . . In fine the defect in *aturals* seems to proceed from want of quickness, activity, and motion, in the intellectual Faculties, whereby they are deprived of Reason: Whereas *mad men*, on the other side, seem to suffer by the other Extreme. For they do not appear to me to have lost the Faculty of Reasoning: but having joined together some *ideas* very wrongly, they mistake them for Truths; and they err as Men do, that argue right from wrong Principles. . . . In short, herein seems to lie the difference between Idiots and mad Men, That mad Men put wrong *Ideas* together, and so make wrong Propositions, but argue and reason right from them: But Idiots make very few or no Propositions, and reason scarce at all. (Locke, 1979, pp. 160–161)

Clearly, Locke has no concern for idiots as such; his interest lies in the utility of their image as an extreme example of humankind; indeed, idiocy would seem to lie outside the range of human nature altogether, for lacking language, it was more closely allied with brutes than with humans.

Goodey and Stainton (2001) pursued this line of thought with an analysis of the way Locke wrote about changelings, which were understood to be indeterminate beings substituted for human infants at birth. Long a mythical creature, the various meanings attached to changelings represented predominantly the presence of the supernatural in the union of physical impairment and spiritual deformity. The concept had little to do with conditions akin to intellectual disability until John Locke argued that changelings, even though born of human parents, were essentially nonhuman: "Ay, but these are *Monsters*. Let them be so . . . your drivling, unintelligent, intractable *Changeling*" (Locke, 1979, p. 571). Thus, Locke concluded that changelings existed somewhere between humans and beasts. As Goodey and Stainton (2001) explained, Locke's ideas about changelings represented an "interstitial species between humans and other animals" (p. 237), a space that offered a new definition of beings with human physical characteristics lacking the essential human quality of reason. Such beings lay outside the spiritual dimensions of humanity as well, suggesting a concept of total exclusion. Although others have argued that Locke's ideas about idiocy made little difference in the ways people thought to be idiots were treated (Andrews et al., 1997), Goodey (2011) took a longer view with his claim that Locke's definition of the changeling fostered modern ways of thinking about and responding to the problem that came to be called intellectual disability.

Cotton Mather (1663–1728), Puritan preacher in the Massachusetts Bay Colony, reflected Locke's assessment of idiocy. In 1713 he reported a visit to a family where he observed two sisters who developed convulsions when just a few months old:

These fits anon left them wholly deprived of almost everything in the world, but only a little sight, and scent, and hunger. Nothing in the whole brutal world so insensible! They move not their limbs: you may twist them, and bend them, and bend them to a degree that none else could bear, and they feel it not. They take notice of nothing in the world, only they seem to see and smell victuals, at the approach of which they will gape, and be very restless, and make something of a bray. . . . They shed no tears. They never sneeze.

They have no speech. They have no way to discover any sentiments of their minds. They never use their hands to take hold of anything. Was *idiocy* ever seen so miserable! (Mather, 1971, p. 139)

Surely Mather's despicable creatures would have suited Locke's interpretation of beings who were neither fully human nor fully beasts. With horror, Mather questioned not only their humanity but their sanctity, for surely, he said, their condition lay outside anything human that God intended. Could Mather's response provide another way to bridge the gap between early modern interpretations of idiocy and current meanings of intellectual disability? There are many who would agree that while contemporary reactions to intellectual disability are more tempered to meet the social times, the dehumanizing, emotional rejection expressed by Mather may currently be found in approaches to intellectual disability.

IDIOCY AND THE ARTS

The language and imagery of idiocy reflects society's responses to people thought to be substantively different. Religious imagery, for example, has represented idiocy with a bifurcated model, discussed previously, that on the one hand sanctified the innocent souls of idiots and on the other hand cast them among the spiritually hopeless, while cultural images of natural fools portrayed a mix of types including, for example, incompetent simpletons and sly court jesters. These representations are central to understanding the concept of idiocy because they helped define the experience of people who were identified as idiots and they permeated the social environment from which concepts of idiocy and then intellectual disability emerged.

Figure 4.1. The "idiot fool" from Hans Holbein the Younger's *Danse Macabre*, circa 1535.
(From Holbein, H. [1538]. *Danse macabre*. Lyon, France: Melchior & Gaspar Trechsel for Jean and Francois Frellon. Retrieved from http://commons.wikimedia.org/wiki/File:Holbein_Danse_Macabre_45.jpg)

The Renaissance period of European history—roughly encompassing the last century of the late Middle Ages and spanning the 17th century—is associated with remarkable developments in science, literature, and art. It is not surprising that some of the concepts associated with the understanding of idiocy during the early modern era are depicted in paintings and literature. An early illustration occurs in Hans Holbein the Younger's masterpiece *Danse Macabre*, or *Dance of Death*, published in 1538. The *Danse Macabre* consists of a series of allegorical images typically depicting Death as a skeleton leading a variety of people to their graves. From Eve (of the Garden of Eden), to the Pope, emperor, and king, to the old woman, physician, and knight, each person is led to his or her final resting place. Also included among the child, the robber, the miser, and the nun, is the "idiot fool" (see Figure 4.1). The idiot fool is shown

Figure 4.2. *The Changeling*, by Henry Fuseli, 1780.
(Retrieved from http://commons.wikimedia.org/wiki/File%3AF%C3%BCssli_-_Der_Wechselbalg_-_1780.jpeg)

prepared to hit Death with his "bauble," an air filled sack or bladder. The Devil follows the fool, blowing his own air bladder—a bagpipe. Dating back as early as the 1400s, these images were probably generated as ways to process or assimilate the sudden death that often occurred in that era from disease, injury, hunger, or war.

The notion of the changeling stirred the imagination of artists from the 16th century onward. For example, Figure 4.2 presents Swiss–British painter Henry Fuseli's painting *The Changeling*, dated 1780, with the image of the changeling. The impetus for a mythology of changelings as not quite human was, of course, usually the birth of a child with physical malformations and perhaps concomitant intellectual impairments. As Fuseli's painting represents, by the latter years of early modern times, changelings were depicted as deformed or hideous children of pairings between humans and nonhumans—elves, trolls, and so forth.

William Shakespeare (1564–1616), widely acknowledged to be the greatest English-language dramatist, knew of idiots and idiocy, as would any Londoner of that time. In Act 5, Scene 5 of the tragedy *Macbeth*, the Scottish king speaks the following soliloquy upon learning that his queen, Lady Macbeth, is dead:

She should have died hereafter.

There would have been a time for such a word.

Tomorrow, and tomorrow, and tomorrow,

> Creeps in this petty pace from day to day,
>
> To the last syllable of recorded time;
>
> And all our yesterdays have lighted fools
>
> The way to dusty death. Out, out, brief candle!
>
> Life's but a walking shadow, a poor player,
>
> That struts and frets his hour upon the stage,
>
> And then is heard no more. It is a tale
>
> Told by an idiot, full of sound and fury,
>
> Signifying nothing.

Macbeth, in his despair, declares that life has no purpose, "a tale told by an idiot, full of sound and fury, signifying nothing." With these words Shakespeare immortalized the association between nothingness and idiocy, or, to put it another way, he portrayed idiocy in terms of absence.

CONCLUSION

Privateer (2006) argued that the Renaissance "produced two new intelligence models: a composite divine-human model and a more radical, totally human form, primarily empirical, material, natural, and scientific in nature" (p. 27). It could be argued that concepts of idiocy represented on one hand aspects of the divine and on the other hand the most abject of humans, despite the fact that the situation of idiocy was largely absent from the developments of the Renaissance, aside from some notable artistic representations. As it emerged from obscurity in the early 1800s, idiocy became increasingly associated with aspects of human nature that were deemed inferior and degenerate, while social, legal, and scientific communities developed approaches to define and control those thought to be idiots. Shedding the obscurity that defined it in early modern Europe, idiocy took on new identities in the modern era that brought unwanted attention aimed at identification, isolation, and eventual maltreatment on a grand scale.

REFERENCES

Andrews, J., Briggs, A., Porter, R., Tucker, P., & Waddington, K. (1997). *The history of Bethlem.* London, United Kingdom: Routledge.

Cranefield, P.F. (1961). A seventeenth century view of mental deficiency and schizophrenia: Thomas Willis on "stupidity or foolishness." *Bulletin of the History of Medicine, 35*(4), 291–316.

Cranefield, P.F., & Federn, W. (1967). The begetting of fools: An annotated translation Paracelsus' *De Generatione Stultorum. Bulletin of the History of Medicine, 41,* 56–74; 161–174.

Cranefield, P.F., & Federn, W. (1970). Paulus Zacchias on mental deficiency and on deafness. *Bul-letin of the New York Academy of Medicine, 46*(1), 3–21.

Geremek, B. (1994). *Poverty: A history* (A. Kolakowska, Trans.). Oxford, United Kingdom: Blackwell.

Goodey, C.F. (2011). *A history of intelligence and "intellectual disability": The shaping of psychology in early modern Europe.* Surrey, United Kingdom: Ashgate.

Goodey, C.F., & Stainton, T. (2001). Intellectual disability and the myth of the changeling myth. *Journal of the History of the Behavioral Sciences, 37,* 223–240.

Jutte, R. (1994). *Poverty and deviance in early modern Europe.* Cambridge, United Kingdom: Cambridge University Press.

Locke, J. (1979). *An essay concerning human understanding* (P. H. Nidditch, Ed.). Oxford, United Kingdom: Oxford University Press.

Mather, C. (1971). *Selected letters of Cotton Mather* (K. Silverman, Comp.). Baton Rouge: Louisiana State University Press.

Midelfort, H.C.E. (1999). *A history of madness in sixteenth-century Germany.* Stanford, CA: Stanford University Press.

Neugebauer, R. (1987). Exploitation of the insane in the new world: Benomi Buck, the first reported case of mental retardation in the American colonies. *Archives of General Psychiatry, 44,* 481–483.

Pestilli, L. (2007). Blindness, lameness and mendicancy in Italy (from the 14th to the 18th centuries). In T. Nichols (Ed.), *Others and outcasts in early modern Europe* (pp. 107–129). Hampshire, United Kingdom: Ashgate.

Platter, F. (1664). *Golden practice of physic.* London, United Kingdom: Peter Cole.

Privateer, P.M. (2006). *Inventing intelligence: A social history of smart.* Malden, MA: Blackwell.

Shurtleff, N.B. (Ed.). (1853). *Records of the governor and company of the Massachusetts bay in New England: Vol. 2, 1642–1649.* Boston, MA: W. White, Printer to the Commonwealth.

Walker, N. (1968). *Crime and insanity in England. Vol. 1: The historical perspective.* Edinburgh, Scotland: Edinburgh University Press.

Wickham, P. (2006). Idiocy in Virginia, 1616–1860. *Bulletin of the History of Medicine, 80,* 677–701.

Willis, T. (1977). *The London practice of physick.* Boston, MA: Longwood Press. (Original work published 1692)

5

The Development of Systems of Supports

Intellectual Disability in

Middle Modern Times (1800 CE to 1899 CE)

Philip M. Ferguson

At the start of the 19th century, the concept of intellectual disability was framed in the terminology and assumptions of the Enlightenment philosophers and the earliest French alienists. Within psychology there was a growing specialization in idiocy—the term established in the Middle Ages, which remained in use for most of the 19th century—as distinct from insanity. It was in this century that the large, specialized, congregate care facilities that we now call *institutions* or *developmental centers* were first created in the United States. By the end of the century, the large, urban public school systems were beginning to establish the system of separate schools and classrooms for backward and feeble-minded children that we now call special education. The basic structure of the systems of supports that grew in the 20th century were established during this period.

*T*he 19th century in the United States was one of the most dramatic in any nation's history. The country went from a small, fragile republic with a largely agricultural economy to the industrial and manufacturing leader of the Western world. It started by mourning the death of its first president, George Washington, barely survived a bitter and deadly civil war in the middle of the century, and saw two more of its presidents assassinated in the span of 16 years. Waves of immigrants from abroad joined rural immigrants from farms and villages to push the percentage of the population living in cities to over 40%, a trend that would continue in the early decades of the 20th century. By 1850, the United States led the world in the production of items and goods requiring the use of precision instruments, and industry was well on the way to mass production methods. By the end of the 1880s, workers in urban settings rode elevators up to their offices in the amazing 10-story skyscrapers that were popping up seemingly everywhere. Once at their desks, they turned on the lights in their electrically lit offices, made calls on one of Bell's amazing telephones, and typed letters on their new Remington typewriters. Even with the depression of the mid-1890s, the end of the century saw renewed economic growth at home and continued expansion of American imperialism in both the Caribbean and the Pacific.

On a social scale, the country also went through dramatic changes. The unfortunate but unavoidable challenges faced by individuals and families who were poor, ill, or otherwise dependent on others became recognized as the social problems of disease, immorality, and poverty. The state replaced the municipality as the main unit of government responsible for responding to the alarming growth of these social maladies. Free public schools—at least at the elementary level—became the norm rather than the exception, supported at the local level but increasingly organized and monitored by states departments of education (Cremin, 1982). The system of state colleges and universities became entrenched in a way that led to expanded citizen access to higher education and encouraged states to sponsor industrial and agricultural research that helped drive their economies upward.

Amid this century of economic, political, and social turmoil and change, people with intellectual disability were never at the forefront of public debate, except as part of a larger group of the dependent classes (Katz, 1985; Rothman, 1980). They were, nonetheless, targets of successive waves of attention from policy makers and social reformers. Although people with intellectual disability seldom drove the engines of change, they were carried along with dramatic shifts in both definition and response to what was perceived to be a growing population of unproductive and dependent people, draining energy from the marketplace and distracting families from their proper role as sources of labor and respite for a hard-working population. Separate national censuses of the "defective and dependent population" were taken to document the extent of the problem (Billings, 1895; Katz, 1985; Wines,1888). Psychology emerged as a distinct profession for clinical practice as much as philosophical speculation (Shorter, 1997). Within psychology there was a growing specialization in *idiocy*—the term established in the Middle Ages and remaining in use for most of the 19th century—as distinct from *insanity*. Gradually, the individual states centralized their governance and control of charities and corrections that led to the patchwork system of social welfare and control that are still largely relied upon (Rothman,

1980). It was in this century that the large, specialized, congregate care facilities that are now called institutions or developmental centers were first created in the United States. Finally, by the end of the century, the large, urban public school systems were beginning to establish the system of separate schools and classrooms for backward and feebleminded children that are now called special education (Osgood, 2008; Winzer, 1993).

In many respects, the current system of care and support for people with intellectual and developmental disabilities had its beginnings in the 19th century. What is more important, in certain fundamental ways it was in this century that the very concept of intellectual disability (in the varied terminology of *idiocy*, *imbecility*, and *feeblemindedness*) began to crystallize around a developmental understanding that could be arranged more helpfully by level than by type. It has been said that "history is anthropology with time rather than place the variable" (Goodey, 2011, p. 2). If so, then the study of intellectual disability in 19th-century America is an ethnography of a culture that is very familiar yet strikingly strange.

Running through the frames that form the examination of intellectual disability in this text—understandings of disability, services and supports for people with intellectual disability during the era, and the lived experiences of people with intellectual disability—will be a larger narrative that tells a story of disability in general and of intellectual disability in particular in the 1800s. It is a story that moves from a belief in the inevitability of a largely preordained social order, to a subject of scientific optimism about human potential and reform, to a return in the final decades to an oppressive pessimism born of failed expectations and a perverted science of heredity (Carlson, 2001; Rafter, 1988; Smith & Wehmeyer, 2012).

IDIOCY IN THE 19TH CENTURY

At the start of the 19th century, the concept of intellectual disability was framed in the terminology and assumptions of the Enlightenment philosophers and the earliest French alienists (i.e., psychologists) from the previous century, as discussed in Chapter 4. From a professional point of view, the terms of choice were *fatuity* or *idiocy*. Benjamin Rush—a signer of the Declaration of Independence and the so-called father of American psychology—defined fatuity in *Medical Inquiries and Observations Upon the Diseases of the Mind* as an affection of the mind that "consists in a total absence of understanding and memory. It has different grades, from the lowest degree of manalgia, down to that which discovers itself in the vacuity of the eye and countenance, in silence and garrulity, slobbering, lolling of the tongue, ludicrous gestures of the head and limbs" (Rush, 1812/1962, p. 291). Rush's views echoed the past much more than they foreshadowed the future. For the most part, his ideas were less sophisticated versions of the approach taken by French psychologists, such as Pinel, in viewing fatuity as a reduction in intellectual functioning, regardless of cause or age of onset. Idiocy was seen not as a developmental disability, as it is now, but as a permanent diminution in cognitive ability, whether congenital or acquired (Simpson, 2007). Indeed, to a great extent, idiocy was mainly understood in comparison with lunacy. It was conceived as an absence of thought, compared to other forms of insanity, where thought was present but distorted. For

Pinel, as for Rush, idiocy was to be understood as a special, and most hopeless, type of insanity, not a separate condition all its own. It was insanity that received the greatest attention; the idiot was simply the untreatable cousin of the treatable lunatic. Of course, this process was not purely linear. By the 1830s, the prominent American insane asylum superintendent Isaac Ray published a treatise on the law and insanity (Ray, 1838) that would remain throughout most of the century. It set out idiocy and imbecility as two of the four main divisions of insanity (mania and dementia were the other two). At the same time, Etienne Esquirol (1838/1845) was making a much stronger distinction between insanity and idiocy: "Idiocy is not a disease, but a condition in which the intellectual faculties are never manifested; or have never been developed sufficiently to enable the idiot to acquire such an amount of knowledge as persons his own age and placed in similar circumstances with himself are capable of receiving" (p. 446).

Over the course of the century, however, the concept of idiocy evolved and formed into something much more closely resembling current usage (at least in the context of a medical model). Two main changes evolved over the 19th century. First, there was the triumph of a developmental approach to understanding the concept of idiocy, ending with a burst of quantitative techniques to locate individuals with supposedly increasing precision along a developmental continuum, from almost typical to permanently infantilized. Second, there was a dramatic elaboration of categories and levels of idiocy. In the 19th century, idiocy became viewed as a condition originating in childhood and subject to location along a continuum of severity. The evolving definitions gave an intellectual justification for the dramatic changes in policy and practice that emerged over the course of the 19th century.

VICTOR, ITARD, AND THE EVOLUTION
OF THE DEVELOPMENTAL CONCEPT OF IDIOCY

Along with viewing idiocy as a defective condition rather than as a developmental deficiency came pessimism about prospects for improvement. The case of Itard and his interventions with the boy he named Victor—the so-called Wild Boy of Aveyron—illustrated the prevailing pessimism at the beginning of the 1800s, at the same time that it provided empirical support for the optimistic efforts of Séguin and others who followed Itard in Europe and the United States in the middle decades of the century. Figure 5.1 provides a scan of the frontispiece and title page for the first English printing of Itard's important book, including the now-familiar image of Victor.

The story of the Wild Boy of Aveyron and his teacher, Itard, has been told by many (e.g., Lane, 1976; Shattuck, 1980). It is often and rightly used as one of the earliest examples of special education and behavioral intervention with children with intellectual disability. The story, however, is also an example of how the concept of idiocy was still a curious mixture of developmentalism and organic defect at the beginning of the 1800s.

Jean-Marc Gaspard Itard was only 26 years old when he became a physician at the National Institute for Deaf-Mutes in Paris and began to work with Victor. When he undertook his experimental efforts to educate the Wild Boy he was probably only 12–14 years older than his pupil. Itard, however, was mature enough in his convictions

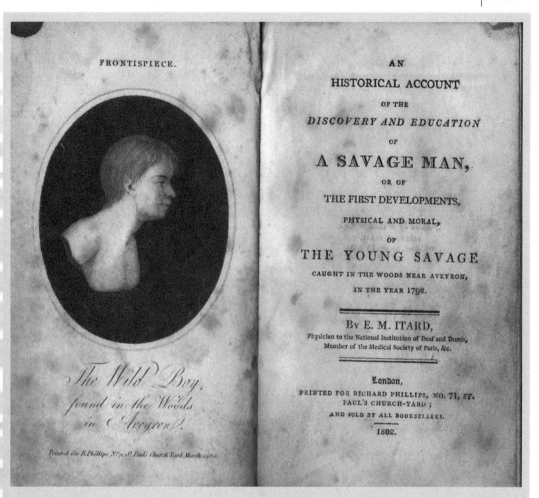

FRONTISPIECE.

AN

HISTORICAL ACCOUNT

OF THE

DISCOVERY AND EDUCATION

OF

A SAVAGE MAN,

OR OF

THE FIRST DEVELOPMENTS,

PHYSICAL AND MORAL,

OF

THE YOUNG SAVAGE

CAUGHT IN THE WOODS NEAR AVEYRON,

IN THE YEAR 1798.

By E. M. ITARD,

Physician to the National Institution of Deaf and Dumb,
Member of the Medical Society of Paris, &c.

London,

PRINTED FOR RICHARD PHILLIPS, NO. 71, ST.
PAUL'S CHURCH-YARD;

AND SOLD BY ALL BOOKSELLERS.

1802.

Figure 5.1. Frontispiece and title page for the first English language printing of *The Wild Boy of Aveyron*, by Jean Mark Gaspard Itard. (Author's personal collection.)
(Image from author's personal collection. From Itard, J.-M.G. [1802]. *An historical account of the discovery and education of a savage man: Or, the first developments, physical and moral, of the young savage caught in the woods near Aveyron in the year 1798.* London, United Kingdom: Richard Phillips.)

that he took on the challenge of educating Victor when his own teacher—Philippe Pinel, regarded as the founder of psychiatry—declared the boy to be incurably defective. After his examination of Victor, Pinel rendered his pessimistic evaluation: "Do we not then have every reason to think that the child of Aveyron ought to be considered in the same category with the children or adults fallen into insanity or idiocy?" (Pinel, as cited in Lane, 1976, p. 69). Note the lack of a developmental distinction in Pinel's diagnosis. Idiocy and insanity could befall both children and adults. In this case, Pinel was arguing, the boy was not an idiot because he had been left in the woods, rather he was left in the woods because he was an idiot (Lane, 1976, p. 5). Itard, on the other hand, approached Victor as an instance of developmental deficiency: a "noble savage" whose development had been impeded by his deprived circumstances growing up. Itard was not, however, challenging Pinel's pessimism about the ineducability of idiots; he was arguing that Victor was not an example of true idiocy. Itard's optimism was based on the claim of misdiagnosis, not a rejection of the prognosis if the diagnosis were true.

By the end of his experiment with educating Victor, Itard thought that Pinel had been right all along: Victor was organically defective, not simply developmentally deprived. The progress that Victor showed under Itard's tutelage was deemed to be simply insufficient (D.L. Ferguson & Ferguson, 1986). Itard, in short, believed that his experiment with Victor was a failure, not because he could not teach him anything but because he could not teach him enough. As Itard explained in his summary report, Victor's development was "the slow and laborious result of a very active education in which the most powerful methods are used to obtain most insignificant results" (Itard, 1806/1962, p. 100). At the same time, Itard foreshadows the optimism that others would take from his efforts as demonstrations that idiocy—not just deprivation—was, in fact, amenable to intervention and instruction. If not curable, idiocy was thought to be at least a state that could be substantially remediated with individualized and systematic instruction.

Between 1806, when the experiment with Victor ended, and 1848, when the first public asylum for idiots was started in the United States, the ambivalence of Itard about the origins and prospects of idiocy was to make its way across the Atlantic and continue to influence the way in which disability was framed. For American legislators and the general public of the 1840s and 1850s, idiocy was something that was at once irredeemably tragic and evil and also potentially curable, or at least salvageable. Indeed, in a narrative version that is suggestive of the before-and-after advertisements that are now familiar, the written characterizations of idiocy by social reformers and asylum professionals—first in Europe and later in the United States—became extreme portrayals of how bad idiocy was when left untreated and how much it could be erased or diminished when subjected to the newly discovered techniques of intervention and training. The work of Itard's protégé, Edouard Séguin, became the singular connection between the developments of asylum doctors in France and England and the subsequent wave of asylum development in the United States. Where Itard wrote only of "true" or "false" idiots, Séguin (and his Paris contemporary, Etienne Esquirol) began to make distinctions by level and type. Where Itard was, at best, ambivalent about the possibilities of improvement of true idiots, Séguin was eager to demonstrate the efficacy of institutional care and training. When the progressive British superintendent of the Hanwell Insane Asylum, wrote of his visit to the Bicetre hospital and private schools in Paris in 1844, he spoke of how impressed he was with the progress of seemingly hopeless idiots under the tutelage of Séguin. Conolly described the successful attempts by Séguin to educate children with as much or more severity of disability as Victor. The efforts taken with a boy of 15 named Charles Emile were particularly impressive to Conolly:

> The crowning glory of the attempt is, that whilst the senses, the muscular powers, and the intellect have received some cultivation, the habits have been improved, the propensities regulated, and some play has been given to the affections; so that a wild, ungovernable animal, calculated to excite fear, aversion, or disgust, has been transformed into the likeness and manners of a man. It is difficult to avoid falling into the language of enthusiasm on beholding such an apparent miracle; but the means of its performance are simple. (Conolly, 1845, p. 295)

By the time he came to the United States in 1850, Séguin's work was well known to Samuel Gridley Howe, George Sumner, Horace Mann, and other reformers in the Boston area. The wave of optimism about the treatment of people previously thought beyond help and hope swept over the United States as quickly as it had parts of Europe. At the same time, the optimism was couched in a crystalizing belief that idiocy was a developmental deficiency that demanded that the focus of remediation must be on young children.

SÉGUIN AND HOWE AND THE EMERGENCE OF THE DEVELOPMENTAL PARADIGM

By the middle of the 19th century, the prospect of improving the lot of those previously thought irretrievably lost to the debasement of idiocy became something that social reformers and asylum doctors in the United States began to put forth as a realistic hope. The optimism of possible improvement did not replace the florid assessments of idiocy's state of human debasement, however. Indeed, if anything, the first generation of reformers calling on legislators to invest in the specialized care—if not cure—of idiocy was promoted as a promising new development that could remove a large and growing community burden.

Even Séguin, while writing his influential treatises on the education and training of children with idiocy, would still use the strong language of hopeless debility in his descriptions. In words that were often cited by American reformers (e.g., Brockett, 1856; Howe, 1848/1972), Séguin defined idiocy as

> a disorder of the nervous system in which the organs and faculties of the child are separated from the normal control of the will leaving him controlled by his instincts and separated from the moral world. The typical idiot is one who knows nothing, thinks nothing, wills nothing, and can do nothing, and every idiot approaches more or less this sum of incapacity. (Séguin, as cited in Trent, 1994, pp. 45–46)

Despite the extreme language ("thinks nothing, wills nothing"), however, there is, in this new conceptualization of idiocy, room for intervention. For Séguin, the focus had shifted. The key was the separation of the senses from the will, and the will from the mind. L.P. Brockett, writing in 1856 about Séguin's influence in the United States, proposed his own variation on Séguin's definition. Idiocy, said Brockett, could be seen *"as the result of an infirmity of the body which prevents, to a greater or less extent, the development of the physical, moral and intellectual powers"* (Brockett, 1856, p. 599, emphasis in original). While not yet restricting idiocy to those cognitive impairments that arise during childhood, there was an implication that idiocy was a matter of degree, more than type. Idiocy was then not the result of the absence of mind (à la John Locke) but a flawed interaction of the child's nervous system and the will that affected the mind (Trent, 1994, p. 46). While the damage may have been severe and the potential limited, the necessary parts for development were still present in the idiotic child. The connections must be restored between what Séguin called "the will" and the senses, but early and methodical training of the child could do that. What had been seen as an immutable defect of nature was now approached as mutable deficiency. This, in turn, made the proper understanding of the levels of idiocy and their relative susceptibility

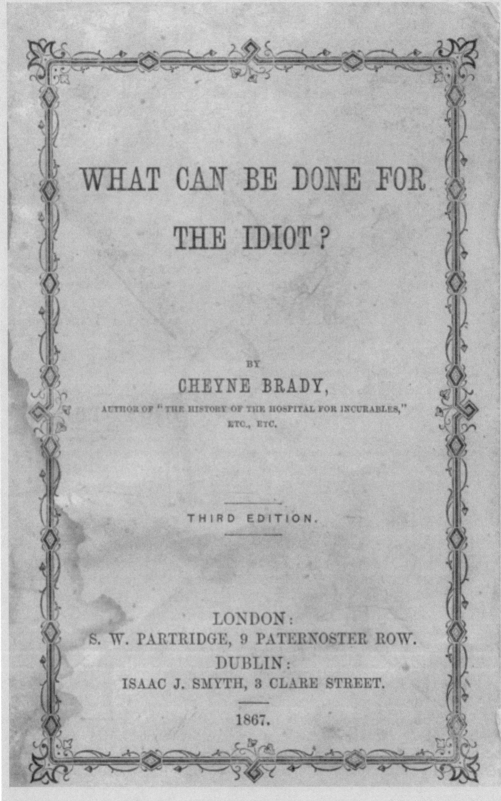

Figure 5.2. Cover of *What Can Be Done for the Idiot?*, by Cheyne Brady.
(Image from author's personal collection. From Brady, C. [1867]. *What can be done for the idiot* [3rd ed.]. London, United Kingdom: S.W. Partridge.)

to improvement under care much more consequential than had previously been the case with Itard and Pinel. This sense that something could be done about the problem of idiocy began to take shape in Europe and in the United States. Cheyne Brady, a London attorney and social reformer, wrote the following in his tract *What Can Be Done for the Idiot* (see Figure 5.2):

> Idiocy is unquestionably one of the most fearful of the host of maladies, which pass like gloomy shadows over the brightest spots of human civilization. Its intensity has also been much increased by the impression which so long prevailed, that it was almost incapable of any palliative, and certainly of anything in the shape of a remedy. Modern science and an enlarged philanthropy are, however, gradually removing this unhappy idea, and are showing that there is no class of unfortunates of our species to whom enlightened treatment may be applied with a more cheering hope of success. (Brady, 1867, p. ii)

Having heard of Séguin's work in Paris, Samuel Gridley Howe and his Boston colleagues began to push for the creation of similar "schools" in the United States. However, he was first commissioned by the Massachusetts legislature to produce a report on just how extensive was the "problem" of idiocy in the Commonwealth (see Figure 5.3). Howe's report was one of the earliest assessments, focused specifically on the prevalence and condition of idiots in the population. The report is instructive because it reflects the transition that the concept of idiocy was undergoing. Howe describes the levels and types of idiocy he finds in moralistic terms. Idiocy was a sign of man's departure from the natural laws of God. Indeed, the British writers of the era were struck by how much time Howe spent on indicting parents as the primary cause of their children's defects. His argument presented idiocy as "most often the consequence of the morally degenerate behavior of the parents, enhanced by the immoral proclivities of the afflicted offspring themselves" (McDonagh, 2008, p. 226). The need for special schools to train these children was, for Howe, as much about getting the children away from the evil influence of a debased home life as it was about getting them into a specialized educational facility.

Howe also began a pattern of taxonomical elaboration that would become the virtual hallmark of professional expertise over the course of the century. Before this era, idiocy was idiocy, distinguished from insanity perhaps, but with little refinement beyond that. By the time of Howe's report, even Séguin had distinguished only "profound idiocy" and "superficial idiocy." Howe went slightly further, presenting a three-part classification of "pure idiocy," fools, and simpletons. Behind his typology, Howe meant to find room for intervention. If there were levels of idiocy, then part of the need for expert care was precise diagnosis to find those for whom the spark of intelligence remained dormant but present. As with his earlier work with blind and deafblind children, Howe's effort was aimed at demonstrating that the divine spark of humanity was still present in children with even the most visible disability. For Howe, it was society's duty to "redeem" the wretched souls from the legacy of degeneration that their families had visited upon them. In many ways, Howe's report can be seen as an early example of the "family studies" that would come later in the century, in support of the theory of degeneracy (Rafter, 1988). These studies (e.g., *The Jukes,* by Richard Dugdale), which are discussed in greater detail in Chapter 6, gradually evolved into

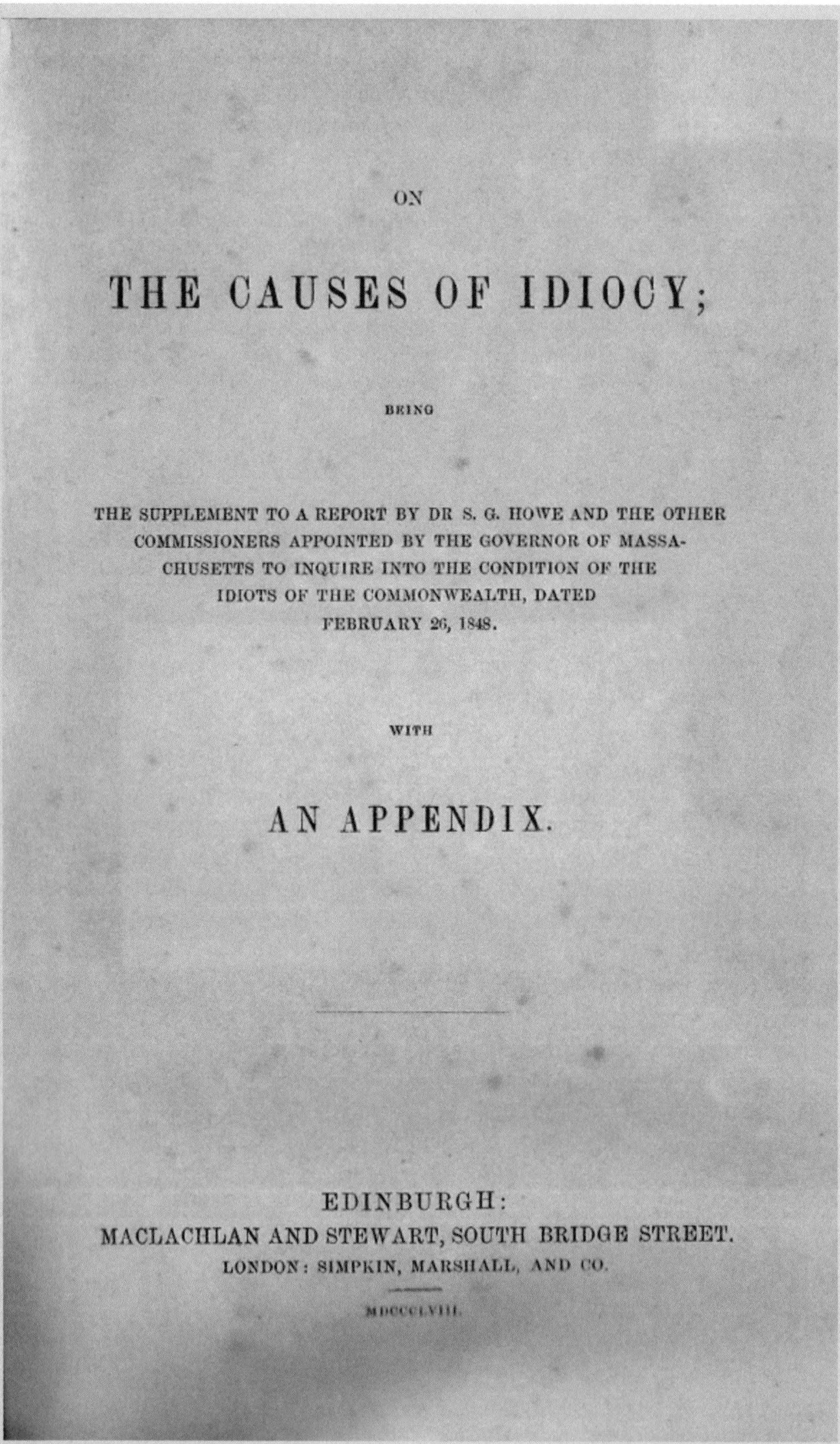

ON

THE CAUSES OF IDIOCY;

BEING

THE SUPPLEMENT TO A REPORT BY DR S. G. HOWE AND THE OTHER
COMMISSIONERS APPOINTED BY THE GOVERNOR OF MASSA-
CHUSETTS TO INQUIRE INTO THE CONDITION OF THE
IDIOTS OF THE COMMONWEALTH, DATED
FEBRUARY 26, 1848.

WITH

AN APPENDIX.

EDINBURGH:
MACLACHLAN AND STEWART, SOUTH BRIDGE STREET.
LONDON: SIMPKIN, MARSHALL, AND CO.

MDCCCLVIII.

Figure 5.3. Title page of *On the Causes of Idiocy*, by S. G. Howe.
(Image from author's personal collection. From Howe, S.G. [1858]. *On the causes of idiocy*. Edinburgh, Scotland: MacLachlan and Stewart and London, United Kingdom: Simpkin, Marshall, and Co.)

the more explicitly eugenic accounts (e.g., Goddard's "Kallikak" study) of the early 20th century. Howe's use of the term *heredity* was a much vaguer notion of generational inheritance than the later theorists and polemicists would develop. His report is full of case descriptions that illustrate the deplorable state of idiot children, when left to the ineffective care of their families:

> No. 410. E. G., aged 8 years. This poor creature may be taken as a type of the lowest kind of idiocy. He has bones, flesh, and muscles, body and limbs, skin, hair &c. He is, in form and outline, like a human being, but in nothing else. Understanding he has none; and his only *sense* is that which leads him to contract the muscles of this throat, and swallow food when it is put into his mouth. He cannot chew his victuals; he cannot stand erect; he cannot even roll over when laid upon a rug; he cannot direct his hands enough to brush off the flies from his face; he has not language—none whatever; he cannot even make known his hunger, except by uneasy motions of his body. His habits of body are those of an infant just born. He makes a noise like that of a very sick and feeble baby, not crying, however, in a natural way. His head is not flattened and deformed, as is usual with idiots, but is of good size and proportion.
>
> The probable causes are hereditary ones. The grand-parents were very scrofulous and unhealthy. The parents were apparently healthy, but gave themselves to excessive sensual indulgence. They lost their health in consequence of this, and were so well aware of it as to abstain and to recover again. In the meantime, five children were born to them—two of whom were like E. G., and died at five or six years of age: two others were very feeble and puny, and died young. (Howe, 1848/1972, pp. 7–8)

Howe and the two other individuals assigned to the commission were making the case in this report that for most of these dire examples of idiocy, improvement was possible. In one of the summary tables attached to the report, approximately 488 out of 574 cases of idiocy were identified as "capable of improvement" (Howe, 1848, p. 55). The result of the report was the first public facility created specifically "for the purpose of training and teaching . . . idiotic children" (Howe, 1848, p. xv).

Part of the conceptual foundation for the newfound optimism about the prospects for improvement of idiocy was the elaboration of classification schemes that emphasized child development over brain dysfunction (Simpson, 2007, 2011). Although Howe devoted much attention in his report to the supposed causes of the idiocy that he found in Massachusetts, he also began a trend, which became the norm for the remainder of the century, of elaborating a multileveled taxonomy of the condition arranged by severity. Pure idiocy was the lowest class, and individuals at this level were described as barely human: "mere organisms, masses of flesh and bones in human shape" (Howe, 1848/1972, p. 7). However at the two higher functioning levels of fools and simpletons, much more optimism was justified. With simpletons, for example, "the harmony between the nervous and muscular system is nearly perfect," giving such individuals "considerable activity of the perceptive and affective faculties" (Howe, 1848/1972, p. 7).

In the mid-19th century there was a burgeoning optimism paired with the dramatically pessimistic portrayals of an earlier era. Both were important. The new optimism was used to argue for public funding of schools and asylums dedicated to demonstrating the premise that careful training and instruction could yield dramatic improvement or even cures. The pessimism however, also played a vital role.

By maintaining a category of such severe disability that the individuals were still beyond help, an intellectual explanation remained available should the newly funded intervention fail to demonstrate the promised improvements. Just as Itard explained that Victor's limited improvement was because he was, in fact, a true idiot rather than a noble savage, so would Séguin, Howe, and others in the first generation of asylum leaders explain that any failures to improve were cases of mislabeling rather than incorrect theories. The failure to improve would only demonstrate the severity of disability, not the inadequacy of instruction.

KERLIN, WILBUR, AND THE CONCEPTUAL FOUNDATIONS OF PESSIMISM

The optimistic conceptualizations of idiocy put forth by Howe in Massachusetts and Hervey Backus Wilbur in New York would quickly encourage legislators in numerous states to establish "experimental schools" for such children. It was a conceptualization of idiocy that came close to promising cures where just a few decades earlier Itard had felt defeated by the magnitude of Victor's deficit. Together with Howe in Massachusetts and Isaac Kerlin in Pennsylvania (with Séguin circulating among all three locations and finally settling in New York City), Wilbur was one of the first generation of asylum leaders who vigorously argued for an understanding of idiocy as deficit rather than defect. Having begun a private school for idiotic children in Massachusetts, even before Howe's public experimental school was authorized in 1848, Wilbur would be most closely associated with the founding and supervision of the New York State Asylum for Idiots. Figures 5.4 and 5.5 are early advertisements for this private school, though were produced after Wilbur had left to take the superintendency of the New York institution.

From the opening of the New York facility in 1851 until his death in 1883, Wilbur was an active and vigorous spokesperson for what he saw as the need for expanded institutional care for idiots. His advocacy began with the optimism of success that he shared with Howe and Séguin. Although cautious in places, Wilbur came close to promising "cures" for at least some of those children who were admitted to his institution:

> There is a class of children who are in the early periods, of infirm or imperfect bodily organization. As a consequence, they are deficient in intellect; they are idiots, with all the absence of mental manifestations, and with the habits and tendencies of this state.... Exposed to the educational and elevating influences of a well regulated institution, the effects produced seem almost like regeneration. The individual entirely emerges from the condition of idiocy. *The effect produced may be spoken of as a cure.* These are spoken of sometimes, to prevent public misapprehension, as exceptional cases, but they constitute a class. (Wilbur, 1858, p. 25, emphasis added)

Even when stated with caution, Wilbur's early optimism would make clear the hopes of dramatic improvement. His use of a developmental approach of reconnecting the senses to the *will* and from there to the *mind* allowed for gradations of success, and an explanation for failure:

> We do not propose to create or supply faculties absolutely wanting; nor to bring all grades of idiocy to the same standard of development or discipline; nor to make them all

IN the little New England village of Barre, located on a plateau high among the blue hills of Central Massachusetts, with extended views of hill and valley, is one of the unique schools of our country—the Private School for the Education and Training of the Feeble-Minded.

The surroundings are ideal in many ways. With an altitude of 1,000 feet above the sea, broad views with beautiful scenery on all sides, the large extent of grounds, consisting of two hundred and fifty acres, the advantageous position of the school, so closely adjacent to the beautiful country village, yet so separated as to secure the necessary privacy —all combine to make the spot peculiarly appropriate.

The number of the pupils is limited, and the classification of the subjects received is carefully made. The arrangements and accommodations for all aim to supply every proper home comfort in the several buildings, which are spacious and elegant. Pupils are received from the age of six upward ; the earlier the better.

This was the first institution of the kind in America. Many years' experience and thought have brought it to its present condition of excellence. The Institution includes a school and a home department. The living buildings are on the cottage system and comprise the boys' cottage, girls' cottage, farm cottage, epileptic boys' cottage, home and custodial building, each with appropriate grounds and appliances. There are large stables and recreation buildings, gymnasium, play grounds, a fine water supply and sewage system.

Dormitories or wards are here unknown. Bodily deformities are corrected as far as possible, and epilepsy treated if present.

The school is strictly under a family organization and is in session all the year round. A competent person is always in attendance upon the recreations. There are several teachers, and an ample number of general assistants, and every child is thus supplied with all necessary general attendance, and medical treatment when needed, the Superintendent being a practical physician. Younger children are taught by a modification of Kindergarten methods, proceeding upward to the ordinary work of the public school. Instruction is individual. Specialized effort is put forth according to the needs of each pupil. Education of the senses by long continued special exercises is arrived at, and habits of precision and accuracy inculcated, so far as possible.

In connection with the regular school work, particular attention is paid to gymnastics and manual training. For instance there is one pupil who works daily at a Sloyd bench, and several others who have made for themselves tool-chests, writing-desks and many other things of use, and who work in wood regularly with enthusiasm, with intelligence and with remarkably good results. The pupils are patiently instructed in work that is plainly useful ; work that is not only a means to the end but is both means and end in one ; work that trains hand and eye and heart, and develops character. Music is taught as a mental exercise and a recreation to the older pupils. In short, symmetry of growth is aimed at, and all methods for arriving at mental development and leading to spontaneous thought are employed to advance the mentally backward person on the path toward normal mentality.

In the Home Department no pains are spared to provide for the comfort and well-being of the children. Their daily exercises and amusements are carefully planned out according to individual requirements.

The school is now in charge of Dr. George A. Brown, A.B. (Yale), who has made a special study of the wants and care of this class of persons. Associated with him is Madam Catherine W. Brown, for forty-five years a noted laborer in the Institution for the welfare of the pupils. Circulars and all information will be sent upon request. Address Barre, Worcester County, Mass. Barre is sixty miles from Boston on the Boston & Maine Railroad, Southern Division, and also on the Ware River Branch of the Boston & Albany Railroad, twenty-five miles from Palmer.

Figure 5.4. Early advertisement for first private institution for feebleminded youth in Barre, Massachusetts. (Image from author's personal collection. From Institution for the Education of Feebleminded Youth, Barre, MA. [n.d.]).

Private Institution for Youth of Feeble Mind.

BARRE, MASS.

THIS Institution offers the best educational advantages for children and youth, whose different phases of mental infirmity unfit them for receiving instruction by the ordinary methods, and at the same time provides a permanent home for those who desire it, where every comfort which wealth can procure is furnished. The limited number of pupils, and ample corps of teachers and assistants supply the individual care required, whilst association with others of equal capacity in the varied exercises of the school-room, or still wider range of amusements, removes the ennui and discontent which the deficient one often experiences in his own home. Twelve years' devotion to the care and education of this class of unfortunates, but increases our desire to elevate their condition and add to their happiness. We would append to this general statement, for parents seeking such a home, the opinion of a Western Clergyman concerning our school: — "Go, for example, to the little village of Barre, reposing among the hills and streams of Worcester County, Mass. Here is the Institution first opened by Dr. Wilbur, in 1848, and since 1851 under charge of Dr. George Brown. You enter an area of many acres, beautifully variegated by nature, and adorned by art. The buildings are elegant and ample. . . . . If you desire to see the establishment, you will be taken at once into a school-room, where a class of lads and misses are reciting History or Geography; and you might easily believe that you had happened into an ordinary village school, only that the wide-awake and thoroughly earnest efforts of the young lady who is teaching, contrast strongly with the methods of too many teachers, and that here and there a singular smile, or restless motion, or awkward utterance, may indicate something peculiar in the pupils. But what were they a few years, perhaps only two or three years, ago? Unable to read or write, unacquainted with the most common facts, helpless, stupid, or mischievous. Now they are attaining slowly, indeed, but truly, the elements of self-support, and of respectability. I cannot take time to go with you through the different departments down to the nursery. Everywhere are evidences of the most scrupulous care, self-denying kindness, persevering energy, and encouraging success. Out of doors you will see some of the pupils working in the garden, sawing wood, feeding, or driving the horses, using the machinery of the gymnasium, or otherwise gaining pleasure and health from exercise. In the evening you may see a happy company assembled in the drawing-room, and may listen to the music of voices and instruments; for many of the pupils exhibit a decided musical taste and talent. In systematic, thorough, and liberal method, I doubt whether this school has a superior among the schools of the land."

We would cordially invite all interested in the subject to come and see for themselves, if the above opinion published a few years ago in a Western Periodical, is still a correct one.

Persons from the West can stop at West Brookfield, a station thirty miles east of Springfield, where a stage runs to Barre, fourteen miles distant, every afternoon.

For terms &c., apply to

BARRE, MASS., 1864.   GEO. BROWN, M. D., SUPT.

Figure 5.5. Description of a private institution, circa 1864. (Author's personal collection.)
(Image from author's personal collection. From Institution for the Education of Feebleminded Youth, Barre, MA. [n.d.]).

capable of sustaining, creditably, all the relations of a social and moral life; but rather to give dormant faculties the greatest practicable development, and to apply those awakened faculties to a useful purpose under the control of an aroused and disciplined will. At the basis of all our efforts lies the principle that the human attributes of intelligence, sensitivity and will are not absolutely wanting in an idiot, but dormant and undeveloped. (Wilbur, 1852, p. 15)

From the beginning, however, there was also a tension between optimism and a dour outlook of the possibilities for change. Just as was true of Howe's facility in Massachusetts, the by-laws for the New York asylum stated that children judged to fit in one of three diagnostic categories (i.e., epilepsy, insanity, and deformity) were to be excluded from admission as being insusceptible to improvement. Children under 7 and over 14 years were not to be admitted. Children were supposed to be in a "teachable condition," although Wilbur admitted that this was often a matter of judgment (Wilbur, 1860, pp. 9–14). In his report on progress at the early institutions in Europe and the United States, L.P. Brockett probably reflected the more cautious version of the claims by Wilbur and other asylum leaders: "Not far from one-fourth of all the idiots in any State or country, are susceptible of improvement by the treatment we have described" (Brockett, 1856, p. 602). The problem for the new superintendents quickly became the identification and response to that 25% of the idiot population that was deemed unsalvageable.

The intellectual foundation for the identification of those who were not improvable led to a distinction between those whose impairments were purely developmental and those for whom the deficits were inextricably tied to some type of underlying organic defect. Physical deformity, insanity, and epilepsy were considered obvious clinical signs of the presence of such organic defects. Thus, individuals with these conditions were usually excluded from admission. However, Wilbur and the other superintendents also explained that for many children, the only proof of such organic defects came with the failure of these children to improve after admission to the institution. In other words, in a classic example of "blaming the victim," the superintendents argued that the failure was the child's fault, not the program of identification and intervention. Just as Itard had explained Victor's inadequate progress as the ultimate proof of his "pure idiocy," so did Wilbur and others infer organic defect in those children who failed to respond to institutional care.

In certain conditions of the central nervous masses, the brain or spinal cord, there will result a degree of idiocy or a form of idiocy that, so far as any marked or permanent results are concerned, may be considered hopeless. In other words, the organic defect and the diseased condition cannot be remedied, and therefore the resulting mental deficiency cannot be obviated. The peculiar conditions however upon which idiocy is based are so beyond the reach of one's observation, are oftentimes so subtle in their character and pathological symptoms, that they can only be inferred, (scarcely said to be proved) by a failure after a fair trial of the most approved means to obviate them. (Wilbur, 1865, p. 11)

By 1870, Wilbur's pessimism had deepened to the point of a grudging admission of overestimating success in the early years:

This institution has now been in operation for more than eighteen years. Its success has met all reasonable expectations. If disappointment there has been, it has arisen mainly from two sources. The general truth of the teachableness of idiots has been established. The number of the class in reference to whom it may be said that education is practicable, may have been less than some had supposed. So, too, the degree and extent of education for the class may not have been as great as was at first predicted.

In other words, limiting the scope of the institution to the work of training and instruction, and viewing this in the cold light of political economy, the proportion of teachable to unteachable is a little less than at first hoped. (Wilbur, 1870, p. 11)

Similar disappointment was reported by the Massachusetts State Board of Charities. In its first annual report in 1865, the director, F.B. Sanborn, gave a mixed review of results at Howe's asylum: "It cannot be doubted that the Idiot School has effected much good, though probably less than was expected" (Sanborn, 1865, p. 167).

As will be discussed subsequently, the main response to this disappointment by asylum leaders in the last three decades of the 19th century was to call for the expansion of both the number and size of the institutions and to more directly take on a purely custodial function. There was also a need for them to discuss in more detail how to think about the disappointing outcomes. If the expertise of the first generation of asylum leaders had been the main evidence for the initial optimism of dramatic improvement among the children admitted to their care, then how could the disappointing results be interpreted in a manner that did not challenge that expertise? One of the main responses was to develop evermore detailed classification schemes that provided elaborate diagnostic "space" for the exercise of professional judgment about who among the idiot population was and was not educable.

CLASSIFYING CUSTODY

In many ways, the conceptual treatment of idiocy in the last half of the 19th century was an example of "*involutionary* change." In Daniel Fischer's wonderful phrase, involutionary change characterizes those historical eras in which things become "more elaborately the same" (Fischer, 1978, p. 101). For the concept of intellectual disability from roughly 1860 to 1900, definitions became more elaborate, typologies expanded, and variations more detailed. However, for the most part, the increased intricacy of diagnostic schemes simply refined rather than redirected the developmental pessimism that started to grow again soon after the first experimental schools of Howe and Wilbur began.

Definitions of intellectual disability during the last decades of the century saw a further emphasis on the developmental approach and came to endorse—at least implicitly—a theory of degeneracy (Rafter, 1988; Talbot, 1898) as the underlying explanation of all forms of human dependency (e.g., deafness, blindness, insanity, drunkenness, delinquency). Classification remained observational, however, and diagnosis remained speculative. Without the scientific advances of rediscovered Mendelian genetics, which would come after the turn of the century (see Chapter 6), medical accounts focused on vague notions of evolution that saw any broad characteristic (such as poverty or disability, or wealth and genius) shared by more than one generation as signs of inherited weakness or strength. Gradually, by the end of the century, *feeblemindedness* came to be favored over *idiocy* as the generic term for entire range of intellectual deficiency.

The most influential classification schemes were probably those developed by William Ireland in England and Isaac Kerlin in the United States. In 1877, Ireland, a physician and asylum superintendent, published an influential nosology that focused on etiology. His general definition, however, showed the increasingly clear emphasis on idiocy as a developmental condition, originating in childhood. "Idiocy is mental deficiency, or extreme stupidity, depending upon mal-nutrition or disease of the nervous centres, occurring either before birth or before the evolution of the mental faculties in childhood" (Ireland, 1877, p. 1). He distinguished in certain terms how idiocy was not to be confused with brain damage or the dementia of old age:

> Dementia begins with average intelligence, which gradually diminishes; idiocy begins with a low amount of intelligence, which gradually increases. The intelligence of the dement and of the idiot may be for a time about equal; but the one has reached by the process of subtraction; the other by the process of addition. (Ireland, 1877, p. 2)

Beyond his developmental emphasis, Ireland was most concerned with the pathological origins of idiocy, thinking that this approach would have greater implications for care and instruction but creating a diagnostic morass with multitudinous types of idiocy, including 1) genetous idiocy; 2) microcephalic idiocy; 3) eclampsic idiocy; 4) epileptic idiocy; 5) hydrocephalic idiocy; 6) paralytic idiocy; 7) cretinism; 8) traumatic idiocy; 9) inflammatory idiocy; and 10) idiocy by deprivation (Ireland, 1877, pp. 40–41). This classification scheme (expanded from the original 10 to 12; Ireland, 1898) was still being used well into the 20th century by asylum superintendents in the United States (Barr, 1904).

Like Howe and Wilbur, Isaac Kerlin was one of the first generation of asylum superintendents. In many ways, his influence in terms of actual institutional practice was greater than either of the other two. Through his writing and his long prominence in the Association of Medical Officers of American Institutions for Idiotic and Feeble-Minded Persons (now the American Association on Intellectual and Developmental Disabilities), Kerlin exerted a dominant influence on the professional view of idiocy in the United States throughout the last half of the 19th century. Kerlin became superintendent of the Pennsylvania Training School for Feeble-Minded Children (the third public idiot asylum to be started in the United States and now known simply as Elwyn) in 1863. He continued to serve in that capacity for the next 30 years, until his death in 1893. His main influence was in the area of disability policy rather than the conceptual approach to intellectual disability. However, his prominence alone made his definitions and classification schemes important.

Kerlin, in contrast to Ireland, paid much more attention to level of functioning rather than etiology. Beginning with the two basic categories of idiots and imbeciles, Kerlin added an intermediate level between the two, called "idio-imbeciles." Perhaps more significantly he added a separate category of "moral imbecile" that was analogous to what he referred to as "juvenile insanity." Within each of his main functional levels, Kerlin added yet another layer of categorization. The final scheme (Kerlin, 1884, p. 248) was something that was "more elaborately the same" as versions developed by Howe, Séguin, and Esquirol.

1. Idiocy

    a. Apathetic

    b. Excitable

2. Idio-imbecile

3. Imbecile

    a. Lower grade

    b. Middle grade

    c. High grade

4. Moral imbecility

For Kerlin, the levels of apathetic and excitable idiocy were equally hopeless, though very different in behavior. The apathetic idiot to Kerlin was little more than "a helpless gelatinoid creature" with intelligence "below that of a trained seal" (Kerlin, 1884, p. 249). At the other end of his developmental spectrum, Kerlin used very different language to describe the "high grade imbecile":

> The mental deficiency or deviation [of the high grade] is often so slight, or the imperfection is found in such a limited range . . . that it may seem strange that several of these boys and girls should be under the care of an institution.
>   In this first rank are often found children who have been typical cases of idiocy from deprivation, who, under the advantages of educational influences especially adapted to the infirmity, rise to the first rank, many to become self-supporting under kindly guidance, but who, left to themselves, sink lower in their enforced isolation. (Kerlin, 1884, p. 251)

For his final category of moral imbecile, Kerlin reflected the growing theories of degeneracy (see Chapter 6 for an expanded discussion) in extending the label to almost all of those considered to be a menace to (e.g., criminals, prostitutes) or a drain (e.g., alcoholics, tramps) upon society. For Kerlin, the very "contentment" of some of these individuals was evidence of their feeblemindedness. Who in their right minds would enjoy such a life (Kerlin, 1884, p. 257)? For Kerlin, it was this class of deviant in all of its specific variations of social maladjustment that required the most active study and treatment. In the words of Frederick Wines, when reporting on special census of the "defective, dependent, and delinquent classes" there was a "morphology of evil" (Wines, 1888) that needed to be studied and understood. How that evil erupted—idiocy, insanity, prostitution, pauperism—was not as important as the underlying lack of moral judgment that degenerated from one generation to another (Katz, 1985).

For Kerlin, and virtually all of the professionals now claiming a newly accredited expertise in idiocy and its treatment, the task of remediation was secondary to that of custody. The optimism of Howe, Séguin, and Wilbur was increasingly challenged by both theory and experience. Whether helplessly disabled beyond all educational efforts, or hopelessly evil because of weakened moral judgment, these individuals needed to be confined for both their own and society's well-being. The developmental perspective that distinguished idiocy in all its forms from dementia, brain damage, and other diseases of adulthood had been one of the conceptual sources of optimism in the midcentury. By the end of the century, the developmental perspective remained as a classificatory tool to distinguish levels of functional impairment but was now divorced from the previous hopes of cure and substantive remediation. Kerlin's successor as superintendent at the Pennsylvania School for the Feeble-Minded summarized the new pessimism in his turn-of-the-century textbook:

> The mistaken idea of seeking a cure for mental defect doubtless has its root in a misapprehension of terms and in confounding idiocy with insanity. In the latter there may be found cure as for any other disease; but idiocy is not disease, it is defect, and one might as reasonably talk of restoring limbs to one born without them as of curing a defective brain. (Barr, 1904, p. 130)

Improvement was possible. Classification was helpful. But above all, custody was essential. A new era of incarceration was to become the legacy of the 19th century.

GRUBB

In 1858, Isaac Kerlin published a small book titled *The Mind Unveiled: A Brief History of Twenty-Two Imbecile Children* (Kerlin, 1858; see Figure 5.6). There were no true first-person narratives by people with intellectual disability in the 1800s, but Kerlin's case studies and many of the annual reports of the various institutions and asylums describe the inmates in ways that provide a glimpse of what life was like for them, albeit with the inevitable spin placed on the narratives by the writers to serve their purpose, typically which was to justify the existence of the institution. Kerlin's book has, as its subtitle suggests, 22 case studies divided into 12 sections with one to four case studies per section. The titles of the sections are informative with regard to how Kerlin and his contemporaries viewed the inmates: "Our Household Pets"; "Blighted by Disease"; "Two Low Cases"; "The Sewing Girls"; "Two Interesting Semi Mutes"; and, a repeat, "Four Low Cases." The children classified as "pets" were named Beckie and Bessie. Of them, says Kerlin, "two children have attached themselves to all of us, on account of their infancy and beauty, and are justly entitled to the appellation of 'pets' in our household" (p. 2).

Both girls are described as helpless infants, though oddly the last paragraph of the description of Beckie indicates she had learned to read, do simple math, and so forth. Kerlin is less sympathetic to the children in the "Blighted by Disease" section, Georgie and James, or Jimmie. Georgie is described as "idiotic in the extreme" (Kerlin, 1858, p. 30), as having hydrocephalus, and his appearance as being "more swinish than human" and his habits as "maliciously filthy" (p. 30). James, or Jimmie, who also has hydrocephalus, is presented a bit more charitably, or at least is not compared to a pig.

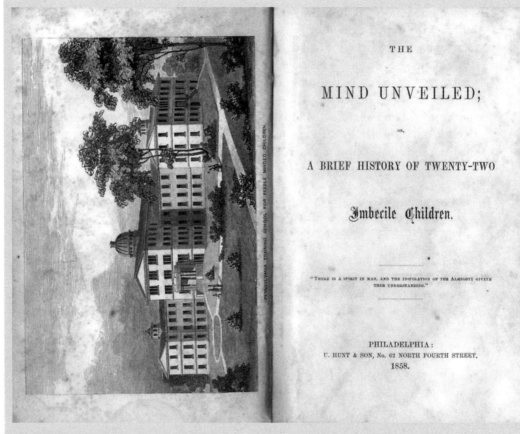

Figure 5.6. Frontispiece and title page for *The Mind Unveiled*, by Isaac Kerlin. (Author's personal collection.)
(Image from author's personal collection. From Kerlin, I. [1858]. *The mind unveiled*. Philadelphia, PA: U. Hunt & Son.)

The lone case study in the section titled "A Boy that We Are Proud Of" contains what may be the most written about person with intellectual disability in the 19th century since Itard's Victor. Given the pejorative nickname "Grubb," this young man appears not only as the sole case study in the "Proud Of" section, but is described in annual reports from the Pennsylvania school and in Kerlin's writing throughout that time period. Grubb was Kerlin's go-to example because he exemplified the type of inmate Kerlin and his colleagues sought so as to prove the worth of their late-19th-century institutions. Grubb was what Henry Herbert Goddard would refer to as a moron (see Chapter 6); mildly cognitively impaired, not visibly impaired, and a menace to society in the views of later 19th century professionals—a moral idiot in Ireland's typology. Grubb was admitted to the Pennsylvania school around 1856, and promptly ran away, escaping the grounds of the asylum and jumping a train to take him home.

> He was a moral idiot, he recognized no obligation to God nor man, and having some appreciation of the value of money and property, nothing that could be appreciated was safe within his reach. With his innate propensity, he had a good share of secretiveness

too, so that the most disguised cross questioning rarely discovered the truth. His honest face, covered the most mature dishonesty. (Kerlin, 1858, pp. 48–49)

Grubb was, like most inmates, required to attend school during the day, though his resistance to "female authority," presumably meaning the teacher, had to be overcome by "a few days of discipline"; the discipline was undefined but apparently was very effective in reversing Grubb's temper. His day, however, was more likely to be spent working on one of the institution's farm enterprises, as was the fate for many inmates:

If a load of hay came—Grubb helped stow it away; if corn in the field was to be husked—Grubb was employed—he was constituted cow-boy, boot-black and errand-boy . . . the school room was a secondary matter for him." (Kerlin, 1858, pp. 50–51)

Religious training was part of Grubb's life, perhaps more so because of his personality: "He became a willing and instructed listener, to the stories of good and bad boys, of duty to God, and of the life, sufferings, and death of our Saviour" (Kerlin, 1858, p. 51). Grubb became the trustee in charge of the collection taken at the Sunday services, passing his hat around among his fellow inmates. It is not surprising that these collections were sparse: "sometimes a few cents, and as many sticks and buttons" (Kerlin, 1858, p. 52). Grubb was not entirely unsuccessful in academic affairs. Kerlin ludicrously attributes a "marked elongation of the tongue" to Grubb's "free exercise in phonetics" (Kerlin, 1858, pp. 52–53).

Because Grubb's rehabilitation from moral idiot and threat to society was so complete in the eyes of Kerlin, he (Grubb) was sent on a tour of the state to show his salvation at the hands of the institution personnel. Grubb presented trinkets made at the institution to dignitaries, including the governor of New Jersey.

Grubb's daily routine was substantially less interesting than his tour of the state on behalf of the institution. All inmates were required to rise at 5:30 a.m., dress, and be at the schoolroom by 6:30 a.m., following breakfast. The classroom day began with light physical exercise, followed by more vigorous exercise using dumbbells (these classes were usually called, double entendre intended, the "dumb-bell class"). Figure 5.7 depicts one such class at a different institution.

In fact, only the younger inmates participated in the dumbbell classes; the older inmates engaged in "moderate out-door work, bed-making, etc." (Kerlin, 1858, p. 139). Of course, this exercise looks suspiciously like the maintenance work that was needed to run the institution. Following "exercise," inmates were lined up and marched single-file into the medical room to undergo inspections. Finally, the instructional period began, after the recitation of the Lord's Prayer. They also chanted the 121st Psalm. Following this, the younger children were dispersed to separate classes, usually accompanied by a teacher and several older inmates whose days were spent corralling the younger children. That evening, the dinner bell would ring and all the inmates would proceed to the dining hall, where they were seated on benches at a long table and served family style. Light exercise followed the dinner hour.

These routines were in place for every day but Sunday, during which religious instructions replaced the academic instruction. The inmates' routine were disrupted by periodic plays and performances, and in most institutions, inmates could participate in a band or orchestra.

1. Dumb-bell class.
2. Band, band-stand, one of four groves.
3. Ring class.

Figure 5.7. A "dumb-bell class." (Author's personal collection.)
(Image from author's personal collection. From *Twenty-ninth annual report of the trustees of the Massachusetts School for Idiotic and Feebleminded Children*. [1876, October]. Boston, MA: Albert J. Wright, State Printer.)

POLICY AND PRACTICE: LOCATING
CUSTODY AND CONGREGATE CARE

In 1914, the New York State legislature created a commission to "investigate the subject of the public provision for the care, custody, treatment and training of the mentally deficient, including epileptics" (New York State, 1915/1976, p. 5). Education was no longer deemed a prominent enough part of the institutional response to people now called *feebleminded* to be mentioned in the official charge to the committee. In its place, custody was now an overt part of the mandate. The report resulting from the work of the committee briefly explained its perspective on how that change in emphasis had occurred:

> On the basis of the work done under Séguin in Paris, the New York State School for Feeble-Minded Children was begun in Albany in 1849 under the direction of Dr. Wilbur who was one of Séguin's disciples. Two years later the school was moved to its permanent quarters at Syracuse. It soon became apparent that this "education of the idiot" did not mean regeneration to normal mentality, but only the training possible within the boundaries of the pathological condition of the patients. Thus sprang up the ideal of custodial care for the feeble-minded which must always be the complement of the educational work in any truly constructive program. (New York State, 1915/1976, p. 24)

Despite the account given in 1915, however, the notion of custodial care as the cornerstone of social policy toward people with intellectual disability did not arrive newborn and untested in last decades of the 19th century. Certainly, leaders such as Wilbur and Kerlin came to voice misgivings about their midcentury optimism and wrote openly about the need for increased provisions (e.g., space, money, staff) for custodial care for a large number of those admitted to the institutions. Still, what actually changed over the course of the 19th century was not *whether* custody and control were needed for a significant majority of the idiotic population but *where* that custody should occur. At the beginning of the century, the policy of choice was confinement in the city or county almshouse. As the call for specialized asylums grew in the middle of the century, the almshouse lost its appeal, replaced (more in official policy than actual practice) by the experimental schools and therapeutic regimes provided there. Even in this period of reform, however, the distinction was made between the curative and the custodial populations. With the end of the century, then, what became the official policy of using large, congregate care facilities for overt purposes of social control and segregation was actually only a specialized version of an earlier policy that authorized abandonment in the basements of almshouses at the beginning of the century.

ALMSHOUSES AND THE "TRULY NEEDY"

In the early part of the 19th century, the idiot was seen almost exclusively in economic terms as someone incapable of managing his or her own affairs. The local "simpleton" was a familiar presence in most towns and neighborhoods, much like the village idiot of the Middle Ages; someone who, like the poor, was "always with us." Only when family and neighbors could not provide for such individuals would the city or county step in with a haphazard system of "placing out" individuals with willing families or placing the idiotic person with the other "deserving poor" in the local almshouse. For the most part, then, government involvement in the lives of people judged to be intellectually disabled in the 19th century began with the rise of the almshouse. Despite the rise of the specialized asylum and professionalization of care, for most of the century there were more so-called idiots living in these county and municipal facilities than in the large, specialized asylums. For the most part, their treatment in these almshouses can only be described as abominable: a sort of passive neglect was the best they could hope for (P.M. Ferguson, 1994).

Beyond confining many of the idiots from poor families, however, the almshouse is important because it began in both policy and practice the approach to custodial care that became the basis of asylum organization in the last decades of the 19th century. Making the connection between the early almshouse and the later institution allows one to highlight the thematic strands of medical incurability, economic uselessness, moral intractability, and aesthetic offensiveness that weave their way through the official justifications of care that characterized patterns of practice throughout the century. Those strands were first stitched together in the patchwork of county and city almshouses that arose throughout the Northeast in the first half of the 19th century.

While large population centers (e.g., New York, Boston, Philadelphia) founded their almshouses in the colonial period, the big push for these facilities came in the period running roughly from 1820 to 1850. During these decades, the almshouse went from an unpopular last resort in a few large cities and towns to the common practice of counties and cities across the Northeast and Midwest. In 1824, there were approximately 83 almshouses in Massachusetts. By 1850, the number had grown to 204 (Klebaner, 1976, p. 74). In the state of New York, 56 of the 60 counties reported having an almshouse by 1857 (New York State, 1857/1976), not counting the facilities in the large cities that continued to operate.

The official and unofficial calls for the installation of an almshouse system of poor relief almost always made two points. First, the care of lunatics, idiots, the aged, and the infirm was said to be much more humane with centralized and enlightened administration and housing (see Yates, 1824/1901, p. 952). The second, more negative type of argument was that "outdoor relief" was needlessly extravagant and unavoidably supportive of the very habits that produced the able-bodied pauper's indigence. In his report to the Massachusetts legislature about the status of poor relief in the Commonwealth, reformer Josiah Quincy concluded that "of all the modes of providing for the poor, the most wasteful, the most expensive, and most injurious to their morals and destructive of their industrious habits is that of supply in their own families" (Quincy, 1821/1971, p. 9). By the middle of the century, the custodial view triumphed over almost all pretensions to reform or remediation. The goal of the almshouse was to clear the home and marketplace of the unproductive and dependent. Poverty was either the avoidable result of individual laziness or intemperance, or, if unavoidable, the empirical proof of chronic incapacity. In other words, it was poverty that had to be explained rather than disability. The quest was to either convince the malingerers to learn the "habits of industry" enough to rejoin their communities or to provide a point of disposal for those who were "truly needy" through infirmity or disability. Much like the later quest of the asylum superintendents, the poorhouse operators were clear about the overall custodial purpose of their facility; it was just the details of the individual sources of poverty that provoked discussion.

Despite the rise of the specialized asylum and the exposés of deplorable almshouse conditions by Dorothea Dix (Dix, 1976) and others, the reliance on the county almshouse as a facility to house idiots and lunatics continued throughout much of the 19th century. In 1857, a survey was completed of almshouse residents in New York State. A total of 424 inmates (5.5% of the total almshouse population) were identified as idiots and another 1,644 (16.8%) as lunatics (Report of the Select Committee, 1859/1976). By contrast, the institution at Syracuse, run by Wilbur, had been open for about 5 years at this point and had 104 children in residence. (Most of the almshouse residents were over 16 years of age and were, therefore, ineligible for admission to the Syracuse asylum.).

By the end of the century, the almshouses were increasingly becoming homes for the elderly poor. Even at this point, however, after 50 years of official policy supporting specialized institutions as the proper location of custody and care for people with intellectual disability, there were still approximately 540 "feeble-minded or idiotic" people living in county facilities, or what amounted to almost 10% of the total county almshouse population (New York State Board of Charities, 1901, pp. 75, 80). Even with the gradual shift of emphasis from the almshouse to the idiot asylum, the purpose remained similar: rehabilitation if possible, but custody in any case.

THE CUSTODIAL ASYLUM AND THE "BACK WARD"

In the last 30–40 years of the 19th century there was an official shift in policy surrounding the purpose and function of the specialized idiot asylum. As classification schemes expanded in a developmental direction, they served as administrative blueprints for institutional organization. The tone of the superintendents' annual reports gradually changed from redemption narratives full of remarkable cures or dramatic progress to calls for institutional expansion to provide lifelong—or at least much extended—care of those residents who "refused" to improve. In reality, of course, this pessimistic counternarrative to the redemption story had always been there from the earliest almshouse. From the very start of their facilities, Howe and Wilbur excluded potential child admissions as too idiotic or too severe to be helped. Two things changed with the new sense of custodial. First, there was the obligation to the adult who couldn't make it on the outside but who was very capable of contributing to his or her own care within the institutional confines (the asylum version of the "able-bodied poor" focused on by the almshouses). Second, there was the need to house those who were too severe to be helped (the "failures"). In addressing both of these needs, the only remaining debate was whether to create separate institutions for the "curable" and the custodial, or to house the entire range of the population—from the so-called "apathetic idiot" to the "high-grade imbecile"—within large, congregate care facilities.

The debate was actually a one-sided affair. Those arguing for large, congregate facilities far outnumbered those supporting the creation of separate, custodial facilities while maintaining the small, educational facilities for their original purpose. For the most part, those supporting separate custodial facilities were part of the New York State system of institutions and charities. Wilbur became, perhaps, the most prominent proponent of the separate facilities, and New York State had some of the most prominent examples of institutions that were established specifically to house individuals who were judged incapable of improvement (e.g., the Rome Custodial Asylum for Unteachable Idiots, opened in 1895 in upstate New York). Defenses of the large, congregate facility came from many sources outside of New York but were perhaps most prominently voiced by Isaac Kerlin from the Pennsylvania asylum.

Soon after the start of his institution at Syracuse, Wilbur acknowledged that the facility was filling up with individuals who he felt had not improved enough to return to society. Despite efforts to first screen out the most disabled children from admission to the asylum, Wilbur found himself confronted with a growing population of residents who both failed to improve and persisted in growing older. Wilbur said that the accumulation of the unteachable inmates in his facility "embarrasses the general management" (Wilbur, 1870, p. 11). The growing presence of adults represented a daily challenge to Wilbur's original conception of who he was and what he did. For him the developmental model of feeblemindedness was more about physical age than about mental age. Adults did not belong in a school, even one exclusively designed for feebleminded children. For Wilbur, there was a clear line of demarcation: People who had not moved far enough along the developmental scale to function independently or with only moderate supervision in the community were custodial once they reached adulthood. This also helps explain why Wilbur argued for several years after the opening of the Willard asylum for the chronically insane in New York that custodial idiots could also be housed there. The point was that they were unimprovable adults; the source of their chronicity was not as important as its undeniable presence.

Arguing strongly for the idea of large, congregate care asylums, Kerlin never confronted Wilbur directly and, indeed, minimized their differences. However, the Pennsylvania superintendent saw his position triumph in almost every state other than New York. In a report to his fellow superintendents in 1888, Kerlin laid out many of his reasons for preferring these larger asylums that housed all levels of idiots at one location, though separated into different buildings or cottages (the so-called cottage plan). In such facilities, Kerlin argued, there were economic benefits to the state, therapeutic benefits to the inmates, and what might today be called professional development opportunities for the staff, including the following benefits:

- Better medical care can be arranged for the "epileptic, paralytic, and scrofulous" children.

- Under the expert eye of the superintendent, inmates may be easily moved back and forth from the "asylum branch" to the "education branch" as progress or deterioration occurs with specific individuals. Such movement would be much more difficult if the educational and custodial departments were not "in proximity."

- Only in congregate institutions could the "custodials" benefit from the entertainment and cultural events provided by and for the higher functioning inmates (e.g., institution bands, theatrical productions, "stereopticon" showings).

- The agricultural and industrial work of the physically able custodial inmates would have a "local market" in the institution. "The gardening, laundering, and cobbling of our feeble-minded employés [*sic*] find here an exchange which will never be criticized by outside 'labor unions,' nor reached by 'labor legislation' " (Kerlin, 1888, p. 80).

- Just as inmates can be shifted around from one level of cottage to another, so may staff be moved from fairly unskilled work with custodial residents to more preferred (and better paid) work as matrons or teachers in the educational department.

- Finally, Kerlin maintained that the stigma and pessimism surrounding the hopeless care of custodial idiots would inevitably lead to an unhealthy atmosphere if they were isolated from other inmates more amenable to remediation. By contrast, when located within an "all-purpose" facility, the custodial department is maintained as a "medical philanthropy" so that it "can never sink to the hopeless, uninviting, and deplorable condition which attaches to the common thought of an utter and complete asylum for neglected idiocy" (Kerlin, 1888, p. 80).

Kerlin summarized his defense of the congregate facility by citing his own facility:

> In short, the experience at Elwyn attests to the economy, reasonableness, and humanity of embracing under the central administration of a general institution all the grades and classes of the idiotic and feeble-minded, living in segregate buildings, it is true, but allowed legitimate contact; each divisible from the other by a classification scientific but not rigid, yet no one group isolated from the Divine influences of hope and the human helps to improvement. (Kerlin, 1888, pp. 80–81)

At the same time that Kerlin made his case for his "all-comprehensive" institution, he made clear that the most severely disabled inmates—those who were assigned to the so-called asylum department—should be located at the back of such facilities, not the front. Cottages for these individuals were to be "more remote" and positioned "at some distance from the other departments,—say from one-half to three-quarters of a mile" (Kerlin, 1884, p. 260). For these facilities, big was better. Not only did size offer economies of scale, it offered a large enough population with which to demonstrate the diagnostic expertise of the asylum professionals. As mentioned previously, taxonomic complexity—finding gradations and categories of idiocy where none had been found before—became for Kerlin and other leaders a key indication of specialized knowledge. All of that was possible only with facilities of a certain number and variety of inmate. As a result of this calculation, the very idea of small, custodial asylums was morally problematic for Kerlin:

> It is the small institution against which may be pronounced the objection of moral "hospitalism." The large, diffuse, and thoroughly classified institution is another affair, and can be to its wards and employés [*sic*] as cosmopolitan as a city. (Kerlin 1884, 262)

By the time of Kerlin's death in 1893, his plan for custodial cottages was fully implemented (see Figure 5.8). The Elwyn facility had a four-building "Hillside" complex matching Kerlin's policies for type of resident and distance from the other cottages. It was purely custodial in character. One building, for example, was designated for "helpless, idiotic and epileptic boys." Another (called "the chalet") was for "epileptic and paralytic girls" (as cited in Hurd, 1916, p. 507). Other states were gradually following the same model.

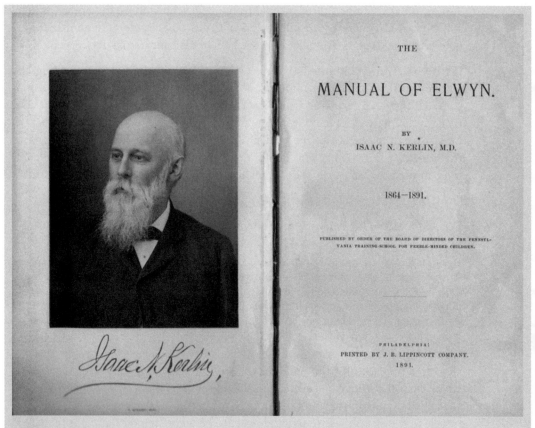

Figure 5.8. Frontispiece and title page for "The Manual of Elwyn: 1864 to 1891," by Isaac Kerlin, an early "how to run an institution" manual. (Author's personal collection.)
(Image from author's personal collection. From Kerlin, I.N. [1891]. *The manual of Elwyn: 1864–1891.* Philadelphia, PA: J.B. Lippincott Co.)

What is to be made of this debate and its outcome? The immediate reasons for the triumph of the congregate care asylum are fairly easy to surmise. First, there were simple economies of scale to be had by building a smaller number of large facilities rather than a larger number of small ones. Indeed, the use of inmate labor to help run the asylums became a source of pride among superintendents. Walter Fernald of Massachusetts described the use of higher functioning female inmates to care for "the lowest grade idiots, paralytics [and] the helpless" as a way of showing the people of Massachusetts that "these trained girls can be of benefit to the state by caring for their more helpless associates" (Fernald, 1891, p. 215). Kerlin bragged about maintenance costs at Elwyn decreasing from $250 to $100 per person because of the use of unpaid inmate labor. The male residents, for example, completely managed the institution bakery, "baking four to six barrels of flour daily at no expense for wages" (Kerlin, 1891, p. 217).

A second reason was the administrative usefulness of having all of the clients in one setting, available to be moved and shuffled on relatively short notice. As Kerlin noted when listing his reasons for congregate care, the convenience of having the two populations—educational and custodial—in close proximity at one institution allowed such reassignments to happen more often. Of course, this also gave the administrator a handy explanation for therapeutic failure: If a resident did not respond to intervention efforts, it was because of misclassification, not poor instruction. The failure to improve became a "success" of classification by simply moving the individual to the proper cottage following prolonged observation. Indeed, one senses that Kerlin's greatest sense of triumph came with the "thoroughly classified" institution that he was able to oversee at Elwyn. Elaborate classification of inmates became a powerful demonstration of professional legitimacy, even if some of those classifications involved admission of therapeutic impotence.

Finally, it can be argued that the rapid adoption of the cottage plan was as much a cause as an effect of the move to large congregate care facilities. By moving to a model of institutional design that emphasized the use of small, separate, simple, cheaply constructed units (or cottages), the states could have their custodial cake and eat it too. Instead of building entirely separate custodial facilities, they were able to build the first "back wards"—institutions within institutions.

So the issue of congregate versus separate can be seen as a debate over not only where inmates of various levels could best be served but also how professional claims to specialized knowledge could best be secured. A strategy of separate care would allow the superintendent to have the discretion of demonstrating the power of classification and assessment while focusing treatment on the salvageable minority. It gave the superintendent dominion over a smaller population, but one with better prospects for valued treatment outcomes. The congregate care facility gave the superintendent control over the full range of individuals—the power to sort and serve as the superintendent saw fit on a continuing basis—where expertise is demonstrated by administrative efficiency as much as by treatment efficacy (P.M. Ferguson, 2002).

THE EXPERIENCE OF INTELLECTUAL DISABILITY

This chapter is like most of the historical accounts of both the concept and the reality of intellectual disability in the 19th century. It has focused almost exclusively on the writings and policies of the emerging class of professionals who took a special interest in the lives and well-being of this class of individuals previously thought to be largely incapable of improvement. In the first half of the century there were early efforts of French alienists and insane asylum superintendents to distinguish more clearly the so-called insane population—which they were most interested in—from the so-called idiots and imbeciles who were less amenable to treatment. By midcentury there were the initial reports of people such as Edward Séguin, Samuel Gridley Howe, and Hervey Backus Wilbur, bemoaning the social causes of idiocy but also proclaiming a new optimism about their capacity for improvement when placed under the care of experts. By the end of the century there were the treatises by Kerlin, William Ireland, and others laying out ever more elaborate classification schemes for both types and degrees of idiocy.

What is largely missing from these historical accounts is the viewpoint of the so-called idiots or their families—people like the aforementioned Grubb. From the beginning of the century in Europe, the history of Itard had been the focus more than the history of Victor. From the first rise of specialized idiot asylums and experimental schools in the United States in the middle of the century, the perspectives of Howe and Wilbur had been the focus rather than the perspectives of the children (and their families) placed under their care in those facilities. By the end of the century, the focus was on the detailed case studies of supposedly degenerate families written by the supporters of the emerging eugenics movement (e.g., Dugdale on "The Jukes"; Rafter, 1988). The opposite perspective of the poor families struggling to make ends meet in a community with few safety nets is absent.

Yet most so-called idiots resided there, even at the end of the century. The triumph of the large, custodial, congregate asylum over smaller, specialized facilities as the accepted model for state policy toward feebleminded citizens must be kept in perspective in this regard. The special report on "defective, dependent, and delinquent" populations, based on the census of 1890 (Billings, 1895) identified only 20 public and four private asylums for idiots, housing a total of 5,254 inmates—this in a country that had grown to a general population of more than 62 million people (P.M. Ferguson, 1994, p. 83). As was discussed previously, even by the end of the century, there were thousands of people identified as idiots remaining in almshouses around country, or remaining in insane asylums. Still, individuals viewed as idiots, imbeciles, or feebleminded lived at large in the community, either with their families, on their own, or in some system of outplacement (what would now be called foster care). Still, far more is known about the lives of those in the institutions.

Much of this imbalance of perspective is understandable, perhaps even inevitable. People with intellectual disability seldom wrote their own accounts of their daily lives. Itard's reports of his training efforts with Victor remain, not a diary or other account by Victor about what he thought. Kerlin's depiction of Grubb remain, set forth to justify his (Kerlin's) beliefs about the importance of congregate settings. It is hard to view history from the bottom up because social history has sometimes been described on an individual basis. At the same time it is ill advised to simply accept the versions of events that those in power produced. Even if it is largely speculative or inferential, it seems worthwhile to consider what life was like in the 19th century from the perspectives of people with intellectual disability and their families.

Personal and family narratives come in many forms. What might be called "generated narratives" are those created artifacts of research or journalism whereby individuals and families are sought out to record their perspectives through in-depth interviews and oral histories (P.M. Ferguson, 2008). These are, of course, hard to come by when dealing with 19th-century experiences. A second category of personal experiences might be called "received narratives." These are published accounts written by individuals or a family member. In short, these are personal memoirs received from the individuals. While such memoirs about the disability experience are common today, they were rare in the 19th century, at least when it comes to the experience of intellectual disability. For the historian, then there are two other narrative sources that are more promising when dealing with time periods before the lifetimes of current generations. First, there are found narratives. These are simply the "primary sources familiar to historians, consisting of diaries, letters, scrapbooks, and other unpublished accounts" (P.M. Ferguson, 2008, p. 49) that are created by individuals and families with no intention of sharing them with a larger public. Second, there is a category that is at once blurrier and essential. These might be called "inferred narratives." For individuals who have no language or no access to writing especially, their stories are sometimes only available through educated speculation. In usually partial and incomplete ways, we infer what someone's experience must have been through the accounts of others. It these last two types of narratives that this section will use in an attempt to move beyond the voices of those in power to those on whom that power was exerted.

AN EARLY TOLERANCE

There is some evidence that the family view of idiotic children changed over the course of the century in ways that both differed and resembled the evolving portrayals of asylum professionals over that same time period. Richards' work with family diaries, letters and other documents finds evidence that—at least for middle-class and wealthy families—the experience of having a child with intellectual disability was not viewed in the pathologized and moralistic terms that would come to dominate the professional literature (Richards, 2004; Richards & Singer, 1998). Certainly the stereotypes abound in the family accounts, but "the stereotypes were at least generally benign" (Richards, 2004, p. 69). The Cameron family of North Carolina is one example. Thomas, the oldest son, was soon recognized by his father to have both physical and intellectual disability. Yet in 1824, after straightforwardly describing these "weaknesses," Thomas' father describes (in a letter to a prospective teacher) the many praiseworthy characteristics he also finds in his son: "He is amiable in his disposition, mild of temper, docile & obedient, affectionate, and of morals most pure—in short I know of no defect in his character, which is susceptible to self-remedy" (as cited in Richards, 1998, p. 453).

In the early decades, in many parts of the country, education for children was still a hodgepodge of public and private efforts with wildly varying approaches to curriculum and instruction. There was no alternative system of special education. Indeed, there was little system at all. For wealthier families there was the option of the private tutor; however, this also created opportunities for children with learning disabilities who were physically able:

> From the family's perspective, this jumble held many possibilities. It was flexible (age grading, for example, lay far in the future), ideally allowing resourceful parents to choose the curriculum, pace, method, and intensity of each child's education at each step. (Richards, 1998, p. 450)

For poor families, life with a disabled child, while certainly difficult and undesirable, was not viewed by others as a cesspool of moral degradation and irretrievable despair. Just as the poor were "always with us," so were simpletons and idiots simply a part of the natural scheme of things. While far from a golden age of tolerance, there was also a kind of grudging acceptance rather than shame and disdain in the first decades of the century (Richards, 2004; Trent, 1994). The policy that followed of more aggressive incarceration and subsequent abandonment reflected and influenced the changing perception of families as well.

DAMNATION AND REDEMPTION

The juxtaposition of professional portrayals of idiocy were at once condemnatory and redemptive, moralistic and medical, pessimistic as to current state and optimistic as to prospects. This shift can be seen in lay accounts of idiocy as well. Perhaps best known from this era are the numerous memorials presented to state legislatures by the social reformer Dorothea Dix. Throughout the 1840s and 1850s, Dix traveled extensively throughout the United States as well as Europe, writing detailed exposés of prisons and almshouses and the condition of those in the facilities who were described as idiotic or insane (Lightner, 1999). Her accounts, though criticized as hyperbolic and even fanciful by some (Lightner, 1999, p. 3), provide an indelible and cumulative record of how cruel daily life had become for many citizens who happened to be both poor and idiotic. The litany of abuse in description of Massachusetts almshouses in 1843 becomes almost dulling in its repetitive style:

> *Lincoln.* A woman in a cage. *Medford.* One idiotic subject chained, and one in a close stall for seventeen years. *Pepperell.* One often doubly chained, hand and foot; another violent; several peaceable now. *Granville.* One often closely confined; now losing the use of his limbs from want of exercise. *Charlemont.* One man caged. *Savoy.* One man caged. *Lenox.* Two in jail, against whose unfit condition there the jailer protests. (Dix, 1976, p. 7)

In 1848, when Howe was asked to survey idiots in the state, his accounts used the descriptions of the living conditions of the children that he found to focus on the conditions of supposed moral degradation in the homes and families that had led to the disabilities in the first place. The benign stereotypes that families and the general public might have used before were increasingly replaced by narratives of economic degradation, moral damnation, and aesthetic repugnance. The life of the idiot was sad, often short. The families—at least the poor ones—were said to be pitiable at best and blameworthy at worst. With the bureaucratization of the government and the capitalization of the marketplace, the daily life of those who were seen as unproductive became harsher and at odds with how the country saw itself.

As these tales of abomination spread in both popular and professional accounts, so did the newly optimistic tales of potential salvation. Once the Massachusetts legislature authorized funds to establish an experimental school for Howe to operate, his accounts of the idiot children who came under his care became full of hope and redemption. At the end of the second year of his school's operation, Howe reported about on the progress his students had made, using language reminiscent of that used 30 years earlier, by the father of Thomas Cameron:

> A great change has come over them. They have improved in health, strength, and activity of body. They are cleanly and decent in their habits. They dress themselves, and for the most part sit at table and feed themselves. They are gentle, docile, and obedient. They can be governed without a blow or an unkind word. They begin to use speech, and take great delight in repeating the words of simple sentences which they have mastered. They have learned their letters, and some of them, who were speechless as brutes, can read easy sentences and short stories. They are gentle and affectionate with each other; and the school and the household are orderly, quiet and well regulated, in all respects. (Richards, as cited in Scheerenberger, 1983, p. 104)

The middle of the 19th century shows what must have been a somewhat muddled scene for both individuals with intellectual disability and their families. The optimism of some families was shown in the professional portrayals of idiots. At the same time, the mood of the country—along with its policies toward more blame, more distancing, and more control—was clearly shifting.

NARRATIVE AND COUNTERNARRATIVE AT CENTURY'S END

As others have noted, over the last half of the 19th century the portrayals of idiocy and feeblemindedness in both the popular and professional literature became increasingly alarmist and pessimistic in tone (Richards, 2004; Trent, 1994). Even as the developmental model came to dominant professional definitions, parental accounts came to reflect the burden and tragedy motifs that filled the newspapers and magazines. Wellknown parents who happened to have a child with disability would use that experience as object lessons for others. Richards cites the proclamations of temperance crusader Carry Nation, that her daughter's disabilities were explained by the alcoholism of the child's father: "Oh, the curse that comes through heredity, and this liquor evil, a disease, that entails more depravity on children unborn, than all else, unless it be tobacco" (as cited in Richards, 2004, p. 77).

At the same time, as always, the experience of families was not uniform or monochromatic. Resistance to the dominant narrative also colored the response of at least some families, even at the end of the century. By the end of the century, almost all asylum superintendents echoed Howe's view of 50 years earlier, in seeing the family and home life of poor, disabled children as the core of the problem. One such asylum leader saw it as the duty of the state to extract the idiot from the household environment so as to minimize damage to both the disabled person and his or her family. This was especially true

> if the parents are poor or in medium circumstances. . . . It is in such families that a large number of children are usually found, and let me impress upon you the fact, that with but few exceptions, it takes more of the time of the mother to look after one idiotic or feeble-minded child than she is able to devote to all her other children. In addition, each idiotic child as soon as it is able to appreciate anything, becomes a source of immoral contamination to other children which is far reaching in its results. (Fitzgerald, 1900, p. 176)

An examination of the family correspondence from that same institution (Rome Custodial Asylum in upstate New York), however, suggests that many families were much less convinced than the superintendent that the asylum was the happiest answer to their problems. While many families welcomed the relief provided by institutionalization of a child, other families actively resisted the process of removing their children from their homes. Letters would show their opposition to institutionalization continuing for years (P.M. Ferguson 1994, p. 146). Even in cases where families went along with the experts and brought their sons and daughters to the asylums, it was also at times for very different reasons than the professionals supposed. For many families, the choice was a simple matter of economics or daily necessity rather than some sort of medical mandate: "In this sense, the decision to seek asylum care may well have been one predicated less on an acceptance of a medical approach to idiocy than on practical issues of household economy and life-cycle poverty" (Wright, 1996, p. 131).

At the end of the century, we are then left with a multilayered account of the experience of idiocy and feeblemindedness by individuals and families. The official narrative was clearly one of people viewed as idiots or imbeciles as a menace or a burden. The official policy was that in response, society had an obligation to separate and segregate such children and adults. The goal was to remediate if possible, but to incarcerate in any case. Custody had replaced cure; therapy had become control. That was the official story. However, daily practice diverged. Only a small percentage of individuals targeted for custody in the institutions actually ended up there. Others were abandoned in almshouses, prisons, or insane asylums. However, many remained in the community, cared for by parents or relatives, moving on to lives of at least survival, if seldom success, as adults. Families often called for more institutional openings for their children, but at the same time often resisted such placements or requested discharge soon after admission. In the end, the experience of disability and the decisions made in response to it were—as almost always is the case—economic at heart. Idiocy and poverty was not a happy combination.

CONCLUSION

The end of the 19th century was as much about beginnings as conclusions when it comes to the history of intellectual disability. As the century ended, the first public school special education classes for backward and feebleminded children were created in the large cities. In many ways, these classes and schools would repeat the cycle of 50 years earlier, with professionals claiming new expertise and jurisdiction over children with specific labels and promising optimistic improvements and social benefits if allowed control. The developmental understanding of intellectual disability triumphed and would quickly become installed as the quantitative language of mental age and IQ that would influence policy and practice for the next century. Perhaps most notably, the eugenic impulses that gained strength in the last half of the century would be taken up with a vengeance by those who saw sterilization as the complement to segregation in the war against social weakness.

The history of intellectual disability in the 19th century gives the impression of something strange yet familiar. The disability rights movement and the resultant reforms of policy and practice in many ways make the language and abuses of the 19th century seem thankfully distant. For all its faults and limitations, the system has gradually moved away from the most extreme cases of segregation and abandonment. There has been real change that is more than involutionary. At the same time, many of the debates in the 21st century seem foreshadowed by the developments of the 1800s. The process of professional specialization and expertise displacing the home and community as sources of support is reminiscent of a system of care that is still too often dominant. The role of families is still contested with rhetoric and practice often at odds with each other. The promises of policy still drastically exceed the realities of practice; segregation and isolation are still the outcome for too many, too often; and the experience of disability still remains troublingly skewed by poverty and race.

At the start of the 20th century, the new science of eugenics made its way from Europe to the United States. The founder of the eugenics movement, Sir Francis Galton, coined the term *eugenics* from the Greek roots meaning "good in birth." It was the science of improving the quality of the human race. In 1904, shortly before his death, Galton delivered a speech to members of the Oxford Socialogical Society titled "Eugenics: Its Definition, Scope and Aims": "Eugenics is the science which deals with all influences that improve the inborn qualities of a race" (Black, 2003). What is meant by improvement?" Galton continued. "What by the syllable 'eu' in 'eugenics,' whose English equivalent is 'good'?"

What indeed?

"A fable will best explain what is meant" Galton suggested.

> Let the scene be the zoological gardens in the quiet hours of the night, and suppose that the animals are able to converse, and that some very wise creature who had easy access to all the cages, say a philosophic sparrow or rat, was engaged in collecting the opinions of all sorts of animals with a view of elaborating a system of absolute morality.
>
> It is needless to enlarge on the contrariety of ideals between the beasts that prey and those they prey upon, between those of the animals that have to work hard for their food and the sedentary parasites that cling to their bodies and suck their blood, and so forth. Though no agreement could be reached as to absolute morality, the essentials of eugenics may be easily defined. All creatures would agree that it was better to be healthy than sick, vigorous than weak, well-fitted than ill-fitted for their part in life; in short, that it was better to be good rather than bad specimens of their kind, whatever that kind might be.
>
> So with men. There are a vast number of conflicting ideals, of alternative characters, of incompatible civilizations; but they are wanted to give fullness and interest to life. Society would be very dull if every man resembled the highly estimable Marcus Aurelius or Adam Bede. The aim of eugenics is to represent each class or sect by its best specimens; that done, to leave them to work out their common civilization in their own way. A considerable list of qualities can easily be compiled that nearly everyone except "cranks" would take into account when picking out the best specimens of his class. Special aptitudes would be assessed highly by those who possessed them, as the artistic faculties by artists, fearlessness of inquiry and veracity by scientists, religious absorption by mystics, and so on. There would be self-sacrificers, self-tormentors, and other exceptional idealists; but the representatives of these would be better members of a community than the body of their electors. They would have more of those qualities that are needed in a state—more vigor, more ability, and more consistency of purpose.

Of course, there were limits to the qualities that would be acceptable: "The community might be trusted to refuse representatives of criminals, and of others whom it rates as undesirable" (Galton, 1904, p. 82).

The specter of eugenics would hang over the lives of people with intellectual disability as the millennium changed to the modern era.

REFERENCES

Barr, M.W. (1904). *Mental defectives: Their history, treatment and training.* Philadelphia, PA: P. Blakiston's Sons.

Black, E. (2003). *War against the weak: Eugenics and America's campaign to create a master race.* New York: Four Walls Eight Windows.

Billings, J.S. (1895). *Report on the insane, feeble-minded, deaf and dumb, and blind in the United States.* Washington, DC: Government Printing Office.

Brady, C. (1867). *What can be done for the idiot?* (3rd ed.). London, United Kingdom: S.W. Partridge.

Brockett, L.F. (1856). Idiots and institutions for their training. *The American Journal of Education, 1,* 593–608.

Carlson, E.A. (2001). *The unfit: A history of a bad idea.* Cold Spring Harbor, NY: Cold Spring Harbor Laboratory Press.

Conolly, J. (1845). Notices of lunatic of Paris. *The British and Foreign Medical Review, 1,* 281–298.

Cremin, L.A. (1982). *American education: The national experience, 1783–1876.* New York, NY: Harper and Row.

Dix, D. (1976). Memorial to the legislature of Massachusetts. In M. Rosen, G.R. Clark, & M.S. Kivitz (Eds.), *The history of mental retardation: Collected papers* (Vol. 1, pp. 3–30). Baltimore, MD: University Park Press.

Esquirol, E. (1845). *Mental maladies: A treatise on insanity* (E. K. Hunt, Trans.). Philadelphia, PA: Lea and Blanchard. (Original work published 1838)

Ferguson, D.L., & Ferguson, P.M. (1986). The new Victors: A progressive policy analysis of work reform for people with very severe handicaps. *Mental Retardation, 24,* 331–338.

Ferguson, P.M. (1994). *Abandoned to their fate: Social policy and practice toward severely retarded people in America, 1820–1920.* Philadelphia, PA: Temple University Press.

Ferguson, P.M. (2002). The legacy of the almshouse. In S. Noll & J.W. Trent Jr. (Eds.), *Mental retardation in America: A historical reader* (pp. 40–64). New York: New York University Press.

Ferguson, P.M. (2008). The doubting dance: Contributions to a history of parent/professional interactions in early 20th century America. *Research and Practice for Persons with Severe Disabilities, 33,* 48–58.

Fernald, W. (1891). Discussion. *Proceedings of the Association of Medical Officers of American Institutions for Idiotic and Feeble-Minded Persons, 15,* 211–218.

Fischer, D.H. (1978). *Growing old in America: The Bland-Lee lectures delivered at Clark University.* New York, NY: Oxford University Press.

Fitzgerald, J. (1900). The duty of the state towards its idiotic and feeble-minded. *Proceedings of the New York State Conference of Charities and Correction, 1,* 172–178.

Galton, F. (1904). Eugenics: Its definition, scope and aims. *Nature, 70,* 82.

Goodey, C.F. (2011). *A history of intelligence and "intellectual disability": The shaping of psychology in early modern Europe.* Burlington, VT: Ashgate.

Howe, S.G. (1972). *On the causes of idiocy.* New York, NY: Arno Press. (Original work published 1848)

Hurd, H. (1916). *The institutional care of the insane in the United States and Canada.* Baltimore, MD: Johns Hopkins University Press.

Ireland, W.W. (1877). *On idiocy and imbecility.* London, United Kingdom: J.& A. Churchill.

Ireland, W.W. (1898). *The mental affections of children: Idiocy, imbecility, and insanity.* Philadelphia, PA: P. Blakiston's Sons.

Itard, J-M.G. (1962). *The wild boy of Aveyron* (G. Humphrey & M. Humphrey, Trans.). New York, NY: Appleton-Century-Crofts. (Original work published 1806)

Katz, M. (1985). *Poverty and policy in American history.* New York, NY: Academic Press.

Kerlin, I. (1858). *The mind unveiled: A brief history of twenty-two imbecile children.* Philadelphia, PA: U. Hunt & Son.

Kerlin, I. (1884). Provision for idiotic and feeble-minded children. *Proceedings of the National Conference of Charities and Correction, 11,* 246–63.

Kerlin, I.N. (1888). Status of the work before the people and legislatures. *Proceedings of the Association of Medical Officers of American Institutions for Idiotic and Feeble-Minded Persons, 12,* 64–83.

Kerlin, I.N. (1891). Discussion. *Proceedings of the Association of Medical Officers of American Institutions for Idiotic and Feeble-Minded Persons, 15,* 211–218.

Klebaner, B.J. (1976). *Public poor relief in America: 1790–1860.* New York, NY: Arno Press.

Lane, H. (1976). *The wild boy of Aveyron.* Cambridge, MA: Harvard University Press.

Lightner, D.L. (1999). *Asylum, prison and poorhouse: The writings and reform work of Dorothea Dix in Illinois.* Carbondale: Southern Illinois University Press.

McDonagh, P. (2008). *Idiocy: A cultural history.* Liverpool, United Kingdom: Liverpool University Press.

New York State. (1976). Report of select committee appointed to visit charitable institutions supported by the state, and all city and county poor and work houses and jails. In *The state and public welfare in nineteenth-century America: Five investigations, 1833–1877.* New York, NY: Arno Press. (Original work published 1857)

New York State. (1976). *Report of the state commission to investigate provision for the mentally deficient.* New York, NY: Arno. (Original work published 1915)

New York State Board of Charities. (1901). *Annual report*. Albany: New York State.

Osgood, R.L. (2008). *The history of special education: A struggle for equality in American public schools*. Westport, CT: Praeger.

Quincy, J. (1971). Report of the committee on the pauper laws of this commonwealth. In *The almshouse experience: Collected reports*. New York, NY: Arno. (Original work published, 1821)

Rafter, N.H. (1988). *White trash: The eugenic family studies, 1877–1919*. Boston, MA: Northeastern University Press.

Ray, I. (1838). *Treatise on the medical jurisprudence of insanity*. Boston, MA: Little, Brown.

Report of the select committee appointed to visit charitable institutions supported by state, and all city and county poor and work houses and jails. (1859/1976). *The state and public welfare in nineteenth-century America: Five investigations, 1833–1877*. New York: Arno.

Richards, P.L. (2004). "Beside her sat her idiot child": Families and developmental disability in mid-nineteenth-century America. In S. Noll & J.W. Trent Jr. (Eds.), *Mental retardation in America: A historical reader* (pp. 65–84). New York: New York University Press.

Richards, P.L., & Singer, G.H.S. (1998). "To draw out the effort of his mind": Educating a child with mental retardation in early-nineteenth-century America. *Journal of Special Education, 31*, 443–466.

Rothman, D.J. (1980). *Conscience and convenience: The asylum and its alternatives in progressive America*. Boston, MA: Little, Brown.

Rush, B. (1962). *Medical inquiries and observations upon the diseases of the mind*. New York, NY: Hafner. (Original work published 1812)

Sanborn, F.B. (1865). *1st annual report of the Massachusetts Board of State Charities*. Boston, MA: Wright and Potter, State Printers.

Scheerenberger, R. C. (1983). *A history of mental retardation*. Baltimore: Paul H. Brookes, Co.

Shattuck, R. (1980). *The forbidden experiment: The story of the wild boy of Aveyron*. New York, NY: Farrar, Straus and Giroux.

Shorter, E. (1997). *The history of psychiatry: From the era of the asylum to the age of Prozac*. New York, NY: Wiley.

Simpson, M. (2007). Developmental concept of idiocy. *Intellectual and Developmental Disabilities, 45*, 23–32.

Simpson, M. (2011). Othering intellectual disability: Two models of classification from the 19th century. *Theory and Psychology* [Advance online publication]. doi:10.1177/0959354310378375

Smith, J.D., & Wehmeyer, M.L. (2012). *Good blood/Bad blood: Science, nature, and the myth of the Kallikaks*. Washington, DC: American Association on Intellectual and Developmental Disabilities.

Talbot, E.S. (1898). *Degeneracy: Its causes, signs, and results*. New York, NY: Charles Scribner's Sons.

Trent, J.W. Jr. (1994). *Inventing the feeble mind: A history of mental retardation in the United States*. Berkeley: University of California Press.

Wilbur, H.B. (1852). *1st annual report: New York Idiot Asylum*. Albany, NY: State Printers.

Wilbur, H.B. (1858). *6th annual report: New York Idiot Asylum*. Albany, NY: State Printers.

Wilbur, H.B. (1860). *8th annual report: New York Idiot Asylum*. Albany, NY: State Printers.

Wilbur, H.B. (1865). *13th annual report: New York State Idiot Asylum*. Albany, NY: State Printers.

Wilbur, H.B. (1870). *18th annual report: New York State Idiot Asylum*. Albany, NY: State Printers

Wines, F.H. (1888). *Report on the defective, dependent, and delinquent classes of the population of the United States*. Washington, DC: Government Printing Office.

Winzer, M.A. (1993). *The history of special education: From isolation to integration*. Washington, DC: Gallaudet University Press.

Wright, D. (1996). "Childlike in his innocence": Lay attitudes to "idiots" and "imbeciles" in Victoria England. In D. Wright & A. Digby (Eds.), *From idiocy to mental deficiency: Historical perspectives on people with learning disabilities* (pp. 118–133). New York, NY: Routledge.

Yates, J. (1901). Report of the secretary of state in 1824 on the relief and settlement of the poor. In *New York State Board of Charities: Thirty-fourth annual report* (pp. 937–1145). Albany: State of New York. (Original work published 1824)

6

In Search of a Science

*Intellectual Disability in
Late Modern Times (1900 CE to 1930 CE)*

Steven Noll, J. David Smith, and Michael L. Wehmeyer

The decades from 1900 to 1930 were years of incredible change in how intellectual disability was understood, defined, and diagnosed. The rudimentary frame of diagnostic procedures was established and scientists—physicians, psychologists, and social workers—vied for primacy in what was becoming a new scientific discipline. Incongruously, though, these advances in the application of science to understanding intellectual disability and to solve societal problems led to the establishment of the eugenics movement and, as a result, people with intellectual disability were forced into burgeoning institutions, denied basic human and civil rights, and, in too many cases, involuntarily sterilized. The term *idiocy* lost its primacy in naming the construct, giving way to "feeblemindedness" and, ultimately, the conceptualization of "the moron." The era closed with the U.S. Supreme Court sanctioning of involuntary sterilization and with institutions for people with intellectual disability transforming from the habilitative efforts envisioned by social reformers in the 19th century to warehouses for a segment of the population who were devalued as human beings.

---

*T*he social context in which intellectual disability was understood from 1900 to 1930 was one of turmoil and change. It was an era of the professionalization of the field of intellectual disability and an era dominated by eugenic thought and practice. The industrial capacity of the United States grew dramatically between the end of the Civil War and the start of World War I, with output of manufactured goods increasing more than 33 times (Johnson, 1998). It is not surprising that this shift in industrial might paralleled a movement away from an agrarian society. In 1880, almost half of American workers were employed in agriculturally related jobs. By 1910, slightly less than one-third, and by 1930, just over one-fifth. As mechanization and industrialization reduced jobs on the farm, urban populations grew. In 1850, half a million people lived in New York City. By 1890, that number had tripled to 1.5 million, and then more than doubled again, to 3.5 million people, by 1900. In Chicago, the population exploded, from less than 30,000 in 1850 to 300,000 by 1870, and 1.7 million by the turn of the century.

The American population as a whole also expanded dramatically. Prior to the Civil War, the population of the United States was just over 31 million. By 1870, it was slightly under 40 million people, growing to 50 million by the 1880 census and to almost 63 million by 1890. By 1900, the population was over 75 million. The increasing numbers of immigrants and the changing nature of immigrant populations also changed. Between 1815 and the start of the Civil War, approximately 5 million people immigrated to the United states, largely from England, Ireland, and Western Europe. From the end of the Civil War to 1890, the number of immigrants doubled to 10 million, again primarily from England and Western Europe, but with more Germans and Scandinavians. However, in less than a quarter century, from 1890 to 1914, another 15 million immigrants landed at port cities in the United States. These immigrants differed from previous travelers not only in sheer volume, but also by point of origin, for most of them embarked on their journeys from Eastern and Southern Europe, Poland, Russia, Ukraine, Slovakia, Croatia, Slovenia, Hungary, Greece, Rumania, and Italy.

Historian Robert Wiebe characterized the period of American history from 1877 to 1920 as "the search for order" (Wiebe, 1967, p. 3), a useful analogy for capturing the essence of the social context in which the American eugenics movement burgeoned (Wiebe, 1967).

IN SEARCH OF A SCIENCE

The rediscovery of Mendel's experiments with garden peas was but one of several events that changed the face of science at the beginning of the 20th century and directly affected the lives of people with intellectual disability. In *The Triumph of Evolution: American Scientists and the Heredity-Environment Controversy, 1900–1941*, historian Hamilton Cravens (1978) noted that at the close of the 19th century it had become possible, at least in the minds of scientists and the public, for science to address questions with regard to social progress, questions stirred up by publications such as Richard Dugdale's eugenic family study *The Jukes,* and by the rising tide of social Darwinism, the application to humans of Darwinian (actually Malthusian) principles of survival of the fittest.

"It was in this context," wrote Cravens, "that the new experimental biology and psychology suddenly began to produce spectacular and brilliant explanations of some of the most complex and intractable mysteries of evolution, heredity, and variation, together with the articulation of seemingly well-established explanations of human nature, intelligence, and conduct" (Cravens, 1978, p. 11).

Mendel's experiments with *Pisum sativum,* pea plants, examined the hereditary transmission of seven "characters" of the plant, where the term *character* referred to aspects of the appearance of the plant: its flowers, pea pods, or the peas themselves. Each character was expressed in dichotomous, mutually incompatible ways: either short or tall plants; yellow or green seeds; round, smooth seeds or round, wrinkled seeds; purple flowers or white flowers; inflated or constricted pods; green or yellow pods; flowers along the stem or flowers bunched at the top of the stem.

Mendel found that if a plant from a line that was known to produce only one character (pure dominant) was bred with another plant from a line that was known to produce only the opposite character (pure recessive), all their offspring (the F1 generation) would have the physical appearance (called *phenotype*) of the pure dominant. Thus, breeding a tall plant with a short plant yielded only tall plants. Likewise, flowers on the stem, purple flowers, inflated pods, green pods, yellow peas, and round smooth peas all were dominant, or bred true.

When plants from the F1 generation were bred with one another, however, the recessive character from the original parent reappeared at a 3:1 ratio (i.e., 3 dominant-trait plants for each 1 recessive-trait plant). Mendel conducted monohybrid crosses, crossing plants that varied by only one character (e.g., tall or short, round or angle/wrinkled, etc.). A plant that breeds true (e.g., for tallness, i.e., one that is a pure dominant for tallness, HH, where capital *H* represents dominant character for height; thus, HH, because the plant inherited a dominant tall gene from each parent) is referred to as the organism's genotype, or the genetic makeup underlying a characteristic or trait. A plant that breeds true for shortness, a pure recessive, would be labeled hh (small *h* for recessive for height). All offspring would, then, be hybrids, each possessing a dominant and recessive character, with the plant displaying the physical appearance, or phenotype, of the dominant character, in this case, tallness.

	h	h
H	H h *tall*	H h *tall*
H	H h *tall*	H h *tall*

When, however, two plants from F1 are interbred, each contributing an Hh to potential offspring, the genotype and phenotype options change, as shown:

	H	h
H	H H *Tall*	H h *tall*
h	H h *tall*	h h *Short*

Thus, for the F2 generation there is a 3:1 ratio, at least for the phenotype, with three potential genotypes resulting in the phenotype for tallness (HH, Hh, Hh) and one (hh) breeding true for the shortness phenotype. The F2 generation, however, yields a genotypic ratio of 1:2:1, with one pure dominant (HH) to two hybrids (Hh) to one pure recessive (hh).

Subsequent monohybrid crosses yielded more complex but still predictable ratios, as did dihybrid crosses (i.e., plants that varied by two characters). Mendel was lucky in the plant characteristics he selected. The characters he identified appear on six different chromosomes, and the *Pisum sativum* has only seven chromosomes. In the one exception, the characters are carried on polar ends of a single chromosome. This was fortunate for Mendel because he did not have to worry about circumstances in which traits are coupled because of their location on the chromosome (Henig, 2000, p. 79). It was unfortunate for the inmates at institutions around the United States because American eugenicists assumed that complex human characteristics such as intelligence (and feeblemindedness) were, like the seven characteristics of Mendel's peas, transmitted by single-gene mechanisms.

These single-gene mechanisms were called unit characters. The notion of unit characters that served as a single-gene transmission mechanism was important to eugenicists. "In an understandable initial enthusiasm for this great discovery," wrote Stephen Jay Gould in 1998, referring to the particulate theory of inheritance exemplified by a single-gene transmission theory, "early geneticists committed their most common error in trying to identify single genes as causes for nearly every feature of the human organism, from discrete bits of anatomy to complex facets of personality" (Gould, 1998, p. 12).

"For our purposes Mendel's law may be regarded as consisting of three principles," wrote eugenicist Charles B. Davenport in a 1910 article in the *Journal of Psycho-Asthenics* (the precursor to the *American Journal on Intellectual and Developmental Disabilities*). "First, the principle of the unit characters or inheritable unit, each of which is, in accordance with the second principle, transmitted through the germ by a representative called a determiner. The third principle is that when the germ cells of both parents carry a determiner of a character the fertilized egg and the embryo derived from it have the determiner of the character double, or duplex. When the germ cell of one parent only carries the determiner, this is simplex in the embryo. When neither parent carries the determiner the embryo is devoid of it" (Davenport, 1910, p. 94).

The application of single-gene transmission theories to the heritability of intellectual disability is best illustrated in the publication of the notorious eugenic family narrative, *The Kallikak Family* (Goddard, 1912). Published in 1912 by psychologist Henry Herbert Goddard, this putative "natural experiment" in human heredity and the heritability of feeblemindedness was used by eugenicists as proof of their single-gene transmission theories and to make significant strides in their agenda to segregate people with intellectual disability from the community, to enact marriage restriction acts in states that would prohibit people with intellectual disability from marrying, and to establish laws to forcibly sterilize people seen as unfit. Figure 6.1 provides an accounting of the Kallikak story, its impact on the life of the woman pseudonymously known as "Deborah Kallikak," and a modern look at the veracity of the story.

FROM FEEBLEMINDEDNESS TO MORON

The leading textbook in the field at the beginning of the 20th century was *Mental Defectives,* written by Martin Barr (1904), superintendent at Elwyn, in Pennsylvania. Considered the first modern American text on intellectual impairment, Barr's 1904 perspective also reflected the growing sense of the importance of heredity in understanding the construct and its potentially devastating consequences in the lives of people who were deemed to be feebleminded.

Attempting to resurrect the Jukes saga and spinning its lessons within the new understanding of feeblemindedness as primarily hereditary, Barr proclaimed that "in these [the Jukes] we have surely found evidence . . . that the hereditary transmission of imbecility is at once the most insidious and the most aggressive of degenerative forces; attacking alike the physical, mental and moral nature, enfeebling the judgment and will, while exaggerating the sexual impulses and the perpetuation of an evil growth, a growth too often parasitic" (Barr, 1904, p. 102).

If in previous eras there was little differentiation in how intellectual disability was conceptualized, either by typology or by level of impairment, this changed beginning in the late 19th century (see Chapter 5), and by the early 1900s it had become a cottage industry to introduce classification schemes that detailed every possible difference systematically. As discussed in Chapters 3 and 4, the notion of idiocy, introduced in the late Middle Ages, remained the primary means of discussing the intellectual disability construct through the mid-19th century; but as the growth of the institution system created a professional class of workers within a discipline, the term was viewed as nonscientific, and other terms began to be used, most notably *imbecility*. William Ireland (1877) wrote that "as idiocy is originally a popular, and not a scientific term, it is difficult to frame a definition comprehensive enough to include all of the meanings to which it has been used" (p. 1). As noted in Chapter 5, in Ireland's system as well as that of others, *idiocy* began to refer to people with the most significant cognitive impairments and *imbecility* to people with less extensive impairments.

Idiot, or *idiocy,* as it emerged across the years from the late Middle Ages, referred, in general to the observable "differentness" of people with intellectual disability. The term was derived from the Greek words *idatas* and *idios*. *Idatas* refers to a private person, and *idios* means "peculiar." Together, they refer to a person who is peculiar, set aside, or different.

INTELLECTUAL AND DEVELOPMENTAL DISABILITIES
2012, Vol. 50, No. 2, 169–178

©AAIDD
DOI: 10.1352/1934-9556-50.2.169

Who Was Deborah Kallikak?

J. David Smith and Michael L. Wehmeyer

Abstract

The Kallikak Family was, along with *The Jukes: A Study in Crime, Pauperism, Disease, and Heredity*, one of the most visible eugenic family narratives published in the early 20th century. Published in 1912 and authored by psychologist Henry Herbert Goddard, director of the psychological laboratory at the Vineland Training School for Feebleminded Children in Vineland, New Jersey, *The Kallikak Family* told the tale of a supposedly "degenerate" family from rural New Jersey, beginning with Deborah, one of the inmates at the Training School. Like most publications in the genre, this pseudoscientific treatise described generations of illiterate, poor, and purportedly immoral Kallikak family members who were chronically unemployed, supposedly feebleminded, criminal, and, in general, perceived as threats to "racial hygiene." Presented as a "natural experiment" in human heredity, this text served to support eugenic activities through much of the first half of the 20th century. This article reviews the story of Deborah Kallikak, including her true identity, and provides evidence that Goddard's treatise was incorrect.

Key Words: *history of intellectual disability; Vineland Training School; Kallikak family; Deborah Kallikak; Henry Herbert Goddard*

One bright October day, fourteen years ago, there came to the Training School at Vineland, a little eight-year-old girl.
—Henry Herbert Goddard

So began *The Kallikak Family*, Henry Herbert Goddard's 1912 best-selling addition to the depressingly large eugenic "family studies" genre. Starting with the 1877 publication of Richard Dugdale's study of the Juke family, these pseudoscientific genealogies chronicled the lives of society's least capable families, who were often given pejorative names like the Smoky Pilgrims, the Pineys, the Dacks, the Happy Hickories, and the Nams. Eugenic family studies such as these influenced the public's understanding of what constituted "degeneracy" for nearly half a century.

The Kallikak Family, which Stephen J. Gould called the "primal myth of the eugenics movement" (1981, p. 198), was published in 1912 and authored by psychologist Henry Herbert Goddard, director of the psychological laboratory at the Vineland Training School for Feebleminded Children in Vineland, New Jersey. *The Kallikak Family* told the tale of a supposedly "degenerate" family from rural New Jersey, beginning with Deborah (see Figure 1) who was one of the "inmates" at the Training School. Like most books in the genre, this pseudoscientific treatise described generations of illiterate, poor, and purportedly immoral Kallikak family members, who were chronically unemployed, supposedly feebleminded, criminal, and, in general, perceived as threats to "racial hygiene."

Unlike other such tales, however, the Kallikak story has a plot twist. The progenitor of this putatively degenerate line, an American Revolutionary War soldier called Martin Kallikak, Sr., had purportedly sired his disreputable ancestral line through a dalliance with an allegedly feebleminded barmaid. Martin Sr., however, righted his moral ship, married an upstanding Quaker woman, and became the forefather of a second line of descendants that included, as Goddard (1912, p. 31) put it, "respectable citizens, men and women prominent in every phase of life." Goddard derived the pseudonym *Kallikak* from the Greek words *Kallos* (beauty) and *Kakos* (bad), which was his dramatic way of capturing the essence of the story of the Kallikak family, one branch of which was supposedly good and the other bad (see Figure 2).

INTELLECTUAL AND DEVELOPMENTAL DISABILITIES
2012, Vol. 50, No. 2, 169–178

©AAIDD
DOI: 10.1352/1934-9556-50.2.169

Figure 1. "Deborah Kallikak" as pictured in the frontispiece of *The Kallikak Family.* (Photograph in public domain.)

The Story of Deborah

The story of Deborah's lineage, as told by Goddard, became a national best seller, and it is evident from the onset of the narrative that Goddard (1912) intended *The Kallikak Family* as a morality tale for the masses:

It is true that we have made rather dogmatic statements and have drawn conclusions that do not seem scientifically warranted from the data. We have done this because it seems necessary to make these statements and conclusions for the benefit of the lay reader. (p. xi)

Goddard's version of Deborah's story begins in *The Kallikak Family* narrative as follows:

One bright October day, fourteen years ago, there came to the Training School at Vineland, a little eight-year-old girl. She had been born in an almshouse. Her mother had afterwards married, not the father of this child, but the prospective father of another child, and later had divorced him and married another man, who was also the father of some of her children. (p. 1)

The remainder of chapter 1 relates records from Deborah's years at Vineland. Throughout *The Kallikak Family* narrative, Deborah is depicted in clinical terms emphasizing defect and degeneracy, to paint a verbal picture of the type of "feeble-minded" person Goddard wanted readers to believe she was: "mouth shut," "staring expression," and, even, "jerking movement in walking" (p. 3).

Ultimately, and predictably, Goddard (1912) turned to information from the Binet–Simon intelligence test (Binet & Simon, 1916) to make his case for Deborah's degeneracy. Goddard introduced the Binet test to an American audience and was the preeminent "mental tester" for the

decade thereafter, until Lewis Terman usurped that role.

By the Binet Scale this girl showed, in April, 1910, the mentality of a nine-year-old child with two points over; January, 1911, 9 years, 1 point; September, 1911, 9 years, 2 points; October, 1911, 9 years, 3 points. (p. 11)

Goddard goes on to state that

[t]his is a typical illustration of the mentality of a high-grade feeble-minded person, the moron, the delinquent, the kind of girl or woman that fills our reformatories. They are wayward, they get into all sorts of trouble and difficulties, sexually and otherwise. (p. 12)

Turning even to Deborah's positive qualities to bolster his thesis, Goddard argued that

[i]t is also the history of the same type of girl in the public school. Rather good-looking, bright in appearance, with many attractive ways, the teacher clings to the hope, indeed insists, that such a girl will come out all right. Our work with Deborah convinces us that such hopes are delusions. (pp. 12–13)

He goes on to indicate that

[h]ere is a child who has been most carefully guarded. She has been persistently trained since she was eight years old, and yet nothing has been accomplished in the direction of higher intelligence or general education. To-day if this young woman were to leave the Institution, she would at once become a prey to the designs of evil men or evil women and would lead a life that would be vicious, immoral, and criminal. (p. 13)

Providing an advance organizational paradigm for how to interpret the remainder of the book, Goddard concluded chapter 1 as follows:

We may now repeat the ever insistent question and this time we indeed have good hope of answering it. The question is, "How do we account for this kind of individual?" The answer is in a word "Heredity"—bad stock. We must recognize that the human family shows varying stocks or strains that are as marked and that breed as true as anything in plant or animal life. (p. 13)

Switching topics in chapter 2 to the means by which data on inmates at the Training School were gathered, Goddard continued as follows:

The Vineland Training School has for two years employed field workers. These are women highly trained, of broad human experience, and interested in social problems. They become acquainted with the condition of the feeble-minded. They study all the grades, note their peculiarities, and acquaint themselves with the methods of testing and recognizing them. They then go out to the homes of the children and there ask that all the facts which are available may be furnished. (p. 14)

So out into the slums, the hollows, and the barrens they went: a cadre of women field workers,

(continued)

Figure 6.1. *(continued)*

INTELLECTUAL AND DEVELOPMENTAL DISABILITIES

©AAIDD

2012, Vol. 50, No. 2, 169–178

DOI: 10.1352/1934-9556-50.2.169

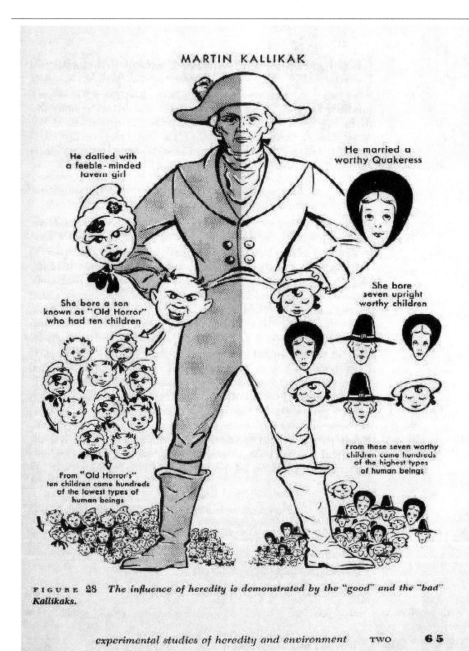

Figure 2. The influence of heredity is demonstrated by the "good" and the "bad" Kallikaks. (Garrett, 1955, p. 65).

INTELLECTUAL AND DEVELOPMENTAL DISABILITIES   ©AAIDD
2012, Vol. 50, No. 2, 169–178   DOI: 10.1352/1934-9556-50.2.169

many of whom were well-educated but unable to break the barrier of gender to secure professional jobs with decent wages. Among them was Elizabeth S. Kite, who had recently returned to Philadelphia from the University of London and was the field worker who tracked down the Kallikak information. And, not surprisingly, they found—or claimed to find—what they were looking for.

> The surprise and horror of it all, was that no matter where we traced them, whether in the prosperous rural district, in the city slums to which some had drifted, or in the more remote mountain regions, or whether it was a question of the second or the sixth generation, an appalling amount of defectiveness was everywhere found. (Goddard, 1912, p. 17)

One family, however, stood out even in this sea of so-called degeneracy.

> In the course of the work of tracing various members of the family, our field worker [Kite] occasionally found herself in the midst of a good family of the same name, which apparently was in no way related to the girl whose ancestry we were investigating. These cases became so frequent that there gradually grew the conviction that ours must be a degenerate offshoot from an older family of better stock. (p. 17)

Goddard then described this putatively degenerate ancestry:

> The great-great-grandfather of Deborah was Martin Kallikak. We had also traced the good family back to an ancestor belonging to an older generation than this Martin Kallikak, but bearing the same name. Many months later, a granddaughter of Martin revealed in a burst of confidence the situation. When Martin Sr., of the good family, was a boy of fifteen, his father died, leaving him without parental care or oversight. Just before attaining his majority, the young man joined one of the numerous military companies that were formed to protect the country at the beginning of the Revolution. At one of the taverns frequented by the militia he met a feeble-minded girl by whom he became the father of a feeble-minded son. This child was given, by its mother, the name of the father in full, and thus has been handed down to posterity the father's name and the mother's mental capacity. This illegitimate boy was Martin Kallikak, Jr., the great-great-grandfather of our Deborah, and from him have come four hundred and eighty descendants. One hundred and forty-three of these, we have conclusive proof, were or are feeble-minded, while only forty-six have been found normal. The rest are unknown or doubtful. (p. 18)

After describing the seemingly endless ways in which this family was worth singling out among the "appalling amount of defectiveness [that] was everywhere found" (Goddard, 1912, p. 17), Goddard stated the following:

> This is the ghastly story of the descendants of Martin Kallikak, Sr., from the nameless feeble-minded girl. Although Martin Sr. himself paid no further attention to the girl nor [to] her child,

society has had to pay the heavy price of all the evil he engendered. (p. 30)

The story of Deborah's putative family concludes in *The Kallikak Family* narrative:

> Martin Sr., on leaving the Revolutionary Army, straightened up and married a respectable girl of good family, and through that union has come another line of descendants of radically different character. All of the legitimate children of Martin Sr. married into the best families in their state, the descendants of colonial governors, signers of the Declaration of Independence, soldiers and even the founders of a great university. There are doctors, lawyers, judges, educators, traders, landholders, in short, respectable citizens, men and women prominent in every phase of social life. There have been no feeble-minded among them; no illegitimate children; no immoral women. There has been no epilepsy, no criminals, no keepers of houses of prostitution. (pp. 30–31)

Good blood. Bad blood. *Kallos. Kakos.*

Impact of *The Kallikak Family*

The impact of *The Kallikak Family* was significant. The book was received with acclaim by the public and by much of the scientific community and was reissued through 12 printings, including a reprinting as late as 1939. It is difficult to locate a biology or psychology text in the years immediately following the publication of the Kallikak book that does not cite the study as conclusive evidence of the hereditary nature of feeblemindedness and, by extension, human intelligence. Eugenicists cited Goddard's study to justify their hereditarian stance as early as 1911, a year before the book appeared in print. The biology text used to teach evolution to students at Rhea County Central High School in Dayton, Tennessee, by John Thomas Scopes, the nominal defendant in the 1925 Scopes trial starring attorneys Clarence Darrow and William Jennings Bryant, was *A Civic Biology Presented in Problems* by George William Hunter, published in 1914. Hunter's text included a presentation of eugenic thought as scientific fact and an overview of the Kallikak story. It is interesting to note that the same text included an argument for the racial inferiority of all people other than those of European origin. No mention of this was made during the trial.

In 1927, *The Callicac Family* [sic] was entered into the record as evidence in *Buck v. Bell*, the case that resulted in the Supreme Court decision establishing that involuntary sterilization of "mentally defective" people was constitutional. *The Kallikak Family* was reprinted in German in 1933,

(continued)

Figure 6.1. *(continued)*

INTELLECTUAL AND DEVELOPMENTAL DISABILITIES   ©AAIDD
2012, Vol. 50, No. 2, 169–178   DOI: 10.1352/1934-9556-50.2.169

the same year Nazi Germany passed the "Law for Prevention of Offspring with Hereditary Defects Act." That Act was based on the model sterilization law drawn up by American eugenicist Harry H. Laughlin, a star witness in *Buck v. Bell*, and legalized involuntary sterilization of Germans with disabilities. From 1934 to 1939, Hitler's Nazi regime sterilized somewhere near 150,000 Germans with disabilities, without their consent or knowledge; and, beginning in the winter of 1939, implemented a program of extermination that, by its end 20 months later, had resulted in the murder of 80,000 disabled Germans.

Deborah Kallikak became the poster child for societal fears, the flames of which were fanned by a select group of well-educated, upper class, White Americans who were joined by an aspiring professional middle class and marching under the banner of the new sciences of genetics and heredity. The name Kallikak would become part of the vernacular: a synonym for backward, inbred hillbillies and slum dwellers. Deborah was only one of many young women whose primary "sin" had been to be destitute, poorly educated, and physically attractive at a time when society viewed this combination as a deadly cocktail leading to, as then President Theodore Roosevelt proclaimed, the threat of "race suicide."

Society's punishments for such transgressions were severe. For Deborah, it was life without parole in an institution. For others like her, it was worse. Before Goddard's "menace of the feebleminded" era ended, somewhere between 40,000 and 50,000 Americans labeled as feebleminded had been sterilized involuntarily.

Emma's Story

The Kallikak Family narrative begins with the chapter titled "Deborah's Story," and it was "Deborah's" story, to the extent that Deborah was an invention of Goddard's, one he needed to tell his story. The story of Emma Wolverton, whom the world has known as Deborah Kallikak, is much richer and more complex, and started with her arrival in the world and at the Vineland Training school.

Emma's entry into the world was as ignoble and anonymous as her arrival at the Vineland Training School that October day in 1897. She was born in 1889 into the wretchedly poor environs of a late 19th-century almshouse to a single mother who had lost her job as a domestic servant as a result of her illegitimate pregnancy (Kellicott, 1911, p. 162). Emma's father, identified as "normal" but as morally bereft as he was financially bankrupt, abandoned the newborn Emma and her mother to the penury of the almshouse. The possibilities in life for Emma, her mother, and her three older siblings improved when they were brought to live in the home of a benefactor. Eventually, though, Emma suffered from the consequences of her mother's poor decisions, who circumvented efforts by the host family to prevent further dissolute sexual behavior and entered into a relationship with another man that resulted in pregnancy. Unnerved by Emma's mother's promiscuity, the benefactor insisted upon and arranged for a marriage between Emma's mother and her man du jour. Soon thereafter, Emma's mother and the rest of her family moved out of the benefactor's home and in with her latest paramour, and after bearing him two children they moved to a farmhouse, where, eventually, Emma's stepfather disappeared and her mother lived openly with the farmer/landlord. Seemingly cut off at every turn, the benefactor arranged for a divorce between Emma's stepfather and mother and for a marriage between Emma's mother and the farmer. The farmer consented, with the caveat that the children who were not his would be sent away—including Emma.

Thus, Emma was brought to the gates of the Training School with the highly suspect explanation that because she did not get along with the other children at school, she might be, possibly, feebleminded. When she entered Vineland, according to school records, she was of average size and weight, with no particularly notable physical anomalies. She could wash and dress herself. She was identified as a good listener and imitator and as active and excitable, though not particularly affectionate. She was not literate and could not count—which is hardly surprising because it is unlikely that she attended school regularly—but she was handy and could use a needle, carry wood, and fill a kettle.

In 1911, the year before *The Kallikak Family* was published, 22-year-old Emma Wolverton was described in institutional records as a skillful and hard worker who lacked self-confidence. She continued to excel in woodworking and dressmaking. Academic subjects were still a problem, but the records indicate that across the years of her confinement at the Training School, she made

INTELLECTUAL AND DEVELOPMENTAL DISABILITIES
2012, Vol. 50, No. 2, 169–178

©AAIDD
DOI: 10.1352/1934-9556-50.2.169

considerable progress in multiple areas of her life, particularly in nonacademic learning and in social skills. She furthered her needlework skills, became a handy carpenter, and worked in the school dining room (see Figures 3 and 4). She learned to play the cornet and performed in the Vineland Training School band. Emma was an avid participant in outings and in the life of the institution (see Figure 5).

But as she got older, Emma became subject to the laws of such institutions, in which more capable inmates were required to perform compulsory labor to meet the demands of these increasingly underfunded and overcrowded warehouses (Trent, 1994). Emma performed a wide array of tasks during her years at Vineland, including serving as a teacher's aide for the kindergarten class. She also was a helper in the wood-carving class. In fact, Emma's capacities earned her the "privilege" of working for the family of Edward R. Johnstone, the institution's then superintendent (Doll, 1988).

In July of 1914, at the age of 25, and after having lived at the Vineland Training School for 17 of those years, Emma was transferred to the women's institution across the street that provided a custodial situation in which feebleminded women could be placed to keep them from "propagating their kind" (Doll, 1988, p. 4). It was to be Emma's home for most of her life.

Figure 4. Deborah as a waitress (from *The Kallikak Family*, Goddard, 1912, p. 4).

In 1985, J. David Smith, co-author of this article, published a book titled *Minds Made Feeble: The Myth and the Legacy of the Kallikaks*. Goddard's thesis of the hereditary nature of feeblemindedness rested, in large measure, on the presumption that Emma Wolverton's ancestors, or a large percentage of them, were feebleminded, although the only family member ever tested using an IQ test was Emma herself. The bulk of *The Kallikak Family* narrative itself involves descriptions of these ancestors: from Emma's purported great-great-grandfather, Martin Kallikak, Jr., the offspring of the ill-advised dalliance with the feebleminded barmaid, on down to Emma herself. Of course, these family members were christened with stigmatizing names by Goddard and Kite; Martin Jr. was referred to, for example, as the "Old Horror." The pictures in the text show Kallikak family members posed in front of what can best be described as hovels, thereby juxtaposing purportedly degenerate people with their paltry homes (see Figure 6).

Minds Made Feeble debunked the assertion in Goddard's narrative that these Wolverton ancestors were degenerate or feebleminded. The present context does not allow for a detailed accounting, but a few examples will suffice to make this point.

It is, of course, Martin Kallikak, Jr., the great-great-grandfather of "Deborah," who is the fulcrum in *The Kallikak Family* narrative. Goddard's description of Martin Jr. is laden with those traits he felt characterized people he described as "morons." In the text, Goddard narrates a conversation with an elderly woman who is, supposedly, part of the "good side of the Kallikak family" (p. 80), who was reported to remember Martin Jr. as ". . . always unwashed and drunk. At election time, he never

Figure 3. Deborah at the sewing machine (from *The Kallikak Family*, Goddard, 1912, p. 4).

(continued)

Figure 6.1. *(continued)*

INTELLECTUAL AND DEVELOPMENTAL DISABILITIES   ©AAIDD
2012, Vol. 50, No. 2, 169–178   DOI: 10.1352/1934-9556-50.2.169

Figure 5. Deborah (lower left) on an outing at the Training School. (From Michael L. Wehmeyer's personal collection.)

failed to appear in somebody's cast-off clothing, ready to vote, for the price of a drink" (p. 80).

According to census data for Hunterdon County, Martin Jr., whose real name was John Wolverton (the spelling of the surname varies by generation from Wolverton with one "o" to Woolverton, with two "o's"), was born in 1776 and was married in 1804, a union that lasted 22 years until his wife's death. Unlike Goddard's description of Martin Jr., John Wolverton appears

Figure 6. Great-grandchildren of "Old Sal" (from *The Kallikak Family*, Goddard, 1912, p. 88).

Figure 7. Emma Wolverton at age 73 (Leiby, 1967).

INTELLECTUAL AND DEVELOPMENTAL DISABILITIES

2012, Vol. 50, No. 2, 169–178

©AAIDD

DOI: 10.1352/1934-9556-50.2.169

to have been fairly successful. He owned land throughout most of his adult life. County records indicate that he purchased two lots of land in 1809 for cash. Deed books for the county contain records of his transferring his property to his children and grandchildren later in his life. The 1850 census record shows that he was living with one of his daughters and several of his grandchildren at that time. That record also lists all of the adults in the household as being able to read. The 1860 census record lists his occupation as "laborer" and his property as valued at $100 (not a meager amount for the average person at that time). John Wolverton died in 1861 (Smith, 1985, p. 93).

But consider Martin Jr.'s fourth child, "Old Sal," whom Goddard described as feebleminded and as marrying a feebleminded man and as having two feebleminded children, who likewise married feebleminded wives and had large families of defective children, some of whom are pictured in *The Kallikak Family.*

"Old Sal" was, in fact, Catherine Ann Wolverton, born in December of 1811. She was married in January of 1834 and died in 1897 at the age of 85 (Macdonald & McAdams, 2001, p. 218). Goddard's nickname of "Old Sal" probably came from Goddard and Kite mistaking Catherine for her sister-in-law, Sarah (Macdonald & McAdams, 2001, p. 811). There is not much known about Catherine herself from the records, but a family history relayed by some of Catherine's descendants reveals many contradictions to Goddard's portrayal of her offspring. Two of her grandchildren, a brother and sister who were retired school teachers living in Trenton, New Jersey, were still living in 1985 when *Minds Made Feeble* was published. One grandson moved from New Jersey to Iowa, became treasurer of a bank, owned a lumber yard, and operated a creamery. Another grandson moved to Wisconsin. His son served as a pilot in the Army Air Corps in World War II. A great-great grandson of Catherine was a teacher in Chicago. A great grandson was a policeman in another city in Illinois. A 1930 newspaper article reported that all of Catherine's sons had been soldiers in the Civil War.

Others of the so-called bad Kallikak family members were land owners, farmers, and, although poor, they were generally self-sufficient rural people. Though many of them had lived with limited resources and against considerable environmental odds, the records suggest that they were a cohesive family. With Emma's grandfather's generation, though, the tides turned for the family. Called "Justin" in Goddard's narrative, Emma's grandfather (also named John Wolverton) was born in 1834, and, like his ancestors, lived in rural Hunterdon, New Jersey, working primarily in agriculture. Like many of his generation, though, John and his family were swept up in the turmoil of the Industrial Age, and by 1880 the family had moved to Trenton, New Jersey, and John worked as a laborer. Times were difficult, the cohesiveness of the family eroded, and Emma's mother's family scraped by in those tough economic times.

Malinda Woolverton was the actual name of Emma's mother. She was born in April 1868, when the family lived in Hunterdon, but by 1885, at the age of 17, she had already moved out of the family home, living with and serving as a domestic and childcare helper in the home of a neighbor. Emma was born to Malinda in February of 1889. Although Goddard indicates that Emma's mother had three illegitimate children who did not live past infancy, before Emma was born in the almshouse, Macdonald and McAdams's (2001) genealogy of the Wolverton family noted that records suggest that Emma was Malinda's only illegitimate child.

The real story of the disfavored Kallikaks, the "other Wolvertons," is not free of troubles and human frailties. The family had its share of skeletons in the closet, but so did many families of that era, particularly those who were faced with poverty, lack of education, and scarce resources for dealing with tumultuous social change. But the family also had its strengths and successes. The tragedy of the disfavored Kallikaks is that their story was distorted so as to be interpreted according to a powerful myth and then used to further bolster that myth. The myth was that of eugenics.

According to Goddard (1912), "(t)his is the ghastly story of the descendants of Martin Kallikak, Sr. from the nameless feeble-minded girl" (p. 29). But, of course, it was not. It was not because it was Goddard's story, constructed by Goddard and Kite to fulfill the need for a eugenics narrative to fit their worldview and to bolster the eugenics myth. It was, perhaps, "Deborah Kallikak's" story, but it was not Emma Wolverton's story. Her story was the story of many American families: people living simply in a rural setting who, for whatever reason, were swept into urban America at the end of the 19th century and start of the 20th century and into a life, like that of many immigrants, that was beset

(continued)

Figure 6.1. *(continued)*

INTELLECTUAL AND DEVELOPMENTAL DISABILITIES
2012, Vol. 50, No. 2, 169–178

©AAIDD
DOI: 10.1352/1934-9556-50.2.169

by hardships for which they were not adequately prepared.

There is one more reason, however, that this was not Emma's story. Wolverton genealogist David Macdonald wrote in 1997 that he was "... certain that Dr. Goddard plugged the [*Kakos*] line into the wrong part of the Wolverton family. He obviously wanted for the [*Kallos*] branch a set of people as good and prominent as possible, and I think that he was not very scrupulous about how he found it" (personal communication, June 23, 1997). In 2001, Macdonald and Nancy McAdams completed their 860-page magnum opus on the Wolverton family. All of the Kalllikaks are to be found there, clearly and carefully documented. In an appendix devoted to the Kallikak study, Macdonald and McAdams wrote the following:

There should be no doubt that John Wolverton (note: referring to the man whom Goddard referred to as Martin Kallikak, Jr.) was a son of Gabriel Wolverton and Catherine Murray. John's parentage would not merit further comment if he had not been described in *The Kallikak Family*, a book published in 1912, as an illegitimate son of John Woolverton and an unnamed feeble-minded tavern girl, when in fact . . . John (Martin, Jr.) and . . . John (Martin, Sr.) were second cousins and both perfectly legitimate sons of their married parents. (p. 807)

Martin Kallikak, Jr. was not the illegitimate son of Martin Kallikak, Sr. Whether the dalliance with a feebleminded barmaid was fiction or fact, Goddard's natural experiment never occurred.

There were no *Kallos*, no *Kakos*, and no Kallikaks. There was no good blood, no bad blood. Some Wolverton family members had access to resources: money, education, health care. Other Wolverton family members had none of those and were swept, with millions of rural Americans and immigrants, into the bowels of America's urban areas, into lives that were often barely livable.

Emma Wolverton moved to the New Jersey State Institute for Feebleminded Women in July of 1914. "[Emma], at this time," stated a social worker who worked with her, "was a handsome young woman, twenty-five years old, with many accomplishments" (Reeves, 1938, p. 195). As she had done at the Training School, Emma assumed childcare responsibilities for the assistant superintendent of the women's facility. For a number of years, Emma worked as a nurse's aide at the institution's on-grounds hospital.

In the early nineteen-twenties, a mild epidemic broke out in the building for low grade patients. Isolation was arranged and the

hospital being short-handed at the time, Deborah was glad to assist the special nurse. She immediately mastered the details of routine treatment and was devoted to her charges. (Reeves, 1938, p. 196)

As was the case with the descriptions of Emma Wolverton's childhood and adolescence in *The Kallikak Family*, hers is not a story without problems by any means. Emma was not an angel. She is described time and again as willful, overbearing, and possessing what could become a vicious temper. On the other hand, those are often exactly the behaviors necessary to survive in an institutional setting.

Inconsistent with Goddard's depiction of her, Emma was literate and well-read. She was a passionate and committed letter writer as well. She wrote letters and sent photographs of herself (see Figure 7) to her friends up to the very end of her life. In her final years, Emma was offered the alternative of leaving the institution. By then, she was in intense pain because of severe arthritis and used a wheelchair most of the time. It is, of course, a cruel irony that the offer of greater freedom in her life came when it was impossible for her to embrace it. Emma declined the opportunity; she knew she needed constant medical attention.

"I guess after all I'm where I belong," Emma had told her support person, Helen Reeves, once in 1938. "I don't like this feeble-minded part, but anyhow I'm not like some of the poor things you see around here" (Reeves, 1938, p. 199).

Emma was hospitalized for the last year of her life, but she "bore the frequent intense pain most bravely and without a great deal of complaint" (Doll, 1988, p. 32). She died in 1978 at the age of 89 years. She had lived in an institution 81 of those years.

The now highly offensive term *idiot*, was the primary term used to refer to people with intellectual disability up until the mid-1800s. It was derived, etymologically, from the Greek words *idatas* and *idios*, both of which refer to a private person, someone who is set apart, peculiar (Oxford University Press, 2011), someone who is different. When we segregate people, we tell them and others that they are peculiar—different from "us." It allows us to then talk about "them" in anonymity, as if they did not really matter. We can refer to them as *morons*, *degenerates*, *trainables*, *retards*, and a million other labels as if they were not really like us. We can lock them away for the rest of their lives or sterilize them without their knowledge.

INTELLECTUAL AND DEVELOPMENTAL DISABILITIES   ©AAIDD
2012, Vol. 50, No. 2, 169–178   DOI: 10.1352/1934-9556-50.2.169

Her name was Emma, not Deborah. We cannot undo the injustices done to her or to others, but we at least owe her the respect of calling her by her name.

References

Binet, A., & Simon, T. (1916). *The intelligence of the feeble-minded.* Vineland, NJ: Training School at Vineland Department of Research.

Dugdale, R. L. (1891). *The Jukes: A study in crime, pauperism, disease and heredity* (5th ed. [1877]). New York, NY: G. P. Putnam's Sons.

Doll, E. E. (1988). Before the big time: Early history of the training school at Vineland, 1888 to 1949. *American Journal on Mental Retardation, 93,* 1–15.

Estabrook, A. H. (1916). *The Jukes in 1915.* Cold Spring Harbor, NY: Eugenics Record Office.

Garrett, H. E. (1955). *General psychology.* New York, NY: American Book Company.

Goddard, H. H. (1912). *The Kallikak family.* New York, NY: MacMillan.

Gould, S. J. (1981). *The mismeasure of man.* New York, NY: W. W. Norton.

Hunter, G. W. (1914). *A civic biology presented in problems.* New York, NY: American Book Company.

Kellicott, W. E. (1911). *The social direction of human evolution.* New York, NY: Appleton and Company.

Leiby, J. (1967). *Charity and correction in New Jersey: A history of state welfare institutions.* New Brunswick, NJ: Rutgers University Press.

Macdonald, D. A., & McAdams, N. N. (2001). *The Woolverton family 1693–1850 and beyond: Woolverton and Wolverton descendants of Charles Woolverton, New Jersey immigrant.* Rockport, ME: Penobscot Press.

Oxford University Press. (2011). *Oxford English dictionary* (3rd ed.). [Online version.] Available at http://www.oed.com.www2.lib.ku.edu:2048/view/Entry/91049?rskey=8j9OXR&result=1&isAdvanced=false#eid

Reeves, H. T. (1938). The later years of a noted mental defective. *American Journal on Mental Deficiency, 43,* 194–200.

Smith, J. D. (1985). *Minds made feeble: The myth and legacy of the Kallikaks.* Rockville, MD: Aspen Systems Corporation.

Straney, S. G. (1994). The Kallikak Family: A genealogical examination of a classic in psychology. *The American Genealogist, 69*(2), 65–80.

Trent, J. W. (1994). *Inventing the feeble mind: A history of mental retardation in the United States.* Berkeley, CA: University of California Press.

Received 8/2/11, accepted 8/26/11.

Editor-in-Charge: Glenn Fujiura

Authors:

David Smith, University of North Carolina, Greensboro; **Michael Wehmeyer** (e-mail: wehmeyer@ku.edu), Department of Special Education, University of Kansas, Lawrence, KS 66045, USA.

Two other terms that emerged in the late 19th century, *mental deficiency* and *feeblemindedness,* began to replace *idiocy* as the term used to refer to the entire class of people with intellectual impairments. With the introduction of terms such as *imbecile, mental deficiency,* and *feeblemindedness,* the terms used to refer to the state of functioning called intellectual disability began to reflect the growing medicalization of the field and of the understanding of the construct. *Imbecile* derives from the term Latin *imbecillus,* referring to weak-mindedness. *Mental deficiency* refers to a defect in or a lack of "mental" capacity—mental, pertaining, of course, to the mind. *Feeblemindedness,* which became the term of choice in the United States, also refers to weak-mindedness. *Mental deficiency* was the comparable term used in England, popularized by A.F. Tredgold's (1920) text, *Mental Deficiency (Amentia). Amentia* refers to the lack of mental capacity, though it derives from the Latin *ament,* which means "insane." A term that surfaced in America at this time was *psycho-asthenics,* which became part of the title of the major journal in the field in the late 19th and early 20th century, the *Journal of Psycho-Asthenics. Asthenia* is from the Latin for weakness; psycho-asthenia refers to weak minds.

At the start of the 20th century, the naming process of trying to describe the condition called intellectual disability had moved from an undifferentiated sense of oddness and differentness to one described by the medical terms that began to dominate how the condition was understood, and referring for the first time to mental processes. The general understanding was one of slow or weak mental functioning, which was reflected in a statement by Henry Goddard, early in his career, before he became the premier mental tester in the nation and formulated the menace of the moron class. Arguing for the potential benefits of studying the feebleminded, Goddard noted: "Most plants ripen fruit every year; some give several crops a year, but there are also century plants. Ours is the century plant. But under favorable conditions of soil and climate the century plant may bear fruit in ten years, sometimes even in eight" (Goddard, 1907, p. 19).

These terms became the umbrella term for the condition called amentia or mental deficiency in England and feebleminded in the United States. Martin Barr's (1904) influential text stated that "feeble-mindedness, including idiocy and imbecility, is defect either mental or moral or both, usually associated with certain physical stigmata of degeneration" (p. 23).

As noted, Barr was an early adopter of both single-gene theories of feeblemindedness and of eugenic approaches to curtail the "unfit," including sterilization. His 1904 definition introduces some ideas that took root in the next decade. First, the "defect" associated with feeblemindedness was either mental or moral, or both. Not only was feeblemindedness associated with slow or weak-mindedness in the sphere of learning but also with weakness in the sphere of morality. Second, Barr clearly associated feeblemindedness with "degeneration."

Degeneration theory was introduced by Benedict Augustin Morel (1809–1873), a French alienist who is best known as the first person to introduce the term *dementia praecox* to describe the condition we now call schizophrenia. According to Morel, "degenerations are deviations from the normal human type which are transmissible by heredity and which deteriorate progressively towards extinction" (Green, 2009, p. 216). Degeneration should be distinguished from our modern understandings of the progress of a disease being accompanied by a gradual *decline* in functioning or of the impact of a disease resulting in the *disintegration* of neural and other systems. Degeneration was "roughly synonymous with *bad heredity* and conceived as an invisible attribute of the 'germ plasm' or 'blood'. . . a tendency to devolve to a lower, simpler, less civilized state" (Rafter, 1997, p. 36).

From viewing feeblemindedness as reflecting weak morals and tending toward degeneration, it is a slippery slope to view people who are feebleminded as menaces to society, moral imbeciles, criminal imbeciles, and as threats to racial hygiene. Although most classification systems of the time included at least three "levels" of feeblemindedness (e.g., idiot, imbecile, moron, ranging in level of impairment from most severe to least severe), the rapidly expanding disability service system fundamentally dealt with two groups: people whose intellectual impairment was deemed to require custodial care (i.e., idiots, imbeciles) and people who were more capable and, ironically, a greater threat to society. Figures 6.2 and 6.3 illustrate how these different groups were understood. Figure 6.2, from Edgar A. Doll's 1917 text *Clinical Studies in Feeblemindedness,* provides pictures of two groups of "idiots." One group of men, in the top picture, is harnessed to a wagon to pull it, much as a team of mules would. Doll (who was Goddard's assistant at Vineland) noted that the picture represents the poor physical tone of the idiot and the psychophysical inferiority, as evidenced by the number of men required to do this work. The bottom picture shows the "physical abnormalities" and "stigmata of degeneration" of a group of men deemed to be of the "idiot grade." These pictures evoke a sense that these people were seen as little more than animals by professionals of the era, degenerating to lower states of functioning.

Figure 6.3, also from Doll (1917) depicts two family groups, each with women who are pointed out to be morons and described in terms of amorality and sloth. One adolescent, called Becky, is described as "an attractive moron who is a center of immorality (or a-morality) wherever she makes her temporary abode" (Doll, 1917, p. 55).

Henry Herbert Goddard's (1912) *The Kallikak Family* illustrates how these distinct groups of people were understood by eugenicists. In considering "what was to be done" about the menace presented by his Kallikak family findings, Goddard noted the following:

> But in view of such conditions as are shown in the defective side of the Kallikak family, we begin to realize that the idiot is not our greatest problem. He is indeed loathsome ; he is somewhat difficult to take care of; nevertheless, he lives his life and is done. He does not continue the race with a line of children like himself. Because of his very low-grade condition, he never becomes a parent.
>
> It is the moron type that makes for us our great problem. And when we face the question, "What is to be done with them—with such people as make up a large proportion of the bad side of the Kallikak family?" we realize that we have a huge problem. (p. 102)

The *idiot* is loathsome, a burden, but not the greatest problem because he or she cannot propagate. It is the *moron,* a term Goddard coined from the Greek word for stupid, who is the threat to racial hygiene. About the subject of his book, Deborah Kallikak, who literally becomes the definition of "moron" in the *Oxford English Dictionary,* Goddard says,

> This is a typical illustration of the mentality of a high-grade feeble-minded person, the moron, the delinquent, the kind of girl or woman that fills our reformatories. They are wayward, they get into all sorts of trouble and difficulties, sexually and otherwise, and yet we have been accustomed to account for their defects on the basis of viciousness, environment, or ignorance.
>
> Here is a child who has been most carefully guarded. She has been persistently trained since she was eight years old, and yet nothing has been accomplished in the direction of higher intelligence or general education. To-day if this young woman were to leave the Institution, she would at once become a prey to the designs of evil men or evil women and would lead a life that would be vicious, immoral, and criminal, though

SOMATIC CHARACTERISTICS OF MENTAL DEFECTIVES

TOP. Group of idiots engaged in serious work pulling a wagon. Observe poor physical tone as expressed in the round shoulders, stooped backs, bent knees, flat feet, inclined heads, shuffling gait, poor carriage, and general inferior physical development. Note also the psychophysical inferiority expressed in the large number needed to pull the wagon, for this is not merely play or "busy work," but productive effort. The metabolism of these "children" requires a differentiated diet, and their low blood pressure makes them susceptible to even slight changes of temperature or altitude. Illustration suggested by Dr. Walter S. Cornell.

BOTTOM. Group of idiots showing physical abnormalities and "stigmata of degeneration." The diagnostic value of these signs is open to question, especially with feeble-minded subjects above idiot grade.

Figure 6.2. "Somatic Characteristics of Mental Defectives."
(Image from author's personal collection. From Doll, E.A. [1917]. *Clinical studies in feeblemindedness* [p. 123]. Boston, MA: Richard G. Badger.)

SOCIAL TYPES OF FEEBLE-MINDEDNESS

LEFT. Mag and her two children at the almshouse. She was able to count the number of her children so long as she had no more than ten, but was very much at a loss when the arrival of the eleventh taxed her number sense beyond its narrow limits. This woman and her social life are vividly pictured in reference 59.

RIGHT. Feeble-minded family picking cranberries. Individual feeble-minded pickers *can* earn as much as two or three dollars a day at this work, but a little money soon allays their working enthusiasm. The girl at the left, Becky, is an attractive moron who is a center of immorality (or a-morality) wherever she makes her temporary abode. Her marital relations are described in reference 58. The girl in the center is the mother of the children shown opposite page 54. The girl at the right is the third wife of the man described opposite page 24; he was married to her by a minister while his two other wives were still living and undivorced. The little girl in the center is the daughter of the girl in the back center. She is the same girl shown opposite page 54, taken four years later.

Figure 6.3. "Social Types of Feeblemindedness."
(Image from author's personal collection. From Doll, E.A. [1917]. *Clinical studies in feeblemindedness* [p. 55]. Boston, MA: Richard G. Badger.)

because of her mentality she herself would not be responsible. There is nothing that she might not be led into, because she has no power of control, and all her instincts and appetites are in the direction that would lead to vice.

We may now repeat the ever insistent question, and this time we indeed have good hope of answering it. The question is, "How do we account for this kind of individual?" The answer is in a word "Heredity,"—bad stock. We must recognize that the human family shows varying stocks or strains that are as marked and that breed as true as anything in plant or animal life. (Goddard, 1912, pp. 11–12)

Goddard (1912) proposed two solutions to the problem of the moron: segregation through institutionalization, and "to take away from these people the power of procreation" (p. 107). Both means are implemented to tragic results over the remaining two decades of this era.

THE EXPLOSION OF THE INSTITUTION SYSTEM

When Samuel Gridley Howe and his socially progressive 19th century colleagues championed the cause of establishing "schools" for people who were deemed idiots, as discussed in Chapter 5, the intent was habilitative. Their purposes, albeit still cloaked in the moral and religious tones reflecting how people viewed intellectual disability from the Middle Ages onward, were to educate people who, to that point, had not been educated. By the late 1800s, the mission for state-supported institutions had changed to support the protection of their inmates from the rigors and potential abuses of everyday society. In the early 1900s, this mission again changed; with people with intellectual disability understood as menaces to society, institutions became places to segregate them for the benefit of society and to impose social control over the "unfit" to the benefit of the "fit."

The facilities that had been built to house people with intellectual disability were changing in the first decades of the 20th century. Early institutions were often built using the Kirkbride plan, named after Thomas Kirkbride (1809–1883), a founder of what is now the American Psychiatric Association. Kirkbride was superintendent of the institution for the insane in Pennsylvania and in 1854 published *On the Construction, Organization and General Arrangements of Hospitals for the Insane,* which soon became the standard handbook for institution construction.

While Kirkbride buildings were often architecturally magisterial, as depicted in Figure 6.4, there were problems inherent with these large complexes, particularly once the populations of institutions exceeded their original design capacity by three- and fourfold. For one, diseases spread rapidly among the inmates housed together on wards, including whooping cough, scarlet fever, smallpox, and measles. At the Pennsylvania Training School, 10% of its inmate population died in the flu pandemic of 1918. Being in a hospital for the feebleminded could be bad for your health.

An alternative adopted by numerous institutions was the cottage system. Separate cottages made it possible to contain a disease outbreak and to quarantine the sick inmates. In addition, the cottage system protected against the massive loss of life potentially associated with fires that were common in that era. The cottage system had administrative benefits as well. Primarily, the smaller units made it easier to segregate inmates by condition or level of impairment, leading to a system of segregation within an already-segregated setting. Cottages for "low grade boys," "high grade girls," "moral imbeciles," young children, "epileptics," "mongoloid idiots," and every other configuration proliferated (see Figure 6.5). As historian James Trent (1994) noted, "high" and "low" grades were determined mainly by an inmate's capacity to perform the myriad types of complex work activities that comprised the running of an institution, and by 1910 much of the routine experienced by more capable institution inmates involved compulsory labor to meet the demands of the increasingly under-funded and overcrowded institutions.

"The most common inmate activity, apart from work on the farm, was the care of custodial cases and small children," observed Trent. "Inmate work at the institution was assigned on the basis of both sex and ability. Predictably, males labored on the farm; worked the heavy machinery in the laundry, print shop, or boiler room; and tended to the institution's assortment of animals. Females performed domestic

Bloomingdale Insane Assylum, Worcester, Mass.

Figure 6.4. Contemporary postcard of the Bloomingdale Insane Asylum in Worcester, Massachusetts. (Image from author's personal collection.)

chores, did the sewing and mending and the constantly needed hand laundry" (Trent, 1994, pp. 103–104).

Inmate work was framed by superintendents in terms of its importance for the rehabilitation of the inmate, but the truth is that like an addict needing a fix, once the institutional system got hooked on free, inmate labor, it became a hard habit to break. Superintendents relied on the more capable inmates to perform the unskilled labor required to run the institution: mopping floors, preparing meals, laundering clothes, and watching younger or more disabled inmates. The bigger the institution became, the more this unpaid labor became necessary. Like a vicious cycle, the availability of more skilled inmates to watch their less skilled counterparts enabled superintendents to meet the increasing demand from the public to take in more severely disabled inmates, thus increasing the demand for the skilled "high grade" laborer. These inmates, then, became too valuable for the superintendents to release and were retained at the institution, independent of any rehabilitation goal. Nobody left the institution: not the skilled and certainly not the unskilled.

No type of labor went unused. Trent noted that "when Martin Barr published his highly respected *Mental Defectives* in 1904, he thanked three 'boys' for their help in the preparation of his book. One inmate had taken photographs for the book, another had done translations, and the third had typed the entire manuscript" (Trent, 1994, p. 103).

Social historian Wolf Wolfensberger identified three trends in institutionalization—isolation, enlargement, and economization—which by 1910 dictated many aspects of these daily routines (Wolfensberger, 1975). Initially, institutions were built to isolate inmates from society, "in order to spare him the stresses he [sic] was believed

DEFECTIVE DELINQUENT BUILDING

The urge for the accommodation of the Morally Defective or Defective Delinquent type of patient became so pressing during the winter of 1912 that the admission of a large number of such cases was made without the suitable provision for their care. The Legislature, upon visiting our Institution, became so impressed with the need for the separate classification of our Defective Delinquents already in the Institution, and the admission to the Institution of the pitiable cases in the jails and detention homes, that they voluntarily appropriated us sixty thousand dollars in excess of our budget request especially for this building. We accommodate in this building at the present time one hundred and sixty patients, making a per capita building cost of three hundred and seventy-five dollars. The building, however, is overcrowded, but inasmuch as all of our buildings are excessively overcrowded we would say that the condition was normal for us, nor do we expect to adjust ourselves otherwise, until the full twenty-five hundred patients, for whom we feel responsible, are provided for.

IMBECILE BUILDING

In a further effort to reclassify our patients, in April, 1915, an appropriation was granted of forty thousand dollars for a building for imbeciles, with a capacity of one hundred patients, a per capita building cost of four hundred dollars. The building is fireproof and sanitary, consisting of three floors, each offering accommodations similar to a cottage—that of dormitory, day room, private baths for patients and nurses, and a beautiful veranda with southern exposure. For the present in addition to providing for our imbeciles, our idiots will also be forced to share this building in order to relieve the hospital of the idiot class to permit of the wider use of that building for medical types. The imbeciles, being industrially trainable, act as assistants according to their daily schedule. High-grade imbeciles make excellent laundresses, housemaids, and general factotums throughout the Institution. They are a happy group of patients, appreciative and easily taken care of. More of such buildings are urgently required for the central parent Institution that the large waiting list of idiots and imbeciles may be admitted and properly provided for.

Figure 6.5. "Defective Delinquent Building" and "Imbecile Building" from undated report from the New Jersey Institution for Feebleminded Women. (Image from author's personal collection.)

incapable of bearing, and to provide him with protection from the persecution and ridicule of the nondevient" (Wolfensberger, 1975, p. 29). Wolfensberger cited two early examples of this. Isaac Kerlin, Martin Barr's predecessor, who had been appointed superintendent of the Pennsylvania School for Idiotic and Feeble-Minded Children in 1864, noted in 1884 that the "grounds of the institution should be hedged or fenced to keep off improper intrusion but be freely used by the inmates for walking, exercise and work" (Wolfensberger, 1975, p. 29). Hervey Wilbur, who in 1848 opened the first private school for the feebleminded in America, wrote in 1879 that institution grounds be "fenced for the privacy of the inmates" (Wolfensberger, 1975, p. 29). Kerlin referred to institutions as "cities of refuge" for the feebleminded (Wolfensberger, 1975, p. 29).

By 1910, the causal direction for isolation had changed from protecting the inmate from society to protecting society from the inmate. The fences, hedges, and other barriers kept inmates in, not the public out. Even so, some inmates had more freedom than others. "Higher grade" males "had free range of the institution grounds" (Trent, 1994, p. 102), wrote Alfred Wilmarth, who after a stint at the institution in Elwyn, Pennsylvania, became superintendent of the Wisconsin Institution for Feebleminded Children. Because of fears about females becoming pregnant, however, women, "higher grade" or not, did not share the same privilege, and even within the institution grounds were curtailed in their freedom to move about (Trent, 1994).

The pressures applied by growing public demands for segregation, the burgeoning size of the institutional population, and the demand for economizing increasingly eroded any sense of individualization. The feebleminded were lumped together as causing societal problems, and they were treated as such. In many institutions inmates wore uniforms.

EUGENICS AND SOCIETY

In the first two decades of the 20th century, eugenic belief was pervasive. This was not a fringe movement populated by a few rabid adherents. It is hard to locate anyone in the early 20th century who didn't believe the eugenic rhetoric, at least to some level. There was the emphasis on "the fit" having more children so as to offset the proposed excessive fecundity of the unfit. Theodore Roosevelt, voiced the public's opinion in a 1902 speech warning against the dangers of "race suicide": "But the man or woman who deliberately avoids marriage and has a heart so cold as to know no passion and a brain so shallow and selfish as to dislike having children, is in effect a criminal against the race, and should be an object of contemptuous abhorrence by all healthy people" (Roosevelt, 1903, p. 2).

Theodore Roosevelt was anything but a man of moderation and his views concerning industry, labor, foreign policy, and social welfare embodied and embraced the Progressive perspective that emerged in the first decade of the 20th century. He consorted with avid eugenicists such as Charles Davenport and rabid racialists like Madison Grant and Lothrop Stoddard, and bugled loudly about race suicide or wanting to rid the United States of the underclasses. Yet Roosevelt's views about the poor and downtrodden, and the views of his Progressive movement, were complex and not easily categorized, a description true of many Americans' viewpoints in the first decade of the 20th century.

One of the paradoxes of the American eugenics movement is that it arose in the midst of what may be the most progressive era in the nation's history. Roosevelt was the dominant political force in America during the inaugural decade of the 20th century. His words—and there were many of them in speeches, letters, and books—formed public opinion and his actions created public policy. While the leaders of the eugenics movement held monochromatic images of people who were poor, immigrants, or feebleminded, for the rest of America such images had more than one wavelength, though they were often blurred.

The Progressive movement extended from the end of the Gilded Age, approximately 1890, to the United States' entry into the "Great War" in 1917. Characterized by historian Michael McGerr (2003) as representing "a fierce discontent," progressivism was a backlash against the excesses of the Gilded Age, industrialization, and the post–Civil War forces that rent the fabric of America. The scope of Progressivism was genuinely breathtaking. "The progressives developed a stunningly broad agenda that ranged well beyond the control of big business, the amelioration of poverty, and the purification of politics to embrace the transformation of gender relations, the regeneration of the home, the disciplining of leisure and pleasure, and the establishment of segregation," wrote McGerr. "They intended nothing less than to transform other Americans, to remake the nation's feuding, polyglot population in their own middle-class image" (McGerr, 2003, p. xiv).

The Progressive movement, however, did not approach social reformation with the pre-Darwinian understandings of 19th-century reformers, such as Samuel Gridley Howe, who viewed disease and disorder as a direct manifestation of sin. Instead, this new wave of reformers adopted the explanations for pathology offered by science and applied that in a social Darwinian fashion to their social agenda. Science was seen as providing direction to the betterment of humankind through social control and social hygiene. Eugenics was, in Progressive America's estimation, a road to human betterment.

By the early 1900s, the scientific community had adopted the twin doctrines of social control (efforts to control the population lest the unfit take over), and social hygiene, which through science and education sought to explore and curtail the causes of prostitution, sexually transmitted diseases, drug addiction, juvenile delinquency, criminology, homosexuality, and mental illness. These social ills, and the concomitant threat they were perceived to hold for society and the race, were attributed to weaknesses, illness, and laziness. One popular poster of the era depicted a monocled Theodore Roosevelt staring out at the viewer, the message "Sickly and frail when a boy, Roosevelt by faithful training achieved the vigor of manhood" in bold letters below.

Progressives readily adopted the notions of social control because they fit well with the overall intent of the Progressive movement to change other Americans to behave like they (i.e., Progressives) behaved. "For the Progressives, social control was not a problem," observed author Matthew Crenson, "it was the solution. They made no secret of their determination to impose order on America. It was what the society needed. Indeed, an emphasis on the control of marginal populations may have been most likely to win over an audience of middle-class taxpayers, state legislators, or wealthy philanthropists. In general, Progressives were determined to demonstrate that social reform could be businesslike, and their expressions of compassion for the weak and unfortunate were balanced by confident assertions that what was needed in the lower orders of society was more discipline" (Crenson, 1998, p. 40).

The primary tool of social control was segregation, and the Progressive era employed this tool efficiently. "Segregation was a complicated social phenomenon," observed McGerr, "and it served a complicated purpose for the progressives. True to their mission to create a safe society for themselves and their children, the progressives turned to segregation as a way to halt dangerous social conflict that could not otherwise be stopped. True to their sense of compassion, the progressives turned to segregation as way to preserve weaker groups, such as African-Americans and Native Americans, facing brutality and even annihilation. Unlike some other Americans, progressives did not support segregation out of anger, hatred, and a desire to unify whites; but they certainly displayed plenty of condescension and indifference, as well as compassion" (McGerr, 2003, p. 183).

Such a mix of seemingly incongruous motives and compassions was exhibited time and again. For example, in 1901, Roosevelt deliberated on the "negro problem": "I have not been able to think out any solution of the terrible problem offered by the presence of the Negro on this continent, but of one thing I am sure, and that is that inasmuch as he is here and can neither be killed nor driven away, the only wise and honorable and Christian thing to do is to treat each black man and each white man strictly on his merits as a man, giving him no more and no less than he shows himself worthy to have" (Bishop, 1920, pp. 166–167).

Despite their rhetoric, Progressives believed "that some social differences would not be erased for many years . . . [and] some differences could not be erased at all" (McGerr, 2003, p. 183). In cases when Progressives believed that only the slow advance of time would bridge the gap of social differences, segregation "allowed reform to continue" at its necessary pace (McGerr, 2003, p. 183). The "necessary pace" for institutions for people with intellectual disability was rapid.

"THIS PLACE AIN'T FOR YOU ANYWAY": THE SOUTH AND THE FEEBLEMINDED

In 1924, Dr. C. Banks McNairy, superintendent of North Carolina's Caswell Training School, reported to his board of trustees that "the problem of the care of the feeble-minded or mentally defective in the south is at least a three-fold more difficult problem than in the northern states, if not more so, because we thrust upon us every type of defectiveness—the feeble-minded, the ne'er-do-well, the defective delinquent, the criminally irresponsible, the wholly immoral and anti-social elements that cannot be handled elsewhere" (McNairy, 1924, p. 345). During the first third of the 20th century, Southerners developed particular strategies for handling the perceived menace of the feebleminded. Based on models established by leaders in the rest of the country, these programs focused on protection of and from the feebleminded. As a 1919 *Atlanta Constitution* article titled "The Feeble-Minded" concluded, "the system at present in vogue is one not only detrimental to the normal children but fraught with serious consequences to the subnormal and defective" (p. 7).

By the early 1920s, every Southern state had implemented some sort of program to handle the burgeoning problems associated with feeblemindedness. These initiatives focused on the development of institutions designed specifically to house individuals who, in accord with the Jim Crow climate of the times, were all white, who had been labeled as feebleminded or mentally defective.

Southern institutions, like their more established Northern and Midwestern counterparts, were caught between the requirements to protect society from deviant feebleminded inmates (who were usually involved in criminal or sexual activities) and the need to shelter other feebleminded people from the problems of an increasingly complex society. Though not necessarily mutually exclusive tasks, these dual functions proved far enough apart to prevent institutions from providing even a basic level of care for their patients. These facilities operated in a social context that conflated feeblemindedness with poverty, criminal behavior, and sexual indulgence, therefore demanding institutionalization for those people who exhibited or seemed to exhibit those characteristics. Yet the internal dynamics of institutional life required facilities that ran smoothly and free from discord and strife. Superintendents often seemed reticent to admit patients whose conduct would cause problems in their institutions, although these people were the very ones society demanded be placed in those facilities, where they could be controlled and guarded.

With the establishment of Southern institutions for the feebleminded by the early 1920s, institutional leaders and superintendents struggled to implement their vision of housing and training inmates placed in their facilities. Beset by inadequate funding, poorly trained staffs, and an ill-defined sense of purpose, institutions often failed to provide even a basic custodial level of care. Southern institutions, mirroring their counterparts across the country, never accurately defined whom they served or why they served them. Consequently, institutions rarely provided protection from high-level feebleminded people (morons), as called for by society, or protection for low functioning individuals (idiots), as demanded by families and social welfare agencies. Southern institutions for the feebleminded opened with the fervent hope that these facilities would, in a 1910 speech by Dr. Ira Hardy, founding superintendent of the North Carolina Training School, "offer light, happiness, and opportunity" to their mentally defective residents. Simultaneously, however, concern for society never appeared far from the thoughts of institutional officials. In his same speech, Hardy continued, "Let us build an institution . . . and place into it these unfortunates early in their youth, who if allowed to run at large, will most assuredly become criminals." These two beliefs, protections for and from society, proved unable to be reconciled as institutions developed throughout the South. But another, more pragmatic assumption also lay at the heart of professional thinking about these facilities. Leaders seemed to decide on the institutional solution to the feebleminded problem based on financial considerations rather than on any concern for either society or for those labeled as feebleminded. Hardy (1910) concluded his speech by declaring that "this institution would be in the course of time the *least expensive* [emphasis added] method of providing for these unfortunates" (p. 2). Nineteen years later, these monetary matters still seemed paramount in a region where social welfare spending remained negligible. "From the economic standpoint, it must be agreed that institutionalizing the recognized feeble-minded," Dr. C.V. Akin (1929), superintendent of the Louisiana State Colony and Training School, stated, "is the most efficient and least expensive procedure to be suggested as capital outlay, maintenance, and overhead are reduced when the individual subjects are removed from the home and community environment and collectively cared for at suitably located colonies and schools" (p. 163).

The belief that high-level feeblemindedness was curable, or at least remediable, led Southern institutional leaders, following in the footsteps of their Northern brethren, to center their attention on children and adolescents. Five of the 10 Southern states named their institutions "training schools" to publicly verify their ostensible commitment to younger patients. The 1917 annual report of the Virginia State Colony for the Feeble-Minded concluded that "all mental defectives possess criminal potentiality in a greater or lesser degree. . . . Therefore, the removal of young children ascertained to be defective, from unfavorable surroundings, and placing them where their association and education are proper, becomes the duty of the State as a matter of social economy" (pp. 18–19). As in many aspects of Southern institutional life, the reality of patient age often belied the wishes and pronouncements of superintendents. In 1925, patients over the age of 20 comprised more than 46% of the Virginia State Colony institution's enrollment. Both the increasing age of patients and their lengthening of their stays behind institutional walls would only increase in the following 20 years.

While officials lobbied for younger patients for a variety of reasons, institutional staff generally treated all patients, regardless of age or mental ability, as children.

In 1920, South Carolina Training School Superintendent Dr. Benjamin Whitten continued on this theme of institutions as parent. "The inmates of this Institution are commonly referred to as 'children' regardless of their ages," he wrote. This term is used both to enable us to avoid the use of the term 'inmate' and also to serve as a reminder that our charges are entitled to the tactful and affectionate treatment that all young children require" (Whitten, 1920, p. 3). This paternalistic relationship—which mirrored similar feelings among elite white males towards poor people, females, and black people—set the tone for daily care within southern institutions. It helped to ensure that custodial care, rather than habilitation, became the norm by not allowing patients to break out of the bonds of institutional dependency.

The small size of southern institutions and their lack of adequate funding caused significant problems as societal concerns about protection from the assumed menace of the feebleminded increased. The 1917 report of the Virginia State Colony verified this attitude. "Until the public mind is so enlightened," it concluded, "that it realizes that it is best for mental defectives . . . to be withdrawn from society, and placed in a custodial institution of the state, the field of activity and usefulness of this or any other institution for the feeble-minded must necessarily by contracted" (Virginia State Colony, 1917, p. 5). These institutions remained small and underfunded, which meant that a significant proportion of those individuals labeled as feebleminded never saw the inside of places like the Virginia State Colony.

That did not mean, however, that families, public welfare agencies, and court systems did not try to place more people within the institutional setting. High demand for placement in institutions that did not have adequate space manifested itself in long waiting lines to enter these facilities. Nationwide, institutions for the feebleminded rapidly reached capacity by the 1920s, but the situation proved especially critical in the South. In 1939, for example, Georgia's Gracewood Training School, the state's only institution for the feebleminded, housed only 336 patients, while the list of those seeking admission numbered more than 400. By operating at or over maximum capacity, Southern institutions put an added burden on already overworked staff and ward attendants.

While all those committed to these facilities were labeled feebleminded, that definition proved incredibly elastic and, as in other institutions, were often tied more to the issues of criminality, sexuality, and poverty than to mental defectiveness. In 1922, for instance, the Florida Farm Colony admitted a young woman who had a recorded IQ score of 60. Her patient record reported, "While the patient may have had convulsions, most, if not all, of the alleged seizures while in this institution, were purely hysterical, with a large element of malingering." Two years later, with the revelation of a sexual relationship with an institutional staffer, she was discharged from the institution. She promptly married the workman and wrote to a Florida Farm Colony matron in 1926 that she and her husband and her father "were living on a farm outside Lakeland and were getting along fine."[1] This woman managed to circumvent institutional prohibition on patient–staff interaction and live a life of her own choosing.

A similar situation occurred at North Carolina's Caswell Training School, where two high-functioning patients (labeled morons) carried on a surreptitious flirtation without the knowledge of staff or the superintendent. Their undated correspondence (discovered after their administrative discharge) survived as both a testament to their ability to circumvent the institutional system and an example of how the system labeled individuals as feebleminded when clearly they were not. The male patient, admitted in 1924 at age 18, confessed in his first letter that

> I know that I have been a bad boy in my past for the past five years I have been trying to show the world what a boy that has been a wreck all his life could do and be.

His female confidante was admitted to Caswell in 1918 at the age of 10 years. Their correspondence lasted for approximately a year, until Caswell discharged her in the summer of 1925. In one of their letters, she reported the means necessary to meet her friend:

> But Doc McNairy [the superintendent] told Miss E. [the ward attendant] to count us choir girls and if there were any one missing in chapel just report it to him. But there will be a chance after chapel if you can get around there. Now don't forget to come around there where you said. When I see you coming down the walk after chapel I will go around there.

The male patient also showed he understood how to manipulate the attendant system to his advantage:

> When Mr. S. relieves Mr. R, then we will try our luck in the old kitchen.

In June 1925, he showed his frustration at life in Caswell in his only dated letter.

> "Darling," he plaintively wrote, "I don't see how I can stand to stay here much longer."[2]

Many patients had those same feelings toward institutionalization, understanding that they had been labeled as feebleminded for no discernible reason. Often they acted on those ideas by destroying institutional property or attempting escape. In 1921, Grace Kent, a psychologist at the South Carolina Training School, wrote to her parents that the institution had just received "a dozen girls" who seemed "more delinquent than deficient." She explained that "the windows [in the girls ward] are about four feet above the ground and there is nothing to hinder the children from getting out. Their clothes are locked up at night, but they have abundant opportunity in the daytime to steal clothing and secrete it outside" (Whitten, 1967, p. 51).

Caswell Training School in North Carolina experienced many of the same problems with high-functioning patients whose problems seemed to be more social than intellectual. In 1918, the superintendent there lamented that "our greatest problem . . . is the high grade girls' building. . . . They will curse, fight, destroy clothing, steal, put their clothing, drinking cups, towels or anything in the sewer pipes, break down doors and knock out windows and run away."[3]

Superintendent McNairy's concerns proved well-founded when in December 1918 and January 1919 three female patients burned down two dormitories at Caswell, killing three residents. He reported to the institution's board of directors that "A group of girls formed a pact. . . . The plan was guarded as only a defective mind can guard." In analyzing this tragedy, McNairy explained the dual purposes of his institution. On the one hand, he viewed these young women as "poor, unfortunate, fiendish, yet irresponsible enemies of themselves, society, and the State." Yet "humanitarianism demands their protection, care, and training." But protection from these individuals remained the major objective of this, and every other institution. McNairy concluded that "society and good citizenship demand their segregation and asexualization."[4]

In fact, social problems often provided the rationale for labeling and institution-alization. In 1931, the Florida Farm Colony received an application for admission for an 18-year-old female from Tampa, categorized as a moron by the Hillsborough County Court, which had initiated the commitment procedures. The paperwork, marked "Urgent," noted the girl's "kleptomaniacal proclivities" and concluded that "she will probably live the life of a common prostitute unless she is given institu-tional care." Though the facility was already over its capacity, the superintendent quickly replied that "it is probable that we shall be able to take her in the near future."[5] As in so many of these situations, no records exist documenting what happened to this young woman. For inmates identified as idiots, thus indicating more severe impairment, institutionalization often provided not protection for society but help for beleaguered families often overburdened with the care of a difficult child. A 1926 publication reported the story of a 13-year-old Georgia boy who had just been admit-ted to the Gracewood Training School. He had "lived with his widowed mother and a fifteen year old brother on a small farm" before being committed to Gracewood. The report noted that "the boy has never been able to sleep normally and rocked himself into a state of exhaustion. He could not talk, feed himself, nor attend to his natural wants" (U.S. Department of Labor, 1926, p. 59).

The promise of sterilization gave hope that feeblemindedness and its heredi-tary transmission could be extinguished completely and relatively inexpensively. The targets for such efforts were women of reproductive age. Class stereotypes worked with gender concerns to place poor women labeled as feebleminded in a particu-larly vulnerable position. Categorized as childlike and simple by virtue of their sex, these women were institutionalized for their own protection, placed in asylums in the original definition of that term. Yet as members of the lower classes, reform-ers and institutional leaders viewed these same women as temptresses, as cauldrons of erotic energy waiting to boil over, and even more alarmingly, as transmitters of feebleminded genes to succeeding generations. Lower class feebleminded women therefore had to be institutionalized, not only for their own benefit but also for the greater benefit of society.

Southern attitudes mirrored and even heightened national feelings about women categorized as feebleminded generally, and lower class ones in particular. The 1914 report of the Virginia Colony for the Feeble-Minded verified those concerns about these individuals when it concluded that "as a matter of choice most of these women lead evil lives" (Virginia State Colony, 1914, p. 16). A year later, a survey of conditions in Georgia covered many of the same issues. "An institution for defective delinquent girls will be a charter of liberty for this most helpless, unfortunate, and potentially dangerous class," it reported, "taking them from the streets and highways, where they have been the defenceless [*sic*] prey of lust and greed. . . . Finally, not the least important of all these benefits is the protection such an institution will afford society" (Anderson, 1919, p. 546). While some Southerners saw the threat of feebleminded women as a consequence of their depraved nature, others viewed it as a result of these women's childlike nature and their inability to ward off the advances of unscrupu-lous males. Regardless of the rationale for placement in institutions, Southern women struggle under a double burden from which escape was difficult.

Eudora Welty's short story "Lily Daw and the Three Ladies" (Welty, 1943) reflected these conflicting attitudes well. In the story, three upper middle class matrons of the small Mississippi town of Victory conspire to get Lily Daw, a young lower class resident of their town, committed to Ellisville State School for the Feeble-Minded. They try to convince her to go, telling her, "It's a lovely place . . . they will let you make all sorts of baskets" (p. 8). Their reasoning for removing Lily from the town echoed their desire for protection of and from Lily. "Lily lets people walk over her so," reported one of the women (p. 11). Another concluded that "Lily has gotten so she is very mature for her age. . . . And that's how come we are sending her to Ellisville" (pp. 4–5). The women looked after Lily when she was growing up and provided her family with "all her food and kindling and every stitch she had on" (p. 7). They decided that Lily could no longer remain at large in the community when assumed evidence pointed to her inability to deal with men in an appropriate manner. Lily's experience was replicated throughout the South, as community leaders viewed young women of her type as dangerous and problematic.

The admission of women such as Lily Daw led superintendents and other officials to institutionalize females for longer periods of time than males. At North Carolina's Caswell Training School, for example, 52.1% of the males admitted from 1914 to 1939 were discharged within three years of admittance. That compared to only 31% of the females. Figures from Florida verify the North Carolina data. While males constituted 55% of the 1,165 admissions to Florida Farm Colony from 1822 to 1937, they constituted 66% of those discharged during that same time period. Whereas males tended to remain in institutions for shorter periods of time, they also were admitted at earlier ages. 1921 to 1949 Florida Farm Colony admission figures from a surrounding county reveal a mean average male admission age of 10.4, which contrasted to a mean average female admission age of 12.4.[6] This 2-year differential placed female admission to the institution at approximately the onset of puberty. Both longer retention rates and later admission ages for female patients demonstrated an official concern that "girls and women of the child-bearing age be given preference in the admission process," recognizing their assumed threat to the social order.

Concerns about hereditary transmission of metal deficiency and the conflation of promiscuous sexual activity with feeblemindedness distorted the admission procedures of Southern institutions. Females constituted the majority of inmates committed for such sexual issues. Compilers of state surveys, developed by Northern social welfare advocates and designed to reveal the extent of the social problems besetting Southern states, often cataloged cases of feebleminded prostitutes and brazenly immoral women. In 1919, the Florida Commission for the Study of Epilepsy and Feeblemindedness (instrumental in the state authorization of the Florida Farm Colony two years later) reported a case study of a female classified as feebleminded. The "girl . . . has been openly immoral for years," the survey taker observed. "In the War Department Records, she is classified as a feebleminded moral degenerate" (Florida Commission for the Study of Epilepsy and Feeblemindedness, 1919, p. 705). No records exist as to whether the young woman ever entered the institution. A Virginia case, however, reveals a direct relationship between alleged female sexual misconduct and institutionalization. In 1928, a Strasburg, Virginia couple wrote Virginia governor Harry Byrd, requesting his help "to get our daughter from the State Colony near Lynchburg. . . . She is feeble-minded. She was not feeble-minded when she went there. . . . She was sent there by the Red Cross because she was coaxed away from her people by outsiders [and gave birth to an illegitimate child]." The parents, acting now as parents to their grandchild, affirmed "the baby is a well, healthy, and able-bodied child." Of course, this contradicted the accepted scientific belief in the inherited nature of feeblemindedness. Not wishing to get involved in this dispute, Byrd curtly responded to the parents that "there is nothing I can do about her discharge."[7]

Other Southern state institutions also struggled with the problems associated with the assumed direct relationship between female sexuality and the label of feeble-mindedness. In 1914, the superintendent of the Children's Home Society of North Carolina wrote to the superintendent of the newly established Caswell Training School regarding a female patient admitted as one of the institution's first residents. "I would not know how to categorize her special form of feeblemindedness," he wrote, "though a report from a recent home she was in indicated that the sexual instinct was very strong. . . . Her future safety," and presumably the safety of society from her feebleminded offspring, "depends on her being segregated and receiving institutional care."[8] The 1916–1917 South Carolina Report on the Feeble-Minded, which investigated high-functioning mental defectives living in their communities throughout the state, also verified prevailing perceptions. Of the 23 Columbia women identified in the report as feebleminded, 18 were categorized as immoral or sexually active. One young woman met that criterion because she married without her mother's consent and "went out in automobiles with men." Report authors categorized another young woman as feebleminded in spite of her "claim to be a junior at Lander College." She was dubiously classified as feebleminded because of her illegitimate pregnancy, which left her "family very much disgraced at her conduct."[9]

Superintendents saw several causes for the preponderance of females being sterilized behind their institutional walls. Concerned that people might have concerns that women were being singled out for the procedure at the Virginia State Colony (of the first 447 people sterilized there, 328 were female), superintendent J.H. Bell addressed the issue in 1931 as he spoke before the Virginia Medical Society. "There has been no disposition on our part to create the difference," he assured his fellow doctors. Males "of a suitable type for sterilization and release" simply "are able to evade serious contact with welfare agencies and local officials" and "therefore are not in a position to be sterilized." Females should be sterilized for their own protection, he argued, since they "fall an easy prey to those of her [sic] own mental level." Conversely, "the feeble-minded male cannot enter into serious competition with the normal male for the affections of the feeble-minded female." Bell concluded by announcing that "the female defective is, generally speaking, more dangerous eugenically than the male . . . and it is, therefore, evident that if all mentally defective women were sterilized, there would be but little reproduction of feeble-minded persons from these sources."[10]

It's little wonder that, in the 1920s, while writing to a female patient at Caswell Training Center, a male patient summarized not only his feelings toward institutionalization but the broader concerns about an entire era of treatment. He wrote simply, "This place ain't for you anyway."[11]

FEEBLEMINDEDNESS IN THE ARTS

One of the reasons that eugenic thought was so widely accepted was because of popular fiction and media. Among the most conspicuous writers spreading eugenic dogma through their novels were H.G. Wells and Edgar Rice Burroughs.

Edgar Rice Burroughs, a Chicago native, published his iconic *Tarzan of the Apes* in 1912 and by 1923 was successful enough to begin printing and distributing his own books. Though several of his books, notably 1918s *The Land that Time Forgot* did well, it was the Tarzan series that became Burroughs's legacy. Publishing a Tarzan book almost every year between 1912 and 1940—including *The Son of Tarzan* in 1914, *Tarzan and the Ant Men* in 1924, and *Tarzan and the Leopard Man* in 1933—the series became an American standard and franchise. In addition to the numerous sequels, Burroughs marketed movies and cartoons, as well as other Tarzan paraphernalia and ephemera.

Tarzan's story is both familiar and more complex than most childhood readers' recall, most of whom today know the story from the animated movie and television versions. The infant Tarzan is raised by a family of apes and the child grows up stronger than his peers and conquers his environment. According to Burroughs's book, though, Tarzan thrives and becomes the "master" of his jungle community for one very compelling reason. Millions of years of evolution had prepared people of his race and class to do so. "I was mainly interested in playing with the idea of a contrast between heredity and environment," Burroughs wrote in 1930. "For this purpose I selected an infant child of a race strongly marked by hereditary characteristics of the finer and noble sort, and at an age where he could not have been influenced by associations with creatures of his own kind. I threw him into an environment as diametrically opposite to that which he had been born as I might well conceive" (Burroughs, 1930, pp. 29–30).

Edgar Rice Burroughs was fascinated with eugenics. *Tarzan of the Apes* was not written for children; it was written as Burroughs's epic of eugenic triumph. He believed that human heredity had reached its zenith in British aristocracy. The story began when mutinous sailors maroon Tarzan's English parents on the coast of Africa. Early in the novel, Burroughs described the father, Lord Greystroke, as "the type of Englishman that one likes best to associate with the noblest monuments of historic achievement upon a thousand battlefields—a strong, virile man—mentally, morally, physically" (Burroughs, 1912, p. 2). Tarzan's mother, also of the English nobility, dies shortly after he is born following an assault by a great ape. His father is killed when a group of apes returns to the family's cabin. Hearing a cry from the crib and intending to destroy him, the male apes are persuaded to spare the infant by a female, Kala. She is in mourning over the death of her own child, and, against the advice of the other apes, she adopts the human baby.

In his earliest developmental years, Tarzan lags behind the young apes in his group in climbing, running, and swinging through trees. In an interesting turn on arguments made about withholding care and treatment from infants with disabilities for eugenic reasons, Kala's husband urges that they abandon this clearly defective child.

"He will never be a great ape," he argued. "Always you will have to carry him and protect him. What good will he be to the tribe? None, only a burden . . . let us leave him quietly sleeping among the tall grasses, that you may bear other and stronger apes to guard us in our old age." . . . "Never . . . " replied Kala. "If I must carry him forever, so be it" (Burroughs, 1912, pp. 55–56).

Soon, however, Tarzan's physical development catches up with that of his ape peers, and by adolescence he has surpassed them in physical prowess; he has become the young "King" of his environment. Even more remarkable, however, are his intellectual feats. His reasoning and problem-solving skills make him clearly superior to all of the other inhabitants of the jungle. Most astounding, Tarzan returns to the cabin home of his parents and discovers picture books, a primer, and a dictionary. Using these, he teaches himself to read and write.

Soon Tarzan becomes aware of the presence of other humans in the jungle. He observes a group of African warriors and studies their skin color and other physical features. Burroughs described in detail Tarzan's thoughts about what he perceived to be the human-like, but not fully human, creatures. He also provided an account of the thoughts and feelings Tarzan expressed when he kills one of these warriors, a sense of relatedness but distance from this "other kind" of man.

Race is a dominant theme in Burroughs's book. Tarzan announces himself to the newly arrived white people by leaving a printed message. He warns them, "This Is The House Of Tarzan, The Killer Of Beasts And Many Black Men. Do Not Harm The Things Which Are Tarzan's. Tarzan Watches. Tarzan Of The Apes" (Burroughs, 1912, p. 170).

It is Jane, of course, who fully elicits Tarzan's innate emotional and intellectual superiority. Unlike the early movie descriptions of a "Me Tarzan. You Jane" relationship, the Tarzan of Burroughs's novel is soon speaking fluently to her, claiming Jane as his love and subsequently discovering his rightful title as Lord Greystroke. Burroughs presented this rapid and remarkable transformation as the inevitable flowering of latent genetic excellence. In describing Tarzan's response to his encounters with the Anglo-Saxon world, he wrote: "It was the hallmark of his aristocratic birth, the natural outcropping of many generations of fine breeding, an hereditary instinct of graciousness which a lifetime of uncouth and savage training and environment could not eradicate" (Taliaferro, 1999, p. 277).

Burroughs continued to be intrigued with eugenic ideas and proposals. This fascination was expressed in a number of Tarzan squeals. In *Tarzan and the Last Empire*, for example, he created a city originally overrun with criminals and vagrants. A new emperor, however, established a stern policy of genetic laundering. According to Burroughs's story, the emperor "made laws so drastic that no thief or murderer lived to propagate his kind. Indeed, the laws of Honus Hasta destroyed not only the criminal but all members of his family, so that there were none to transmit to posterity the criminal inclinations of a depraved sire. . . . the laws of Honus Hasta prevented the breeding of criminals" (Burroughs, 1929, p. 59). After two millennia of this policy, Tarzan finds a city completely free of crime.

Burroughs's inspiration for the eugenic laws of Honus Hasta appears to have come from a nonfictional source. A month before he began work on *Tarzan and the Last Empire*, Burroughs reported on a 1928 murder trial for the *Los Angeles Examiner*. The defendant, William Hickman, was charged with the brutal murder of a 12-year-old girl. In his accounts of the trial for the *Examiner,* Burroughs ridiculed the defense argument that Hickman was insane:

"Hickman is not normal. But abnormality does not by any means imply insanity. Hickman is a moral imbecile and moral imbecility is not insanity" (as cited in Taliaferro, 1999, p. 229). This abnormality, Burroughs asserted, was "genetic—an inborn brutality of will. . . . If we hang him we have removed . . . a potential menace to peace and happiness and safety of countless future generations, for moral imbeciles breed moral imbeciles, criminals breed criminals, and murderers breed murderers, just as St. Bernards breed St. Bernards" (Taliaferro, 1999, pp. 229–231).

Across the Atlantic, Burroughs's contemporary, H.G. Wells, produced a body of science fiction that, if not as prodigious as Burroughs's output, made up for it in impact. Wells and Burroughs dominated the science fiction genre during the Progressive era, and their utopian visions mirrored the era's axioms.

Wells was, of course, the enormously popular author of *The Time Machine*, *The Island of Dr. Moreau*, *The Invisible Man*, and *The War of the Worlds*. The plot of the latter is familiar to modern audiences through the frequent movie and television reproductions. An anonymous narrator tells the story from the appearance of the Martian invaders, to the devastation wrought by these aliens, to their demise from viral or bacterial agents. What may be less obvious to modern audiences, who, as with the Tarzan stories, have only seen screen-based interpretations of *The War of the Worlds*, was Wells' underlying meaning.

"The underlying lesson of the book," Wells biographer Michael Coren explained, "is an ethical one. He reminds us that our strength is nothing to that of others, just as the strength of the colonized peoples of the world is nothing to that of the European and North American nations" (Coren, 1993, p. 52).

In 1901, Wells published a utopian novel titled *Anticipations*. "The idea," observed Coren, "was that one part of the world's population would benefit by killing or enslaving the rest. Civil, economic, and political freedom would be severely limited and controlled; racial and social homogeneity would be enforced; an omnipotent state would, by a combination of education and social engineering, produce a world of content and obedient citizens" (Coren, 1993, p. 63).

"And the ethical system which will dominate the world-state," wrote Wells in *Anticipations*, "will be shaped primarily to favour the procreation of what is fine and efficient and beautiful in humanity—beautiful and strong bodies, clear and powerful minds, and a growing body of knowledge—and to check the procreation of base and servile types, of fear-driven and cowardly souls, of all that is mean and ugly and bestial in the souls, bodies, and habits of men" (Coren, 1993, p. 64).

THREE GENERATIONS OF IMBECILES

The involuntary sterilization of people with intellectual disability as a means of social control began in the first decade of the 20th century, and at the end of the 1920s was codified as the law of the land. In 1907, Indiana became the first state to pass a compulsory sterilization law for "all confirmed criminals, idiots, rapists and imbeciles" who were confined in state institutions. Even as early as 1894, however, institution superintendents were experimenting with this practice. In that year, Dr. F. Hoyt Pilcher, superintendent of the Kansas institution in Winfield, began "asexualization operations" on inmates of the asylum. At the 34th annual meeting of the American Association for the Study of the Feebleminded held in 1910 in Lincoln, Illinois, F.C. Cave, by then superintendent of the same Kansas institution, reported on results of asexualization operations performed on 58 inmates of the institution under Dr. Pilcher's watch. "These operations prevent the begetting of defective off-spring and also limit lewdness and vice," proclaimed Dr. Cave, closing his report by observing that "it is time some drastic action were taken to stem the ever increasing tide of weak-minded individuals who are demanding more and more room in our charitable institutions by their increase" (Cave, 1910, pp. 124–125).

Pilcher's enthusiasm for sterilization, however, exceeded the appetites of the citizens of Winfield. Headlines in the Saturday, September 1, 1894 edition of the *Topeka Lance* trumpeted "Mutilation by the Wholesale Practiced at the Asylum" (Seaton, 2004–2005, p. 253). By 1899, Pilcher had been forced to resign his position as superintendent, though as much because of the governorship changing political parties as the furor his experimental methods created.

Between 1907 and 1921, 18 states passed sexual sterilization statutes (Landman, 1932, pp. 291–292), and by January 1, 1921, an estimated 3,233 people had already been forcibly sterilized (Whitney, 1934, p. 302). The majority of people sterilized during this period were people in institutions for the insane, for the simple reason, observed medical historian Philip Reilly, that they were more likely to be released from the institution than were people who were feebleminded, and their release was made contingent upon undergoing sterilization. Reilly estimated that more than 400 people who were feebleminded were forcibly sterilized during the years before 1921 (Reilly, 1991, p. 48). Beginning in 1912, however, many states began to declare these laws unconstitutional. Between 1912 and 1921, laws in 7 of the 18 states were struck down.

Enter Harry Hamilton Laughlin, who was recruited by Charles Davenport to become the assistant director of the Eugenics Records Office (ERO) in October 1910. It was through the tireless efforts of Laughlin over the next decade and with the endorsement of the United States Supreme Court that asexualization, forced sterilization, became the law of the land. In February 1914, the ERO published two reports from the Committee to Study and to Report on the Best Practical Means to Cut Off the Defective Germ-Plasm in the American Population. Both reports were authored by Laughlin and issued by a subcommittee of the American Breeders' Association's Eugenics Section, established in May 1911. Bulletin Number 10A identified the committee members, the committee's mission—conveniently identical to its name—a stock explanation of the "problem" in terms of unit characters and human traits, and a classification of the "cacogenic varieties of the human race." *Cacogenic* means pertaining to or causing degeneration in offspring. It is a term that was created by eugenicists from the Greek *cac* or *caco* (bad) and eu(genics). Bulletin 10A concluded with suggested remedies, including life segregation or segregation during the reproductive period, sterilization, restrictive marriage laws, eugenical education, eugenical mating, environmental betterment, polygamy, and euthanasia. Polygamy may appear to be an odd solution, but the committee was referring to the animal-breeding model in which an animal of high quality sires many offspring through multiple partners. The polygamous solution to the menace of the moron, then, would be to have "high-quality human stock" reproduce madly through multiple partners.

Bulletin 10B bore all the fingerprints of Laughlin's modus operandi. It began with a state-by-state analysis of the text and a legislative history of existing sterilization laws. Next was a summary of laws that had been vetoed, revoked by referendum, or introduced but not passed. The Bulletin then described litigation and legal opinions about and criticisms of the existing laws. Finally, Laughlin, under the guise of the committee, provided the principles and details for a model sterilization law.

Fast forward from 1914 to 1922, when Laughlin published the highly influential *Eugenical Sterilization in the United States*. Unlike Bulletins 10A and 10B, which appeared at a time when sterilization laws were proliferating and, as such, probably had limited impact on the movement, *Eugenical Sterilization* was published as state laws were being struck down and, expanding the model sterilization law originally proposed in Bulletin 10B, had a catalytic effect on the sterilization movement. One reason that *Eugenical Sterilization* was able to galvanize the passage of state laws was because it was published by the Municipal Court of Chicago. Judge Harry Olson was chief justice of the court and president of the Eugenics Research Association. Through Olson, Laughlin was able to secure an appointment as a Eugenics Associate of the Psychopathic Laboratory of the Municipal Court, thus having *Eugenical Sterilization* published and distributed by an entity with credibility in legal circles.

In 1924, Laughlin was approached with an opportunity to test the validity of his model sterilization law. Laughlin had mailed a copy of *Eugenical Sterilization* to Albert Priddy, superintendent of the Virginia Colony for Epileptics and Feebleminded in Lynchburg (Black, 2003, p. 113). Priddy, with others, used the model law to craft sterilization legislation for Virginia, which was passed in March 1924 and implemented in June (Black, 2003, p. 113).

Priddy's beliefs were, essentially, exactly those that Goddard wanted people to have about his morons—particularly women. Priddy wrote the following in a 1922–1923 report:

> The admission of female morons to this institution has constituted for the most part of those who would formerly have found their way into the red-light district and become dangerous to society. . . . These women are never reformed in heart and mind because they are defectives from the standpoint of intellect and moral conception and should always have the supervision by officers of the law and properly appointed custodians. (Smith & Nelson, 1989, p. 32)

Among the women admitted to Priddy's institution who, in his estimation, fell into this category of moron and moral imbecility, was Carrie Buck (see Figure 6.6). Buck was admitted to the Virginia Colony on June 4, 1924. Carrie Buck's early years were less than ideal. Her mother, Emma, had herself been committed to the Virginia Colony in 1920 for prostitution and "moral delinquency." Carrie was raised in foster homes and it was her foster family, with whom she had lived since she was three, who petitioned to have Carrie incarcerated, alleging that she was feebleminded and epileptic. The 14-year-old Carrie was also pregnant.

Figure 6.6. Carrie and Emma Buck, 1924.
(From Arthur Estabrook Papers, Special Collections & Archives, University at Albany, SUNY; reprinted by permission.)

Priddy also shared Laughlin's perspective that segregation should lead inevitably to sterilization. With the newly minted Virginia sterilization law implemented in the same month that Carrie Buck was incarcerated at the Virginia Colony, and given her family history of apparent feeblemindedness, Carrie was, Priddy and others felt, the perfect case with which to test the strength of the new law.

In October 1924, Priddy sent Laughlin a letter in which he explained his careful adherence to the guidelines provided in *Eugenical Sterilization in the United States* when drafting the Virginia statute, how the law was needed to ease the burden on the state and his institution with regard to the number of morally and intellectually degenerate women in Virginia by sterilizing them so as to be able to discharge them from the Colony, and then providing Laughlin a rough case history of Carrie's life (Smith & Nelson, 1989, p. 58). Priddy closed his communication with Laughlin with the request for the ERO eugenicist to provide a deposition for the trail, which was to begin later in the month. Laughlin had no hesitancy providing the requested deposition.

"Laughlin made two major points to the court," summarized Stephen J. Gould in a 1984 essay on the case. "First, that Carrie Buck and her mother, Emma Buck, were feeble-minded by the Stanford-Binet test of IQ, then in its own infancy. Second, that most feeblemindedness is inherited, and Carrie Buck surely belonged with this majority" (Gould, 1985, p. 310).

The deposed Laughlin reported, predictably, that "generally, feeble-mindedness is caused by the inheritance of degenerate qualities; but sometimes it might be caused by environmental factors which are not hereditary. In the case given, the evidence points strongly toward the feeble-mindedness and moral delinquency of Carrie Buck being due, primarily, to inheritance and not to environment" (Gould, 1985, p. 311).

Shortly after the trial ended, the judge for the Commonwealth of Virginia found in favor of the state. Carrie Buck was to be sterilized. In 1925, Virginia governor Elbert Trinkle wrote to the staff of the Virginia State Colony. "I notice from the paper the Sterilization Law has been declared constitutional by the [Virginia] Supreme Court. I do hope you people will get busy and use the law as fast as it can be used."[12] And use it fast they did. From 1928 to 1944, Virginia sterilized 2,825 individuals labeled as feebleminded.

The case was then—in close collusion between the prosecution and defense—appealed to the Virginia Court of Appeals, where the verdict was upheld. In September of 1926, papers were filed to have the case considered by the United States Supreme Court. By then, Albert Priddy had died and had been replaced by Dr. J.H. Bell, so when the Supreme Court agreed to hear the case, in April 1927, it would be known as *Buck v. Bell*.

The opinion of the Supreme Court was written by Justice Oliver Wendall Holmes Jr., one of the most celebrated jurists in the history of that institution. The son of one of America's most important 19th-century poets, Holmes Jr. was a thrice-wounded Civil War veteran who had been appointed to the court in 1902 by President Theodore Roosevelt. Holmes was a towering intellectual, known for his pithy, eminently quotable opinions. Unfortunately for Carrie Buck and thousands of others after her, he was also a eugenicist and a social Darwinist (Alschuler, 2000).

It should not be surprising then, that when he delivered his opinion for the majority of the court, upholding Carrie Buck's sterilization, it was with a sharp wit that cut deeply, literally, and figuratively for many Americans such as Carrie Buck.

> Carrie Buck is a feeble-minded white woman who was committed to the State Colony. She is the daughter of a feeble-minded mother in the same institution, and the mother of an illegitimate feeble-minded child. We have seen more than once that the public welfare may call upon the best citizens for their lives. It would be strange if it could not call upon those who already sap the strength of the state for these lesser sacrifices. It is better for all the world, if instead of waiting to execute degenerate offspring for crime, or to let them starve for their imbecility, society can prevent those who are manifestly unfit from continuing their kind. The principle that sustains compulsory vaccination is broad enough to cover cutting the Fallopian tubes. (Gould, 1985, p. 311)

"Three generations of imbeciles are enough," Holmes's decision famously concluded (Gould, 1985, p. 311).

Carrie Buck was sterilized the morning of October 19, 1927 (Smith & Nelson, 1989, p. 179). Not surprisingly, Virginia's sterilization enthusiasts took full advantage of their newly granted privilege and in the next decade sterilized 1,000 institutionalized Virginians against or in oblivion of their will.

NOTES

1. Deceased Patient Record #146, Vault files, Tacachale Community, Gainesville, Florida.
2. Letters between PME and GWR, Notebooks, Caswell Training School Records, Caswell Center, Kinston, North Carolina. Information regarding admission and dismissal of both patients was obtained for Patient Admission Book, Caswell Center Medical Department. These letters were only discovered after the dismissal of the female patient in August 1925.
3. C. Banks McNairy to board of directors, March 23, 1918, *Minutes of the Executive Committee Board of Directors of Caswell Training School,* Caswell Center, Kinston, North Carolina.
4. Superintendent's Report, January 10, 1919, *Minutes of the Executive Committee Board of Directors of Caswell Training School,* Caswell Center, Kinston, North Carolina.
5. Application from November 20, 1931, and Colson reply, November 23, 1931, Vault files, Tacachale Community, Gainesville, Florida.
6. Patient Admission Book, Medical Records Office, Caswell Center, Kinston, North Carolina; 1921–22—1935–37 *Biennial Reports of the Superintendent of Florida Farm Colony;* Alachua County Commitment Records, 1921–1940, Alachua County Courthouse, Gainesville, Florida.
7. Mr. and Mrs. Burner to Governor Harry F. Byrd, February 20, 1928, Papers of Governor Harry Byrd, Record Group 3, Box 29, State Colony Folder, Virginia State Archives, Richmond, Virginia.
8. William Streeter to C. Banks McNairy, May 11, 1914, and patient information from Patient Record #4, Caswell Center Medical Department, Kinston, North Carolina.
9. Cases 76 and 57, *Working Papers of the South Carolina Report on the Feeble-Minded,* South Carolina State Archives, Columbia, South Carolina.
10. Bell, J.H. (1931, October 7). *Eugenic sterilization and its relationship to the science of life and reproduction.* Paper presented at the meeting of the Virginia Medical Society, Roanoke, Virginia. Richmond: Virginia State Library.
11. GWR to PME, undated correspondence, Notebooks, Caswell Training School Records, Caswell Center, Kinston, North Carolina. See Note 2.
12. E. Lee Trinkle to hospital superintendents, November 24, 1925, Box 24, State Commissioner of Hospitals Folder, Elbert Lee Trinkle Papers, Virginia State Archives, Richmond, Virginia.

REFERENCES

Akin, C.V. (1929). Discussion of a paper. *New Orleans Medical and Surgical Journal, 82,* 163.

Alschuler, A.W. (2000). *Law without values: The life, work, and legacy of Justice Holmes.* Chicago, IL: University of Chicago Press.

Anderson, V.V. (1919). Mental defect in a southern state. *Mental Hygiene, 3,* 546.

Barr, M.W. (1904). *Mental defectives.* Philadelphia, PA: P. Blackistone's & Sons.

Bishop, J.B. (1920). *Theodore Roosevelt and his time, shown in letters* (Vol. 1). New York, NY: Charles Scribner's Sons.

Black, E. (2003). *War against the weak: Eugenics and America's campaign to create a master race.* New York, NY: Four Walls Eight Windows.

Burroughs, E.R. (1912). *Tarzan of the apes.* New York, NY: Bust.

Burroughs, E.R. (1929). *Tarzan and the lost empire.* New York, NY: Metropolitan Books.

Burroughs, E.R. (1930). The Tarzan theme. *Writer's Digest, 10,* 29–31.

Cave, F.C. (1910). Report of sterilization in the Kansas State Home for Feeble-Minded. *Journal of Psych-Asthenics, 15,* 123–125.

Coren, M. (1993). *The invisible man: The life and liberties of H.G. Wells.* New York, NY: Atheneum.

Cravens, H. (1978). *The triumph of evolution: American scientists and the heredity-environment controversy, 1900–1941.* Philadelphia: University of Pennsylvania Press.

Crenson, M. (1998). *Building the invisible orphanage: A prehistory of the American welfare system.* Cambridge, MA: Harvard University Press.

Davenport, C.B. (1910). Application of Mendel's law to human heredity. *Journal of Psycho-Asthenics, 15,* 93–95.

Doll, E.A. (1917). *Clinical studies in feeblemindedness.* Toronto: R. G. Badger.

The feeble-minded. (1919, June 2). *Atlanta Constitution,* p. 7.

Florida Commission for the Study of Epilepsy and Feeblemindedness. (1919). *Florida's feeble minded* (Survey 42). Tallahassee, FL: Author.

Goddard, H.H. (1907). Psychological work among the feeble-minded. *Journal of Psycho-Asthenics, 12,* 18–30.

Goddard, H.H. (1912). *The Kallikak Family.* New York, NY: MacMillan.

Gould, S.J. (1985). "Carrie Buck's daughter." In S.J. Gould (Ed.), *The Flamingo's Smile* (pp. 307–313). New York, NY: W. W. Norton & Company.

Gould, S.J. (1998). The internal brand of the Scarlet W. *Natural History, 102*(2), 10–18.

Green, B. (2009). *Problem-based psychiatry.* London: Radcliffe Publishing Co.

Hardy, I. (1910). *What it costs.* Kinston, NC: Caswell Training School Records.

Henig, R.M. (2000). *The monk in the garden: The lost and found genius of Gregor Mendel, the father of Genetics.* New York, NY: Houghton Mifflin.

Ireland, W.W. (1877). *On idiocy and imbecility.* London, United Kingdom: J.& A. Churchill.

Johnson, P. (1998). *A history of the American people.* New York, NY: HarperCollins.

Kirkbride, T.S. (1854). *On the construction, organization, and general arrangements of hospitals for the insane.* Philadelphia, PA: Lippincott.

Landman, J.H. (1932). *Human sterilization: The history of the sexual sterilization movement.* New York, NY: MacMillan.

McGerr, M. (2003). *A fierce discontent: The rise and fall of the progressive movement in America, 1870–1920.* New York, NY: Free Press.

McNairy, C.B. (1924). *Superintendents report to the board of directors of Caswell Training School.* Kinston, NC: Caswell Training School Records.

Rafter, N.H. (1997). *Creating born criminals.* Chicago: University of Illinois Press.

Reilly, P.R. (1991). *The surgical solution: A history of involuntary sterilization in the United States.* Baltimore, MD: The Johns Hopkins University Press.

Roosevelt, T. (1902). Introduction. In B. Van Vorst & M. Van Vorst (Eds.), *Women who toil: Experiences of two ladies as factory girls.* New York, NY: Doubleday, Page.

Seaton, F.D. (2004–2005). The long road toward "The Right Thing to Do": The troubled history of the Winfield State Hospital. *Kansas History, 27,* 250–263.

Smith, J.D., & Nelson, K.R. (1989). *The sterilization of Carrie Buck: Was she feebleminded or society's pawn?* Far Hills, NJ: New Horizon Press.

Smith, J.D., & Wehmeyer, M.L. (2012). Who was Deborah Kallikak? *Intellectual and Developmental Disabilities, 50*(2), 169–178. Washington, DC: American Association on Intellectual and Developmental Disabilities.

Taliaferro, J. (1999). *Tarzan forever: The life of Edgar Rice Burroughs, creator of Tarzan.* New York, NY: Charles Scribner's Sons.

Tredgold, A.F. (1920). *Mental deficiency (amentia).* New York: William Wood & Co.

Trent, J.W. (1994). *Inventing the feeble mind: A history of mental retardation in the United States.* Berkeley: University of California Press.

U.S. Department of Labor. (1926). *Dependent and delinquent children in Georgia.* Washington, DC: U.S. Printing Office.

Virginia State Colony. (1914). *Annual report.* Lynchburg, VA: Author

Virginia State Colony. (1917). *Annual report.* Lynchburg, VA: Author.

Welty, E. (1943). *A curtain of green.* Garden City, NY: Doubleday, Doran.

Whitney, L.F. (1934). *The case for sterilization.* New York, NY: Frederick A. Stokes.

Whitten, B. (1920). *Annual report.* Clinton, SC: South Carolina State Training School.

Whitten, B. (1967). *A history of Whitten Village.* Clinton, SC: Jacobs Press.

Wiebe, R.H. (1967). *The search for order: 1877–1920.* New York, NY: Hill and Wang.

Wolfensberger, W. (1975). *The origin and nature of our institutional models.* Syracuse, NY: Human Policy Press.

7

Isolation, Enlargement, and Economization

Intellectual Disability in Late Modern Times (1930 CE to 1950 CE)

J. David Smith, Steven Noll, and Michael L. Wehmeyer

Before the end of World War II, the problems set in motion during 1900–1930 exploded. The number of institutions in America increased by 50%. The size of these institutions dramatically increased, with the population of people who were institutionalized more than doubling. These mega-institutions, heavily regulated but still underfunded by state bureaucracies and struggling to hire and retain workers, came under increasing attack, and the impact of the Great Depression exacerbated conditions. The lack of privacy, gross overcrowding, and restrictions of freedoms of the inmates resulted in dehumanizing conditions, violations of basic human rights, and a diminution of basic human dignity. Unsanitary conditions, inadequate medical and nursing staff, fire and safety hazards, improper use and regulation of medication, poor nutrition, and the lack of staff created health and safety hazards for residents. The lack of habilitative and educative efforts in facilities resulted in the deterioration of physical, cognitive, and communication skills and abilities among inmates, and the use of involuntary sterilization escalated. Budget pressures resulted in too few paid employees, which led to the use of inmates as unpaid labor. The growing professional class in the field continued to make all decisions pertaining to the lives of people with intellectual disability. There was, however, some progress. Conceptualizations of intellectual disability changed from the prevailing use of the term *moron* to *mental deficiency*, and professionals began to use difficulties in adaptive behavior and daily living to understand the construct. Additionally, at the end of World War II there emerged a ray of light that became the parent movement.

*I*n 1930, the American novelist Pearl S. Buck left her daughter, Carol, at the Vineland Training School, in Vineland, New Jersey. Buck first came to the attention of the American public when *East Wind, West Wind* was published in 1930. It was a novel that portrayed the conflicts created by cultural change in China. She wrote with the authority of personal experience and actual observation, because she had grown up in China as the daughter of Presbyterian missionaries. In 1931, *The Good Earth,* a novel about Chinese peasant life, brought her increasing fame and a Pulitzer Prize. For the next 40 years, Pearl Buck continued to be a prolific and respected writer, and in 1938 she was awarded the Nobel Prize in Literature, the first American woman to receive this honor.

In addition to her writing, Buck was known for her humanitarian actions. She worked to foster racial tolerance and to promote the welfare of immigrants to the United States. She was a visible advocate for disadvantaged Asian people, particularly children. In 1941 she founded the East and West Association, with the goal of promoting greater harmony and understanding among people of different cultural backgrounds. In 1949 she founded Welcome House, an adoption agency for Asian American children. She and her second husband had raised a large family of adopted children of diverse racial and ethnic origins.

It was her experiences with her own child, Carol, however, that shaped the future for people with intellectual disability. Pearl Buck's first child, Caroline Grace Buck, was born in May of 1920. It soon became apparent that Carol's rate of development was noticeably slower than that of other children. When the Buck family returned to the United States, Pearl sought the opinions of physicians more knowledgeable about developmental problems than those she had consulted in China. At the Mayo Clinic, in Rochester, Minnesota, she received the news that her daughter was "severely retarded" (Buck, 1950, p. 21). Although Buck would not learn it until much later in her life, her daughter was born with a metabolic disorder called phenylketonuria, or PKU. Left untreated, the blood stream of children with PKU accrues high levels of unsynthesized phenylalanine, an amino acid found in a host of foods—including breast milk, meat, chicken, fish, nuts, and dairy products—resulting in, among other symptoms, cognitive disability as a function of neural damage.

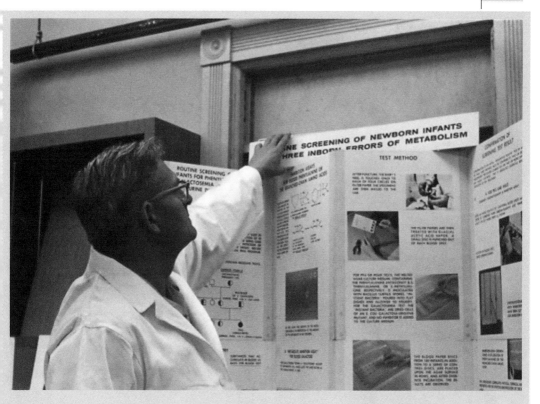

Figure 7.1. Robert Guthrie presenting findings from his research on PKU. (Image from author's personal collection.)

In the early 1960s, pediatrician and microbiologist Robert Guthrie, with funding from the National Association for Retarded Children, a parent advocacy organization, developed a blood test that could detect the presence of PKU. Known as the Guthrie Spot, newborns worldwide are screened for the presence of PKU. If detected early, children with PKU can be placed on phenylalanine-restricted diets and experience typical developmental outcomes (see Figures 7.1 and 7.2).

Of course, this knowledge did not exist in the 1920s, and circumstances and the times soon made it seem to Buck that she would have to institutionalize Carol. In 1929, Buck sojourned back to the United States to locate an institution in which Carol could live the remainder of her life. Her quest led her, eventually, to the front porch steps of the Vineland Training School (see Figure 7.3).

"I knew," wrote Buck about the end of her search, "when I entered the office and shook hands with the quiet, gray-haired man who greeted me with a gentle voice that I had found what I wanted. He was sympathetic, but not with effort. He was not eager. He said diffidently that he did not know whether I would be satisfied with his school, but we might look around. So we did look around, and what I saw was that every child's face lit when he came into the cottages, and that there were a clamor of voices to greet him and call his name—Uncle Ed, they called him" (Buck, 1950, p. 44). "I saw a certain motto repeated again and again on the walls, on the stationery, hanging above the head's own desk. It was this: Happiness first and all else follows" (Buck, 1950, p. 45).

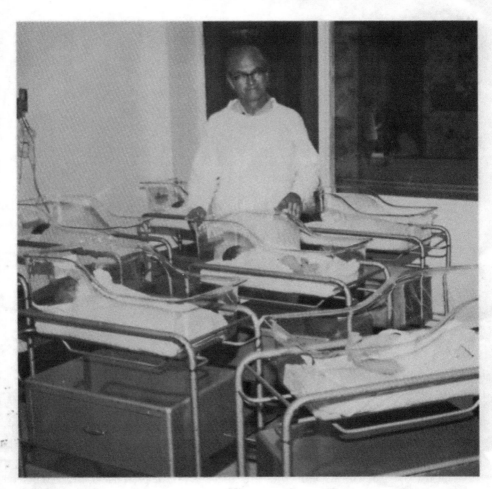

Dr. Robert Guthrie cares

You may have never heard of phenyl-ketonuria (PKU) and thanks to Dr. Robert Guthrie, you probably never will. PKU is a crippling metabolic disorder that can cause severe mental retardation if not diagnosed early. Dr. Guthrie's simple blood-spot test for PKU is widely used and is the basis for broader screening to detect other inborn errors of metabolism.

This ounce of prevention is already saving lives around the world and pays for itself. Dr. Guthrie's pioneering effort in preventive medicine research is an ex-ample of the progress that promises a better tomorrow through a more careful today.

Help dedicated men like Dr. Guthrie help protect our most important national resource — the next generation. Support the National Association for Retarded Citizens.

National Association for Retarded Citizens
2709 Ave. E East, Arlington, Texas 76011

This Space Contributed By The Publisher As A Public Service

Figure 7.2. Advertisement of Robert Guthrie's PKU test.
(Image from author's personal collection. From the National Association for Retarded Children, n.d.)

Figure 7.3. Maxham Cottage, Vineland Training School for Feebleminded Children, Vineland, New Jersey. (Image from author's personal collection.)

Edward Ransom Johnstone was the superintendent of the Vineland Training School, and his motto for the institution had won Pearl Buck's heart. "You must remember," Buck recalled Johnstone telling her, "that these are happy children. They are safe here. They will never know distress or want. They will never know struggle or defeat, nor will sorrow ever touch them. No demands are made upon them which they cannot meet. The joys which they can appreciate they have. Your child will escape all suffering. Will you remember that and let it be a comfort to you?" (Buck, 1950, p. 47).

In 1932, Buck donated $50,000 to Vineland for the construction and maintenance of a cottage, called Carol's Cottage, on the campus in which her daughter could live (Trent, 1994, p. 233). She was a long-time member of the board of directors for the Training School, and even after her death, in 1973 from lung cancer, her contribution to the Training School continued in the person of her adopted daughter, Janice, who became Carol's guardian and an active member of the Vineland board of directors (Finger & Christ, 2004, p. 50).

As important as Pearl Buck was to the Vineland Training School, it was her impact on other parents of children with intellectual and developmental disabilities for which she is most remembered by disability advocates. In an article in the *Ladies Home Journal* in May 1950 titled "The Child Who Never Grew," Buck told the story of her daughter, Carol (see Figure 7.4). Later that year, the article was reprinted as a book by John Day Publishing, and it was condensed for inclusion in the September 1950 issue of *The Reader's Digest*.

Figure 7.4. Cover of May 1950 *Ladies Home Journal,* in which *The Child Who Never Grew* was printed. (Image from author's personal collection. By Pearl S. Buck. Originally published in the May 1950 *Ladies' Home Journal*® Magazine.)

ISOLATION, ENLARGEMENT, AND ECONOMIZATION

Pearl Buck's fame and wealth enabled her to provide care for Carol that, even if she had not paid to have a cottage built for her, would still eclipse the standards under which most of Carol's peers with intellectual impairments were living. Social historian Wolf Wolfensberger's identification of three trends in institutionalization (i.e., isolation, enlargement, economization), discussed in Chapter 6, continued to dictate many aspects of the daily routines in the institution and thus the quality of the lives led by people in that institution. The number of institutions in the United States continued to grow, from approximately 60 in 1930 to almost 90 in 1950. The sheer numbers of people residing in these state institutions increased, from approximately 60,000 in 1930 to almost 140,000 in 1950. Finally, the percentage of the general population incarcerated in institutions for "the feebleminded" rose from 43 per 100,000 in 1930 to roughly 80 per 100,000 in 1950. Institutions that were built to hold 1,000 residents now held three or four times that amount, and that didn't include the waiting list to get into the institution.

These mega-institutions, heavily regulated but still underfunded by state bureaucracies, struggling to hire and retain workers, came under increasing attack. The lack of privacy, gross overcrowding, and restrictions of freedoms of the inmates resulted in dehumanizing conditions, violations of basic human rights, and a diminution of basic human dignity. Unsanitary conditions, inadequate medical and nursing staff, fire and safety hazards, improper use and regulation of medication, poor nutrition, and the lack of staff created health and safety hazards for residents. The lack of habilitative and educative efforts and facilities resulted in the deterioration of physical, cognitive, and communication skills and abilities among inmates. The lack of paid staff led to the use of inmates as unpaid labor. Many times, the institution's most capable residents would care for residents with the most intensive support needs. Figure 7.5, an article in the October 1946 issue of *The Catholic Worker,* illustrates the depth of many of these problems.

Klein and Strully (2000) wrote about the life of Bill, whose experiences were typical for people with intellectual disability during this period:

> Bill was born to a loving and caring family in 1932. Sadly, his mother died during his birth, leaving Bill in the care of his father, grandmother, and two older siblings. Like all young children, Bill loved to explore, but walking was difficult because he could not see and was unsteady on his feet. He often fell, sometimes resulting in serious injuries. By the age of 5, Bill was beginning to dress and feed himself with a great deal of assistance and had not yet learned to speak or use the toilet. His frequent violent seizures, challenging behavior, and trouble moving about on his own made it difficult for his family to care for him.
>
> When his grandmother's health began to fail, there was no one to care for Bill while his father worked. Unlike the other children in the family, he did not go to school, and there were no services available to support the family to take care of him or to enable him to be educated at home. When Bill was 5 years old, the family doctor, the pastor from the family's church, and Bill's aunts, uncles, and grandparents advised his father to send Bill to live at the state institution 50 miles away. Reluctantly, Bill's dad took him there.
>
> For the next 45 years, Bill remained in the institution. He shared a ward with 20 to 40 other boys, and later men, with disabilities. As a child, Bill was energetic and liked to be on the move, and his adventures often led to injury. Since there were not enough staff to accompany Bill on his explorations, he was tied to a chair or to his bed for up to 20 hours each day. This practice continued into his adulthood. Having never learned to speak, Bill shouted loudly if he needed assistance, or was hungry, bored, frustrated, or lonely. Eventually, Bill was forced to wear a helmet to keep him from hurting himself.

Slaves or Patients?

Rosewood and Enforced Labor

The Rosewood State Training School for mentally deficient children is located about 12 miles outside of Baltimore. The institution houses about 1,200 patients, almost equally divided as to sex and ranging from the idiot class to high level moron and borderline cases. The latter group were placed there principally because of delinquent trends that led to their rejection by society. Policies of the institution lie in the hands of an administrative staff including five doctors and psychiatrists, a business administrator, the principal of the Rosewood School, etc. Actual care of the children is the responsibility of the attendant staff -- whose members are sadly underpaid and required to work 12-hour shifts. A Board of Visitors, consisting of prominent professional people, meets monthly to theoretically approve and supervise all matters concerning the patients' care. Final authority over the general affairs of the institution lies with the Maryland Board of Mental Hygiene.

With so much professional talent devoted to the patients' care -- and considering, in addition, the spacious grounds and substantial buildings of Rosewood -- one might assume that the people of Maryland deserve high credit for providing so well for the unfortunately handicapped children of their State. Only by knowing through actual experience what goes on behind this splendid scenery can one realize what a subtle viciousness Rosewood actually represents.

Patients Are Trapped

Twelve hundred patients, many of whom should be capable of ultimate return to society as useful citizens, are trapped there -- subject to the absolute authority of an administration characterized by a tone of official stagnation and torn by personal feuds and bitter frustrations, an administration held together principally by the common realization that in the preservation of the "status quo" lies the continuance of a steady and relatively easy livelihood. The children are often denied true friendly care from the attendants because the salary is so low and the workday so long and trying that the job is unattractive to individuals of the moral, social and emotional caliber that should be required for such work.

Work Program Well Developed

Virtually all of the actual work involved in the operation of the institution is done by the children. The more capable boys are assigned to the farm, the dairy, the powerhouse; the girls to the laundry, the kitchen, the dining rooms. Specialized employees such as the painter, plumber, mason, etc., are assigned patients as assistants. In the cottages, patients do all of the cleaning as well as the feeding, bathing and changing of incontinent or helpless patients under the supervision and direction of the attendant.

Within the limits of justice such an arrangement could be commended. A just work program could be used as a factor in developing a sense of self-assurance and habits of self-reliance. By training the "patient-student" in the various trades and manual arts, a just work program could equip him with the basis for earning his livelihood in the event of ultimate parole. Such a program *planned for the patients' welfare and training* would be a credit to Rosewood. Too often, however, we encounter the proposition that these children *owe* their labor to the State to repay it for the cost of their care. Rather, it should ever be borne in mind that Society took these children into its custody, usually against their will; it is, therefore, Society's obligation to provide for them. Unfortunately, however, from the distorted principle that places the obligation upon the patient has come the practice of *punishing* children who do not work by depriving them of of [sic] the few limited pleasures Rosewood does offer.

Rosewood's program of "work therapy", if it can seriously be so named, goes beyond the limits of justice and is instead an outright exploitation of patients' labor. There are children there who work *every day of the year*

Figure 7.5. "Slaves or Patients?" An article by Gordan Zahn in the October 1946 issue of *The Catholic Worker*. (From Zahn, G. [1946, October]. Slaves or patients? *The Catholic Worker*. Available at http://www.disabilitymuseum.org/dhm/lib/detail.html?id=1720&&page=all)

without respite! Since most of these jobs (on the dairy, in the powerhouse, in the cafeteria and kitchen, etc.) entail early work hours or heavy labor or both there can be no excuse for not arranging the work schedule so as to provide at least one day of rest each week for every worker patient. On more than one occasion this was suggested to the Rosewood authorities -- with no satisfactory result.

The exploitation is evidenced again in the fact that patients who do valuable work are sometimes neglected in parole considerations. For example, one girl who proved herself reliable and efficient as a nurse's aide was kept in such work until she reached a point near indispensability. When her grandmother suddenly took an interest in her and moved toward obtaining a parole for her, the entire hospital staff began trying to persuade the girl to accept a limited parole-employment arrangement under which she would continue doing her work *at a regular salary*! It is to be noted that not until faced with *the threat* of losing her by parole did they consider her worthy of employee status. It is reasonable to assume that if the grandmother has since lost interest in parole efforts, the girl will continue doing that work as a *patient -- and without pay*!

In most cases patients assigned as "helpers" to the specialized employees are stooges for these employees -- doing the actual work while the others "supervise" and collect the pay. It is ridiculous to refer to this arrangement as "occupational training". Once a specialized employee has trained a patient, to the point that his work is done for him in a satisfactory fashion, it is almost impossible to get that patient away from him for training in some other occupation, as would be done in a valid training program.

Overworked

The more capable and willing a patient is, the more he or she is overworked. One patient does practically all of the heavy work in a cottage having a large proportion of helpless patients; his workday *every day* begins at 5:30 AM and continues to about 7 PM. A young girl works as a nurse's aide in the clinic. After the morning treatment period is over, she (and the other clinic assistants -- patients, of course) wash the entire basement floor, offices and all, and at frequent intervals wax and polish the floor as well. This should be enough to be considered a full day's work, extending as it does from 8:30 to 5; but, because she is such a capable worker, this girl is kept in a cottage housing children much younger than herself, so that she may help with the care of the little patients *before and after* her duties in the hospital. In addition, after a thoroughly exploited day, she frequently cleans the attendants' private living quarters to earn a little spending money. Most of her friends and two of her sisters are at a different cottage that houses girls of her age; however, she is so valuable at the small girls' cottage that, in spite of her many pleas and the consideration her other work should entitle her to, she is consistently refused a transfer to that cottage wherein she rightfully belongs.

It is to be admitted that many of these patients are overwilling and take great pride in extra responsibilities. Nevertheless, it should be expected that the people placed in charge over them will have enough sense to keep their work within reasonable limits.

Instead the opposite is often true. One boy assigned to night duty as a helper on the hospital ward was observed by one of the administrative officers in the act of watching some other boys install posts along a roadway. Twice the official ordered the boy to "get to work" installing posts; twice the boy objected explaining that he was on night duty and was then on his "free time." The final result of confusing justice with this particular official's orders was that the boy was punished by being ordered indoors for the rest of the day -- that is, until he was due to report for his night duty! Many other injustices could be described here to further illustrate the extent of Rosewood's labor exploitation -- child labor exploitation, at that -- by the State of Maryland. It should be to the shame of every person that such a situation can exist.

Gordan C. Zahn, The Catholic Worker, October 1946

Over the years, there were a few caring staff people who taught Bill some sign language and helped him learn to better feed and dress himself. Occasionally, someone would even take Bill to the pool, which he loved. Aside from the considerations and actions of a handful of people, Bill's life was devoid of any kindness or compassion. (pp. 165–166)

Early in 1983, at the age of 51, according to Klein and Strully (2000), Bill left the institution and moved into his own home in the community. With careful planning, he received the assistance he needed and became part of his community. He established relationships with his neighbors, was recognized as a citizen in his small town, became a volunteer for various community organizations, and voted in the local elections.

FROM MORON TO MENTALLY DEFICIENT

Bill's ability to achieve successful outcomes once he moved out of the institution illustrates that it was how disability continued to be understood that limited people with intellectual disability in this era, not their abilities. In the 1930s through the 1950s there was a subtle shift in how the construct of intellectual disability was understood. For much of the 30 years prior, the term *feebleminded* had been used, initially to refer to people with intellectual impairments who were the most capable and later to refer to the entire class of people with intellectual impairments, with subcategories of *idiot, imbecile,* and *moron* designating differences in level of intellectual ability. In June 1933, the American Association for the Study of the Feeble-Minded held its annual meeting in Boston. Founded in 1876 as the Association of Medical Officers of American Institutes for Idiotic and Feeble-Minded Persons, and now known as the American Association on Intellectual and Developmental Disabilities, the association was the principal home for professionals in the field and was (and remains) the most recognized body for defining the construct in the world. At the association's 57th meeting in Boston, the delegates adopted a proposal to change the association's name to the American Association on Mental Deficiency. In 1940, the name of the association's flagship research journal (now the *American Journal on Intellectual and Developmental Disabilities*) was changed from the *Journal of Psych-Asthenics* to the *American Journal on Mental Deficiency.*

With these changes, the field modified prior conceptualizations of the condition that emphasized a "weak mind" (e.g., psycho-asthenics, feebleminded) that had proliferated and it embraced the idea that the underlying problem identified by the construct was one of a defect within the mind, not just of a weak mind. The assumption was that to have a "mental deficiency" was to be "mentally defective." Though the term *mental deficiency* and its adjectival form *mentally defective* were prominently used, the field also used terms that were variations of the same underlying mechanism. The term *mental subnormality* was also used, suggesting that the nature of the "mental defect" was inferior mental performance, characterized by mental slowness, or mental retardation. The latter term, *mental retardation,* eventually adopted to replace the inevitably stigmatizing term *mental deficiency,* did not really herald a change in how the construct was understood, but instead, a refinement—to *have* mental retardation was to *be* defective. The locus of that defect was the mind. The term *mental,* which is common to all of these terms, means "of or pertaining to the mind." The nature of the "defect" of the mind (mental deficiency) was inferior mental performance (mental subnormality), characterized by mental slowness (mental retardation).

This shift toward a defect model also adopted a functional component, as is best illustrated by the inclusion of adaptive behavior in the definition. In 1941, Edgar Doll, considered the father of adaptive behavior, proposed six criteria for "mental deficiency":

1. Social incompetence;
2. due to mental subnormality;
3. which has been developmentally arrested;
4. which obtains at maturity;
5. is of constitutional origin; and
6. is essentially incurable.

In 1953, Doll operationalized his notion of social incompetence in the Vineland Social Maturity Scale, adopting the term *social maturity* to refer to items in nine domains: "1) communication skills; 2) general self-help ability; 3) locomotion skills; 4) occupation skills; 5) self-direction; 6) self-help eating; 7) self-help dressing; 8) self-help general; and 9) socialization skills". Doll's social maturity scale sought to measure behavior—what is now referred to as adaptive behavior—directly.

By the end of the 1950s, even as the term *mental deficiency* was being replaced by *mental retardation,* the idea that impairments in adaptive behavior were part of what should define the construct had taken hold permanently. The American Association on Mental Deficiency (AAMD) 1959 fifth manual on terminology and classification (see Figure 7.6) was notable for two reasons: it was the first to define the construct using the term *mental retardation* and it was the first to elevate adaptive behavior and development as elements of the definition. Mental retardation "refers to subaverage general intellectual functioning, which originates during the developmental period and is associated with impairment in one or more of the following: (1) maturation, (2) learning, and (3) social adjustment" (Heber, 1959, p. 3). The manual identified maturation, learning, and social adjustment as "aspects of adaptive behavior." A supplement to the 1959 manual, published two years later, simplified the issue by repeating the definition, verbatim, except replacing "in one or more of the following:" with "in adaptive behavior" (Heber, 1961, p. 3).

THE GREAT DEPRESSION AND
CHANGING INSTITUTION POPULATIONS

The economic hardship induced by the Great Depression affected institutions in the country, limiting resources and contributing to the growing population boom in these facilities, especially in institutions in the South. The Great Depression exacerbated the continuing conflict over the levels of patients admitted to Southern institutions as many families searched desperately for relief in handling children with more severe disabilities. In 1931, with the Depression in full force, the Georgia Department of

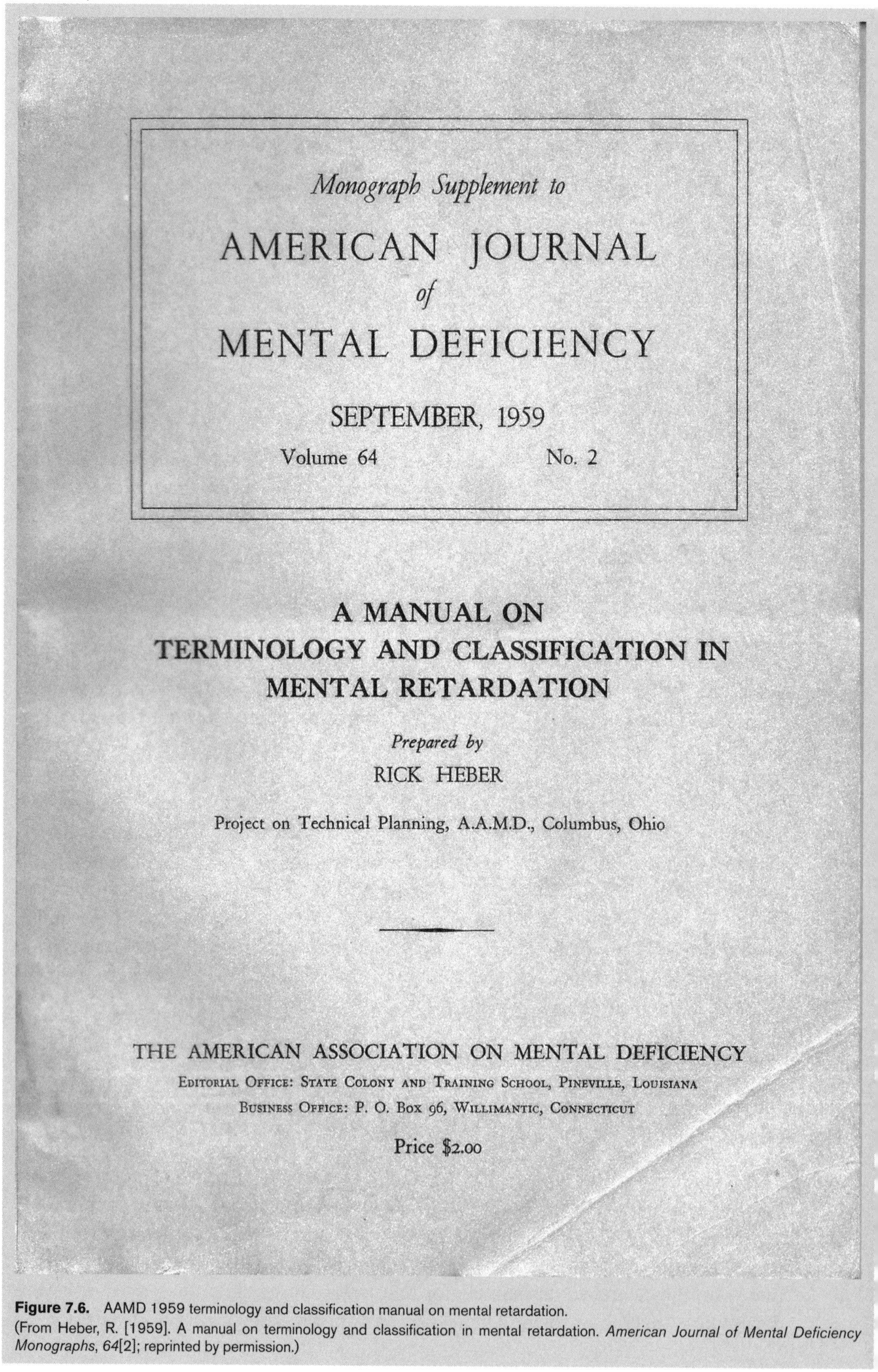

Monograph Supplement to

AMERICAN JOURNAL

of

MENTAL DEFICIENCY

SEPTEMBER, 1959

Volume 64   No. 2

A MANUAL ON
TERMINOLOGY AND CLASSIFICATION IN
MENTAL RETARDATION

Prepared by

RICK HEBER

Project on Technical Planning, A.A.M.D., Columbus, Ohio

THE AMERICAN ASSOCIATION ON MENTAL DEFICIENCY

EDITORIAL OFFICE: STATE COLONY AND TRAINING SCHOOL, PINEVILLE, LOUISIANA
BUSINESS OFFICE: P. O. BOX 96, WILLIMANTIC, CONNECTICUT

Price $2.00

Figure 7.6. AAMD 1959 terminology and classification manual on mental retardation.
(From Heber, R. [1959]. A manual on terminology and classification in mental retardation. *American Journal of Mental Deficiency Monographs*, 64[2]; reprinted by permission.)

Public Welfare reported that "the problem at present is accentuated by the economic depression; many families who in ordinary times are able to care for their own unfortunate children, find it difficult or impossible to do so now. Gracewood has functioned to the limit of its capacity" (Georgia State Department of Public Welfare, 1931, p. 36). The situation appeared as bleak in South Carolina, where the State Training School foundered as economic conditions worsened within the state: "The demands upon the Institution at this time are greater than ever," reported superintendent Whitten in 1931. "Many families are completely disorganized because of their inability to properly care for a defective child . . . when the economic condition is such that this necessarily places a very heavy burden upon them." Whitten ended by reemphasizing the gender-based notions of feeblemindedness that permeated the institutional thought of the time. "You can readily realize what a deplorable situation this is," he concluded, "particularly in the case of girls, who are being held solely to protect them from the depravities of mankind" (Whitten, 1931, pp. 7–8).

By forcing many families of marginal economic means to turn to the state for assistance, the depression accelerated the trend towards lower functioning patients in Southern institutions. A 1940 admission request to North Carolina's Caswell Training School epitomized the new type of patient crowding facilities during these tough economic times. A community social worker asked for admission for a 6-year-old boy "not only for his welfare but because of the effect . . . the strain and worry of having him in the home had on his mother. Constant anxiety is breaking down her health." Caswell's psychologist responded that "the above named child is obviously a very low-grade idiot and physically entirely incapacitated. Caswell Training School at the present has little room for patients of this type." In spite of this admonition, the institution accepted the boy and placed him "on the Junior ward," where he "seems happy and has made a good adjustment."[1] Figures from the Florida Farm Colony reflect that admissions of lower functioning individuals ("idiots") became more common during the depression era of the 1930s, reflecting the economic difficulties of families in providing care. Admissions of patients labeled as idiots jumped from 8.5% in 1928 to 31.5% in 1938.[2]

Institutional leaders quickly recognized the problems associated with this shift in patient demographics. The level of care at these facilities, which were never very high to begin with, devolved rapidly into custodial warehousing. In 1936, the superintendent of the Virginia State Colony announced that "there is little we can do for the idiots, except to feed them clothe them, and give them medical attention. The 'turnover' in the idiot class is only as great as the death rate" (Virginia State Colony, 1936, pp. 9–10). While contemporary Southern newspapers portrayed the "congenital idiot as lower than the lowest animal . . . a monster who should have never seen the light of day" ("Idiots, Imbeciles, and Morons," 1922), superintendents expressed their concerns about these patients in similar language. In his same 1936 report, the Virginia superintendent concluded that the "psychic trauma wrought upon the normal children in the family by an idiot sibling is incalculable. The typical idiot child gibbers, drools, utters the most animal-like sounds, and soils himself at convenience" (Virginia State Colony, 1936, p. 10). The increasing numbers of these low-level patients in Southern institutions brought into sharp focus the problems of small, underfunded facilities, caught between budgetary crises bought on by the depression, forcing the slashing of already-meager state expenditures, and the needs of relief for families from the dual burdens of the economic downturn and the presence of a child with severe disabilities.

The increasing numbers of lower functioning patients in state institutions strained slim resources to the breaking point. In 1933, the superintendent of the South Carolina Training School warned the public that "applications continue to come in with greater frequency and regularity." This occurred in spite of "the unbroken failure and neglect of the Legislature to provide an additional bed at this Institution during the past six years" (Whitten, 1933, p. 4). Overcrowded facilities and long waiting lists characterized Southern institutions during the depression years of the 1930s. Pushed on the one hand to admit more patients because of the dire economic conditions and prevented on the other from discharging large numbers of residents, superintendents often faced an unpleasant dilemma. The number of people waiting to enter the facilities was often higher than the institutional rolls. In 1935, Caswell Training School in North Carolina had a population of 621, while its waiting list numbered more than 800. Similarly, while 319 patients resided in Georgia's Gracewood facility in 1939, officials reported 375 individuals waiting to enter.

The overcrowding of Southern institutions, hastened by increasing admissions of low-level patients, led to dangerous conditions on the wards. In December 1939, a fire in the high-level boys' dormitory at Gracewood, the Georgia Training School, killed 6 of the 24 inmates housed there. As tragic as this was, the superintendent reported, "One can imagine what the loss of life would be if one of the frame buildings at Gracewood, now housing 130 low grade mental cases, some bedridden, should burn" (Georgia State Department of Public Welfare, 1939, p. 194). That same year, the superintendent of the Florida Farm Colony wrote that "the wards are so crowded we are having to place some of the patients on an open sleeping porch, during both summer and winter."[3] The pressures of long waiting lines and overcrowded facilities gradually filling up with low-functioning patients exasperated institutional leaders. "All the purposes of the school as laid down by the law creating the school," wrote a North Carolina official in 1936, "have never been attained in its [sic] fullest sense" (Caswell Training School, 1934–1936, p. 16). Florida Farm Colony superintendent Maxey Dell expressed this idea in more descriptive terms a year later when he wrote to a Pinellas County judge concerning that admission of another low-functioning patient. "We feel like a keg of powder," he warned, "waiting for someone to apply the match."[4]

In February 1935, 200 leading citizens of Augusta, Georgia, wrote an open letter to members of the Georgia state legislature supporting the call for eugenic sterilization of Georgia's feebleminded population. In the letter they asked, "How much of our money are you willing to contribute to the growth of a yearly increasing crop of half-wits?" They concluded by warning that "within the next hundred years, there will not be enough normal people to care for the sub-normal" ("Leading Augusta Citizens," 1935).

The sterilizing of people labeled as mentally deficient was, of course, well underway by then, having been endorsed as constitutional by the U.S. Supreme Court. In a rather perverse way, institutional leaders viewed the operations as beneficial to their patients. "Without sterilization we would not dare to have patients of both sexes dance together, view movies together, work and play together . . . because of eugenic sterilization we have been able to permit our patients to lead as normal lives as possible while institutionalized—to carry on reasonably normal social intercourse—all with benefit to them and to us" (Arnold, 1938–1939, p. 176). However, the main function of the procedure remained, in the words of a 1935 *Atlanta Constitution* editorial, "the recognized right of society to protect itself" ("The Feebleminded Menace," 1935). When Georgia passed its eugenic sterilization statute two years later, the paper praised the law as "a definite advance of modern civilization in the prevention of increase in insanity and crime" ("Sterilization Progress," 1937).

By 1940, ten Southern states operated 11 public institutions designed specifically to house individuals labeled as mentally deficient or feebleminded. These facilities cared for a multiplicity of individuals, from low-functioning "incompetent" idiots who required constant care and supervision to high-functioning "deviant" morons who needed vocational training and community instruction. Opened in a blush of Progressive era optimism about the efficacy of institutionalization, these facilities gradually (or in some cases quickly) devolved into custodial warehouses where maintenance rather than training became the watchword. "Our institution has become very largely a custodial one," a Florida Farm Colony report announced in the mid-1940s. "While this same situation appears to exist in varying degrees in all institutions of this type, it nevertheless creates a very real problem."[5]

The road to custodial care was neither straight nor well marked. The optimism that signaled the opening of Southern institutions seemed legitimate. Institutions, so the prevailing logic went, would protect both society and those individuals labeled as feebleminded. The marriage of state intervention and scientific practice, embedded in the institutional ideal, would solve the problems associated with the feebleminded menace to the benefit of all. Continuing the rhetoric of early 20th-century Progressive moralism, institutional advocates waxed poetic about the prospects of these new facilities. In 1915, Sarah Shaw, principal of North Carolina's newly opened Caswell Training School, addressed the state legislature, requesting an increase in funding for the institution. From Caswell, she reported, came "a cry, a weak, pitiful cry, a Macedonian cry, from hundreds of throats, begging that they may have a chance of a home and an opportunity to grow, both in body and soul."[6]

Whereas sympathetic observers such as Shaw viewed institutionalization as a benefit for all concerned, too often the opposite proved true. From the beginning, signs pointed to problems with the institutional solutions designed for individuals viewed as feebleminded. Among the most prominent was an inability to adequately define the condition of feeblemindedness. Even if institutional leaders cleared the definitional hurdle, they still faced the predicament of fitting their facilities within the spectrum of state services. Viewed by some state officials as prisons for low-functioning offenders, by others as training schools for retarded people to learn the life skills necessary for reintegration back into society, and by still others as permanent homes for those unable to function outside institution walls, institutions never managed to develop a coherent function. When combined with their *actual* function as a dumping ground for individuals with a myriad of problems, sometimes only peripherally related to mental deficiency, institutions often failed to help society or the patients.

Institutions did not exist in a social vacuum, of course. Decisions concerning location, staffing, funding, and control were often made with little concern for the patients admitted to these facilities. Local, state, and even national political considerations often impinged on the daily running of institutions. Superintendents walked a tight-rope between the internal needs of their facilities and the external demands of the wider world. Too often they subsumed patient needs to institutional political survival. Institutions proved susceptible to economic vagaries as well. The Great Depression had a devastating effect on state facilities, especially in the South, where state legislatures provided only a minimum amount of funding before the economic downturn. The crisis of the Great Depression forced states to slash even those meager budgets to a minimum, straining already overburdened facilities to the breaking point. It also destroyed the fabric of many families, forcing them to institutionalize family members previously cared for at home. The combination of reduced expenditures and increased admission pressures forced many institutions into custodial care.

Federal funding, usually allocated through New Deal public works programs, provided some relief from the problems caused by the Great Depression. These expenditures marked the beginning of federal intervention into the mental health field that would profoundly reshape the fiscal landscape of mental retardation by the 1960s. Many long-postponed large capital improvement projects were constructed under the auspices of the Works Progress Administration (WPA) and the Civil Works Administration. These allowed institutions to better serve their changing populations, since dormitory construction gave superintendents some flexibility in separating patients of differing mental levels, raising the possibility of better patient care. In 1935, for example, South Carolina administrators used Public Works Administration funding to build three new dormitories as well as a small hospital. Three years later, WPA monies were used to "develop an additional water supply, build a dormitory housing more than 90 individuals, construct an 11 room house for employees, and provide a recreational center consisting of a swimming pool, bath house, and park" (Whitten, 1967, pp. 94–95). These infusions of federal dollars, however, did not solve the underlying institutional problems. Superintendents still had to grapple with concerns about patient care and the ambiguous nature of feeblemindedness.

These problems existed nationwide in institutions; indeed, the pages of publications such as the *Journal of Psycho-Asthenics* during the 1930s are filled with the protestations of superintendents concerned about the fate of their facilities. Yet Southern institutions faced even greater challenges. They operated in a region that had little experience with institutional solutions to social problems. Legislatures created institutions, often with great publicity and fanfare, but rarely supplied the funds necessary to keep them operating in a position that would provide even a basic level of care to the patients housed there. More basically, even if legislatures had the foresight to allocate more funds for better institutional care, this money was simply not available in the poorest region of the country. The Great Depression forced Southern states to reduce already meager social welfare appropriations to miniscule levels.

A DESIRABLE PROGRAM . . .

In November 1930, President Herbert Hoover convened the White House Conference on Child Health and Protection to discuss issues affecting the lives of children. More than 3,000 experts and advocates in child health and welfare gathered in the nation's capital. The conference reports spanned 32 volumes, and among the notable outcomes

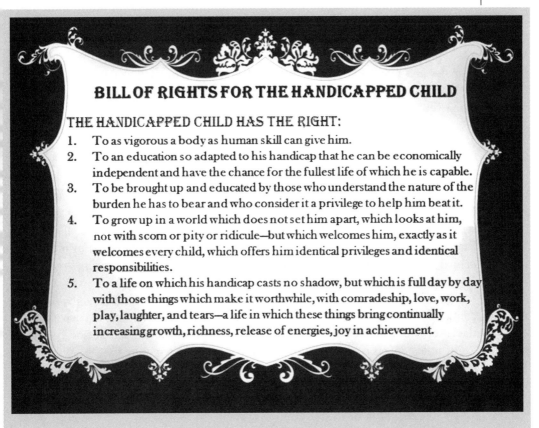

Figure 7.7.   Bill of Rights for the Handicapped Child issued by subcommittee on mental deficiency, 1930.

from the meeting were the establishment of a Children's Charter, containing 19 proposed requirements for children's education, health, welfare, and protection, and the creation of the American Pediatric Society. Vineland's Edward Johnstone chaired the subcommittee on mental deficiency, and their report was prefaced with the first Bill of Rights for the Handicapped Child (see Figure 7.7).

In its report, the subcommittee advanced the concept of "a desirable program" for the education of children with disabilities that included access to 1) identification and registration; 2) early diagnosis; 3) therapeutic prevention, including special classes and modified curricula, institutional care and training, and colonization and parole; 4) community supervision, vocational training follow-up, and supervision of home conditions and parental training; 5) sterilization; and 6) research.

If the juxtaposition of a bill of rights with the identification of access to sterilization as one of six elements of a desirable program of education for children with disabilities seems incongruous, it is illustrative of the relative ubiquity of the acceptance of involuntary, forced sterilization among professionals in the field of intellectual disability.

In 1921, people in institutions who had been forcibly sterilized in the United States totaled 3,233. By 1927, just prior to the *Buck v. Bell* decision (discussed in Chapter 6), the count stood at 8,515. That is in 20 years, from 1907 to 1927, approximately 8,500 inmates of institutions for the insane and the feebleminded and criminal penitentiaries were involuntarily sterilized. It took only five years after *Buck v. Bell* to double that 20-year mark, with 16,066 people forcibly sterilized by 1932; 27,869 by 1937; and 38,087 by 1941. Although before the Supreme Court ruling the proportions of males and females who were sterilized were approximately equal, after the ruling that ratio was almost 2 to 1, with twice as many women undergoing the operation than men (Reilly, 1992).

"Institutional reports," noted Philip Reilly in his book *The Surgical Solution: A History of Involuntary Sterilization in the United States*, "show that young women who were at most mildly retarded were often admitted for the sole purpose of being sterilized. Officials then discharged them, confident that they could not become pregnant" (Reilly, 1992, pp. 98–99). In large measure, Reilly argued, this was a result of the Great Depression. Prior to the market crash of 1929, the primary purpose of the forced sterilization programs was to prevent the birth of children with supposedly genetic-based and hereditary disorders. After the crash, the emphasis moved to preventing people who were thought to be unable or incapable of raising and caring for children from doing so, as a means to reduce the state's financial liability.

State-sanctioned sterilization programs reached their peak in the 1930s, but many continued into the 1940s and 1950s. It would be nice if the reduction in such efforts in the latter two decades was a function of moral and ethical changes in society, but as Reilly noted, it was as much a function of the fact that there were too few civilian physicians available during World War II. It is estimated that, during the 20th century, between 40,000 and 50,000 Americans who were deemed to be "feebleminded" were "involuntarily" (e.g., forcibly) sterilized.

. . . IT IS UP TO MY PEOPLE

After her sterilization shortly after the *Buck v. Bell* decision, Carrie was "paroled" from the Virginia State Colony and placed with a family in rural Bland County. She performed household chores as a condition of her release. She was later formally discharged from the institution. In 1932, she married a widowed carpenter who was also a deputy sheriff. They sang together in their church choir. He died in 1941 and she moved to Front Royal, Virginia, to be close to her sister. There she remarried and worked as a caretaker for elderly and ill people in their homes. The relatives of those she cared for refuted the diagnosis of feeblemindedness that had attributed to her. They described her as a capable and helpful woman whom they had trusted unconditionally with their loved ones.

Carrie died in 1983 in a nursing home in Waynesboro, Virginia. It is ironic that the woman who had been denied motherhood was asked to play the role of Mary in the District Home's Christmas pageant shortly before her death.

The practice of involuntary sterilization continued in Virginia until 1972, and the enabling statute remained in effect until 1974. In 2002, Governor Mark Warner issued a formal apology for Virginia's forced sterilization of thousands of its citizens. His statement coincided with the 75th anniversary of the Supreme Court decision that made Carrie Buck's sterilization legal. When her case was first heard in a circuit court, she was asked if she was worried about the prospect of having the sterilization surgery performed. Her reply in a typical Southern reference to family was that she was not concerned because "it is up to my people." Unfortunately, Carrie had no "people" who could protect her from the judgments that had already been made about her lack of value as a person.

Carrie had saved carefully and asked that she be buried in Oakwood Cemetery, in Charlottesville. Vivian, Carrie's supposedly feebleminded daughter from whom Carrie had been separated shortly after her birth, is buried on an adjacent hillside in the family plot. Vivian was an honor student when she died of complications of an infectious disease at age eight. "Three generations of imbeciles are enough" (*Buck v. Bell*, 1927), Oliver Wendell Holmes had arrogantly proclaimed to the nation. But, of course, that wasn't the case—it was three generations of injustice.

Although the Carrie Buck story illustrated the tragic human side of the hereditability issue, data on the first 1,000 patients sterilized at the Virginia State Colony showed that the matter was not easily resolved. Only 50% of these patients "had definite bad family histories (233 had one ancestor with mental defect, 267 had more than one)" (Arnold, 1937–1938, p. 60). That left the other 500 sterilized individuals, ostensibly operated on for eugenic reasons, with no hereditary history of intellectual disability. North Carolina went even further than Virginia in explicitly rejecting a strictly eugenic rationale for a procedure that was supposedly based entirely on hereditary reasoning. A 1936 state survey reported that "turning to the environmental viewpoint, we often find more reasons than appear from the standpoint of eugenics. A person with a mental age of 10 or less can scarcely be expected to be an adequate mother or father regardless of whether the offspring are normal, superior, or retarded." The survey continued stating concerns about the ability of individuals with intellectual disabilities to handle the responsibilities of parenthood. "If the early family life is as important as we think in shaping the personalities of children," it reported, "then mentally handicapped parents are a liability." This liability could be overcome by increasing the number of sterilizations of people labeled as feebleminded, regardless of the hereditary component. The survey concluded that "the Sterilization program of the state Eugenics Board should be continued . . . on a larger scale."[7]

If family history did not provide a reason for sterilizing all feebleminded individuals, then concerns about their moral character became increasingly important in the decision to sterilize. In December 1938, a Polk County, Florida, judge wrote to the superintendent of the Florida Farm Colony concerning a "white girl 15 years of age . . . known as a habitual sex delinquent . . . with an IQ of 51." The judge asked, "If I could send this girl to you after an adjudication of feeble-mindedness, could you have such an operation [sterilization] performed?" The superintendent replied, "It is not only justifiable but definitely indicated that she be sterilized." But he regretfully informed the judge that because Florida had not passed a sterilization statute, performing such an operation would place him "in position for severe criticism or criminal persecution."[8] These supposed histories of immorality and antisocial behavior often constituted the sole legal reasoning for the initiation of sterilization procedures. This belief dovetailed with concerns about the class-based nature of feeblemindedness. The report on the first 1,000 people sterilized in Virginia concluded that "812 came from families of the definitely lower class" (Arnold, 1937–1938, p. 61). A similar 1948 study of 48 sterilized women in North Carolina came to analogous conclusions.

"A predominance of un-educated low-income and highly fertile women" composed the sample (Woodside, 1950, p. 387).

In the years after *Buck v. Bell* upheld the constitutionality of eugenic sterilization, the procedure provided a negative alternative to institutionalization for many young Southern women labeled as feebleminded. Institution leaders seemed much more likely to initiate sterilization procedures on female patients than on males. Females represented 64.1% of the 24,957 officially reported procedures in the Unites States from 1907 to 1949. In Virginia and North Carolina, the two Southern states that sterilized the most patients, the figures are 60% and 80% females sterilized, respectively (Wellborn, 1940).

While the vast majority of sterilization procedures took place on institutionalized inmates, North Carolina's 1933 statute allowed for the operation to be conducted on people in the community upon the recommendation of county welfare agencies. This made North Carolina unique in that other state laws pertained only to institutionalized people, usually as a prerequisite for discharge. The sexual disparity appeared even more pronounced in North Carolina's non-institutional cases than in the rest of the south, with women constituting nearly 90% of the 229 people sterilized between 1933 and 1939 (Wellborn, 1940). In examining the implications of this wide disparity, Benson (1936) concluded that "we tolerate the actions of men where we do not tolerate similar actions in women" (p. 59). In his study of 19 extrainstitutional sterilizations from 1934 to 1936 (17 of which were performed on women), he reported that sexual delinquency was the major rationale for the procedure. One young woman, sterilized for sexual delinquency, was considered "very obviously a case for Caswell Training School, but authorities were unable to get her into the School" (Noll, 1995, p. 76). Another young woman, listed as poverty-stricken and afflicted with venereal disease, was sterilized for being "boy-crazy." The operation did little for that malady, "for she is as boy-crazy as she ever was. However," the report concluded, "she will not propagate her kind" (Noll, 1995, p. 76).

TIERGARTEN STRASSE #4

In 1932, the Third International Eugenics Congress was held in New York City. The eugenic sterilization movement had not run its course in America at the time of the Third International Congress—through the 1930s and 1940s the number of sterilizations mounted, particularly in California and Virginia—nevertheless, the movement's momentum was waning.

"In the United States," wrote medical historians Andre Sofair and Lauris Kaldjian (2000), "a combination of public unease, Roman Catholic opposition, federal democracy, judicial review, and critical scrutiny by the medical profession reversed the momentum of the eugenics movement" (p. 312).

Conditions in Germany had the opposite effect. Sofair and Kaldjian noted that "economic crisis, radical nationalism, Hitler's totalitarianism, and the medical professions willing participation and attraction to Nazism for financial and ideological reasons" swung the momentum the other way (Sofair & Kaldjian, 2000, p. 312). The "golden era of the forced sterilization of the helpless" began one year after the Third International Eugenics Congress when, in July 1933, Germany passed the Law for

Der jährliche Aufwand Deutschlands für

Erbkranke =

1200 Millionen RM für 880000 Erbkranke (1936)

713 Millionen RM

die Verwaltung { von Reich, Ländern u. Gemeinden

Figure 7.8. A 1938 propaganda poster stating that in 1936 the total cost of caring for 880,000 people with hereditary disease was 1,200 million Reichsmarks, which was almost double the 713 million Reichsmarks spent on the local, state, and federal German government.
(Image from 1938, provided by United States Holocaust Memorial Museum. © United States Holocaust Memorial Museum; reprinted by permission.)

Prevention of Offspring with Hereditary Defects Act (see Figure 7.8). The act legalized involuntary sterilization for people suffering from hereditary physical or mental diseases, including feeblemindedness. The Law for Prevention of Offspring with Hereditary Defects Act owed much to the work of American eugenicists (Sofair & Kaldjian, 2000, p. 312). It was, in essence, modeled after Harry Laughlin's (1922) sterilization law propagated in the work *Eugenical Sterilization in the United States* (Kuhl, 1994, p. 39).

The influence of the American eugenics movement began earlier than 1933, however, with its influence on Adolph Hitler (Smith & Wehmeyer, 2012). While in prison, from April to December 1924, Hitler wrote *Mein Kampf.* Among the books he read in the course of writing the book were eugenicist Madison Grant's *The Passing of the Great Race* and the two volume *Grundriss der menschlichen Erblichkeitslehre und Rassen-hygiene* [Foundation of Human Heredity and Race Hygiene], published in 1921 by German eugenicists Erwin Baur, Fritz Lenz, and Eugen Fischer. It is not surprising, then, that *Mein Kampf* incorporated the American eugenic dogma pertaining to sterilization.

"In *Mein Kampf*," Philip Reilly noted, "Hitler wrote: 'To prevent defective persons from reproducing equally defective offspring, is an act dictated by the clearest light of reason. Its carrying out is the most humane act of mankind. It would prevent the unmerited suffering of millions of persons, and, above all would, in the end, result in a steady increase in human welfare.' Perhaps the most striking aspect of these words is their similarity to those of Justice Oliver Wendell Holmes, who wrote the opinion in *Buck v. Bell*" (Reilly, 1991, p. 106).

The Law for Prevention of Offspring with Hereditary Defects Act went into effect on January 1, 1934. Its implementation relied on caregivers and medical personnel—mainly physicians, health care workers, and institution superintendents—to "denunciate" people suffering from one of the hereditary diseases. Denunciations were sent to hereditary health courts established by the law, consisting of three members: a judge, a physician from the public health services, and a physician knowledgeable about heredity. If the hereditary health court ruled in favor of sterilization, the operation was compulsory, even to the extent of having police use force to ensure compliance (Friedlander, 1995, pp. 26–27). "It is generally agreed that at least 300,000 persons were sterilized during the years preceding World War II" (Friedlander, 1995, p. 30), with more than half of those being people identified as feebleminded.

In August 1939, the German *Reichsministerium des Innern* [Reich Ministry of Interior] issued a decree requiring "midwifes and physicians to report all infants born with specified medical conditions," including idiocy and mongolism, microcephaly, hydrocephalus, and physical deformities, so as to evaluate whether an infant should be euthanized (Friedlander, 1995, p. 45). Informants were also to report children up to age three who had these conditions. The forms were turned into state and provincial health offices, which then transmitted them to a false governmental agency called the Reich Committee for the Scientific Registration of Severe Hereditary Ailments, or simply the Reich Committee. Functionaries there would pass forms on to three "experts;" physicians who based their decision to kill an infant or child exclusively on information from the form (Friedlander, 1995, p. 46).

To implement the killing program, the Reich Committee established wards at state hospitals and clinics; there were eventually 22 such wards (Friedlander, 1995, p. 46). Once a child was determined to be "defective" and targeted for the killing program, he or she was transferred to a nearby Reich Committee children's ward. If the child was in an institution or a hospital, the transfer was straightforward. There was no parental notification, no appeals, just the transfer of the sentenced child. If the child was at home, public health officers were sent to "persuade" the parents to release the child, though the program's real intent was strictly secret (Friedlander, 1995, p. 56). "Because many records of the killings have not survived," wrote Auschwitz survivor and genocide historian Henry Friedlander, "it is impossible to calculate the number of children killed in the children's wards during World War II. The best estimate is a total of at least 5,000 murdered children" (Friedlander, 1995, p. 61).

From infants and children, the systematic murder of Germans with disabilities moved to include adults in the summer of 1939. The offices of the adult killing program were housed at Villa Number 4 on Tiergarten Strasse, in Berlin, which had been confiscated from its previous Jewish owners. The adult killing program soon became known by the address of the headquarters, Tiergarten Strasse 4, or eventually, just T4.

On September 21, 1939, the Reich Ministry of Interior issued a decree requiring that all local governments provide a list of institutions for the feebleminded, insane, and epileptics by mid-October of that year. Thereafter, each institution individually received a questionnaire requesting information about the facility, including the number of patients and information about its proximity to transportation networks (Friedlander, 1995, p. 75).

In addition, each institution received a form to be completed about each of its inmates or patients who had been institutionalized for five years or more. The form, to be completed by a physician, was one page in length and required information about "name, date of birth, citizenship, race, length of time in institution, names of nearest relatives and whether they visited on a regular basis, name and address of guardian and of those responsible for payments, and whether the patient was committed as criminally insane" (Friedlander, 1995, p. 75).

The forms were to be returned, and then were submitted to a larger body of medical experts, who numbered up to 40 physicians, "including nine university professors of medicine" (Friedlander, 1995, p. 78). These medical professionals decided who, among the names submitted, would be killed. These names were sent to the T4 transport office, which handled the logistics of transporting the condemned to killing chambers. *Surrendering institutions,* the institution at which the patients had previously lived, were notified of the transfer and of the day and time a T4 vehicle would pick up the patients.

"All personnel reports and medical records had to accompany the patients," explained Friedlander. "Patients were to have pieces of tape with their names attached to their backs between the shoulder blades; sedatives were to be administered to disturbed patients" (Friedlander, 1995, p. 84).

"On the designated day," chronicled Friedlander, "Gekrat [the T4 transportation entity] arrived to move the patients in large gray buses . . . . The patients, who usually suspected their fate, often had to be coerced before they entered the notorious vehicles" (see Figure 7.9) (Friedlander, 1995, p. 84). Their families were told, simply, that their sons, daughters, husbands, and wives had been sent to another institution.

The people were bussed to one of six killing centers established by T4—Grafeneck. Brandenburg. Hartheim. Sonnenstein. Bernburg. Hadamar. Located in previously empty buildings, the centers were renovated to include examination rooms; autopsy rooms; administration, physician, and nursing offices; and a gas chamber and crematorium (Friedlander, 1995, p. 87).

"The gas chamber was constructed to resemble showers," Friedlander described the killing chamber in Brandenburg. "Three by five meters large and 3 meters high, it was paneled with ceramic tiles. Benches for the patients lined the walls. About 10 centimeters above the floor, a pipe with a circumference of about one inch ran along the wall; in this pipe there were small holes through which gas could enter the chamber" (Friedlander, 1995, p. 87). Showerheads were added to the room later to convince inmates they were entering a shower room.

The patients arrived at the killing center and were led to an examining room, where they were told to undress. Their clothes and their worldly possessions were labeled and numbered; each person was examined by a physician, a procedure absurdly said to be a "final safeguard against the possible errors made during the medical evaluation process" (Friedlander, 1995, p. 94).

Each person was assigned a number, which was stamped or taped on his or her body, then was photographed. In groups and still naked, the condemned were then led into the gas chamber. They were told they were to be bathed, but many knew their fate and had to be sedated or forcibly moved into the killing chamber.

Figure 7.9. Disabled prisoners at Buchenwald.
(Image from 1938, provided by United States Holocaust Memorial Museum courtesy of Robert A. Schmuhl. © United States Holocaust Memorial Museum; reprinted by permission.)

The door was closed and bolted, the gas valve turned on. Unconsciousness came in five minutes, though those five minutes were not pain free . . . victims gasped for air, screamed, collapsed and, eventually, sank into unconsciousness and, five minutes after that, death. Their bodies were dragged from the gas chambers, pronounced dead, then taken to the crematorium ovens. "The killing center thus, 'processed' living human beings into ashes in less than 24 hours" (Friedlander, 1995, p. 98).

It was the constant smoke bellowing from the crematorium chimneys and the smell from that smoke that gave the killing centers away for what they were. Hitler ordered the killing program to halt in August 1941. The public and clergy had begun to suspect what was really happening, and some among those protested. The decision to halt the program was based on concern about the impact of the killing program on the Nazi party's image.

From 1939 to 1941, 70,273 people were "disinfected," as the Nazis described the murders. The estimates of the number of Germans with disabilities murdered by their government—but also by the physicians, nurses, public health officials, and others responsible for the health and well-being of these vulnerable people—is estimated to be at 80,000.

THE CHILD WHO NEVER GREW

"I have been a long time making up my mind to write this story," began Pearl Buck in *The Child Who Never Grew.* "It is a true one, and that makes it hard to tell" (Buck, 1950, p. 5). A long time indeed. Until the publication of *The Child Who Never Grew* (see Figure 7.10), Buck actively concealed Carol's existence from the public (Finger & Christ, 2004). But tell it she did, and the impact was swift. Speaking a few years later

Figure 7.10. Excerpt of "The Child Who Never Grew." (Author's personal collection.)
(Image from author's personal collection. By Pearl S. Buck. Originally published in the May 1950 *Ladies' Home Journal*® Magazine.)

to a group of parents, Pearl Buck noted that she had received letters from parents and family members of children with disabilities from all over the world. One of those parents who read Buck's story was Dale Evans Rogers, whose own impact on the lives of children with intellectual disability would unfold in the coming decade.

Carol's birth and condition affected Buck's life as well, in ways that go beyond the requirement for caregiving, as documented by Finger and Christ (2004). In *The Good Earth* (Buck, 1931), which won the Pulitzer Prize and is Buck's best known book, the Chinese farmer who is the protagonist of the book has a daughter who has an intellectual impairment.

Besides *The Child Who Never Grew,* Buck discussed being the parent of a child with intellectual disability in 1954's semiautobiographical *My Several Worlds* (Finger & Christ, p. 53). In the clearly autobiographical novel *The Time is Noon*, published in 1967, the female lead character is the mother of a son with an intellectual disability. In addition to her support for the Vineland Training School, Buck became an active volunteer and spokesperson for National Association for Retarded Children (see Figure 7.11).

In 1965, Buck coauthored a book titled *The Gifts They Bring: Our Debt to the Mentally Retarded,* in which it is suggested that the gift "they" bring—*they* meaning children with intellectual disability—is love. Buck and her coauthor close the book with a story that speaks to Buck's own regret, perhaps, of institutionalizing Carol:

> And what folly to think that one can forget a child by putting him in an institution while he is a baby!

Figure 7.11. Pearl Buck also served as a spokesperson for the National Association for Retarded Children. (Image from author's personal collection.)

"Our doctor says it would be better for all of us if we put our mongoloid baby boy in an institution as soon as we leave the hospital," a father said. "But I wonder if he is right?" the mother added.

"We think you would be wrong," we replied. "You would rob your little boy of the early environment to which he is entitled since he was born into your family—yes, even as he is, it is still his right, for it was not his fault any more than it is yours that the chromosomes he inherited are in faulty arrangement. Yet he is not defective in every way. He can feel the warmth of your love, he can respond. He would know in his own fashion in the institution where you put him that something was lacking. It is love that would be lacking. He will be washed and fed and cared for, the necessities of physical life will be provided, but without love he will never reach his best." (Buck & Zarfoss, 1965, p. 147)

Carol Buck died in 1992, succumbing to lung cancer. She was buried at the Vineland Training School, her only home for more than 60 years (Finger & Christ, 2004, p. 51).

A SELF-MADE MAN

In 1994, Raymond Gagne, who at the time was a leader in the self-advocacy movement, wrote his autobiography titled *A Self-Made Man*. He begins his story talking about his life during the 1940s, during which time he lived at home, and into the 1950s, when he was moved to an institution.

My name is Raymond J. Gagne. This is my story about my life and why self-advocacy and self-determination are important to me. I was born on January 10, 1945. I am a person with cerebral palsy.

I lived with my mother, grandmother, uncle, two brothers, and a sister in a large house in Attleboro, Massachusetts. My mother felt there was something wrong with me. She took me to many doctors and hospitals to see if they knew how to help me. They told my mother I would never walk.

When I lived at home, I used to sit in a rocking chair next to a yellow window. I would sit there for hours watching people and cars go by. When my family went out, they put me in my baby carriage and usually included me in the activities. My brothers and sister went to school. At the time, there was no school for me. I stayed home with my grandmother, who took care of me. She had her hands full. I could not walk, talk, feed myself, or dress myself. She had to carry me upstairs each time I had to go to the bathroom. I crawled on the floor to get around.

When I was 8, my mother told me I was going away. She put my name on my clothes and packed my new suitcase. I remember the night before I left. I was bathed and my fingernails and toenails were cut. On February 19, 1953, two ladies picked my mother and me up for the drive to a state school. I didn't know where we were going. My mother had just told me I was going away and that I would be better off.

After arriving at the state school, I was put in Building 7. An orderly brought me to a ward. He put me in a bed and took all my clothes off. He put a johnny on me. My mother left, and I didn't see her any more that day. I was scared because I didn't know where I was or why I was there. I had arrived early in the afternoon. The rest of the day and night I was in bed. The bed was different from mine at home. The ward itself was drab. The windows were high with white shades. There were no curtains or decorations on the wall, not even a clock or calendars. There was a radio. The first song I heard was "Pretend You're Happy When You're Blue." It made me sad to hear it. I cried for 3 days.

Later, I was moved to Building 15. They put me on the floor. The other patients stepped all over me. I cried all day because I wanted to go back home. That evening they gave me a group bath with five other boys. The bathtub looked like a bird bath. There were water sprayers all around the inside of the bath. I was put to bed after the bath. At midnight, the attendants woke everybody up to go to the bathroom. I hated that, but I went. Every morning we would wake up at 6:00 a.m. An attendant would help me put on the clothes he had laid out the night before. I didn't have any say about what I wore. What they put on, I wore. Sometimes they wouldn't put underwear on me.

The first time I had a visitor was a month after being left at the state school. My mother came to visit me. I cried all the time she was there. I told her I wanted to go home. During this visit, she asked me about taking me home for a 1-day visit. When the visit was over and they got ready to take me back, I acted up. I hit and bit my mother. I also hid underneath the bed so she couldn't get me. She finally returned me to the state school.

As I look back on my childhood, I realize that I have been on my own since I was 8 years old. Some people would disagree and say that I was taken care of for many years. However, I felt as though I had no love or understanding from anyone.

That spring, I went to the dentist for the first time ever. The dentist pulled out eight teeth. He did not use any Novocain or any pain killers. I tried to be brave and not cry.

On Sunday afternoons in the summer, I used to spend the day lying on the floor of the ward waiting for company. No one ever came. Once I waited a full day for my mother to come and pick me up. I had to wait on a bench all day because the attendants didn't know when my mother was coming. During my visit, my grandmother fell down the steps and had to be hospitalized. A few days after I returned to the state school, my grandmother died. I wasn't told until Christmas day, 5 months later.

Looking back, I feel my strength and stubbornness helped me to survive these years of my life when I had so little control. Once I went to Building 5 and saw that people had more freedom there. I asked the staff if I could move to this building. In the new building, I could go to bed at 9:30. I never actually had my own personal bed. It made me think that, even in prison, you at least have your own cell. At the state school, I didn't have any living space of my own.

The staff who worked at the state institution were insensitive and cruel. There was one attendant who would take me to a back room and beat me up. Other times, he would hit me right in front of everybody. Another attendant hit the residents on the head with his keys.

The staff never seemed to prepare me for living outside the institution. They didn't seem to think I would make it on my own. I never had support, role models, or mentors to guide me in growing up. Very few of the staff ever assisted me in developing my identity, creativity, or self-esteem. (Gagne, 1994, pp. 327–330)

Ray Gagne titled this section of his autobiography "A Life of No Power: 18 Years in the Institution," an apt description of the lives of many people with intellectual disability in this era: powerless.

NOTES

1. All information is from files contained in Patient Record #2, Caswell Center Medical Department, Kinston, North Carolina.
2. Patient Admission forms, Vault files, Tacachale Community, Gainesville, Florida.
3. Dell to Board of Commissioners of State Institutions, May 6, 1939, Vault files, Tacachale Community, Gainesville, Florida.
4. Dell to Judge Jack White, Clearwater, Florida, January 29, 1937, Vault files, Tacachale Community, Gainesville, Florida.
5. Florida Farm Colony, 1943–1945, *Biennial Report,* 9.
6. C. Banks McNairy and Sarah Shaw, An Appeal to the Appropriations Committee of 1915 for the North Carolina School for the Feeble-Minded, Raleigh, North Carolina, February 12, 1915, North Carolina Collection, Wilson Library, University of North Carolina, Chapel Hill.
7. *A Study of Mental Health in North Carolina; A Report to the North Carolina Legislature of the Governor's Commission Appointed to Study the Care of the Insane and Mental Defectives* (Ann Arbor, MI: Edwards Brothers, 1937), 301, 364.
8. Judge Chester Wiggins to J. Maxey Dell, December 1, 1938 and Dell reply, December 3, 1938, Vault files, Tacachale Community, Gainesville, Florida.

REFERENCES

Arnold, G.B. (1937–1938). A brief review of the first thousand patients eugenically sterilized at the State Colony for Epileptics and Feeble-Minded. *Journal of Psycho-Asthenics, 43,* 60–61.

Arnold, G.B. (1938–1939). What eugenic sterilization has meant to the Virginia State Colony. *Journal of Psycho-Asthenics, 44,* 175–177.

Benson, J.M. (1936). *Sterilization, with special reference to Orange County, North Carolina.* Chapel Hill: University of North Carolina.

Buck, P. (1931). *The good earth.* New York, NY: John Day.

Buck, P. (1950). *The child who never grew.* New York, NY: John Day.

Buck, P., & Zarfoss, G.T. (1965). *The gifts they bring.* New York, NY: John Day.

Buck v. Bell, 274 U.S. 200 (1927).

Caswell Training School. (1934–1936). *Biennial report.* Kinston, NC: Author.

Doll, E.A. (1941). *The essentials of an inclusive concept of mental deficiency. American Journal of Mental Deficiency, 46.*

Doll, E.A. (1953). *The measurement of social competence: A manual for the Vineland Social Maturity Scale.* Minneapolis, MN: Educational Test Bureau, Educational Publishers.

The feebleminded menace. (1935, February 17). *Atlanta Constitution,* p. 12.

Finger, S., & Christ, S.E. (2004). Pearl S. Buck and phenylketonuria (PKU). *Journal of the History of the Neurosciences, 13,* 44–57.

Friedlander, H. (1995). *The origins of Nazi genocide: From euthanasia to the final solution.* Chapel Hill: The University of North Carolina Press.

Gagne, R. (1994). A self-made man. In V.J. Bradley, J.W. Ashbaugh, & B.C. Blaney (Eds.), *Creating individual supports for people with developmental disabilities* (pp. 327–334). Baltimore, MD: Paul H. Brookes Publishing Co.

Georgia State Department of Public Welfare. (1931). *Report for the years 1929, 1930, and 1931.* Atlanta: Georgia State Printing Office.

Georgia State Department of Public Welfare. (1939). *Official report, 1939.* Atlanta: Georgia State Printing Office.

Heber, R. (1959). A manual on terminology and classification in mental retardation. *American Journal of Mental Deficiency Monographs, 64* (2).

Heber, R. (1961). A manual on terminology and classification in mental retardation. *American Journal of Mental Deficiency Monographs, 64* (2, 2nd ed.).

Idiots, imbeciles, and morons at Caswell: Weeds grow rank in our garden, their spread threatens our state. (1922, December 10). *Greensboro Daily News,* p. 3.

Klein, J., & Strully, J.L. (2000). From unit D to the community: A dream to fulfill. In M.L. Wehmeyer & J.R. Patton (Eds.), *Mental retardation in the 21st century* (pp. 165–180). Austin, TX: PRO-ED.

Kuhl, S. (1994). *The Nazi connection: Eugenics, American racism, and German national socialism.* Oxford, United Kingdom: Oxford University Press.

Laughlin, H.H. (1922). *Eugenical sterilization in the United States.* Chicago, IL: Psychopathic Laboratory of the Municipal Court of Chicago.

Leading Augusta citizens urge passage of pending selective sterilization bill. (1935, February 17). *Atlanta Constitution,* p. 4.

Noll, S. (1995). *Feeble-minded in our midst: Institutions for the mentally retarded in the south 1900–1940.* Chapel Hill: University of North Carolina Press.

Reilly, P.R. (1992). *The surgical solution: A history of involuntary sterilization in the United States.* Baltimore, MD: The Johns Hopkins University Press.

Sofair, A.N., & Kaldjian, L.C. (2000). Eugenic sterilization and a qualified Nazi analogy: The United States and Germany, 1930–1945. *Annals of Internal Medicine, 132*(4), 312–319.

Smith, J.D., & Wehmeyer, M.L. (2012). *Good blood, bad blood: Science, nature, and the myth of the Kallikaks.* Washington, DC: American Association on Intellectual and Developmental Disabilities.

Sterilization progress. (1937, February 23). *Atlanta Constitution,* p. 7.

Trent, J.W. (1994). *Inventing the feeble mind: A history of mental retardation in the United States.* Berkeley: University of California Press

Virginia State Colony. (1936). *Annual report.* Lynchburg, VA: Author.

Wellborn, E. (1940). *Eugenical sterilization in the United States, with particular attention to a follow-up study of non-institutional cases in North Carolina, April 5, 1933 to January 1, 1939.* Chapel Hill: University of North Carolina.

Whitten, B. (1931). *Annual report.* Clinton: South Carolina Training School.

Whitten, B. (1933). *Annual report.* Clinton: South Carolina Training School.

Whitten, B. (1967). *A history of Whitten Village.* Clinton, SC: Jacobs Press.

Woodside, M. (1950). Social and legal aspects: Sexual and psychological adjustment after sterilization: A follow-up of 48 married sterilized women in North Carolina. *Obstetrical & Gynecological Survey, 5,* 387.

8

The Parent Movement

Late Modern Times
(1950 CE to 1980 CE)

Michael L. Wehmeyer and Robert L. Schalock

With the end of World War II, America emerged as an economic force, and parents of children with intellectual disability began to question the necessity of the options being provided to them by professionals. Concurrent with the scientific progress in eradicating diseases such as polio and tuberculosis, parents began to believe that there might be "help for the retarded" and that their sons and daughters might be cured and, if not cured, at least live with them and go to school like other children. The crown jewels of the parent movement's impact were the dramatic shift in institutional populations, which by the 1970s began rapidly declining and being replaced by community supports, and the passage of federal laws guaranteeing children with disabilities free access to public education. The term *mental retardation* replaced *mental deficiency*, and while the lives of many children with intellectual disability improved dramatically, the basic understanding of intellectual disability still emphasized charity and pity. The legislative protections and advances of the parent era provided a foundation for new ways of understanding disability and intellectual disability that were to emerge in the late 20th century.

---

*I*n September 1950, one month after the birth of her daughter Robin, Dale Evans read Pearl Buck's *The Child Who Never Grew,* excerpted in *Reader's Digest* (Trent, 1994). Evans was acutely interested in the story because Robin, the only biological child of American icons Roy Rogers and Dale Evans, had been born with Down syndrome.

Like virtually every family whose child was born with Down syndrome in 1950, the Rogerses were told to put the child in an institution. They rejected this advice and in doing so eventually helped to change what was expected for people with intellectual and developmental disabilities and their families.

In their era, Roy Rogers and Dale Evans were the most recognized movie and television couple in America, and maybe, in the world. In the 1940s and 1950s, Roy Rogers made as many as six movies a year that were seen by more than 80 million fans, more than half the population of the United States. By 1950, more than a thousand Roy Rogers fan clubs had sprung up around the world. The fan club in London, England, boasted a membership of 50,000 adoring aficionados of Roy and Trigger, his horse (Rogers, Evans, Stern, & Stern, 1994, p. iv). Beginning in 1951, *The Roy Rogers Show* captured the hearts of television-viewing Americans and made Roy, Trigger, Bullet (Roy's dog), and Dale television stars. The show aired 100 episodes before its final episode ran in 1957. In 1962 and 1963, Roy and Dale hosted *The Roy Rogers and Dale Evans Show,* a musical variety show that included guests such as Martha Raye, Cliff Robertson, as well as The Sons of the Pioneers—a country swing group that had been founded as a trio in the early 1930s by Bob Nolan, Tim Spencer, and Leonard Slye, the latter of whom would adopt the stage name Roy Rogers, eventually making The Sons of the Pioneers his permanent band. Roy, Dale, and The Sons of the Pioneers recorded more than 400 songs and spoken-word recordings together or separately. Fans fondly remember their images on lunch boxes and the resonate sounds of their theme song, *Happy Trails to You,* written by Dale and sung at the end of all of their performances.

"Roy Rogers and Dale Evans were simply the most popular cowboy and cowgirl the world has ever known," wrote Jane and Michael Stern in their foreword to the Rogerses autobiography, *Happy Trails to You, Our Life Story*:

> Their West was a magical American landscape full of promise and hope in which goodness was always rewarded and bad guys always got what they deserved. They reigned at a time when the cowboy ideal seemed to signify everything decent about a nation in which all things were possible if you were a good guy with a solid handshake and a sense of honor. They were, in the words of H. Allen Smith, "purity rampant" at a time when we Americans wanted heroes pure and yearned to believe that dreams come true. They fought fair and didn't swear or even grumble when the going got tough. The adventures they had were thrilling and fun and wholesome, filled with rollicking songs, mile-a-minute horse chases, and a dash of fresh romance

(but not too much mushy stuff). Whatever trouble came along, you knew that Roy and Dale could handle it—with skill and certainty, good humor, and grace. (Rogers et al., 1994, p. iv)

"This is the story of what a baby girl named Robin Elizabeth accomplished in transforming the lives of the Roy Rogers family," wrote Dale Evans (1953) in the foreword to *Angel Unaware* (see Figure 8.1), the book she wrote about Robin's short life. "At year's end," observed historian James Trent, "only two other books that year had sold more copies, the *Revised Standard Version of the Bible* and the *Power of Positive Thinking*" (Trent, 1994, p. 234).

Angel Unaware was the vehicle by which Dale Evans worked through the grief accompanying her daughter's death, at the age of two, from mumps and encephalitis (Trent, 1994, p. 235). She began writing the book on August 26, 1952, the day of Robin's funeral and, the day that would have been her second birthday (Garrison, 1956, p. 13). *Angel* was written as a conversation between Robin and God. Its saccharine prose hides the radically new way in which intellectual and developmental disability was portrayed; the overtly Christian message overlies, and to some degree disguises, what was becoming a secular 1950s message about hope, possibility, and potential for children with disabilities.

The message about intellectual disability conveyed during most of the first half of the 20th century was crafted by eugenicists and professionals; a message

Figure 8.1. Dust jacket cover from *Angel Unaware*, by Dale Evans Rogers.
(Image from author's personal collection. From Rogers, D.E. [1953]. *Angel unaware*. New York, NY: Revell.)

intended to solidify the role of professionals in the diagnosis and treatment of people with disabilities—a role justified by society's putative needs and, eventually, ratified by the public's acceptance. That message was conveyed in the terms used to describe people who were different: *moron, criminal imbecile, menace,* and *degenerate.*

Dale Evans delivered a very different message in *Angel Unaware.* Her message was targeted not to the professionals who had made decisions to that point but to the parents of other children like Robin. At the heart of that message was the notion that Robin, and children like Robin, were God's gifts to parents and families and to society, and that such children should be accepted and loved . . . at home.

Figure 8.2. Dale Evans Rogers and Roy Rogers. (Image from author's personal collection.)

In *Angel Unaware*, Dale Evans uses Robin's perspective in the third person to talk about Robin's impact on Dale's life. Robin has observations about the medical profession's insistence that she be put in an institution, how a "mongoloid" baby could not live in a typical home, and other standard medical opinions of the day.

> Mommy asked [the doctor] what she and Daddy should do. What did anybody do with a Mongoloid baby? Doctor said gently that there wasn't much anyone could do; the few institutions for such babies were over-crowded, and the State homes and hospitals wouldn't take in "one of these children" until he was four years old. Then he said something fine: "Take her home and love her. Love will help more than anything else in a situation like this—more than all the hospitals, and all the medical science in the world." (Rogers, 1953, p. 15)

In *Angel Unaware,* Dale Evans Rogers addressed the universal and most difficult question faced by any parent whose child experiences illness or disability—*Why?*

Like parents of all ages, Dale and Roy sought the reasons that their daughter was so different. Dale Evans, at times, attributed Robin's presence in their life as part of a divine plan to have the Rogers family reach out to other families with children like Robin. Other times, Dale Evans worried that Robin's disability was a punishment for past sins. Ultimately, for Dale Evans, the answer to the question *Why?* was simply that it was part of a divine plan, and that her role was to be faithful. Just before Robin turned one, she was diagnosed with a heart problem, not uncommon for children with Down syndrome. A leading pediatrician advised Roy and Dale to put Robin in an institution. But Dale remained faithful to the divine plan. *Angel* provided a checklist for others to respond to that plan:

- First, parents should just trust.

- Second, parents should just love: "They loved me, all of them, and maybe when I laughed it was in joy and thankfulness for their love. They weren't ashamed of their little 'borderline' Mongoloid!" (Rogers, 1953, p. 25–26).

- Third, parents should just learn, essentially, that all people matter and that children with disabilities belong with their families.

Before her second birthday, Robin came down with the mumps, and as her temperature escalated and encephalitis developed, the medical doctors attending to her told Roy and Dale that she was near death. "He told Mommy that she and Daddy had done the right thing in keeping me at home, loving me like they had. His own wife was going to have a little baby soon, he said, and if it were a baby like me, he would do the same thing" (Rogers, 1953, p. 60).

The Child Who Never Grew and *Angel Unaware* promoted the idea that having a child with a disability was no longer simply a failing on the part of the parent or, as proclaimed by eugenicists, a direct result of the parents' degeneracy and heredity. What is more important, these visible women gave parents of children with disabilities permission to do one thing that all parents want to do: be proud of their child. Disability scholar Dick Sobsey (2001), who is also the parent of a child with a disability, wrote the following:

> For me and thousands of other people like me . . . Dale's greatest contribution wasn't her songs, or singing voice, or those old shows, although I liked them all a lot, too, Dale touched our lives in a much more important way because we were parents of kids with developmental disabilities. A lot of us believe that Dale Evans set us free.
>
> As much as the lives of the Roy Roger's family were transformed by Robin Elizabeth, Dale's book transformed a lot of other families. For some of those folks, that transformation might have been spiritual like it was for Dale, for others it was just down to earth. For all of us who are parents to kids with serious disabilities, however, Dale's work made a difference in how we fit into the world even for those who don't realize it.
>
> For me, the important thing is that Dale Evans made being the parent of a child with a disability something to be proud of and I am extremely grateful for that. When Dale Evans had the strength of character to speak proudly of having a child with a developmental disability, she blazed a trail through a frightening wilderness for other parents. (Sobsey, 2001, pp. 402–403)

"I want to thank you personally for your book, *Angel Unaware*," began one of the thousands of letters Dale Evans received, and answered, after the publication of *Angel*. "I have just read it for the third time. It helps to make easier the painful ordeal." "I am so glad you had the courage to admit your child Robin was a handicap Angel," wrote another mother, as I am sure she has a special place in God's heaven. My Son Joe is a Mongaloid [*sic*] of 13 yrs. Now, and you are an inspiration to the Mothers and Fathers of the world who have children like ourse [*sic*], people all over the world will stare and talk. Joe goes to School and is learning to write and read, he is able to do lots of things for himself and it makes me so proud of him and I thank you again for Writing [*sic*] the book.

    P.S. I can hold my hed [*sic*] up a little bit higer [*sic*] to know someone like you is helping our kids. (Sometimes it does droop a bit). (Garrison, 1956, pp. 123–124)

EXPERIMENTAL SUBJECTS UNAWARE

Why did parents of children with disabilities such as Dale Evans in the late 1940s and 1950s begin to challenge the system and to question professionals about what was best for their children, while parents in the 1920s and 1930s accepted that segregation and, to a lesser extent, sterilization were best for their sons and daughters? What had changed in the intervening years?

For one, the conditions in institutions had deteriorated to such an extent that they engendered media exposure and became the target of social reformers. The overpopulation that began earlier in the century had long since created institutions that were, at best, warehouses of unfortunate humanity. The available workforce had been seriously depleted by the war; the institutions were understaffed and inmates assumed a greater share of the burden for caregiving and facility upkeep. Postwar exposés of these conditions focused the nation's attention on the situation (Trent, 1994, p. 237).

In 1950, when *The Child Who Never Grew* was published, 124,304 people lived in large, state-run institutions for "the mentally retarded." The institution census peaked in 1967 at 194,650 people. The census fell below 100,000 by 1988, and as of 2005 was down to 40,532 people residing in state-run institutions for people with intellectual and developmental disabilities. Simultaneously, the number of smaller, community-based residential settings skyrocketed. By 1977, the number of people with intellectual and developmental disabilities living in state-funded or private community-based residences with six or fewer people totaled 20,400. By 1992 that number had risen to 119,675 and by 2005 by slightly less than 300,000 people. An additional 50,000 people lived in slightly larger community residences supporting 7–15 people (Prouty, Smith, & Lakin, 2006). As more options for living in the community became available, more families sought them rather than the dehumanizing conditions brought about by institutional settings.

Science also had a role in the changing trend toward deinstitutionalization. After World War II, the accumulation of scientific advances that had begun in many cases in the 19th century culminated in stunning reversals in the course of several epidemic diseases—tuberculosis and polio, most notably. The bacterium causing tuberculosis, *Mycobacterium tuberculosis,* had been identified in 1882 by Robert Koch, and a viable vaccine had been developed as early as 1921 by French bacteriologists Albert Calmette and Camille Guerin, but the vaccine's wide adoption in the United States didn't occur until after World War II. Furthermore, the discovery in 1943 of the antibiotic streptomycin and its application to treat cases of tuberculosis resulted in the near elimination of the disease, at least in North America.

The discovery of a polio vaccine by Jonas Salk in 1952, and its implementation nationwide in 1962, similarly affected the incidence of that disease, which had so frightened baby-boomer parents. These conquests seemed to signal that, with science, all things were possible.

Finally, the war created a new awareness of disability. Of the hundreds of thousands of returning service people, thousands had physical and other disabilities caused by the war. Disabled World War II veterans, such as future Senate Majority Leader and presidential candidate Robert Dole, held the country to its moral obligation to provide support for their reintegration into American life. One legacy of the World War I had been the Soldier's Rehabilitation Act, which had provided employment rehabilitation and retraining services for American soldiers injured in "the war to end all wars." In 1920, a civilian version of the Rehabilitation Act was established, and in 1935 that act became permanent as part of the Social Security Act. In 1943, people with intellectual disability and mental illness were added as eligible classes under the Rehabilitation Act.

With the 1954 expansion of the Rehabilitation Act, the federal presence in disability rehabilitation became a true force. Propelled by the high number of disabled veterans entering the system and by the advances that such large populations bring in terms of innovation in rehabilitation and treatment, disability joined tuberculosis and polio as something that, potentially, could be defeated by science.

These legislative and scientific changes were not, however, good for all people with intellectual and developmental disabilities. Along with the growing trend toward community-based supports and the steady decrease in the national institution census, the treatment of people with intellectual impairments as something less than humane continued.

Most notorious, perhaps, was the use of inmates from the Walter E. Fernald State School in experiments to examine the absorption of calcium and iron. In the late 1940s and early 1950s, some of the inmates at the Fernald School were recruited to join a science club, which offered them larger food portions, parties, and trips outside the institution. These science club members were given iron-enriched cereals and calcium-enriched milk for breakfast, and then given, either orally or intravenously, radioactive calcium tracers to track absorption. The inmates, all boys, had never been told that they were eating oatmeal contaminated with radiated milk (D'Antonio, 2004).

Frederick L. "Freddie" Boyce was one of the inmates who involuntarily participated in the Fernald experiments. Years later, in 1994, testifying at a hearing before a congressional inquiry into the episode, Boyce explained, "We didn't commit any crimes. We were just 7-year-old orphans." "You really feel like you must have been someone really insignificant" (D'Antonio, 2004, p. 57), Boyce told *Newsday* reporter Michael D'Antonio, in a 2004 interview. "I mean, if they could do that to you, and nobody said anything, then how were you any more important than a bug or rat in a laboratory" (D'Antonio, 2004, p. 57).

In a similar instance in 1951, researchers subjected a live virus polio vaccine to 20 children with intellectual disability, again without their knowledge or their parents' consent (see Figure 8.3). Finally, at the Willowbrook State School on Long Island, New York, researchers in the 1950s and 1960s infected inmates with the

MENTAL RETARDATION   VOLUME 39, NUMBER 5: 405–409 | OCTOBER 2001

Sacrifices for the Miracle: The Polio Vaccine Research and Children With Mental Retardation

J. David Smith and Alison L. Mitchell

The classic fairy tales of Hans Christian Anderson and the Brothers Grimm are testaments to the enduring fascinations and fears that children have shared across the generations. The Grimm's "Hansel and Gretel" and "Cinderella" and Anderson's "Ugly Ducking" and "The Emperor's New Clothes" continue to entertain children and to reassure them of the ultimate conquest of good over evil. There are other joys and anxieties of childhood, however, that are more generation-specific. For the children of the 1990s, for example, school violence and the horror of AIDS had an impact unimaginable to previous generations. The decade of the 1950s, on the contrary, is often portrayed as a period of idyllic childhood. What is forgotten in the nostalgic accounts of this period, however, is that along with Davey Crocket and coonskin caps, the children of the 1950s were taught to crouch under school desks in case of a Russian nuclear attack. Another nightmare for the children of that generation was polio.

Polio, commonly called infantile paralysis because it most frequently affected children, reached epidemic proportions in the early 1950s. This viral disease paralyzed and killed thousands of children each year. Images of patients and the "iron lungs" used to enable them to breathe terrified both children and their parents. Although the means by which the disease was transmitted was uncertain, swimming pools were closed, public gatherings were avoided, and school cancellations were common during the worst outbreaks (Klein, 1972).

Then, in early April 1955, newspaper headlines announced that a safe and effective polio vaccine had been developed by Dr. Jonas Salk. Before the end of that month, thousands of children were vaccinated against polio. By 1961, an oral vaccine for polio had been developed by Dr. Albert Sabin. In 1971, only one case of polio was documented in the United States (Chase, 1982).

Polio: Memories of the Senior Author

My personal reflections on the terrors of polio are embodied in three waves of thoughts and feelings. My first memory is of the death of a boy in my neighborhood. News that Billy had polio came as a shock to the community. He died within days. My parents' fears could not be concealed even from a 6-year-old. I accepted their restrictions willingly and played alone in my own backyard. I was terrified.

My second recollection is of standing in line for my first polio shot. I watched as some of my friends and classmates were inoculated, dreading my turn. That scene was to be repeated twice before the series of vaccinations was complete. The next time I was vaccinated was as an adult, this time with the Sabin technique. The sugar cube with a dot of vaccine was much more pleasant than the needle.

My final reflection on polio concerns the role of people with mental retardation in the development of the polio vaccine. I have only recently become aware of their largely involuntary and exploitive participation in the research that led to the availability of the vaccine. For my childhood peers and myself, the eradication of polio was a miracle. For people with mental retardation and their advocates, the development of the vaccine is a disturbing saga. It is also a testament to the degree to which the lives of people with mental retardation were devalued through most of the last century. Reviewing the story may encourage us to think carefully as we look at the meaning of their lives in the new century.

The Salk Vaccine and "Institutionalized" Research

Vaccination is accomplished by introducing a tiny amount of a virus into the body of the vaccinee. The immune system of the vaccinated person

Figure 8.3. "Sacrifices for the Miracle: The Polio Vaccine Research and Children with Mental Retardation."
(From Smith, J.D., & Mitchell, A.L. [2001]. Sacrifices for the miracle: The polio vaccine research and children with mental retardation. *Mental Retardation, 39*[5], 405–409; reprinted by permission.)

MENTAL RETARDATION   VOLUME 39, NUMBER 5: 405–409 | OCTOBER 2001
Perspective: Polio vaccine miracle   J. D. Smith and A. L. Mitchell

responds by producing antibodies. The vaccinee is thus protected against the "wild" form of the virus and the disease it causes. Vaccines may be created with either a weakened live virus or a dead virus. In general, both weakened and dead viruses produce antibodies but not the disease. Given the unique characteristics of a particular disease, however, either a live or a dead virus vaccine may not prove to be preventative. More important, some vaccines may actually produce the disease that is being targeted for immunity. Research and trials are important, therefore, in producing a safe yet effective vaccine (Hooper, 1999).

Medical research is usually an evolutionary process. The work of one scientist provides a platform or stimulus for the research of the next. One of the pioneers in polio vaccine research was Howard Howe of Johns Hopkins University. In 1952, Howe produced a polio vaccine using a dead virus that he tested on chimpanzees. It seemed to be safe and to produce antibodies against polio. Howe then tested the vaccine on children at the Rosewood Training School in Owings Mills, Maryland. He described these children as "low grade idiots or imbeciles with congenital hydrocephalus, microcephaly, or cerebral palsy" (Howe, 1952, p. 265). In reporting on the response to the vaccine, Howe wrote, "Both children under five years of age and chimpanzees develop readily demonstrative neutralizing antibodies . . . following the injection of small quantities of . . . formalin inactivated poliomyelitis virus" (p. 275).

Jonas Salk may have been inspired or nudged by Howe's work to move ahead more quickly with his own work on a vaccine for polio. He might also have been influenced by Howe's research in his selection of subjects for trial vaccinations. Salk had tried his vaccine earlier on animals, and it appeared to be safe and effective. In a 1952 article, he described testing his vaccine at the D.T. Watson Home for Crippled Children in Pennsylvania. Some of the children he vaccinated had already been disabled by polio and, therefore, had some level of immunity. Others had no immunity at all to the disease. In both groups, Salk found that his vaccine promoted the development of antibodies (Chase, 1982).

Salk continued his research at the Polk State School in Pennsylvania, where he vaccinated institutionalized children. The antibody production stimulated by the vaccine in this group was also encouraging. He was relieved by the fact that none of the children contracted polio, a risk associated with the vaccine because some undetectable amount of virus might not have been killed. Salk was quoted as saying, "When you inoculate children with polio vaccine, you don't sleep well for two or three months" (Chase, 1982, p. 296).

Feeding Live Polio Virus to Children With Mental Retardation

The fact that children and adults with mental retardation were the subjects of choice for medical research at the time of Salk's work on polio is made even more clear through the trials that led to the development of a live virus vaccine. Although the name of Albert Sabin is most often associated with this vaccine, a number of scientists were involved in its development. In fact, a competition developed between researchers for the discovery of the most reliable and effective oral vaccine. Sabin won the competition, but the race could have been won by Hilary Koprowski.

The quest for a reliable live virus vaccine was stimulated by two factors. One, a live virus vaccine could be administered orally rather than being injected. This would make it less expensive and easier to immunize large numbers of people. Second, Salk's dead virus vaccine had not proven to be as effective as originally thought. There were cases where the dead virus did not create immunity. There were also cases where the techniques for killing the virus had not been totally effective. Live virus that remained in the vaccine in these cases had caused polio in some of the people injected with it.

Like Salk and Sabin, H. Koprowski had set out on a personal mission to eradicate polio. Even before the successful development of Salk's vaccine, Koprowski was testing weakened, but live, strains of polio virus. Although he tested the vaccine in monkeys, Koprowski revealed at a 1951 meeting that he had administered a live virus polio vaccine to human subjects.

In his report of feeding the virus to 20 children with mental retardation at Letchworth Village in New York, H. Koprowski, Norton, and Jervis (1952) explained that this decision to administer the virus to humans for the first time was based on

gaps in knowledge concerning the mechanisms of infection and immunity in poliomyelitis . . . due to the fact that, as far as is known, human beings have never been exposed to actual administrations of living poliomyelitis virus for clinical trial purposes (p. 108).

(continued)

Figure 8.3. *(continued)*

MENTAL RETARDATION   VOLUME 39, NUMBER 5: 405–409 | OCTOBER 2001

Perspective: Polio vaccine miracle   J. D. Smith and A. L. Mitchell

Klein (1972) reported in his description of the trial of the vaccine that H. Koprowski requested permission of the New York State Department of Health to test it on the children at Letchworth. In fact, Koprowski did *not* request permission. In her later account of the trials, I. Koprowski (1997) provided her husband's recollections:

I realized then that I would never get official permission from the State of New York. Therefore, we asked permission from the parents of those children. The parents gave us permission to feed vaccine to their children. On February 17, 1950, the first human subject was immunized with poliomyelitis virus by drinking an emulsion. (p. 298)

Koprowski described the vaccinees at Letchworth Village as "volunteers." In fact, "Volunteer No. 1" was a 6-year-old boy with severe disabilities who had to be fed the vaccine through a stomach tube. The other 19 "volunteers" had similar multiple disabilities. There was no mention in the original report of parental permission having been sought or granted (H. Koprowski et al., 1952).

Fortunately, none of the children at Letchworth developed polio from swallowing the live virus vaccine. Koprowski reported that they all developed antibodies. It is clear, however, that he gambled with the lives of those children. The vaccine strand had been problematic in tests with monkeys. In those earlier trials, in fact, half of the subjects were paralyzed and a quarter died (Hooper, 1999).

In discussing his memories of the meeting where he had first disclosed his Letchworth Village research, H. Koprowski referred to Albert Sabin's reaction:

Sabin was quite vociferous at the meeting. . . . he questioned my daring. How did I dare to feed children live polio virus. I replied that somebody had to take this step. Well, he turned round and round saying, "How do you dare to use live virus on children? You are not sure about this, you are not sure about that, you may have caused an epidemic. (I. Koprowski, 1997, p. 299)

Koprowski was also criticized in the medical journal *Lancet* for the lack of evidence that he had obtained the informed consent of his subjects.

Koprowski et al. [1952] tell us in a footnote that for obvious reasons the age, sex, and physical status of each volunteer are not mentioned. The reasons must be more obvious to the authors than to the readers, who can only guess, from the methods used for feeding the virus, that the volunteers were very young and that the volunteering was done by their parents. One of the reasons for the richness of the English language is that the meaning of some words is continually changing. Such a word is "volunteer." We may yet read in a scientific journal that an experiment was carried out with 20 volunteer mice, and that 20 other mice volunteered as controls. (Poliomyelitis, 1952, p. 552)

This criticism, however, does not seem to have deterred Koprowski. Subsequent investigations of the records from a conference on the "Biology of Poliomyelitis" indicate that several further trials of live virus vaccine were very likely conducted at Letchworth but were not published in the mainstream medical literature (Hooper, 1999).

Koprowski and the Children of Sonoma

It is certain, however, that Koprowski conducted his vaccine research on children with mental retardation elsewhere. In July 1952, Koprowski tested his oral vaccine on 61 children at Sonoma State Hospital in California: All of them had mental retardation as their primary diagnosis. The children ranged in age from 8 months to 8 years. This time Koprowski made certain that he had formal permission to conduct his research. With the help of physicians at Sonoma, the appropriate clearance was swiftly obtained from California authorities. The trial was considered a success when 52 of the 61 children showed an increase in antibody levels to polio.

In the course of the vaccine research, Koprowski and his colleagues (H. Koprowski et al., 1956) conducted another study. This experiment is particularly revealing of the attitudes toward children with mental retardation that were prevalent during the research. Koprowski reported that a group of 6 children who had been fed the vaccine were, as a result, excreting virus in their stools. He described them as being kept "in very intimate contact" with another 8 children who lacked antibodies. In fact, the children (who were incontinent) were allowed to play together 3 hours a day on a plastic mat, which, although washed down to remove gross soils, was deliberately not disinfected. In the course of this experiment, 3 of the unvaccinated children became infected with the virus. None of the nurses, however, developed antibodies. Koprowski reasoned that the nurses caring for the children took precautions against infection, wearing protective clothing and washing their hands after every contact with a child. He also concluded that the vaccine virus was not contagious "when the principles of simple personal hygiene are practiced" (p. 959). Again, the disregard for the children as human beings is evident in this report.

Koprowski continued his research on institu-

MENTAL RETARDATION   VOLUME 39, NUMBER 5: 405–409 | OCTOBER 2001

Perspective: Polio vaccine miracle   J. D. Smith and A. L. Mitchell

tionalized populations, including other children with mental retardation and the infants of female prison inmates for several years. In 1957 and 1958, he enlarged his research to include thousands of children in Africa and Russia. His vaccine fell into disfavor, however, when polio cases in Northern Ireland were linked to his research there. Ultimately, Albert Sabin would win the oral vaccine race, and his form of live virus was adopted for use in the United States (Rogers, 1992).

Research and Mental Retardation: Other Cases

As disturbing as the history of the polio vaccine trials are, there are other examples of children and adults with mental retardation being used as devalued subjects in medical research. During the 1940s and through the 1950s, children and adults with mental retardation at Fernald State School were used in a scientific study conducted by the Massachusetts Institute of Technology on the nutritional effects of ingesting radioactive iron. Children who received permission from their parents to join the "Science Club" were fed oatmeal laced with the radiated metal (Higgins, 1998). From 1946 to 1952, over 125 children were exposed to radiation at the Fernald School in this manner (Allen, 1993a).

The Willowbrook State School was another setting in which the questionable use of persons with mental retardation in medical research occurred. The researchers who carried out the Willowbrook studies, conducted from the 1950s to the 1970s, sought to identify a vaccine for hepatitis. A research team systematically infected residents with varying strands of hepatitis, knowing that those children would develop the infectious disease (Grodin & Glantz, 1994).

The value placed on people with mental retardation by some researchers is evident in their choice of human subjects rather than animals. According to the Humane Society, institutionalized children have been used for research purposes because they are "cheaper than calves" (cited in Grodin & Glantz, 1994). During the polio trials, the cost of raising and keeping monkeys for experimental use was so high that doctors frequently sought human "volunteers." Children were given an experimental vaccine after it had been tested on only 62 animals (Paul, 1971).

In the cases of the Fernald radiation studies and the Willowbrook hepatitis experiment, the validity of the parental consent obtained is questionable. According to the permission letter to the parents in the Fernald experiment, the benefits of the Science Club consisted of receiving an extra quart of milk each day, attendance at baseball games, and trips to the beach (Higgins, 1998). There was no mention in the parental consent letter of radiation experiments nor of the potential harm that could come to their children (Allen, 1993b).

Consent in the Willowbrook studies was also obtained in a questionable manner. Parents were asked for consent and promised that their children would be placed on a special ward with extra staff. The researchers failed to tell the parents that the special ward was for individuals infected with hepatitis (Grodin & Glantz, 1994).

Claiming a Place of Value: The Continuing Struggle

Jonas Salk won a victory over the polio epidemic. Albert Sabin won the race for an oral vaccine. Millions of people in the world benefited from these triumphs. It is critical, however, that we reflect on the struggle that continues for people with mental retardation in claiming their human worth in the eyes of their fellow human beings. Perhaps the sacrifice that these people have made for others will eventually be recognized and their value in society secured. Until then, their friends, families, and advocates cannot rest.

References

Allen, S. (1993a, December 31). MIT records show wider radioactive testing at Fernald. *The Boston Globe*, pp. 1, 13.

Allen, S. (1993b, December 26). Radiation used on retarded: Post war experiments done at Fernald School. *The Boston Globe*, pp. 1, 45.

Chase, A. (1982). *Magic shots: A human and scientific account of the long and continuing struggle to eradicate infectious diseases by vaccination*. New York: Morrow.

Grodin, M., & Glantz, L. (1994). *Children as research subjects*. New York: Oxford Press.

Higgins, R. (1998, January 18). Haunted by the "Science Club" monetary offer can't erase his memory. *The Boston Globe*, p. 1.

Hooper, E. (1999). *The river: A journey to the source of HIV and AIDS*. New York: Little Brown.

(continued)

Figure 8.3. *(continued)*

MENTAL RETARDATION   VOLUME 39, NUMBER 5: 405–409 | OCTOBER 2001
Perspective: Polio vaccine miracle   J. D. Smith and A. L. Mitchell

Howe, H. (1952). Antibody response of chimpanzees and human beings to formalin inactivated trivalent poliomyelitis vaccine. *American Journal of Hygiene, 55,* 265–279.

Klein, A. (1972). *Trial by fury: The polio vaccine controversy.* New York: Scribner's.

Koprowski, H., Jervis, G., & Norton, T. (1952). Immune responses in human volunteers upon oral administration of a rodent adapted strain of poliomyelitis virus. *American Journal of Hygiene, 55,* 108–126.

Koprowski, H., Norton, G., & Jervis, G. (1956). Clinical investigation on attenuated strains of poliomyelitis virus: Use as a method of immunization of children with living virus. *Journal of the American Medical Association, 160,* 954–966.

Koprowski, I. (1997). *A woman wanders through life and science.* Albany: State University of New York Press.

Paul, J. (1971). *A history of poliomyelitis.* New Haven: Yale Press.

Poliomyelitis: A new approach (Editorial). (1952). *Lancet, 1*(i), 552.

Rogers, N. (1992). *Dirt and disease: Polio since FDR.* New Brunswick, NJ: Rutgers University Press.

Authors:
J. David Smith, EdD, Dean, and **Alison L. Mitchell, MS,** Graduate Assistant, School of Education and Human Services, Longwood College, 201 High St., Farmville, VA 23909.

hepatitis virus to test a vaccine for that infectious disease. Willowbrook would go on to gain notoriety as the result of a series of events culminating in a 1972 investigative television report by then-fledgling ABC-TV journalist, Geraldo Rivera.

In 2004, journalist Michael D'Antonio published *The State Boys Rebellion,* which, drawing from Fernald records and interviews with former Fernald inmates such as Frederick Boyce, told the story of eugenics, the Fernald experiments, and the efforts of Frederick Boyce and others to reclaim their dignity. In 2004, Boyce wrote a letter to the governor of the state of Massachusetts, asking that his diagnosis as a "moron" be expunged from his records and that he receive an apology. In May 2005, Boyce received a letter from the Massachusetts Department of Mental Retardation stating that he "was not mentally retarded." Boyce died from colon cancer in May 2006, four days after receiving the letter.

ROSEMARY KENNEDY AND THE LAUNCH OF A COMMUNITY SYSTEM

The increasingly affluent parents of the growing baby-boomer generation refused to accept the institution as the only option, and, through parent organizations such as the National Association for Retarded Children, began to lobby for more and better services. In 1960, when a young man whose sister had mental retardation was elected to the nation's highest office, these parents had an advocate like none they had known before. Under the Kennedy administration, a system of government supports that answered Pearl Buck's question, "What will the government do for our community?" was established to support people with mental retardation in their communities.

In 1970, Pearl Buck published a biography titled *The Kennedy Women: A Personal Appraisal,* which was billed as "a woman's view of the tragic deterioration of a proud and powerful family—caused . . . by the standards and failures of the society that spawned it" (Buck, 1970, p. i). Of the matriarch of this family, Rose Fitzgerald Kennedy, Buck wrote the following:

> And yet, she has another cross to carry, this beautiful American woman. Among her many children, four sons and five daughters, one daughter, the eldest, remains forever a child. How shall I write of this cross? I myself have had to bear it for many an endless year. I know all too well the horror of the doctor's decision, "Madame, your child is hopelessly retarded." How well I know that heart-sickening experience! It was once said to me after I had given birth to such a dear yet stricken baby daughter. (Buck, 1970, p. 18)

Pearl Buck and Rose Kennedy were of the same generation, the former born in 1892, the latter in 1890, and both women—Rose Kennedy from birth, Pearl Buck later in life—were wealthy, so the lives of their respective daughters were, in many ways, parallel. Rose Kennedy's daughter, her eldest daughter and third child, christened Rose Marie Kennedy but called Rosemary, was born September 13, 1918. Apparently as a result of oxygen deprivation during the birth process (Shorter, 2000, p. 31), Rosemary's development was delayed, and eventually she was diagnosed with mental retardation. Despite her limitations, Rosemary had an active childhood and was capable of doing many things, from taking care of younger children to playing tennis and swimming (Shorter, 2000, p. 31). She traveled with her family on holidays to Europe, engaging in mountain climbing, rowing, and hiking activities with the rest of the family (Shorter, 2000, p. 32).

In 1940, upon the families return from a 2-year stay in England, during which time Rosemary's father, Joseph Kennedy Sr., served as the American ambassador to Great Britain, Rosemary's behavioral patterns took a turn for the worse, and she engaged in tantrums and episodes of aggression toward others. Because they were concerned about these violent behaviors and Rosemary's increasing tendency to wander the streets at night (Shorter, 2000, p. 32) and the possibility that she "was having sexual contact with men" (p. 32) during these outings, the Kennedy family sought help from physicians and psychologists.

These professionals' predictable recommendation was to institutionalize Rosemary. The family, and particularly Rosemary's father, fought the idea of institutionalization, preferring that "Rosemary should have every opportunity that the rest of us had, even though she could not make the most of such opportunities" (Shorter, 2000, p. 33). Rosemary's unpredictable, violent, and risky behavior moved the family closer to a decision to place her in an institution. In the fall of 1941, in a last ditch effort to avoid this and keep her at home, Rosemary was admitted to St. Elizabeth's Hospital in Washington and underwent a lobotomy—surgery to destroy the prefrontal lobes of her brain. The decision to have Rosemary undergo a lobotomy has been both criticized as a reaction to Rosemary's emerging sexuality based upon fears and stereotypes engendered by the eugenic era and admired as a caring attempt to provide treatment to keep Rosemary at home. It is clear that neither Rosemary nor Rose Fitzgerald Kennedy knew the nature of the surgery. It is also clear that the lobotomy

had the opposite effect intended. At some time in the early 1940s Rosemary was institutionalized, and by 1949 she was living at St. Coletta School in Jefferson, Wisconsin,
where she lived the rest of her life. Just as Pearl Buck's wealth allowed her to build a
separate cottage for her daughter Carol, the Kennedy wealth allowed Joseph Kennedy
to build a separate house for Rosemary, called, not surprisingly, the Kennedy cottage.

Unlike Pearl Buck, though, whose 1950 memoir about her daughter was a coming out of sorts, the Kennedy family was circumspect about discussing Rosemary. She
was visited regularly by her mother and her younger sister, Eunice Mary Kennedy. If
the family was reticent about discussing Rosemary, however, their impact on the lives
of other people with intellectual disability and their families was significant.

Eunice Kennedy Shriver's actions, captured in Figure 8.4 in a tribute to her from
American Association on Intellectual and Developmental Disabilities past president David Braddock, in many ways catalyzed the movement to the community that
defines this era in the history of intellectual disability. Perhaps nothing was as important, though, as her early efforts to publicize the inequity experienced by children
with intellectual disability. Using the bully pulpit provided by her family's wealth and
political power, Eunice Kennedy Shriver published an article in the September 22,
1962 issue of the *Saturday Evening Post* titled "Hope for Retarded Children." The article
launched a movement, and the theme of Hope for the Retarded became the mantra of
that generation's efforts to keep their sons and daughters at home with them.

In 1961, President John F. Kennedy, with the urging of Ms. Shriver, established
the President's Panel on Mental Retardation. The panel issued 97 recommendations,
many of which formed the basis for legislation and funding streams that benefit people with intellectual disability and their families. Only weeks before his assassination,
President Kennedy signed legislation that moved the United States toward a community-based system of supports, and then spoke with members of National Association
for Retarded Children at their annual meeting in Washington, D.C. (see Figure 8.5)
about that historic legislation.

GROWTH OF THE PARENT MOVEMENT

After the release of *Angel Unaware,* a strange phenomenon began to occur. The audiences at the rodeos or the television studios in which Roy Rogers and Dale Evans
performed began to be peppered with children with Down syndrome. Seated among
the children who flocked to their performances were children whose parents had,
before *Angel,* felt ashamed or guilty about taking them out in public, or had been
shamed by society into feeling guilty about having a child who was different.

These parents began to talk with one another and to organize small groups to
meet the needs that arose by keeping their children at home. Even before 1950, a few
pioneering parents had begun to reject the options professionals were offering their
children and banded together to seek out better options. Prior to the organization of
these first local parent groups in the United States in the 1930s and 1940s, families
that had children with mental retardation were alone. At that time little was known
about the condition or its causes, and there were virtually no programs and activities
in communities to assist in the development and care of these children and adults as
well as to support their families.

INTELLECTUAL AND DEVELOPMENTAL DISABILITIES   VOLUME 48, NUMBER 1: 63–72 | FEBRUARY 2010

Perspectives

Honoring Eunice Kennedy Shriver's Legacy in Intellectual Disability

David Braddock

DOI: 10.1352/1934-9556-48.1.63

Eunice Kennedy Shriver: 1921–2009

An entire book needs to be written to do justice to the many achievements of Eunice Kennedy Shriver in philanthropy, public policy leadership, and the International Special Olympics movement. However, my task here is to briefly highlight Mrs. Shriver's most significant and lasting achievements in the field of intellectual disability as they relate to these three spheres of activity. Her striking achievements, spanning more than 50 years, involved formidable challenges and changed the field of intellectual disability forever by advancing human dignity and civil rights, public acceptance, community services, research, health promotion, and the joy and benefits of physical activity and sport.

What Eunice Shriver Faced

We begin in 1958, a significant year in Eunice Shriver's public life and in intellectual disability history as well. According to the medical historian

Edward Shorter (2000), in that year, Joseph P. Kennedy asked his daughter Eunice and her husband Sargent Shriver to take responsibility for the Kennedy Foundation's new program in the prevention of intellectual disability. Imagine Joseph P. Kennedy's pride were he to learn that 50 years after giving this assignment to his daughter, the National Institutes of Health's (NIH) National Institute on Child Health and Human Development (NICHD)—the leading intellectual and developmental disabilities research enterprise in the United States and perhaps the world—would be named in her honor.

However, in 1958, what Eunice Shriver encountered in Washington in the field of intellectual disability (then termed *mental retardation*) was challenging to say the least. The environment was characterized by disinterested bureaucracies in the executive agencies, the judiciary, and, with the notable exceptions of Congressman John Fogarty (Democrat, RI) and Senator Lister Hill, (Democrat, AL), in the U.S. Congress. The late Elizabeth

Figure 8.4. "Honoring Eunice Kennedy Shriver's Legacy in Intellectual Disability."
(From Braddock, D. [2010]. Honoring Eunice Kennedy Shriver's legacy in intellectual disability. *Intellectual and Developmental Disabilities*, 48[1], 63–72; reprinted by permission.)

(continued)

Figure 8.4. *(continued)*

INTELLECTUAL AND DEVELOPMENTAL DISABILITIES | VOLUME 48, NUMBER 1: 63–72 | FEBRUARY 2010
Perspective: honoring Shriver's legacy | D. Braddock

Boggs cofounded the National Association for Retarded Children in 1950 and in 1958 was elected its first female president. Three years later she would be a leading member of President John F. Kennedy's Panel on Mental Retardation. "In the mid 1950's," she wrote, "NIMH [National Institute of Mental Health] staff [at the National Institutes of Health] privately doubted if as much as $250,000 could be well spent on a subject as unglamorous as mental retardation" (Boggs, 1971, p. 107).

The federal presence in intellectual disability had been so modest in the early 1950s that a grant from the Kennedy Foundation of $1.25 million to establish a private school in Illinois exceeded the entire federal budget for intellectual disability services at that time (*New York Times*, 1952). In 1956, "There was not an identifiable program [for services] in the federal government aimed at meeting the problem of mentally retarded children" (U.S. House of Representatives, 1963). By 1958, total federal support for intellectual disability research was still just $4.3 million annually. It was almost exclusively administered by the National Institutes of Health's NIMH and the National Institute of Neurological, Communicative Disorders and Stroke (NINCDS).

However, there would be signs of change. In 1958, then-fledgling Congressman George McGovern of South Dakota sponsored what became Public Law (P.L.) 85-926, the Education of Mentally Retarded Children Act. This statute authorized a modestly funded $1 million training program for teachers of children with intellectual disabilities. The enactment, according to Elizabeth Boggs (1971), responded to the fact that enrollment of children and youth in special education programs had grown nationwide by 150% during the preceding decade. More special education teachers were needed, and they required specialized training. McGovern's legislation was the predecessor of contemporary special education personnel preparation programs. The precedent-setting Education for All Handicapped Children Act of 1975 (P.L. 94-142), the foundation of today's Individuals With Disabilities Education Act (IDEA) as amended, would not become law for another 17 years after McGovern's 1958 legislation.

For adults with intellectual disabilities in 1958, federal grant support for services was essentially restricted to the state–federal vocational rehabilitation grant program. That fiscal year, only 1,578 persons with intellectual disability were reported to be rehabilitated (i.e., placed in jobs) under the auspices of that program across the entire nation. This was 2% of the overall rehabilitation caseload in the states for persons with disabilities of all types. In 2006, the rehabilitation caseload of people with intellectual disabilities was 28,602 persons, 14% of the overall disabilities caseload nationally.

Power to the States

The U.S. Supreme Court ruled in 1954 in *Brown v. Board of Education of Topeka, Kansas* that separate educational facilities segregated by race were inherently unequal and violated the 14th Amendment to the U.S. Constitution. In the 1970s, the 14th Amendment's due process provision was interpreted to apply to people with intellectual disabilities who were inappropriately institutionalized in large state-operated facilities (Herr, 1983). However, in 1954, 173,594 people with intellectual disabilities, many of them children, remained separated from children and adults without intellectual disabilities, in poorly funded, state-operated residential "schools" and in state psychiatric institutions across the country (NIMH, 1956). To say that these facilities were spartan would be too kind. Mrs. Shriver wrote in a 1964 *Parade Magazine* article, after touring institutions, "I have seen sights that will haunt me all my life. If I had not seen them myself, I would never have believed that such conditions could exist in modern America" (pp. 6–7). The "sights" she saw were even more vividly summarized in a moving passage she had written two years earlier for the September 22, 1962, edition of *The Saturday Evening Post*.

I remember well one institution we visited several years ago. There was an overpowering smell of urine from clothes and from the floors. I remember the retarded patients with nothing to do standing, staring, and grotesque-like misshaped statues. I recall other institutions where several thousand adults and children were housed in bleak, overcrowded wards of 100 or more, living out their lives on a dead-end street, unloved, unwanted, some of them strapped in chairs like criminals. In the words of one expert, such unfortunate people are "sitting around in witless circles in mediaeval prisons." This is all the more shocking because it is so unnecessary. Yet institutions such as these still exist. (p. 72)

In 1967, five long years after *The Saturday Evening Post* article appeared, Niels Erik Bank-Mikkelsen, national director of Denmark's intellectual disability services programs, toured Cali-

INTELLECTUAL AND DEVELOPMENTAL DISABILITIES   VOLUME 48, NUMBER 1: 63–72 | FEBRUARY 2010

Perspective: honoring Shriver's legacy   D. Braddock

fornia's Sonoma State Hospital, which at the time had 3,400 residents with intellectual disabilities. "I couldn't believe my eyes," he said. "It was worse than I have seen in visits to a dozen countries. In our country, we would not be allowed to treat cattle like that" (National Association for Retarded Children, 1967b, p. 2). The disclosure of these conditions was not a surprise to the field nationally. A year before Bank-Mikkelsen's comment was widely distributed in the media, Professor Burton Blatt, then at Boston University, and photographer Fred Kaplan, published *Christmas in Purgatory* (1966). An excerpt from this powerful photographic essay on institutional conditions in America was reprinted in *Look Magazine* (Blatt & Mangel, 1967). The graphic photos stirred national attention.

However, very difficult impediments in funding intellectual disability services in the states persisted. "States rights" dominated the landscape of federal–state relations. "The powers not delegated to the United States by the Constitution are reserved to the States respectively or to the people." So reads the 10th Amendment to the U.S. Constitution, thus relegating virtually exclusive oversight of state-operated intellectual disability institutions to state governments, which had very limited tax bases at the time. To illustrate how fiscally neglected state institutions were in the 1960s, the President's Panel on Mental Retardation stated in its 1962 report to President Kennedy that it was "gratified" to learn that average spending per resident in these facilities advanced from $2.05 per day in 1950 to $4.55 in 1960 (p. 132).

State-operated institutions would not begin a steady national decline in their resident populations until after they peaked in 1968, six years after President's Kennedy's panel recommendations were issued. (The resident population of institutions has declined every year since then by between 3% and 6%.) In 1971, federal class action litigation in the states on rights to education and habilitation, stimulated by the advocacy of parents and concerned professionals, provided catalysts for community integration and access to education. Today, 11 states operate residential service delivery systems without reliance on state-operated institutions for people with intellectual disabilities. The vast majority of the 533,000 persons with intellectual disabilities living in supervised "out of home" residential settings nationally, including institu-

tions, now live in community settings with only a few other persons. The 2009 institutional census of state-operated institutional facilities is estimated from projections of 2007 and earlier data to have fallen below 37,000 persons nationally (Braddock, Hemp, & Rizzolo, 2008).

The President's Panel on Mental Retardation and Eunice Kennedy Shriver's Leadership

Eunice Shriver's most catalytic and lasting contribution to the community integration and institutional reform movement was her leadership in 1961 in championing the creation of the President's Panel on Mental Retardation and in subsequently playing "an active role pressing for ever-increasing vigor in the panel's performance" (Boggs, 1971, p. 113). Shriver insisted that only the finest leaders, scientists, and clinicians be appointed to the panel. Panel members included the aforementioned Elizabeth Boggs and Robert Cooke, pediatrics chair at Johns Hopkins University, Kennedy Foundation scientific adviser, and noted administrator. Cooke had led the call for the creation of an NIH "kiddie institute," which became the NICHD in 1962. A parent advocate for two children with cri du chat syndrome, he was instrumental in convincing Mrs. Shriver to shift the focus of the Kennedy Foundation from care and treatment to research into causes.

Other key panel leaders included Leonard Mayo, chair of the 1950 White House Conference on Children and Youth, who chaired the panel, and George Tarjan, the panel's vice chair, a psychiatrist and superintendent of the Pacific State Hospital in California. In 1959, Tarjan was president of the American Association on Mental Retardation (now the American Association on Intellectual and Developmental Disabilities) and was president of the American Psychiatric Association during 1983–1984.

Boggs, who held a doctorate in mathematical chemistry from Cambridge University, was a leader of the panel's Task Force on Coordination as well as vice chair of the Task Force on Law. Boggs later wrote, "The idea of the panel was urged on the president by his sister Eunice Shriver" (Boggs, 1971, p. 112). Donald Stedman and John Throne, directors of the Kennedy Foundation during the early 1960s, both concurred with Boggs' assessment

(continued)

Figure 8.4. *(continued)*

INTELLECTUAL AND DEVELOPMENTAL DISABILITIES | VOLUME 48, NUMBER 1: 63–72 | FEBRUARY 2010

Perspective: honoring Shriver's legacy | D. Braddock

of Eunice Shriver's personal advocacy role with the president to establish the panel (Shorter, 2000, p. 84).

After the panel was established, Shriver personally and passionately lobbied her brother, the president, and his capable long-time aide Myer (Mike) Feldman, as only she could, to generate critical presidential support for the panel's 97 recommendations. Although she was not a formal member of the panel, she was the only consultant listed in the panel's final report to the president. Feldman, now deceased, was a brilliant attorney who had also served as an aide to Kennedy in the Senate and would later serve as Kennedy's presidential aide and as counsel to President Lyndon B. Johnson. He became one of Mrs. Shriver's closest friends, and, for many years, Feldman was vice chairman of the board of directors of the International Special Olympics.

President Kennedy's October 1961 *White House Statement on Mental Retardation*, delivered in the Rose Garden, was likely written by Feldman as a call to action, in the president's voice:

The manner in which our Nation cares for its citizens and conserves its manpower resources is more than an index to its concern for the less fortunate. It is a key to its future. Both wisdom and humanity dictate a deep interest in the physically handicapped, the mentally ill and the mentally retarded. Yet, although we have made considerable progress in the treatment of physical handicaps, although we have attacked the problems of mental illness, although we have made great strides in the battle against disease, we as a nation have for too long postponed an intensive search for solutions to the problems of the mentally retarded. That failure should be corrected. (President's Panel on Mental Retardation, 1962, p. 196)

The panel would have only 11 months to complete its work in time to accommodate the congressional calendar so that recommended legislation might be introduced, enacted, and funded. The panel organized itself into six task forces: Prevention, Education and Habilation, Law and Public Awareness, Biological Research, Behavioral and Social Research, and Coordination. The panel held public hearings in seven large cities, sought technical assistance from a variety of governmental and nongovernmental sources, and traveled to review facilities in Sweden, Denmark, Holland,

President John F. Kennedy hands Eunice Kennedy Shriver the pen he used to sign groundbreaking intellectual disability legislation in October 1963. The legislation implemented recommendations of his presidential panel (photo from the author's collection).

INTELLECTUAL AND DEVELOPMENTAL DISABILITIES   VOLUME 48, NUMBER 1: 63–72 | FEBRUARY 2010

Perspective: honoring Shriver's legacy   D. Braddock

England, and the Soviet Union. The panel's final report was officially transmitted to President Kennedy on October 16, 1962, at a White House event held during the top-secret build up of the 1962 Cuban missile crisis. The president made no mention of the unfolding crisis to the panel as he met with them (Boggs, 1971, p. 107).

As Close as Possible

One overarching theme could be identified in the panel's final report, entitled *National Action to Combat Mental Retardation*: that future services and supports to people with intellectual disabilities should be provided "as close as possible" in community and family settings as opposed to large and remote, state-operated residential institutions. Over 175,000 individuals with intellectual disabilities were institutionalized in large, state-operated intellectual disability residential facilities at the time (U.S. Bureau of the Census, 1975). Many individual facilities had thousands of residents. The Willowbrook State School in New York, for example, reached a peak of approximately 8,000 residents. State-operated psychiatric hospitals for persons with mental illness also housed an additional 37,000 persons with intellectual disabilities nationally in their massive general populations (NIMH, 1961).

The President's Panel on Mental Retardation issued 97 recommendations emanating from its six task forces. Many were subsequently embodied in P.L. 88-156, the Maternal and Child Health and Mental Retardation Planning Amendments of 1963, and in P.L. 88-164, the Mental Retardation Facilities and Community Mental Health Centers Construction Act. Both were enacted just a few weeks prior to the president's death in 1963 and both were noteworthy legislative achievements. P.L. 88-156 doubled the fiscal authorization level for the existing federal maternal and child health state grant program and authorized special grants under Section 508 for maternity and infant care "to help reduce the incidence of mental retardation caused by complications associated with childbearing."

P.L. 88-164 authorized three interrelated construction programs. Under Title I, Part A, $27 million was expended for the construction of Mental Retardation Research Centers affiliated with large universities at 12 sites. Title I, Part B authorized construction of 18 university-affiliated facilities (UAFs), now termed the University Centers of Excellence in Developmental Disabilities Education, Service and Research (UCEDDs). A community facilities construction program was also authorized under Title I, Part C. Between 1965 and 1970, 362 projects involving $90 million were completed for construction of facilities for the diagnosis, education, treatment, training, and personal care of people with intellectual disabilities (Braddock, 1987). The Kennedy Foundation provided the matching grants for numerous original applicants for the UAF grants and several applicants for the research centers. Thus, many of these university centers are named in honor of Eunice Kennedy Shriver and John F. Kennedy. The United States is unique internationally in the breadth, depth, and sheer numbers of UCEDD programs. At present, there are 67 UCEDDs, including at least one in every state, and 21 intellectual and developmental disabilities research centers.

It is notable that P.L. 88-156 legislation also called for the first comprehensive, state-by-state planning in intellectual disability services. This was an important action because it began to penetrate the wall of indifference between federal and state governments regarding institutional conditions and the general lack of educational, rehabilitative, medical, and community residential services in all the states. The state planning objectives were the forerunner of comprehensive, multiagency developmental disabilities planning in the states subsequently authorized in 1970 in the Developmental Disabilities Services and Facilities Construction Act (P.L. 91-517). That comprehensive planning mandate continues to this day. The late U.S Senator Ted Kennedy was an original prime sponsor of the legislation in the Senate.

Thus, in 1963, the federal government's expectation of the reform of intellectual disability services across the states was initiated for the first time in the nation's history. The field would never be the same. The President's Panel on Mental Retardation had been a catalyst for change, but the principal change agent was someone who was not a formal member of the panel: Eunice Kennedy Shriver. Her leadership of the panel in the Office of the President and with the president personally made all the difference. The panel's productivity was a tribute to all its citizen members and to President Kennedy. However, the panel was Eunice Kennedy Shriver's first great and lasting triumph in

(continued)

Figure 8.4. *(continued)*

INTELLECTUAL AND DEVELOPMENTAL DISABILITIES   VOLUME 48, NUMBER 1: 63–72 | FEBRUARY 2010
Perspective: honoring Shriver's legacy   D. Braddock

the intellectual disability field. In November 1966, she would be honored with the prestigious Lasker Public Service Award in Health. The citation read:

Undaunted by public apathy and ignorance, Mrs. Shriver has, in the last few years, focused public attention on the problems of the mentally retarded and accomplished a revolution in research on the causes of mental retardation, the care of the retarded, and the acceptance of the retarded by family and community. (National Association for Retarded Children, 1967a, p. 1)

Eunice Kennedy Shriver never rested on laurels. She would receive many awards in her career, in addition to the Lasker, including, to name a few, the Humanitarian Award from the American Association on Intellectual and Developmental Disabilities; honorary degrees from Yale, Princeton, Georgetown, and numerous other universities; the Presidential Medal of Freedom from President Ronald Reagan; the French Medal of Freedom; the National Collegiate Athletic Association (NCAA) Theodore Roosevelt Award; and the Laetare Medal from the University of Notre Dame. In 2008, she received the inaugural Sportsman of the Year Legacy Award from *Sports*

Illustrated. Two years after receiving the Lasker Award in 1966, one of her first major awards, she promptly launched an enterprise that would have an unprecedented worldwide impact in the field of intellectual and developmental disabilities: the Special Olympics.

Emergence of the International Special Olympics

The President's Panel on Mental Retardation was unprecedented in the history of the intellectual disability field in the United States. However, Eunice Shriver's leadership had only just begun in intellectual disability. On July 20, 1968, 900 Special Olympians from 25 states and Canada gathered at Soldier Field in Chicago, Illinois. By that time, Mrs. Shriver had interacted for several years with key leaders in the emerging field of adapted sports for people with intellectual disabilities. The group included the Canadian adaptive sports innovator and professor Frank Hayden, the late Professor William Freeberg of Southern Illinois

Launching the Special Olympics: 1968, Eunice Kennedy Shriver overlooks Chicago's Soldier Field at the first national Special Olympics games (photo courtesy of International Special Olympics).

INTELLECTUAL AND DEVELOPMENTAL DISABILITIES   VOLUME 48, NUMBER 1: 63–72 | FEBRUARY 2010

Perspective: honoring Shriver's legacy   D. Braddock

University, and Ann McGlone Burke, then of the Chicago Park District and now a justice on the Illinois Supreme Court. According to the biographer Edward Shorter (2000), Mrs. Shriver first called for "a national tournament of athletic contests in the United States among teams of mentally retarded children" (p. 128) in 1965, while speaking in Dallas. "Camp Shriver," a summer sports activity event for children with intellectual disabilities, was first held at the Shriver's Timberlawn home in Maryland beginning on June 7, 1962. Camp Shriver subsequently expanded to numerous additional sites and, most recently, to Nairobi, Kenya.

In Chicago, at the first national games, Eunice Kennedy Shriver would announce a "Special Olympics training program for all mentally retarded children everywhere" (Shorter, 2000, p. 134). Four decades later, in 2009, more than 3.1 million athletes and over 1 million volunteers and coaches from 175 countries would be participating. In many of the world's poorest countries, Special Olympics is a very important development program for people with intellectual disabilities. In the past 13 years, with Timothy Shriver's leadership as chief executive officer and Mrs. Shriver's continuing inspiration as the founder, the Special Olympics has emerged as the leading sports participation and health-promotion development program for people with intellectual disabilities in the developing world.

Mrs. Shriver faced formidable odds in setting the stage for these outcomes to be achieved. Chief among them were the widely held prejudices in the early and mid-1960s that people with intellectual disabilities would suffer physical and psychological harm if they attempted to exercise vigorously, regularly, and competitively; that they could not master team sports; and that they were best served in more sedentary camping and recreational activities like eating hot dogs, singing songs, and sleeping in tents. Overly protective "recreationist" assumptions against carefully planned and monitored athletic training and competitions collapsed as tens of thousands of Special Olympics athletes soon proved skeptics wrong by competing in athletic games throughout the country, and then throughout the world. However, this is another story, a glorious story of the triumph of one determined woman who led millions of Special Olympians into the modern era and gave them and their families pride to be alive, engaged, and active in body, mind, and spirit. Mrs. Shriver's leadership experiences with the Kennedy Foundation and with the president's panel were put to extraordinarily good use on the world stage through the Special Olympics.

Eunice Kennedy Shriver's personal qualities were just as important in her success and a key to understanding her achievements in the intellectual disability field and in leadership generally. To paraphrase her son Timothy Shriver, these qualities included a chemistry of political acumen nationally and internationally, coupled with celebrity pizzazz, and a deep respect for the role of scientific research on the one hand, delicately balanced with an even deeper appreciation of the inner beauty, courage, and potential competence of people with intellectual disabilities on the other. These qualities of mind and spirit were only strengthened by her dedication to her faith, to her family, to the joy of sport, and to citizen activism. The impact of that citizen activism can be characterized by political philosopher John Stuart Mill's (1862) adage that "one person with a belief is equal to a force of ninety-nine who have only interests" (p. 23). In Eunice Kennedy Shriver's case, Mill's adage is an understatement. Shriver spoke with the force of millions in empowering the voices of people with intellectual disabilities and their families around the world. She lived by action, not adage.

Honoring Her Legacy

How do we properly honor Eunice Kennedy Shriver's dedication and leadership in the field of intellectual disability? What goals would she ask us to articulate and address more effectively in the future if she could do so today? Those who knew her might say that she would insist that we continue to support vigorously rights and opportunities for people with intellectual disabilities and their families and that we acknowledge that there is much to do in the United States and in other developed countries to provide better inclusive education and health care and to promote healthy lifestyles, to enhance opportunities for social and employment participation, and to more aggressively level the playing field through improved access to emerging assistive technologies for all people with cognitive disabilities (Rizzolo & Braddock, 2008).

Mrs. Shriver would also remind us that the greatest challenge in intellectual disability of this

(continued)

Figure 8.4. *(continued)*

INTELLECTUAL AND DEVELOPMENTAL DISABILITIES   VOLUME 48, NUMBER 1: 63–72 | FEBRUARY 2010
Perspective: honoring Shriver's legacy   D. Braddock

2007 Special Olympics World Games, Opening Ceremony, Shanghai, China. Photo courtesy of Special Olympics, by Diego Azubel.

generation, and likely the next, lies in recognizing and acting on the fact that the majority of people with intellectual disabilities in the world today are the scores of millions of people who live day-to-day in developing countries where they are denied health care, education, employment opportunity, basic human rights, and personal support. Special Olympics organizations are typically among the most viable nationwide organizations explicitly dedicated to improving the lives of people with intellectual disabilities in these poor countries and they often have excellent access to the business community and government leaders.

Forging stronger partnerships between country-based Special Olympics programs and intellectual disability–related, nongovernmental organizations, such as Inclusion International and local consumer and professional associations, would promote broadly based development of general services and supports for people with intellectual disabilities, and for Special Olympics programs. Potential impacts include the expansion of programs promoting health, social and educational participation, community acceptance, and employment. In addition, the university-based UCEDD model in the United States, launched by the president's panel initiative in 1963, and described

previously, holds promise in the developing world as a possible model for advancing personnel training, clinical services, community and family support programs, and applied research in intellectual and developmental disabilities.

There is no stronger source of inspiration available to surmount these immense worldwide challenges than to reflect back on the challenges Eunice Kennedy Shriver faced in intellectual disability in the late 1950s in the United States. We—the United States of America—were then ourselves a "developing country" attitudinally and in failing to provide decent services and supports for people with intellectual disabilities and their families. Inappropriate institutionalization, denial of educational opportunity, rampant discrimination in employment, and the denial of appropriate health care were the norms, not exceptions, in the 1950s. The President's Panel on Mental Retardation was the clearing in the wilderness, whereupon the foundation for the next five decades of progress in the field was established in the United States. Eunice Kennedy Shriver was the primary moving force behind that effort, just as she has been the soul and the moving force of the Special Olympics worldwide.

INTELLECTUAL AND DEVELOPMENTAL DISABILITIES

VOLUME 48, NUMBER 1: 63–72 | FEBRUARY 2010

Perspective: honoring Shriver's legacy

D. Braddock

Formidable challenges remain to be addressed here in the United States, even given the overall growth of support for intellectual disability services in recent years. However, it is striking how inequitably distributed resources are to states, communities, families, and individual consumers. Thousands of persons with intellectual disabilities are on waiting lists for community services and family support (Lakin & Turnbull, 2005). Tens of thousands more reside inappropriately in state-operated institutions and nursing homes, notwithstanding the U.S. Supreme Court's *Olmstead* (1999) decision promoting access to community residential services and family support options to institutionalization.

Direct support staff wages in community facilities and in family homes are often below the poverty level. Staff turnover is unacceptably high and often exceeds 50% (U.S. Department of Health and Human Services, 1999). Moreover, family support programs receive only a small portion of funding in the field today, participation in supported employment programs nationally is declining, and many students with intellectual disabilities are still educated in segregated classes or separate educational facilities. In addition, there is very limited support for intellectual disability research and research training, as well as for the development, testing, and diffusion of emerging cognitive technologies for people with intellectual disabilities (Braddock, 2007).

Eunice Kennedy Shriver stimulated considerable progress in intellectual disability worldwide during her lifetime. She leaves at least three distinct and enduring legacies in intellectual disability as a guide. First is the 1961–1962 President's Panel on Mental Retardation and its catalytic national agenda in residential and community services, biomedical and behavioral research, education and training, and the prevention of intellectual disability. The 50th anniversary of the presentation of the panel's final report to President Kennedy in the White House will be October 16, 2012. We should celebrate that event and, if invited to do so, assist other nations to launch their own action-oriented panels to stimulate program development in intellectual disability.

The second legacy of Eunice Kennedy Shriver is her half century of leadership of the Kennedy Foundation's path-breaking philanthropy in education, research, and public service in intellectual disability. The foundation has been a beacon of light for many other foundations in the United States that have followed its lead and invested in the field of intellectual and developmental disabilities.

Mrs. Shriver's third legacy is the International Special Olympics and its breathtaking growth to over 3 million participants in 175 countries in 2009. Special Olympics is a leading development organization concerned with intellectual disability in all of these countries. Increasing numbers of athletes today are participating in Special Olympics–sponsored health assessment, medical–dental referral programs, and unified sports with nondisabled friends.

These three multifaceted legacies—the president's panel, the Kennedy Foundation, and the Special Olympics—are each themselves major contributions to the field of intellectual disability over the past half century. The task before us now is clear: Envision and create a better future for people with intellectual disabilities and their families than even Eunice Shriver could have imagined during her long and consequential lifetime.

So, in every country across the globe, in every city, town and remote village—and she touched almost all of them during her life—let the word go forth to honor the legacy of Eunice Kennedy Shriver.

References

Blatt, B., & Kaplan, F. (1966). *Christmas in purgatory.* Boston: Allyn & Bacon.

Blatt, B., & Mangel, C. (1967, October 31). Tragedy and hope of retarded children. *Look Magazine, 41,* 96–99.

Boggs, E. (1971). Federal legislation 1966–71. In J. Wortis (Ed.), *Mental retardation, an annual review,* Vol. 3 (pp. 103–127). New York: Grune & Stratton.

Boggs, E. (1972). Federal legislation (Conclusion). In J. Wortis (Ed.), *Mental retardation, an annual review,* Vol. 4 (pp. 165–206). New York: Grune & Stratton.

Braddock, D. (1987). *Federal policy toward mental retardation and developmental disabilities.* Baltimore: Brookes.

Braddock, D. (2007). Washington rises: Public financial support for intellectual disability in the United States, 1955–2004. *Mental Retardation and Developmental Disabilities Research Reviews, 13,* 169–177.

(continued)

Figure 8.4. *(continued)*

INTELLECTUAL AND DEVELOPMENTAL DISABILITIES   VOLUME 48, NUMBER 1: 63–72 | FEBRUARY 2010

Perspective: honoring Shriver's legacy   D. Braddock

Braddock, D., Hemp, R., & Rizzolo, M. C. (2008). *The state of the states in developmental disabilities: 2008* (Rev. ed.). Washington, DC: American Association on Intellectual and Developmental Disabilities.

Brown v. Board of Education of Topeka, 347 U.S. 483 (1954).

Developmental Disabilities Services and Facilities Construction Act of 1970, P.L. 91-517.

Education for All Handicapped Children Act of 1975, P.L. 94-142.

Education of Mentally Retarded Children Act of 1958, P.L. 85-926 (1958).

Herr, S. S. (1983). *Rights and advocacy for retarded people*. Lexington, MA: D.C. Heath, Lexington Books.

Lakin, K. C., & Turnbull, A. P. (2005). *National goals and research for people with intellectual and developmental disabilities*. Washington, DC: American Association on Mental Retardation.

Maternal and Child Health and Mental Retardation Planning Amendments of 1963, P.L. 88-156.

Mental Retardation Facilities and Community Mental Health Centers Construction Act of 1963.

Mill, J. S. (1862). *Considerations on representative government*. New York: Harper and Brothers.

National Association for Retarded Children. (1967a, February). Lasker award given to Eunice K. Shriver. *Children Limited 16*(1), p. 1.

National Association for Retarded Children. (1967b, December). Retardation expert castigates California hospital. *Children Limited 16*(2), p. 2.

National Institute of Mental Health. (1961). *Patients in mental institutions, 1960*. Washington, DC: U.S. Government Printing Office.

New York Times. (1952). Kennedy Foundation gives $1,250,000 to aid Chicago home for retarded boys. New York: Author.

President's Panel on Mental Retardation. (1962). *National action to combat mental retardation*. Washington, DC: U.S. Government Printing Office.

Rizzolo, M., & Braddock, D. (2008). *Cognitive disabilities*. In S. Helal, M. Mohktari, & B. Abdulrazak (Eds.), *Technology for aging disability and independence: Computing and engineering design and applications* (pp. 203–215). Hoboken, NJ: Wiley.

Shorter, E. (200). *The Kennedy family and the story of mental retardation*. Philadelphia: Temple University Press.

Shriver, E. (1964, February 2). The sun has burst through. *Parade Magazine*, pp. 6–7.

Shriver, E. (1962, September 22). Hope for retarded children. *Saturday Evening Post*, pp. 71–75.

U.S. Bureau of the Census. (1975, September). *Historical statistics of the United States, colonial times to 1970, bicentennial edition, Part 2*. Washington, DC: Author.

U.S. Department of Health and Human Services, Assistant Secretary for Planning and Evaluation, Office of Disability, Aging, and Long-Term Care Policy. (2006). *The supply of direct support professionals serving individuals with intellectual disabilities and other developmental disabilities: Report to Congress*. Washington, DC: Author.

United States House of Representatives, Committee on Appropriations, United States House of Representatives, Committee on Appropriations, Subcommittee on Labor, and Health, Education and Welfare. (1963). *Supplemental appropriations to combat mental retardation*. Washington, DC: U.S. Government Printing Office.

Author:

David Braddock, PhD (E-mail: braddock@cu.edu), Associate Vice President, University of Colorado System; Executive Director, Coleman Institute for Cognitive Disabilities; and the Coleman-Turner Chair and Professor in Psychiatry, University of Colorado, Denver, School of Medicine.

Figure 8.5. President Kennedy addresses the 13th annual convention of the National Association for Retarded Children on October 22, 1963, at the Mayflower Hotel, Washington, DC. (Photograph from author's personal collection.)

The creation of these groups has been described as an act of courage. It required parents "to bring their problem into the open and to challenge both the traditional image of mental defect and the rejection and discrimination practiced by society against them" (President's Committee on Mental Retardation [PCMR], 1977, p. 38). Specifically, they were challenged by the availability of few resources as well as professional indifference, widespread ignorance, and powerful stigma directed against people with mental deficits and, to some degree, themselves.

In September 1950, representatives from 23 parent groups met in Minneapolis, Minnesota, to form the National Association of Parents and Friends of Mentally Retarded Children (Abeson & Davis, 2000, p. 19). Aided by interested professionals, these isolated parent groups were invited to meet to explore the organization of a national association. With 44 delegates representing 23 local organizations in 13 states, the National Association of Parents and Friends of Mentally Retarded Children, now The Arc of the United States, was born. With the founding of The Arc, an umbrella under which to organize, the parent movement grew rapidly. By 1975, approximately 218,000 members were organized in 1,700 state and local chapters.

The stated purposes of the new organization as written in The Arc's original constitution and bylaws were as follows (National Association of Parents and Friends of Mentally Retarded Children, 1950):

- To promote the general welfare of mentally retarded children of all ages everywhere;

- to further the advancement of all study, ameliorative and preventive research and therapy in the field of mental retardation;

- to develop a better understanding of the problem of mental retardation by the public and cooperate with all public, private and religious agencies, international, federal, state and local departments of education, health and institutions;

- to further the training and education of personnel for work in the field of mental retardation;

- to encourage the formation of parent groups, to advise and aid parents in the solution of their problems, and to coordinate the efforts and activities of these groups;

- to further the implementation of legislation on behalf of the mentally retarded;

- to serve as a clearinghouse for gathering and disseminating information regarding the mentally retarded, and to foster the development of integrated programs in their behalf; and

- to solicit and receive funds for the accomplishment of the above purposes.

Building on these purposes, one of the early priorities of the association was to change the public's perception of children with mental retardation. Another was to educate parents and the organization's leaders on the condition of mental retardation, as well as what was possible for people with the condition. A third priority was to procure services for children and adults who were denied education, work, day care, and preschool programs.

From the beginning, The Arc recognized the need to educate the public about mental retardation. Consequently, a national campaign of information and appeal for children with mental retardation began in 1954. It sought to counter the ignorance of America as well as the negative image of "the mentally retarded individual as a destructive menace with a child's mind in a grown body" (PCMR, 1977). Using the slogan "Help Retarded Children" (see Figure 8.6), the campaign sought to present children as innocent beings that have the right to love and affection. Furthermore, the message stated that these children should not be discriminated against, because neither they nor their families could help the presence of mental retardation. With the emergence of this message and with the association, a number of well-known people came forward to tell or write about children with mental retardation in their families. These included the aforementioned Pearl Buck, Dale Evans Rogers, and Eunice Kennedy Shriver, but also Muriel Humphrey—wife of Senator and Vice President Hubert Humphrey, whose granddaughter had an intellectual disability—and popular first lady Eleanor Roosevelt (see Figure 8.7). Although these portrayals were essentially of helpless children who elicited pity, it was a first step in changing the public's image and understanding that mental retardation could occur in any family.

As the organization grew, the founders' children became adults who did not want to be viewed as "perpetual" children. Equally significant was the desire to do away with promoting images of pity because of the emergence of the critical concept that people with mental retardation were citizens like all other citizens, with rights defined and protected by law. Reflecting this logic, the name of the organization was changed in 1973 from the National Association for Retarded Children, which was the name adopted in 1951, to the National Association for Retarded Citizens. Additionally, in 1975, the board of directors banned the use of poster children. The image of an

Figure 8.6. National Association for Retarded Children "Help Retarded Children" campaign image. (Image from author's personal collection.)

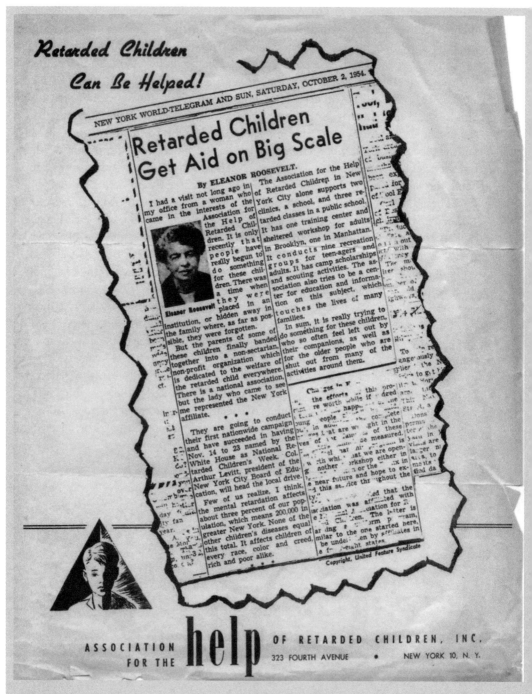

Figure 8.7. Flyer of Eleanor Roosevelt article in the *New York World-Telegram and Sun* (October 2, 1954), produced by the New York state chapter of the Association for the Help of Retarded Children, Inc. (Image from author's personal collection.)

individual with mental retardation projected by the organization at that time was of a person impaired by the condition of mental retardation but having the basic human and civil rights of all citizens.

Dale Evans and Pearl Buck played pivotal roles in the emergence of that national movement. Shortly after the publication of *Angel Unaware,* the director of one of the parent groups aligned with that newly formed national parent association, The Exceptional Children's Foundation, in Los Angeles, contacted Roy and Dale's publicist to inquire about the possibility of having the Rogeres shoot a publicity photo for one of the agency's projects. Dale and Roy had determined that royalties from *Angel Unaware* should go to assist other children like Robin, and when the request for the publicity photo was made to Dale, she asked if the agency was part of a national organization (Garrison, 1956, p. 64). As a result, Evans donated royalties from the book (see Figure 8.8), $50,000 in all, to

Figure 8.8. Dale Evans Rogers presenting check for $10,000 from royalties for *Angel Unaware* to the National Association for Retarded Children. (Image from author's personal collection.)

the National Association of Parents and Friends of Mentally Retarded Children, which enabled the foundling association to hire an executive director (Sobsey, 2001, p. 404).

In a gesture that showed that *Angel* was more than just a book, an opportunity arose for Dale to meet with leaders of the newly founded national association at the Los Angeles chapter, and the book's publisher, Revell, felt it important that some royalties accruing from *Angel* be presented at this meeting. To do this, they provided Dale a check for $5,000 as an advance. When Dale arrived to present the donation, the auditorium in which the ceremony was to be held was overflowing with parents and their children. As Dale approached the presentation platform, a single clap began, immediately joined by others, until it was a thunderous ovation that would not abate. Dale stood, watching the audience, and then dropped her head, and began to weep. She was escorted off to regain her composure before coming on stage again to present the donation.

"This is the first time in my life that I've broken up in public," Dale related to a friend, "but I simply couldn't help it. I looked out there and saw Robin's face in the face of every child. And the look in every parent's face—the pain, the control, the beautiful look in their eyes. It was too much" (Garrison, 1956, p. 150).

Roy and Dale went beyond simply donating money to the organization, however, by lending their valuable image and names to the cause. In the Roy Rogers–Dale Evans "Helping Hand Riders" campaign (see Figure 8.9), Roy and Dale's familiar, smiling, and cowboy-hat-bedecked faces appeared on the front of envelopes distributed by what was then called the National Association for Retarded Children.

"Hi Kids!" the pitch began.

Figure 8.9. National Association for Retarded Children "Helping Hand Riders" campaign with Roy Rogers and Dale Evans Rogers. (Image from author's personal collection.)

We want to tell you about some children in your neighborhood and all over the country who aren't quite as lucky as you. These are mentally retarded children who do not learn as fast as you do and probably never will be able to.

These mentally retarded children need your help. They like to play and have fun just like you. When you play with them try to understand and help them all you can.

These children have to have special care and programs, which cost lots of money. Do you want to help them? If you do, put your donations in this envelope, seal it, and give it to your teacher. You will be making a lot of children happy.

"Remember," the pitch ended, "Retarded Children Can be Helped."

In 1959, Roy Rogers and Dale Evans were recognized by the National Association for Retarded Children for their distinguished service to the association. *Angel Unaware* had, almost literally, created the national association. The book's success surprised everyone associated with it. *Angel* was released on March 16, 1953. Simultaneously, the book was printed, in its entirety, in the *Los Angeles Daily News* between March 15 and 18. On April 12, it debuted at number 15 on the *New York Herald Tribune's* Sunday nonfiction bestseller list. By April 26, it had climbed to number 10; by May 10, to number 5; and by the end of May it was the bestselling nonfiction book in the country, according to *Retail Bookseller* (Garrison, 1956, p. 79).

On March 23, at the Broadway Department Store in Hollywood, Dale was scheduled to appear and autograph copies of *Angel*. The book buyer for the department store expressed low expectations for the turnout—such events typically drew only a dedicated few, and the book had only been out one week. When Dale approached the autograph table from a back room, she saw that they'd underestimated the emotional power of *Angel*. The line of autograph seekers stretched through the store and outside onto the street. Many of them were parents of children with an intellectual disability, waiting silently, almost contemplatively, with their child next to them.

"You knew," wrote the Rogers's publicist Maxine Garrison, whose 1956 book *The Angel Spreads Her Wings* chronicled the story of *Angel Unaware*'s rise, "that this was not a usual thing for them [the parents], to take the children out and know they would be accepted among strangers . . . Dale, they knew, would understand" (Garrison, 1956, p. 89).

Many of the children with their parents had Down syndrome, and it was emotionally draining for Dale to see so many children that reminded her of Robin. It was also an emotional evening for many of the parents as they met the woman who had freed them from years of isolation and guilt.

The Broadway Department Store sold 1,000 copies of *Angel Unaware* that evening. By the time Garrison's *The Angel Spreads Her Wings* was written, only three years after *Angel* was published, the book had sold more than half a million copies. At the turn of the 21st century, *Angel Unaware* had sold more than 1.1 million copies (Sobsey, 2001, p. 404).

Pearl Buck also donated the royalties from *The Gifts They Bring: Our Debt to the Mentally Retarded,* published in 1965, to the National Association for Retarded Children. Although the royalties were not as plentiful as the royalties from *Angel Unaware,* the donation came at a time during which the association was in financial crisis and provided much-needed support.

In October 1958, Pearl Buck presented the keynote address to the growing association at its national conference in Philadelphia (see Figure 8.10).

Figure 8.10. Pearl Buck (left) on the evening of October 11, 1958, when she delivered the keynote address at the National Association for Retarded Children's annual conference in Philadelphia. Dr. Elizabeth Boggs, a founder of the association and a major advocate in intellectual and developmental disabilities during the 20th century, is seated on the right. (Image from author's personal collection.)

"It would be impossible to express to you what it means to be here tonight," the Nobel laureate told those assembled. "Perhaps I, better than anyone else in view of my white hair, can go back and remember what it was when you really, and I too, didn't exist."

"Well, it's been wonderful to watch that change [change in the parent movement]. And as we came from our first awakening of what shall I do about our particular child and where can I find a place that my child can go? To watch the enlargement which tonight is proved by your presence here, an enlargement which says 'what can we do for the whole situation?' Is the whole situation 'what can we do in our community?' What will the state do for our community? What will the government do for our community?"

THE HOPES AND DREAMS OF FRAN PORTER

It is important to remember that during the 1950s, families with children with intellectual disability were still faced with an almost total lack of support in their communities. The community movement was still a decade away. There were few if any alternatives except for institutionalization or home placement. Thus, across small and large towns throughout the country, families began joining together to support one another and plan for needed services. While this would eventually be seen as the start of a movement with international impact, it was not recognized as such at the time.

These families saw themselves as doing what needed to be done. Although they were people with a mission, they had no strategic plan, no funding, no policy statements, no guide to show the way, and yet they steadily moved forward—but they did have a clear goal, as is reflected in the following statement (Crutcher, 1990, p. 17): "All parents have as their goal to live and die in peace, knowing that our children are all right, safe, happy, and living productive lives full of opportunities."

Fran Porter's story, as told to McGill-Smith and Dean (2002), describes the situation of many parents at that time:

> When Dana was nearly 4, we finally met other parents of children with Down syndrome. They not only answered our questions but told us about planned or available services for our son. For us, it was the moment when our isolation ended, when we found that there were others who could understand the doubt and worry and frustration we felt for our son. For our family it was a new beginning . . . and for my husband and me, for the first time, there was hope. (p. 64)

The hopes and dreams of Fran Porter—and thousands of parents like Fran and her husband—were initially channeled into a network of activities centered around establishing parent training programs, 'special education' classes, and work activity centers/sheltered workshops.

One of the first Parent Training Programs was established as part of the ENCOR program in Omaha, Nebraska (Porter, 1978). The philosophy of the program was that parents experiencing a crisis can be helped by parents who have made an exemplary adjustment to their own child with a handicap, and who have the capacity and willingness to help others by sharing their experiences. Furthermore, the philosophy of the program was to share their knowledge with new parents so that no child would be institutionalized due to lack of awareness of services in the community.

There were three prominent features of the Parent Training Program that became the framework for national and international replication. First, a speakers' bureau was established that allowed parents to share their stories with the media, the medical community, and legislators. Second, social events were a regular part of the program which allowed new families to meet many role models. Third, it became a community-wide program that provided community education, outreach to the medical community, media connections, and outreach to the religious community (McGill-Smith & Dean, 2002).

A primary push of the parent movement was to get access to education for their children. In fact, the passage of the Education for All Handicapped Children Act in 1975 might be seen as the crowning accomplishment of the parent movement. One account of such efforts appeared in *A Practical Guide for Nebraskans with Developmental Disabilities* (Schalock, 2002):

> During the 1950s, in Nebraska and around the country, things started to change. Small programs began to appear in local communities. Most of these local programs were school programs run by volunteers. The volunteers were often the parents of the children who were in the program. These little programs continued to grow. Many eventually added a professional teacher. The costs of these programs were often paid for by fees charged to families and profits from local fundraising events. (p. 43)

As chronicled by Ferdinand and Marcus (2002) about the Nebraska effort, the following activities reflect how throughout the country parents established educational services for their children.

- In Fremont (Nebraska) families established the Dodge County Association for the Aid of the Mentally Handicapped. By December 1957, with their mothers as teachers, seven children began attending classes in a school held in the Fremont YMCA. In 1959, a local realty company donated an old house to the association for use as a school, which became known as the Fremont Opportunity Center.

- In 1957, Broken Bow (Nebraska) saw the Custer County Association for Retarded Children offering classes to eight children in their newly established "education facility." These children were also served in a group home, which was known at that time as a living-in facility.

- In Hastings (Nebraska) the parents organized and staffed a school, optimistically named the Hope Training School. The families formed a nonprofit corporation and received several apartment buildings from the city through a federal surplus program. The parents converted one of the apartments to serve as the program's school. The other apartments were rented out to provide income for the corporation to operate the school.

Young children with a disability were not the only focus of parental activities. Families with adolescent or adult members with a disability also needed services, which typically involved establishing work activity centers that in time became sheltered workshops. The original intent was to provide training and employment services as part of a continuing long-term program of accommodating the social and vocational needs of individuals with significant functional limitations. The funding for such programs was initially provided from Title XX funds, combined with state and local public and private financing. To many families and clients the sheltered workshop provided a vehicle whereby individuals could become more productive and valued within a safe environment. Parents were highly committed to these programs, which represented their best efforts to provide meaningful and productive activities (Schalock, 1983).

Collectively, the establishment of advocacy organizations, along with parent training programs, special education classes, and opportunity centers/sheltered workshops reflected both the needs and the aspirations of parents during the critical decades of the 1950s and 1960s. Indeed, during these two decades these activities represented what parents had to do for needed services and supports, and to set the course for what happened next: working collaboratively to change public policies and focus on the need for institutional reform, deinstitutionalization, and community services. Parents played a key role in each of these activities; however, they also worked collaboratively with professionals, legislators, and other key stakeholders.

FROM MENTAL DEFICIENCY TO MENTAL RETARDATION

The period from 1950 to 1980 consisted of rapid changes in prevailing systems of support for children, youth, and adults with intellectual and developmental disabilities and their families, but in truth, not much actually changed about how disability, and in turn, intellectual disability, was understood. The term *mental retardation* replaced the term *mental deficiency* as the term most prevalently used, but the prevailing meaning associated with this term, mental defectiveness manifested in retarded mental development, remained in common usage.

Diagnosis and classification systems were promulgated to meet the needs of diagnosing and classifying children, youth, and adults with intellectual disability to be eligible for the newly emerging community services. The American Association on Mental Deficiency, whose name did not change to the American Association on Mental Retardation until 1987, proposed a tripartite definition of mental retardation that remained fundamentally unchanged for decades, in which mental retardation was diagnosed based upon significantly subaverage intellectual functioning as measured on IQ tests, significantly subaverage adaptive behavior, and manifestation in the developmental period, before the age of 18. The most common classification system divided people with intellectual impairments into five groups: 1) borderline (IQ generally 85–70), 2) mild (IQ 69–55), 3) moderate (IQ 54–40), 4) severe (IQ 39–25), and 5) profound (IQ below 25). These classification group names soon morphed to refer to the people so classified within—the moderately retarded or the mildly retarded.

Three issues pertaining to understanding the construct now called intellectual disability warrant mentioning as being new to this era. First, although the lives of people with intellectual disability and the lives of people who are poor have always intermingled, the effect of poverty in causing intellectual disability was a topic that emerged as important in this era. Second, what to do about or with the population of people whose IQ scores were too high to qualify them as having mental retardation but who clearly had difficulty adjusting to life in society was a topic of consideration. Third, the role of culture and mental retardation emerged as a point of discussion. That these topics affected the same people is of note; people who were disproportionately poor were often people of color, whose educational opportunities were limited.

These discussions moved the field away from the dogma of the first half of the 20th century pertaining to heredity. The nature–nurture controversy wasn't by any means resolved, but there was, at least, a controversy. In the zeitgeist of the 1960s war on poverty and the civil rights movements, the recognition that intellectual impairment was both affected and caused by circumstances associated with poverty, from the ingestion of lead-based paint to the lack of quality maternal health care came full circle. Causes of mental retardation were deemed to be familial or cultural-familial versus organic.

The problems associated with people who were referred to as "borderline retarded" but who, in many cases, were not eligible (or chose not to participate in) services for people with mental retardation was captured by Robert Edgerton (1967) with the now-classic study *The Cloak of Competence: Stigma in the Lives of the Mentally Retarded.* Starting in 1960, Edgerton followed 110 adults who had been deinstitutionalized from Pacific State Hospital in Los Angeles between 1949 and 1958. This longitudinal study found that before being institutionalized, many of these individuals were told, in the terms of the era, that they were feebleminded. Deinstitutionalization presented them with a strong motivation to explain their hospitalization as due to nerves, surgery, alcoholism, and so forth, and to deny their disability. While "passing for normal" was motivated by an attempt to avoid the prior stigma of being identified as "retarded," after leaving the hospital and returning to the real world, these people struggled to adapt (Snell et al., 2009).

The stereotypes of disability that dominated in the pre–World War II era—people with intellectual disability as menaces to society or moral imbeciles—were replaced with more humane, though still in many ways debilitating, stereotypes. People with disabilities were viewed as objects to be fixed, cured, rehabilitated, and, at the same time, pitied. They came to be viewed as "victims" of their disabling condition and worthy of charity. Shapiro (1993) described this phenomenon when discussing the emergence of the poster child as a fundraising tool:

> The poster child is a surefire tug at our hearts. The children picked to represent charity fund-raising drives are brave, determined, and inspirations, the most innocent victims of the cruelest whims of life and health. Yet they smile through their unlucky fates . . . no other symbol of disability is more beloved by Americans than the cute and courageous poster child. (p. 12)

Within this stereotype, people with intellectual disabilities were viewed as so-called holy innocents (e.g., special messengers, children of God) and thus incapable of sin and not responsible for their own actions. Based at least partially on the prevalent use of mental age calculated from intelligence scores, people with intellectual disability began to be perceived as so-called eternal children. Although no longer feared and blamed for all social ills, people with intellectual disabilities were perceived as children, to be protected, pitied, and cared for.

CHRISTMAS IN PURGATORY

Although the years between 1950 and 1970 were critical to the development of a community-based system, it is important to remember that this was also the time that the institution census peaked, and many people with intellectual disability were still institutionalized. Institutions that had existed for a century were by then often massive warehouses characterized by inhumane living circumstances. Like many reform efforts, initial attempts were made to fix the system. People with intellectual disability still needed protection; they were victims, holy innocents.

Events in the mid-1960s would change the course of the movement to one of deinstitutionalization. In 1966, Senator Robert Kennedy, Eunice Kennedy Shriver's younger brother, visited the Willowbrook State School on Long Island, New York, where in the previous decade inmates had been infected with the hepatitis virus to test a vaccine for that disease, without their or their parent's knowledge. Kennedy emerged into

Figure 8.11. Images from *Christmas in Purgatory*. (From Blatt, B. [1964]. *Christmas in purgatory* [p. 12]. Syracuse, NY: Center on Human Policy, Syracuse University; reprinted with permission.)

the light of day from his tour, obviously shaken, and in a press conference said this of the institution, which by then housed 6,000 inmates:

> In state institutions for the mentally retarded, I think—particularly at Willowbrook—that we have a situation that borders on a snake pit; . . . the children live in filth; many of our fellow citizens are suffering tremendously because of lack of attention, lack of imagination, lack of adequate manpower. [There is] very little future for . . . children who are in these institutions. (Minnesota Governor's Council on Developmental Disabilities, 2006)

Figure 8.11. *(continued)*

Propelled by Kennedy's pronouncements, disability scholar Burton Blatt arranged to tour four institutions in the northeast, none of which were named but one of which was almost certainly Willowbrook, and brought with him photographer Fred Kaplan, who surreptitiously snapped photographs of the horrific conditions in the facilities. The resulting photo essay, titled *Christmas in Purgatory,* showed the stark, black and white photographs of naked, apparently starving, severely disabled inmates or rows of iron beds with children confined to them, juxtaposed with poetry verses and essays selected by Blatt (see Figure 8.11).

"There is hell on earth," began *Christmas in Purgatory,* "and in America there is a special inferno. We were visitors there during Christmas, 1965" (Blatt, 1966, p. i).

When an abridged version of *Christmas* appeared in a 1967 issue of *Life Magazine,* reporters from newspapers in cities and towns that hosted institutions turned their attention to conditions in their community's facility (Taylor, 2006, p. 145). One such local exposé was about Willowbrook and caught the attention of journalist Geraldo Rivera.

In January 1972, Rivera aired a series of investigative reports that set off a torrent of public excoriation of Willowbrook and a series of legal challenges that would, eventually, close the institution. He gained entry into Willowbrook from a friend, Mike Wilkins, who was a physician there. Entering the Willowbrook grounds unannounced with Wilkins and a camera and light operator, Rivera entered a shocking scene.

"I've done perhaps 800 stories," Rivera explained. "In that time I have seen families burned out of their homes. I have stepped over people killed in robberies, in family fights, and in mass violence. I've watched people dying from gunfire, from disease, and from drugs. I thought I had seen the most wretched aspects of life in the City . . . I was wrong" (Rivera, 1972, pp. 16–17).

What Rivera saw, and what he and his crew captured on film and aired to the New York City viewing public, were approximately 70 people with severe disabilities warehoused in a "room that looked like the unfinished basement of a cheap home in the suburbs. Wooden benches and hard chairs were scattered randomly around the room. Plaster was peeling off the dirty, greenish cement walls" (Rivera, 1972, p. 17).

The people, who initially struck Rivera as "freaks" and "things" were huddled in corners of the room or lying in fetal positions under benches and sinks. Years of maltreatment and neglect had exacerbated their physical impairments, and many could not walk. Most were unclothed or partially clothed. Many were dirty and caked in their own or others' waste. The scene recalled the horrors of the Nazi death camps to Rivera.

When the story aired that evening in January 1972, Rivera went home, exhausted but confident that, at least as a journalistic investigative piece, he had succeeded. When he arrived at work the next morning, the station had been inundated with more than 700 phone calls from irate citizens. The station was compelled to follow the story on that evening's newscast, during which Rivera promised viewers that we "showed you that film again because it comes with the promise that we're not going to let this story die."

> We're going back to Willowbrook . . . again.
> We're going to talk to the parents . . . again.
> And look at those horrible wards . . . again.
> And show them to you . . . again and again and again.
> Until somebody changes them. (Rivera, 1972, p. 38)

Return he did, and during his visits he got to know the people behind the medically impaired bodies that had been so long neglected. He interviewed and eventually befriended a young man named Bernard Carabello (who is pictured on the dedication page, with his friend and our colleague, Hank Bersani, to whom this book is dedicated), who had lived at Willowbrook for 18 years. Bernard's story struck a chord among the viewing public.

Rivera's coverage began to spark civil outrage, if not unrest. Parents of children in Willowbrook rallied, demonstrating against the institution's administration. New York Governor Nelson Rockefeller restored funds that had been cut to the New York Department of Mental Hygiene.

The week of January 31, Rivera appeared on the *Dick Cavett Show,* the entire 90 minutes of which were devoted to Willowbrook. Toward the end of the show, Bernard Carabello came out and sat next to Rivera. He told how he'd been put into solitary confinement because he refused to confess to a fabricated homosexual relationship between Carabello and Dr. Wilkins, who had exposed Willowbrook to the world's scrutiny. On September 17, 1987, Willowbrook shut its gates for the last time. Every person living there had been moved to a community-based residence.

PL 94-142 AND GROWTH OF EDUCATION

In the 1950s, diagnostic evaluation and education were key concerns of families. In 1949, twenty-four states provided education to children classified as "educable," with IQs of 50–75, but no state mandated education for children with IQs below 50. The National Association for Retarded Children's position was that the opportunity to learn is a universal right and that all children can learn, if not academic skills, then daily living and life-adjustments skills. This was stated in the organization's first position statement on education in 1953: "Every American child, including every retarded child, has the right to help, stimulation and guidance from skilled teachers provided by his community and state as part of a broadly conceived program of free public education" (National Association for Retarded Children, 1953).

In the early days of the parent movement, chapters of The Arc, as the National Association for Retarded Children is now known, organized classes for children denied public education wherever space could be found—in church basements, vacant buildings, and abandoned one-room schoolhouses. They demonstrated that children with mental retardation could learn. By 1959, 49 states provided classes for children considered educable, and 37 states provided classes for children considered "trainable" (i.e., having IQs of 25–50). This still left children with the most severe disabilities unserved in many states, and no state served children classified as "dependent" retarded (i.e., having IQs under 20). They were considered to be unable to learn, needing only custodial care (PCMR, 1977).

Part of the problem of states providing adequate education for children with mental retardation was the lack of qualified teachers. New educational methods and approaches were necessary in order to individualize instruction for children who exhibited diverse learning styles, functional levels, and needs. In response, The Arc advocated for legislation and funding, and in 1958 Public Law (PL) 85-926, an Act *To Encourage Expansion of Teaching in the Education of Mentally Retarded Children Through Grants to Institutions of Higher Learning and to State Education Agencies,* was enacted (Weintraub, Abeson, Ballard, & LaVor, 1976). It was the first federal legislation passed that provided support for university training programs that served leaders and teachers in special education for children with mental retardation. Most important, this law also established a federal role in dealing with people with mental retardation and their families in the United States.

The Arc continued to advocate for education for all children with what was then called mental retardation. Decisions made by several state chapters, along with The Arc of the United States, that brought successful right-to-education litigation in federal courts was particularly influential. Most notable was the case brought by the *Pennsylvania Association for Retarded Children v. Commonwealth of Pennsylvania* (1971) that sustained the right of all children with mental retardation to a public education. A 1974 goal of the association called for mandatory education laws in each state based on the zero-reject concept, meaning that all children, regardless of the severity of their disability, were entitled to a free and appropriate public education. In 1975, the advocacy begun by parents in the 1950s succeeded with the passage of PL 94-142, the Education for All Handicapped Children Act (now the Individuals with Disabilities Education Act [IDEA]), which required all schools accepting federal funds under the act to educate all children with disabilities, and all truly meant all!

NORMALIZATION AND THE COMMUNITY IMPERATIVE

Perhaps the most significant change in the lives of people with intellectual disability throughout the 20th century was the shift in focus from congregate work and living settings as preferred (indeed, often as the only available) options to the community as the optimal living and working environment. As this chapter has indicated, this focus emerged in the post–World War II era. Braddock, Hemp, Parish, and Westrich (1998) documented that in 1960 there were only 336 community residential settings for people with developmental disabilities in the United States, but that by 2000 there were more than 90,000. Concurrently, in 1967 the nation's institutional census was 194,650; by 2000 it had dropped to less than 50,000.

The importance of the community to the field of mental retardation in the late 1970s was illustrated by *The Community Imperative,* a declaration supporting the rights of all people with disabilities to community living. Issued by the Center on Human Policy at Syracuse University, in 1979, *The Community Imperative* was in response to specific testimony submitted in the *Wyatt v. Stickney* (1974) case, focusing on the deplorable conditions at the Partlow State School and Hospital in Alabama. The purpose of *The Community Imperative* was to serve as a vehicle for persons in the field to communicate their belief to the court and to the nation that all people, regardless of the nature or severity of their disability, have the right to community inclusion. The document was drafted by the Center on Human Policy under the leadership of Dr. Burton Blatt (author of *Christmas in Purgatory*) and was endorsed by more than 300 parents, people with disabilities, and researchers and professionals, including leaders like Gunnar and Rosemary Dybwad, Seymour Sarason, Marc Gold, Bengt Nirje, and other pioneers in the field of mental retardation. *The Community Imperative* stated the following:

In the domain of Human Rights:

- All people have fundamental moral and constitutional rights.
- These right must not be abrogated merely because a person has a mental or physical disability.
- Among these fundamental rights is the right to community living.

In the domain of Educational Programming and Human Services:

- All people, as human beings, are inherently valuable.
- All people can grow and develop.
- All people are entitled to conditions which foster their development.
- Such conditions are optimally provided in community settings.

Therefore:

In the fulfillment of fundamental human rights and in securing optimum development opportunities, all people, regardless of the severity of their disabilities, are entitled to community living. (Center for Human Policy, 1979)

The idea that people with mental retardation should be in the community (and also "of" the community) was planted with the introduction of the normalization principle to the North American audience (Wolfensberger, 1972). Nirje (1969) explained that the normalization principle had its basis in "Scandinavian experiences from the field" and emerged, in essence, from a Swedish law on mental retardation that was passed July 1, 1968. In its original conceptualization, the normalization principle provided guidance for creating services which "let the mentally retarded obtain an existence as close to the normal as possible" (Nirje, 1972, p. 363). Nirje also stated the following:

> As I see it, the normalization principle means making available to the mentally retarded patterns and conditions of everyday life which are as close as possible to the norms and patterns of the mainstream of society. (p. 363)

Nirje (1969), p. 179 identified eight "facets and implications of the normalization principle":

1. Normalization means a normal rhythm of day.

2. Normalization implies a normal routine of life.

3. Normalization means to experience the normal rhythm of the year.

4. Normalization means the opportunity to undergo normal developmental experiences of the life cycle.

5. Normalization means that the choices, wishes and desires [of the mentally retarded] have to be taken into consideration as nearly as possible, and respected.

6. Normalization also means living in a bisexual world.

7. Normalization means normal economic standards [for the mentally retarded].

8. Normalization means that the standards of the physical facility should be the same as those regularly applied in society to the same kind of facilities for ordinary citizens.

Much of the emphasis in the normalization principle related to the importance of people with intellectual disability experiencing the rich stimulation of being involved in their community, in living with family members, and of experiencing friendships. The normalization principle stressed that contact with people without disabilities, and people from both genders, is critically important across all age ranges. The importance of economic self-sufficiency was also highlighted. Finally, Nirje pointed out for the first time that self-determination was critical to the normalization principle.

Ruth Sienkiewicz-Mercer, a woman who lived in a state institution for people with mental retardation, wrote in her autobiography about the importance of community in her life:

> I had never had a place of my own. As a result, I had never worried about buying groceries and planning meals, paying the rent and the phone bill, balancing a checkbook, making appointments, figuring out how to keep the appointments I made—all of the things adults just do. But starting out in society at the age of 28, after living at a state institution for the mentally retarded for sixteen years, I found these everyday tasks confusing and wonderful and frightening. (Sienkiewicz-Mercer & Kaplin, 1989, p. 202)

Sienkiewicz-Mercer's observation acknowledged that living life to its fullest is fundamentally about addressing problems and solving them—about accepting challenges and taking risks. Robert Perske's classic call for allowing people to assume risks illustrated this further:

The world in which we live is not always safe, secure and predictable. . . . Every day that we wake up and live in the hours of that day, there is a possibility of being thrown up against a situation where we may have to risk everything, even our lives. This is the way the real world is. We must work to develop every human resource within us in order to prepare for these days. To deny any person their fair share of risk experiences is to further limit them for healthy living. (Perske, 1972, p. 199)

Robert Perske, Ruth Sienkiewicz-Mercer, Bengt Nirje, and Burton Blatt all wrote about the common theme that life is only worth living if it is in the context of relationships and experiences that enable one to take risks, pursue goals, meet challenges, and make things happen; or to paraphrase another author who wrote on similar themes, to engage in the pursuit of life, liberty, and happiness. A century of experience shows that the place in which such pursuit occurs is one's community.

A LIFE OF POWER

The 1950 through 1980 era was one of progress, and yet one that retained too much of the mindset on intellectual disability from the first half of the 20th century. Progressive ideas of community integration were juxtaposed with horrific incidences of discrimination and abuse. In the early 1970s, physicians from two visible hospitals were accused of withholding treatment from infants with intellectual disability, resulting in an extremely high mortality rate. The resulting court cases, called Baby Doe cases, which continued until the early 1980s, illustrated that many people in the medical community, and in society at large, held low value for the lives of people with intellectual disability.

Along with the growth of community-based residential services and special education, however, this era saw the introduction of an employment movement for people with intellectual disability. The efforts of parents to established sheltered workshops for people with mental retardation resulted in a vast network of such entities, many housed at chapters of the National Association for Retarded Citizens, reflecting the shift from parental advocacy for children to life-span issues. Influenced heavily by the normalization principle, psychologist Marc Gold developed the "try another way" approach, teaching people with severe cognitive impairments assembly skills using a bicycle brake assembly task. Gold's approach was based on mutual respect and an emphasis on abilities, rights, and personal preferences—all themes that would be echoed in the coming decades.

For Raymond Gagne, whose "powerless life" reflected the life of many people with intellectual disability, the 1950s to the 1980s became, instead, a life of power:

When I was 19, I started to work in a workshop. I worked in the workshop for 1 year. We put nails in boxes and then sealed the boxes. I got paid $30 a week. This was the first real money I had to call my own. Within a year I was promoted to the position of supervisor. I learned good work habits such as being on time, doing good work, responsibility, and getting along with others. Although I learned some good things at the workshop, many basic skills were never taught.

When I was in the institution, sometimes I went home for a visit. I didn't want to go back, so I would act up. I didn't know it, but even then I was advocating for myself. At that time, there were no self-advocacy groups like there are now. I wish there had been, so someone could speak up for me. (Wehmeyer, Bersani, & Gagne, 2000, p. 321)

Then, one of the people who worked at the institution in which Ray lived told him that he (the worker) thought that Ray could be successful living in the community. With the belief of that one person, Ray ventured out into a new life.

The day I moved [from the institution to an apartment that I shared with two other men], some staff told me I would be back in a month. They may still be waiting for me to come back. I lived in an apartment for 3 years on my SSI [Social Security Income] income and the income from my job at the institution's workshop. . . . The institution did not have professionals coming to help make the move easier. To be honest, I only saw my social worker a week before I moved. If [I] had a question, [I had to] call the halfway house. . . .

During that fall I moved into my own apartment after a counselor at a camp for people with cerebral palsy told me she thought I could. I did well in living alone for three years. . . .

After living alone for three years, I decided to move near the city where my sister lived. While there I [began to volunteer] with the local chapter of United Cerebral Palsy. I learned about Section 504 of the Rehabilitation Act and helped found an advocacy group named the Massachusetts Coalition of Citizens with Disabilities. I learned the skills of leadership, advocacy, consumer [organization], and assertiveness by watching people, participating in group meetings, and asking questions. . . .

After four years, I moved twice more. I continued to learn new skills and became more involved in self-advocacy and consumer advocacy. I moved to New Bedford, Massachusetts. I was interviewed by the ARC directors and was hired as a public information coordinator. . . . Unlike the staff at the institution, the human service professionals I met at this job treated me with respect. They gave me a chance to contribute my input and feedback, and believed in many of my ideas. My colleagues also adapted the working environment to help me communicate with them. After several years I became the staff liaison to a self-advocacy group of adults with mental retardation. (Gagne, 1994, pp. 332–334)

Ray Gagne was an early pioneer in the self-advocacy movement, and his experiences leading into the last two decades of the 20th century presaged the major themes of those years.

REFERENCES

Abeson, A., & Davis, S. (2000). The parent movement in mental retardation. In M.L. Wehmeyer & J.R. Patton (Eds.), *Mental retardation in the 21st century* (pp. 19–34). Austin, TX: PRO-ED.

Blatt, B., & Kaplan, F. (1964). *Christmas in purgatory: A photographic essay on mental retardation.* New York, NY: Allyn & Bacon.

Braddock, D. (2010). Honoring Eunice Kennedy Shriver's legacy in intellectual disability. *Intellectual and Developmental Disabilities, 48*(1), 63–72.

Braddock, D., Hemp, R., Parish, S., & Westrich, J. (1998). *The state of the states in developmental disabilities.* Washington, DC: American Association on Mental Retardation.

Buck, P. (1970). *The Kennedy women: A personal appraisal.* New York, NY: Cowles.

Center for Human Policy. (1979). *The community imperative.* Retrieved from http://www.freedom clearinghouse.com/do/commimperative.htm

Crutcher, D.M. (1990). Quality of life vs. quality judgments: A parent's perspective. In R.L. Schalock (Ed.), *Quality of life: Perspectives and issues* (pp. 17–22). Washington, DC: American Association on Mental Retardation.

D'Antonio, M. (2004). *The state boys rebellion*. New York, NY: Simon & Schuster.

Edgerton, R. (1967). *The cloak of confidence: Stigma in the lives of the mentally retarded*. Los Angeles: University of California Press.

Ferdinand, R., & Marcus, J. (2002). Doing what we had to do in the 1950s: Parents build the foundation. In R.L. Schalock (Ed.), *Out of darkness and into the light: Nebraska's experience with mental retardation* (pp. 123–134). Washington, DC: American Association on Mental Retardation.

Gagne, R. (1994). A self-made man. In V.J. Bradley, J.W. Ashbaugh, & B.C. Blaney (Eds.), *Creating individual supports for people with developmental disabilities* (pp. 327–334). Baltimore: Paul H. Brookes, Co.

Garrison, M. (1956). *The angel spreads her wings*. Westwood, NJ: Fleming H. Revell.

McGill-Smith, P., & Dean, S. (2002). The pilot parent program. In R.L. Schalock (Ed.), *Out of darkness and into the light: Nebraska's experience with mental retardation* (pp. 63–72). Washington, DC: American Association on Mental Retardation.

Minnesota Governor's Council on Developmental Disabilities. (2006). *Parallels in time II: 1950–2005*. Retrieved from http://www.mnddc.org/parallels2/index.htm

National Association of Parents and Friends of Mentally Retarded Children. (1950). *Constitution and bylaws*. Minneapolis, MN: Author.

National Association for Retarded Children. (1953). *Education bill of rights for the retarded* (Position paper). New York, NY: Author.

Nirje, B. (1969). The normalization principle and its human management implications. In R.B. Kugel & W. Wolfensberger (Eds.), *Changing patterns in residential services for the mentally retarded* (pp. 179–195). Washington DC: President's Committee on Mental Retardation.

Nirje, B. (1972). The right to self-determination. In W. Wolfensberger (Ed.), *The principle of normalization in human services* (pp. 363–392). Toronto, Canada: National Institute on Mental Retardation.

Pennsylvania Association for Retarded Children v. Commonwealth of Pennsylvania, 334 F. Supp. 1257 (E.D. Pa. 1971), 343 F. Supp. 279 (E.D.Pa. 1972).

Perske, R. (1972). The dignity of risk. In W. Wolfensberger (Ed.), *The principle of normalization in human services* (pp. 197–211). Toronto, Canada: National Institute on Mental Retardation.

Porter, F. (1978). *The pilot parent program: A design for developing a program for parents of handicapped children*. Omaha, NE: Greater Omaha Association for Retarded Citizens.

President's Committee on Mental Retardation. (1977). *MR 76: Mental retardation past and present*. Washington, DC: Author.

Prouty, R.W., Smith, G., & Lakin, K.C. (2006). *Residential services for persons with developmental disabilities: Status and trends through 2005*. Minneapolis: University of Minnesota, Research and Training Center on Community Living/Institute on Community Integration.

Rivera, G. (1972). *Willowbrook: A Report on how it is and why it doesn't have to be that way*. New York, NY: Random House.

Rogers, D.E. (1953). *Angel unaware*. New York, NY: Fleming H. Revell.

Rogers, R., Evans, D., Stern, J., & Stern, M. (1994). *Happy trails: Our life story*. New York, NY: Simon & Schuster.

Schalock, R.L. (1983). *Services for developmentally disabled adults: Development, implementation, and evaluation*. Baltimore, MD: University Park Press.

Schalock, R.L. (Ed.). (2002). *Out of darkness and into the light: Nebraska's experience with mental retardation*. Washington, DC: American Association on Mental Retardation.

Shapiro, J.P. (1993). *No pity: People with disabilities forging a new civil rights movement*. New York, NY: Crown.

Shorter, E. (2000). *The Kennedy family and the story of mental retardation*. Philadelphia, PA; Temple University Press.

Sienkiewicz-Mercer, R., & Kaplan, S. (1989). *I raise my eyes to say yes*. West Hartford, CT: Whole Health Books.

Smith, J.D., & Mitchell, A.L. (2001). Sacrifices for the miracle: The polio vaccine research and children with mental retardation. *Mental Retardation, 39*(5), 405–409.

Snell, M.E., Luckasson, R., Borthwick-Duffy, S., Bradley, V., Buntinx, W., Craig, E.M., . . . Yeager, M.H. (2009). The characteristics and needs of people with intellectual disability who have higher IQs. *Intellectual and Developmental Disabilities, 47*(3), 220–233.

Sobsey, D. (2001). Dale Evans and the great rescue: A parent's view. *Mental Retardation, 29*, 401–404.

Taylor, S.J. (2006). *Christmas in purgatory*: A retrospective look. *Mental Retardation, 44,* 145–149.

Trent, J.W. (1994). *Inventing the feeble mind: A history of mental retardation in the United States.* Berkeley: University of California Press.

Wehmeyer, M.L., Bersani, H., & Gagne, R. (2000). Riding the third wave: Self-determination and self-advocacy in the 21st century. In M.L. Wehmeyer & J.R. Patton (Eds.), *Mental retardation in the 21st century* (pp. 315–333). Austin, TX: PRO-ED.

Weintraub, F.J., Abeson, A., Ballard, J., & LaVor, M. (1976). *Public policy and the education of exceptional children.* Reston, VA: The Council for Exceptional Children.

Wolfensberger, W. (1972). *The principle of normalization in human services.* Toronto, Canada: National Institute on Mental Retardation.

Wyatt v. Stickney, 325 F. Supp 781 (1974).

9

The Self-Advocacy Movement

Late Modern Times (1980 CE to Present)

Dianne L. Ferguson, Philip M. Ferguson, and Michael L. Wehmeyer

In 1990, the Americans with Disabilities Act was added to the legal protections afforded to people with intellectual and other disabilities, and as a result of the deinstitutionalization movement, the independent living movement, and an emerging civil rights movement for people with disabilities, people with disabilities began to achieve more positive community living, employment, and education. The burgeoning self-advocacy movement and these dramatic successes in all aspects of life led to the understanding that historic conceptualizations of disability were no longer useful. As a result, disability began to be understood in terms of the fit between a person's capacities and the demands of the environment (instead of as a problem within the person) and the focus began to shift to identify better ways to modify the context to enable people to be successful. There remains much work to be done, but the progress since 1980 places the field at a point where people with intellectual disability can be contributing members of their communities and lead rich, full lives.

Mickey Rooney stars in "Bill," the true story of the successful integration into community life of Bill Sackter, a retarded adult who had spent 44 years in a mental institution on GE Theater Dec. 22 on CBS-TV, 9-11 p.m., ET.

Figure 9.1. Press release photo of Mickey Rooney as Bill Sackter. (Image from author's personal collection.)

*O*n December 22, 1981, the Hallmark channel aired a made-for-TV movie titled, eponymously, *Bill*. Starring Mickey Rooney and Dennis Quaid, the movie was a commercial and critical hit. Mickey Rooney, the venerable child actor, won an Emmy and a Golden Globe Award for the lead actor. Barry Morrow, who would go on to write and direct *Rain Man*, won an Emmy for outstanding writing.

Rooney (see Figure 9.1) played the role of William Sackter, who wanted people to call him Bill. He was an unlikely hero and subject of not only this movie but also of a sequel, also starring Rooney, with Quaid and Helen Hunt; a book (*The Unlikely Celebrity: Bill Sackter's Triumph Over Disability,* by Thomas Walz, 1998); and a feature-length documentary (*A Friend Indeed: The Bill Sackter Story,* www.billsackter.com).

Bill Sackter was born in 1913, the only son of Russian immigrants who operated a grocery store in St. Paul, Minnesota. In 1920, Bill's father died because of a weak heart, a victim of the recurrent flu epidemics from 1918 to 1920. Bill's mother was unable to run the grocery store and tend to her three children on her own, and applied to the State of Minnesota for a "mother's pension." Bill had the unfortunate experience of growing up in the height of the American eugenics era, discussed in depth in Chapter 6. In 1917, Minnesota had passed a law authorizing a State Board of Control to assume guardianship of people deemed to be feebleminded and providing them, through county welfare boards, to make commitments to state institutions. When Mary Sackter applied for a pension following her husband's death, it was granted based upon the requirement that Bill be made a ward of the state and sent to a so-called training school.

That institution was in Faribault, Minnesota, and under the supervision of A.C. Rogers, the Minnesota School for the Feeble-Minded and Epileptics had become one of the most visible such institutions in the nation, hosting national meetings of other superintendents. Rogers, a physician, like other superintendents of his era, was deeply involved in the eugenics movement, chairing the subcommittee on feeblemindedness of the American Breeders Association's committee on eugenics.

In 1920, at the age of 7 years, Bill was taken from home to Faribault. His mother visited him once, though she wrote him periodically and even sent clothes and food, but he never saw his sisters again, and he never heard from his mother after the age of 12. He had an uncle who was also an inmate of the Faribault institution, so he saw his aunts, who came to visit his uncle, periodically. In fact, his mother, in 1925, had written the superintendent of the institution to ask if Bill might be allowed to come home. She had moved, with a daughter, to Detroit. The superintendent, predictably, wrote back that Bill would need lifelong supervision, and his mother gave up hope of seeing her son again, eventually moving to Canada with a second husband (Walz, 1998, p. 10).

Bill was alone, confined to an institution that, like its contemporary counterparts, was growing disproportionate to the original specifications for the buildings and population. From the moment he arrived in Faribault, he was subject to abuse and what amounted to slavery. In one particularly horrific instance, he was literally scalped by an attendant who was physically abusing Bill, and while holding his hair, pushed him down some stairs. Bill wore wigs, many ill-fitting, much of the rest of his life. Like other more capable inmates, he was responsible for feeding younger and more disabled inmates, and working in other tasks in the institution, including working in the institution's garden and pushing food carts from the main kitchen out to the dormitories (Walz, 1998, pp. 23–24).

By 1955, when Bill had lived at Faribault for 30 years, the institution housed 3,355 inmates, far exceeding its original capacity. Up to this point, Bill's story is one that could have appeared in Chapter 6. He was just one of many unfortunate people who were swept into the institution system in the first decades of the 20th century and whose lives were, at best, desperate.

In 1962, however, a woman responded to an ad in the newspaper that asked for correspondents for people without family who lived in Faribault. Through this program, Bill got to know Hally Johnson, who would not only correspond with Bill, but visited him at Faribault, took him out into the Twin Cities area, and brought him to her home for meals. She learned that Bill was gregarious, inquisitive, and loved being out of the confines of the institution. After several near misses, on September 4, 1964, forty-four years after he was admitted, Bill was released from Faribault. He lived in a boardinghouse in Minneapolis and, supported by the boardinghouse's property owner and by Hally Johnson, his friend, Bill made do. Despite his many job-related experiences and skills learned while at Faribault, the best Bill could do was to get a job at a sheltered workshop, making less than a dollar a day. Despite the property owner and Ms. Johnson's attempts, Bill became socially isolated and alone. Bill's case manager from the state, burdened by a large caseload, was unable to do more than just perfunctory checks; but on one of those, the case manager became aware of an ulceration on Bill's leg, which required multiple hospitalizations (Walz, 1998, pp. 28–29).

The boardinghouse was in a rundown section of Minneapolis, and Bill was mugged twice. Finally, in 1970, his case manager was able to get Bill a full-time job at a country club, and later that year Bill moved into a small sleeping room above the kitchen at the club (Walz, 1998, p. 30). It was at the club that Bill met Barry Morrow, a social work student who, with his wife, became friends with Bill, helping him to build a community. An aspiring filmmaker, Morrow took videotape of Bill to document his life—footage which is used in the documentary *A Friend Indeed*. When one of Barry's professors, Dr. Tom Walz, was offered the deanship of the School of Social Work at the University of Iowa, he offered a position in Iowa City to Morrow. Morrow accepted, but because Bill was a ward of the state of Minnesota, Bill was not allowed to move. Shortly after, Bill's ulcerated leg had to be amputated and he was to be sent back to Faribault (Walz, 1998, pp. 37–38).

Morrow petitioned the state to become Bill's guardian and told Walz that if he came to Iowa, so did Bill. Walz readily acquiesced and sought a job for Bill in the School of Social Work at the University of Iowa. After a couple of false starts, Morrow hit upon the idea to have Bill operate a small coffee dispenser in the main corridor of the School of Social Work (Walz, 1998, p. 49).

Thus began Wild Bill's Coffeeshop, a staple of the University of Iowa School of Social Work. To this day, Wild Bill's is operated by a person with a disability and provides opportunities for university students to interact with people with disabilities, as well as providing a social focal point for the school and the university. It was as proprietor of Wild Bill's that Bill Sackter had a chance to show the gifts that the institution had ignored. His gregarious nature, cheerful disposition, and universal goodwill made everyone he met on the job his friend. His status as a local celebrity grew as he became integrated into the broader university community, his religious community, then into the civic community. In 1977, Bill was recognized as the Iowa Handicapped Citizen of the Year. At the award ceremony, Bill pulled out his harmonica and, with the governor of Iowa on the stage with him, played a raucous rendition of the "Too Fat Polka," his favorite song to play, to the delight of the audience. He became a frequent attendee at Bar Mitzvahs in Iowa City, after his own Bar Mitzvah celebration. He was a favorite entertainer and visitor of the university's early childhood center, delighting a whole generation of young Iowa citizens. Friends, claimed Bill, were the basis of his "good life" (Walz, 1998, p. 65). Many people in Iowa City knew and liked Bill Sackter before December of 1981. After that, everyone knew him.

For a period of two years, Bill Sackter became a national celebrity, and not just a local celebrity. He attended, with Barry Morrow, both the Emmy and Golden Globe Award ceremonies. At the Golden Globe ceremony, Bill took the stage with Barry Morrow to accept Mickey Rooney's award on the actor's behalf. Bill's reputation had preceded him, and the television station executives required Morrow to confiscate Bill's harmonica from him. At the end of Bill's short acceptance speech on behalf of Rooney, and as Morrow was heading off the stage, Bill whipped out a backup harmonica, turned back to the microphone, and started playing the "Too Fat Polka." A stunned Morrow froze, but before he could act, Jane Fonda, seated at a table near the stage, began clapping in rhythm with Bill's foot stomping, and soon enough, the entire audience was clapping along with the performance. Bill was finally persuaded by Morrow to end his impromptu concert, but left to a standing ovation from Hollywood's elite (Walz, 1998, pp. 93–94).

More than just a compelling story, *Bill* (the movie) was America's introduction to the notion that a person with an intellectual disability could become a valued member of the community. Bill soon became an unofficial spokesperson for the Association for Retarded Citizens, traveling to speak at chapters around the country (see Figure 9.2).

Bill died at home, asleep in his overstuffed rocking chair, in June 1983, from a blood clot that had traveled out of his long-problematic leg. Seven years at home, then 44 wasted years in an institution, followed by 19 years in his community. Bill's story is one emblematic of the early decades of the 1900s, but it is that short two decades, highlighted by two years of national celebrity after the 1981 movie release, that makes his story more important to be told in this final chapter of the book. His legacy was not of the institution—as was the unfortunate fate for Emma Wolverton (i.e., Deborah Kallikak), who never had the opportunity to live outside the institution—but one of community hero. The Association for Retarded Citizens established a new award in his honor after his death, and the Bill Sackter Award has recognized dozens of people who, like Bill, lived a part of their lives in the oppression of institutions, but went on to become valued and loved members of their communities. On April 13, 2009, the University of Iowa School of Social Work hosted Bill Sackter Day to remember the man who had such an impact on that community's life.

RIDING THE THIRD WAVE OF THE DISABILITY MOVEMENT

Figure 9.2. Bill Sackter at an event hosted by a chapter of the National Association for Retarded Citizens. (Image from author's personal collection.)

The history of the disability movement can be characterized in three distinct waves (Wehmeyer, Bersani, & Gagne, 2000), each discussed in previous chapters. From roughly the mid-1800s to the mid-1900s, professionals dominated, creating a professional field and holding sway over all decisions. After World War II, parents demanded a voice in decisions about the lives of their sons and daughters and, bolstered by visible parents such as Pearl Buck and Dale Evans Rogers, created what became the parent movement: a second wave of the disability movement.

The third wave of the disability movement, the self-advocacy, or self-determination movement, emerged through the 1970s and continued into the 1980s. Several factors contributed to the emergence of this Third Wave: the impact of the normalization principle, progress in deinstitutionalization, the effects of the independent living and disability rights movement, and the emergence of a consumer-organized and consumer-run self-advocacy movement.

Shapiro's book on the disability civil rights movement captures a scene that has played out across the United States since the early 1980s:

> "One thing we're going to vote on is a revolution!" Deepfelt cheers erupt from the crowd at the first-ever convention of People First of Connecticut. "Resolution" is the word that T.J. Monroe wanted, but revolution, really, is more like it. Monroe and the three hundred people in the hotel ballroom are trailblazers of the self-advocacy movement, a new and spreading crusade of people with mental retardation to make their own decisions about everything, from where they live to what they are called. (Shapiro, 1993, p. 85)

"You have to do two things today," Monroe exhorts his rapt followers. "You have to make thunder. You have to speak for your rights" (Shapiro, 1993, p. 86).

The origins of the self-advocacy movement are usually attributed to a small group of people with intellectual disability in Salem, Oregon, who are credited with formulating the phrase "We are people first" (Edwards, 1982). The roots of that movement, however, lie in Sweden in the late 1960s and 1970s. Beginning in 1965 in Sweden, Nirje (1969) described the use of social clubs called *flamslattsklubben* to promote training in Sweden for "the adolescent retardate." This training was embedded within Nirje's development of the normalization principle. Within only a few years, reports on the training for the social groups included instruction in parliamentary procedure (Nirje, 1969). In July 1972, the Spastics Society in England organized the Campaign for the Mentally Handicapped and hosted a conference for people with intellectual disability titled "Our Life" (Dybwad, 1996, p. 8). The first Canadian conference was held in British Columbia in 1973, and a number of people from Oregon attended that event, leading them to organize the first American conference from which the People First language emerged, soon becoming the name of the organization established as a result of the conference (Dybwad, 1996).

Gradually, similar activities were organized and conducted through the United States. It is difficult to get a handle on how widespread the self-advocacy movement for people with intellectual disability is in America; nobody keeps formal statistics and state and local self-advocacy come and go, as is the way of all volunteer-led entities. In September 1990, a national conference for self-advocates was held in Estes Park, Colorado, at which time a decision was made to create a national entity to provide a national umbrella organization for self-advocacy groups. In September 1991, another national conference was held in Nashville, at which the proposed national organization was established, named at the first board meeting in December of the same year as Self-Advocates Becoming Empowered (SABE; Schoultz & Ward, 1996).

Supported by notables such as Justin Dart, considered the father of the Americans with Disabilities Act, and empowered, no doubt, by the passage of that important civil rights act in 1990, the self-advocacy network grew. In 1993, there were state organizations and affiliated chapters in 37 states. Parent advocacy organizations had been early supporters of the self-advocacy movement, and while it was (and is) important that self-advocates have a unique voice, efforts of entities such as the Association for Retarded Citizens to form and support self-advocacy chapters were critical in the emergence of the association. In 1991, in Portland, Oregon, at the same national convention at which the National Association for Retarded Citizens changed its name to The Arc (no acronym), a reflection of the growing stigma associated with the term *retarded* and response to the requests of self-advocates, The Arc held a planning conference setting forth strategies by which chapters of The Arc could involve self-advocates in chapter activities in a meaningful manner (Wehmeyer & Berkobien, 1996). Almost all national disability groups, whether governmental, professional, or parent-focused, now have policies and positions in place to support self-advocacy and to meaningfully involve people with intellectual disability. The self-advocacy network also remains an important presence. An annual SABE conference has been held since the organization of SABE in Nashville in 1991, and recent gatherings have hosted more than 1,500 attendees.

An immediate impact of the self-advocacy movement on how intellectual disability might be understood was the rapid development of leaders in the self-advocacy movement; people with intellectual disability who became visible advocates for themselves and for others. People such as Nancy Ward, Tia Nelis, Barbara Goode, Betty White, Bernard Carabello, Cliff Poetz, Ray Gagne, T.J. Monroe, and many others began changing the way people perceived individuals with intellectual disability. "Nothing about us without us" became the rallying call for the self-advocacy movement.

The importance of people with intellectual disability having their voices heard can be seen in some of the achievements of the movement. Nancy Ward, a self-advocacy leader from Nebraska, who has also served as the president of SABE, among many other roles, wrote about those accomplishments in her state in the early years of the movement:

> One of the things that People First of Nebraska is real proud of is, and this really blows my mind, because you would think that since Nebraska is one of the leading states for community services for people that have disabilities, we would have done this a long time ago. It took People First of Nebraska to notice that we had a lot of obsolete language in our state statutes, like "moron," "idiot," "imbecile," and to do something about it. We got the legislature to get rid of the language. It was a compromise, because we had to replace it with "people who have mental retardation," but at least it's better than nothing. (Ward & Schultz, 1996, p. 209)

In the years since Nancy Ward wrote about vetting obsolete language from state statutes, the self-advocacy movement has been largely responsible for abandoning the use of the term *mental retardation* and for urging organizations to change their names to reflect that; as noted, the Association for Retarded Citizens is now The Arc, the American Association on Mental Retardation is now the American Association on Intellectual and Developmental Disabilities, and the President's Committee on Mental Retardation is now the President's Committee on Intellectual and Development Disabilities. Even more significant, perhaps, was that the term *mental retardation* was replaced by the term *intellectual disability* in all federal legislation in 2010, and states are now adopting similar language in their statutes.

VOICES OF THE PAST: RESIDENTS OF AN INSTITUTION REMEMBER

By the 1980s, the deinstitutionalization movement was in full swing. The notorious Willowbrook State School closed its doors to the last inmate in 1987. A 2005 report from the University of Minnesota found that the total population of people with intellectual disability living in public institutions was just over 40,000 people in 2004. A recent report places that number at just over 30,000 people remaining in state institutions for individuals with intellectual disability (Lakin, Larson, Salmi, & Webster, 2010, p. iii).

Between 1960 and 1976, according to Lakin et al.'s report, eight state institutions closed, while between 1976 and 2004, 166 state institutions or state-supported living units of 16 people or more closed. In that time, 38 states closed at least one institution, and 10 states (and the District of Columbia) had closed all of their state institutions (Research and Training Center on Community Living, 2005). More states followed

Figure 9.3. Oregon State Institution for the Feeble-Minded, circa 1920.
(From Carey, C.H. [1922]. *History of Oregon*. Portland, OR: Pioneer Historical Publishing Co. Image retrieved from http://commons
.wikimedia.org/wiki/File:Oregon_State_Hospital_1920.jpg)

suit, with Virginia being the latest state to declare that it would close its remaining institutions. It is reasonable to predict that by 2025, there will not be a single state-funded institution remaining.

Still, institutional life was a reality for too many people throughout the 1980s and 1990s. In the early 1980s, when Oregon was the epicenter of the People First movement in the United States, the population living in Fairview was still around 1,000 people. In 2000, the Fairview Training Center in Salem, Oregon, closed. Opened in 1907 as the Oregon State Insane Asylum, and boasting one of the magisterial Kirkebride buildings that were popular in early institutions (see Figure 9.3), like most institutions of its era, it was the epicenter for sterilization in Oregon.

It was not the first in the nation, or the last. Even at its peak population, it was not the biggest. As those who lived there know too well, it definitely was not the best; but for others who lived elsewhere, it was also not the worst. Nevertheless, during its existence, almost 10,000 people with intellectual and developmental disabilities lived all or part of their lives at Fairview, and it remains an indelible part of their memories and experience. The very "ordinariness" of Fairview makes its history important, not so much for those who knew it well, but for those future generations who will never have to know it at all (Ferguson, Ferguson, & Brodsky, 2008).

For most of the 20th century, Fairview exhibited all of the practices and policies that have gradually led society to move away from such models of large, congregate care, which have been documented in previous chapters, to a variety of smaller, community-based residential arrangements.

When Fairview closed, a history was produced in honor of all of the people who lived and worked there over the years (Ferguson et al., 2008). It seems worthwhile, as part of understanding the experience of intellectual disability in the most recent era, to consider interviews with previous residents of Fairview, for although the institution is now closed, the experiences of those times continue to influence the lives of Fairview former-residents, as they do all people who have lived in such settings. Furthermore, neither the official story of Fairview nor the unofficial story revealed by letters, case files, and other documents fully captures the lived experience of the residents. Ferguson and colleagues (2008) met former residents, all now living in the community and most participating in various chapters of People First, and invited them to talk about their experiences, interviewing them individually, in couples, and in small groups.

Of course, not all residents had the same or even similar experiences. From the 1950s through the 1970s, the population of Fairview began to shift toward people with more severe intellectual and developmental disabilities, and many of these people were not able to directly describe and reflect on their experiences. In interviews conducted for their history, Ferguson et al. (2008) interviewed 20 people born between 1934 and 1967, who spent from 4 years to 45 years living at Fairview, and described their experiences that spanned three decades of life there. Many were in their 50s or older when interviewed, so their memories for specific dates were sometimes hazy. Still, they all shared very clear descriptions of life at Fairview from their own experiences (Ferguson et al., 2008, p. 47).

As the following quotations illustrate, these experiences differed:

- "I don't have any least favorite about it. Everything was okay when I was there."

- "There are some bad points and some good points about Fairview."

- "I was handicapped, but it made me sicker to be there. It was like a prison. Handcuff. Shut door."

- "I didn't like it there. People mean."

- "It was a good place, you know, but most people liked it. Most people didn't. Most people got different opinions on it."

All who were interviewed expressed some ambivalence about their time at Fairview, and quite a few were very clear that they had not liked their experience. One man elaborated the "good points" as "you've got a roof over your head, a meal to eat, a bed to sleep" (p. 47). "Bad points" varied from person to person, but perhaps the most philosophical reflection came from the same man, who elaborated the good points and bad points:

> Fairview was a good place. I know it's called an institution. It's not our fault, we were put there . . . because our parents didn't take care of [us] and they didn't have no choice . . . so that means the choice we got—we have to live with it, deal with it if you're going to survive—gonna make it out. . . . We made it. We are here. We're still alive. We talk about it today. (Ferguson et al., 2008, pp. 47–48)

In 1961, the sociologist Irving Goffman offered a definition of a "total institution" as any situation when "a group of individuals, cut off from the wider society for an appropriate period of time, together lead an enclosed, formally administered round of life" (Goffman, 1961, p. xii). Much of what the respondents shared about their lives at Fairview echoed this definition. Consider this account of a typical day:

> The attendants woke everybody up at 5:30 in the morning [others said 6:00, but all agreed on *early*]. And if you didn't get up, they would give you a spanking, they will. I put my clothes on. I went up to the boys' dining room and eat at 6:00 in the morning. At 6:30 I worked in the pantry by the boys' and girls' dining room. Monday through Friday, I worked from 6:30 to 8:00. At 9:00, the boss [would] tell me to go back to the cottage. And then come 8:30, about 50 boys had to stand in line and we go to school by two. We'd get out at 11:30 and go to the boys' dining room and eat from 11:30 to 12:00. Then we'd go back to the cottage and get ready to go back to school from 12:30 to 3:30. Then at 4:30 we'd go back to the boys' dining room and then I would work from 5:00 to 7:30. On school nights we went to bed at 8:00 at night. Then on Friday and Saturday nights we'd go to bed at 9:00 at night. But everybody would get up at 5:30 *every* morning. (p. 48)

Every ex-resident we talked to remembered school and work as the twin activities of daily life. For those who stayed in Fairview until they aged out of school, work—which sometimes included multiple jobs—consumed more of the schedule.

Residents were assigned to cottages that were rigidly segregated by sex. The only time men and boys might see women and girls was sometimes going to and from meals and "if you go outside in the playground, we could see them across in another playground." As they got older, dating was not officially allowed—"no, we didn't have no choice"—but more than one clever resident found "ways to sneak around." They would "go into the kitchen and steal food out of the kitchen" (Ferguson et al., 2008, pp. 48–49), or the boys would find ways to sneak over to the girls' cottages. Ferguson et al. heard from several that some residents figured out how to use the maintenance tunnels that connected buildings at Fairview to sneak out and get to friends in other cottages. Like all young people, the goal was not to "mess up," but to bend the rules, or escape them when possible to spend time with friends.

Some of those friendships made at Fairview lasted. One couple who later married—after trying to "elope" by escaping from Fairview only to be found by the police and brought back[1]—described their first meeting:

> I was on H cottage as a little toddler and she was on T cottage. She was sitting by a fence and she had a bag full of candy on her lap and I reached my little hand to her and I got a piece of candy. So that's how I met her. Do you want to add something onto that?
>
> Yeah. We'd been going together for a long time before we got married. (Ferguson et al., 2008, p. 49)

Many people who lived together in Fairview during this period see each other still, have gotten married, or live together. As one person explained, "Tony[2] means the world to me, like Peter does. I don't know what I'd do without Peter and Tony in my life" (Ferguson et al., 2008, p. 49). These long-ago forged friendships have endured for many and continue to provide them with the comfort of shared experience and memories as they forge their lives in the community—although not all friendships had the same happy endings. One man wanted most to "let everyone know that I met true friends for 40 wonderful years now." Another man explained "I made a lot of friends in there" but "I lost one friend. And me and him used to do almost everything together"" (Ferguson et al., 2008, p. 49). When asked what happened, he explained that he "passed away" from seizures:

> He had them [seizures] when he was in there. I knew when he was going into 'em, when he was going to have 'em. He was in the same group home as I was and the paramedics and the cops and everybody asked the staff about how often does he have them and they said "I don't know, ask the guy sitting at the table." That was me. I said I know when he's going into them. I know how long he goes into 'em. And he had one he couldn't come out of. (Ferguson et al., 2008, p. 49)

For everyone, living at Fairview was about "a lot of people. They got big rooms and lots of beds in there." Although the numbers varied over the period of time the respondents lived there, cottages could have as many as 40 residents living in shared space. There was "no privacy. You had to go to the bathroom to get some privacy." One person said that because his bed was by a window, he "went to the bathroom to change" and that everyone "wanted privacy" (Ferguson et al., 2008, p. 50). The communal nature of so many people living in relatively small spaces sometimes led to fears and vulnerability beyond lack of privacy:

> I was fighting to stick up for myself. Okay, now take this for an example. You're laying in bed. There's a divider like a wall where someone could get up and look over. If someone did get up there they could pounce on you down below. So, you gotta fight to stick up for your rights. If you don't, they're going to walk all over you. (Ferguson et al., 2008, p. 50)

Fear was a strong part of memories. Frank reported that "being around people all the damn day—I was so damn scared all the time. I didn't know what to do, which way to turn." Some reported being bullied in some of the cottages—"sometimes kids would kick on you," or sometimes "when you come into the dining room and they want to trade for pancakes for milk. But I didn't like that." The same man that worried about being "pounced on" (Ferguson et al., 2008, p. 50) when sleeping complained about the public nature of the shower routine:

> Every time a kid takes a shower, again there's no privacy. Mrs. Williams is sitting in a chair watching all of the boys strip naked. No privacy . . . if you happen to drop a bar of soap, you gotta scoot your back towards the wall and get your bar of soap. Yeah, just like prison. (Ferguson et al., 2008, p. 49)

Several mentioned being "embarrassed" by the shower routine: "they used to make us sit naked in line, they did. On bath day. I don't think that was right." For one man the lack of privacy and autonomy felt like incarceration:

> The best way I can put it, it was like being in prison. . . . Cause you had guards all the time around you. When you walked around the grounds you never dared walk by yourself. You had somebody with you all the time. When you went on bus rides to the Fair or down to the coast, it didn't make no difference where it was, you had somebody with

you every day. Anywhere. Anyplace. You had a staff person. Work. Walking around the grounds, telling you a certain time to be back. When to be back. What time to be back. When we went to the dining hall at night, you had somebody watching you all the time. The bus to go home, you had somebody watching you get on the bus. (Ferguson et al., 2008, pp. 50–51)

Over time, routines changed and although not everyone interviewed had the same memories of some details, the rules and the lack of privacy emerged frequently in these accounts. One woman complained that inmates were only allowed to take showers at night; others described suddenly being moved to a new cottage with no warning or explanation. People typically reported living in many different cottages, sometimes as many as 5 or 6. A move came suddenly—"They move you. They pack our clothes and take us over there [to the new cottage]" (Ferguson et al., 2008, p. 51). Everyone who talked about the sudden moves talked about them as a surprise. They thought the moves sometimes had to do with their age. Others had the perspective that being moved to cottages meant more autonomy, with permission, for example, to cook for themselves instead of eating in the dining rooms.

Not having to eat in the dining room seemed to be a real benefit, as most of the people interviewed reported not liking the food—"It wasn't good. People got sick." Some apparently didn't like the food so much they threw it against the wall, but that came with consequences: "Wall. Bounce back. All that meat. Soup like water. Punish you if you didn't eat it. Go in the little room again." Another respondent put it succinctly: "Too much grease. It wasn't good." One of the more poignant expressions of the lack of autonomy came from a man who explained, "You couldn't have what you wanted. It's my birthday. You can walk in the store, buy what you want to buy. Right?" (Ferguson et al., 2008, p. 51). Not, however, at Fairview.

Respondents depicted life at Fairview as one of control, rules, and congregate living. Many chafed under the rules and found ways to

sneak off my cottage any time I wanted to. And in our minds, it's the right thing to do. Sometimes we ask, they say no. Most of the time we're going to do it. They don't like it. That's too bad. (Ferguson et al., 2008, p. 52)

As might be expected, accounts of rules, breaking rules, and suffering consequences was a big part of the stories about life at Fairview. Respondents talked about "spankings" for various infractions. Sometimes everyone in a cottage received this form of corporal punishment. Some reported staff spanking with their hands, others with "cow whips or razor straps. ("And it stings really bad.") "They used their shoes to spank us also. They used to take their shoes off and spank us with that too, they did." You could get spanked for "talking in line" and for turning the TV off when a staff person wanted to watch it. And sometimes "he would make you face the wall and you had to stay that way for awhile" (Ferguson et al., 2008, p. 52).

"They were strict at Fairview" was the general consensus. Several felt that "we were treated wrong by the staff. You got beat up, yelled at. They put us in closets." In fact, several individuals talked to us about how "if we didn't do what we were told to do they'd put us in a lock up or something." Others described it as a "little room" (Ferguson et al., 2008, p. 52), such as a bathroom, with bars on the window.

Sometimes "being mean" seemed unrelated to breaking rules, but it was their experience of having staff working with them, or supposedly helping them, as in this woman's account of her experience with staff helping her to shower and wash her hair:

> They put your head underneath the water, and then they'd wash your hair for you and practically drown you underneath the sink when they washed your hair and they turned the cold water on you in the shower. (Ferguson et al., 2008, p. 52)

Being put in a cold bath for "messing my pants" was another example or having to take baths with water hot enough to scald—"If you don't behave yourself, they'd get you with the scalding hot water" (Ferguson et al., 2008, pp. 52–53). or being strapped down, shackled, or put in strait jackets. Some described having bags put over their heads, and one man remembered being put in a laundry bag and hung from a pipe. Kevin described being frightened by staff who threatened to put him in a vat of acid. He went on to say,

> Yeah. Just like prison. . . . I was constantly fighting. I got thrown in lock up. I was fighting these people off and I got full restraints. I got the wet sheet when they strap you down to the bed they put it across you and its wet. It's very uncomfortable. (Ferguson et al., 2008, p. 53)

Betty described "haircut day" as a punishment. One man reported that residents who were found kissing were made to kneel down and kiss the table as punishment:

> I had a beautiful set of hair. I combed it up into a French roll. I had a little spit curl right here (pointing). You know what that is dontcha? I was sitting down and they called me to sit down and I like to run away and they said, "Here's your punishment." Zip. There went my hair. (Ferguson et al., 2008, p. 53)

One man talked about "these great, big, huge blocks, about like so (gestures about a foot square) and that baby was heavy. They had a deal going into the neck, like a little eye where they could strap you to it and put a padlock on. There was a rag on the bottom of it." Residents would be made to push the block as a form of punishment. A former staff person we interviewed described the "punishment block" a bit more (Ferguson et al., 2008, p. 53).

> Actually it was kind of a big, about a 60 or 70 pound block and they had to push it up and down the hall. Some of them had handcuffs—you'd literally get handcuffed to this thing and have to push it back and forth up and down the hall. If you didn't do it, they'd beat you while you were doing it or put you in time out and beat you in time out. (Ferguson et al., 2008, p. 53)

When graduate students visited Fairview in the 1980s and early 1990s, they often saw the punishment block, and were told that it was for the people for whom staff couldn't find anything to do—and so they would just keep them on this punishment block.

Sheila talked about how "we had punish blocks, too, on the girls cottage." She goes on to explain, they did lots of things to girls. . . . Well, they did more to the men, the boys I mean, than to the girls. I think us girls were scared. You know, we were frightened and scared. If we say something, they would yell on you and we'd get, you know in trouble. . . . Yeah. If we say anything, we would be in trouble. If we said something we would be punished for it and they would tell us, "Don't say nothing to anybody about this." (Ferguson et al., 2008, p. 54)

The respondents remembered school as a good experience. "It was fun" and "at least we'd get off the cottage for awhile" seemed to be the most common assessments. "The teacher treated us much better" was one reason, but also because they went on trips (to nearby towns and cities), learned to read and write, and participated in band and choir. There was also physical education, volleyball, "and in winter time we'd play basketball." "They had me do arithmetic, and spelling and reading." Some, however, reported that "they kicked me out of school" (Ferguson et al., 2008, p. 54) though they couldn't recall the reason.

School ended for most of people while they were still living at Fairview, and then work became the center of their daily routine. There were chores and jobs, and it was sometimes difficult to distinguish them in the conversations. Certainly, "make beds. Only one way to make beds. If a quarter didn't bounce, she'd rip it off and make you do it over" (Ferguson et al., 2008, p. 54), could be a chore or a job. Like the tradition of most similar congregate care institutions, the residents did many of the jobs that kept the institution functioning. As one man explained,

We [took] care of Fairview. All they [staff] did, they just sat around don't do nothing. As you got older—we were the ones that took over the jobs. We're the ones that did all the work. (Ferguson et al., 2008, p. 54)

When Fairview was still called the Fairview Home, before it was renamed the Fairview Hospital and Training Center, Tony remembered working at the institution's farm where groups of residents would "pick strawberries, beans, and pick potatoes." Others would work in the gardens—"go on rounds on the grounds and check the beds . . . water them and turn on the sprinklers. Sometimes we'd pull them up and plant some more" (Ferguson et al., 2008, p. 54).

Work fell into two broad categories: caring for and maintaining Fairview and caring for less able residents. Although respondents talked eagerly about these jobs, they rarely talked about either liking them or not liking them. Work was simply a fact of life at Fairview. Most residents had a number of different jobs over their tenure (Ferguson et al., 2008, p. 55):

- "They put me in H Cottage in the basement in the coal room."

- "I used to work in the canteen and then I used to work in the dining room serving customers when they came in for meals. Then I used to work in the workshop out there."

- "I worked in the boiler room, the laundry room and in the orchard. I went out to pick up potatoes and carrots and all that stuff. Big boiler room, burn sawdust and then had to take the ashes out and dump them."

- "I worked in a workshop up there and I made palettes and stuff. Tony worked at the dairy and milked cows."

- "Doing custodial work down at the main office. Running the buffer, mopping the floors, cleaning the sinks. Just about anything they had to do around there."

- "The chicken house. Number one, you feed the chickens. Number two, you clean up the chicken mess. See, they make a big mess every day. Number three, you take a basket and you get all the eggs. And you take that in the house and you wash all the eggs in hot water. Then you put the eggs into a cage, some type of cage or something to take down to the main kitchen. Oh, I didn't like it at first, but I did like it as time goes by. I also worked at the laundry."

Keeping Fairview running or "doing all the work" was one type of job. Caring for other residents was the other type. Both men and women were assigned to these jobs, but—at least for Ferguson et al.'s (2008) respondents—they seemed to fall more often to the women. Several talked about working with residents with physical disabilities in the "department called hydro," where some residents received physical therapy. "You had to sit by the tank and watch the patients and make sure they didn't slide into the water. If they did then you had to pull them up." One man talked about how much he enjoyed watching his wife take care of the babies, and helping. "My wife loves tiny babies, she does. I remember walking those little babies out there in Fairview, I did" (Ferguson et al., 2008, p. 55).

Albert reported working on a cottage where he would "feed some people and made beds. Then I went to Coulter delivering charts" (Ferguson et al., 2008, p. 56). But for some, the assignment of caring for less able residents was not a good one:

> I think they were water heads [a slang term for individuals with hydrocephalus]. I would work on that. That cottage was Snell. I bathed them and changed their diapers. They had clothes everywhere. They didn't take care of them very good. It was terrible. It made me kind of sick. In fact, you know, I didn't really want to be there. It was really bad. (Ferguson et al., 2008, p. 56)

When asked if they were paid for their work, most respondents said "No," or "They didn't pay us nothing." Some pointed out that "you get your haircut free. You get to live in the cottage free too. You get the food free too" (Ferguson et al., 2008, p. 56), which was a way to understand working for your keep. However, some of the individuals who entered Fairview later reported that they were paid, after a fashion:

> You get paid and you put your money at the office. [It was like a bank?] Right. Then they got this thing—you go to the barber shop and they cut hair and then you go up there and get the stuff you want to get at the canteen. They give you a card or something and they punch it. (Ferguson et al., 2008, p. 56)

One individual who was among the youngest interviewed reported that they were paid with a check and "I went off the grounds to cash it" (Ferguson et al., 2008, p. 56).

Going off grounds was a privilege that more able and well-behaved residents enjoyed, but as one person put it, you "gotta earn it." Living in cottages that permitted more autonomy, such as cooking for oneself or getting to go to the canteen, were other privileges that had to be earned. Residents were allowed to go into town to see movies on some occasions, and as part of school went on a variety of field trips, but for most, these had to be "escorted." As one woman explained, "We needed sponsors to take us out. We needed to sign all this crap" (Ferguson et al., 2008, p. 56).

The pattern was that after a resident "was there for a long time" they might be able to leave Fairview unaccompanied, but they had to be back by 5:00. Ralph explained, "You could sign a blue piece of paper; then there's a pink piece. The proctor'd keep the blue paper, you keep the pink paper. You'd tell them how long you'd be gone then what time you going to be back" (Ferguson et al., 2008, p. 57).

"Nathan and I took the bus to downtown Salem and we went to movies together. They gave you a pass." At this point in our interview, Peter showed us his pass that he had saved for years. It was old, wrinkled, and pink, but you could still read "Fairview Community Pass. Peter Wilson." When we asked why he had saved it, his reply captures the experience of living at Fairview—a place that is "mean," "embarrassing," where you get spanked and punished, learn to read and write, and have some fun. "Well, I wanted to save this in case someone wanted to ask me about my home" (Ferguson et al., 2008, p. 57).

A couple of respondents reported regular visits from family: "They let me go every weekend to visit my family. My dad and mom lived right down the way from Fairview." Peter's dad visited him regularly: "On Sunday my Dad would come and see me every single week. And my Dad [would] take me home for Christmas, Easter, and sometimes I'd go home for one whole week." For most, however, there were no visits and a family was only the brothers and sisters that also lived at Fairview, though often "they were on a different cottage" so the only time you might see your sibling was at school. Parents divorced or were struggling with their own challenges, like "my mother was in the State hospital in Salem, Oregon. She came out to visit my brother and I. She did a couple of times, she did" (Ferguson et al., 2008, p. 57).

As described in the complete history (Ferguson et al., 2008), arriving at and leaving Fairview were critical times for both families and residents. In the early years, the case files held the handwritten letters poignantly showing how families wrestled with the emotions of having a son or daughter either sent to Fairview or discharged. Decades later, the memories of respondents also focused on the same episodes. As with the parents of an earlier generation, respondents described a process that often seemed vaguely imposed on them by the authorities.

The life at Fairview described by respondents was a given because people were sent there. It was involuntary, not a choice. All tried to make the best they could of the experience. There seemed to be two patterns in how respondents came to be at Fairview. Several recalled going as young children for school or "training": "I went to Fairview because my brother was there already going to school . . . and I wanted to be with my brother" (Ferguson et al., 2008, p. 58). A few went to Fairview as even younger children, but more found themselves entering Fairview as young teenagers, often after encounters with courts and judges.

> Well, somebody accused me of trespassing and harassment, which I didn't do, and so the judge gave me a choice of spending my time in jail or going to Fairview, so I said, "Okay, I'll go to Fairview." (Ferguson et al., 2008, p. 58)

Others reported trouble with "sex," "getting arrested by the police and hand-cuffed," and having a judge send them to Fairview. Still others told of spending time in foster homes—"then I burned the barn down" and "they didn't send me to a judge, they just sent me to Fairview." Getting into trouble was part of the recollections of several of the men we interviewed, including one who remembered the final event occurring when he was living with his grandmother: "I hit my grandmother in the face and, my grandpa called the police and the police took me to jail for a little while until they got me to Fairview." This man may have actually been in Fairview before this incident, as he refers to "going back to Fairview" after having lived in a group home, which may have been an early community placement. After "getting into trouble" in the group home and the unsuccessful experience living with grandparents, however, the return to Fairview lasted longer. At least two others we spoke to experienced leaving Fairview only to run into some kind of difficulty in the community and being sent back. A third reported that his "worst memory" of Fairview was "when they were trying to send me back to Fairview because I wasn't working fast enough [at my job] in central Oregon" (Ferguson et al., 2008, p. 58).

One woman struggled with school remembering that the teacher described her as "so retarded she can't keep up with the other children," until she remembered being told that "you can't come back to school no more" (Ferguson et al., 2008, p. 58). After several unsuccessful foster home placements, she finally ended up in Fairview when she was 12 years old. Sometimes family exigencies resulted in being sent to Fairview:

> My dad couldn't take care of me because my mother died. I had my sister and a brother—the 3 of us and he couldn't take care of us. My Aunt took care of me for awhile and she's the one that finally put me there. (Ferguson et al., 2008, p. 59)

Difficult home situations, which sometimes included abuse or neglect, figured in the lives of some of the residents we interviewed and often served as one of the reasons they ended up going to Fairview. One man felt that, had his family been able to provide better care and "work with me," he might not have gone to Fairview:

> A lot of people tell me that my parents should have been locked up instead of me. I should have been in a foster home. I should have been adopted out if they didn't want me. (Ferguson et al., 2008, p. 59)

Leaving Fairview was a bit hazier for some respondents, in part because they were only minimally involved in the process. Just as arriving at Fairview, living there, following rules, and having things simply happen were common, leaving was just one more event that others controlled:

> What they do, they ask at the office meeting. [They] get together and talk about [things]. Then they pull this record out, the record I have, and they say "Is this person ready to get out? Where're we going to put him? We're going to put him out in the community to try him out for a 6 month trial basis to see how it goes." (Ferguson et al., 2008, p. 59)

Others just remembered someone coming up to them and saying, "You getting out?": "We'd get packed up, we move, we move and then try it for six months to a year.

If we do good, we just continue." Some were told they were leaving because they'd been "prepared" by learning, for example, to work in the laundry. Others thought they were allowed to leave because they had made "progress." Most were worried about having to go back: "I didn't have to go, well I went back at first, then my boss wanted me back so I got to go back" (Ferguson et al., 2008, p. 59). A few had family members who advocated for the move, but for most the event of leaving was like most other parts of the experience—someone else decided and it happened. For some there were strings attached. Here are two accounts:

> They said, "Sign these papers and you can get out in the community." We didn't know how to read and write. They didn't tell us what these papers were. Do you know that those papers took us right to the sterilization table? They tied me and I came untied. But the thing is I feel pain every once in awhile. My wife got cut the wrong way. She feels heavy scar tissue pain. And I wake up in a cold sweat, like from battle fatigue. I wasn't in the armed forces, but you might as well say when you're out in Fairview, it's the same thing. (Ferguson et al., 2008, p. 60)

And this:

> Well, they asked me to sign some papers for [being] sterilized and I said no, I ain't going to sign it. I'm going to get out without being sterilized. And they told me, they threatened me, they said you'll never get out of Fairview until you have it done. Yes. I had to be sterilized. I went through the surgery. I did it just to get my ass out of there. Excuse me. (Ferguson et al., 2008, p. 60)

No one was sad about leaving Fairview. Most reported, in one way or another, "We were happy" and "it felt good." When asked, all said they preferred living in the community "cuz you get more freedom" (Ferguson et al., 2008, p. 60).

For anyone in Oregon who was at all close to the process of closing Fairview and the shift to community programs, it was clear that the process was not without problems and bad press. Over the last two years of Fairview's existence, not only were approximately 300 residents moved to the community, but also nearly 1,400 employees had to find new jobs (Shipley, 2000). The unions fought the deinstitutionalization plans, some families felt their family members would be safer at Fairview, and some community members resisted the development of group homes in their neighborhoods (Gustafson, 2000b). Human resources administrators had to deal with rampant staff turnover (up to 85% per year), concerns about staff competence, lack of quality assurance systems, and very high case management loads, as well as several deaths from neglect or incompetence in community settings. The last two residents, however, left Fairview on Thursday, February 24 (Gustafson, 2000b). A handful of staff remained for a few more weeks to move furniture and secure the now-empty buildings. Fairview Training Center officially closed its doors on March 1, 2000.

Walter Feist was not the last resident to leave Fairview, but only four remained for a few days after he left. Like Jack Broderick, Fairview's first admission 92 years earlier, Mr. Feist had come to Fairview when he was 9 years old. When he left Fairview, Mr. Feist had spent 33 years as a resident there. After some early misgivings about his move, Feist reportedly was happy to make the transition to a group home closer to his family (Hunsberger, 2001). From Jack Broderick to Walter Feist, more than 9,700 people were admitted to the Fairview Training Center. Each of them had stories of their own, and most will never be known to those beyond their immediate families. The collective story of Fairview, however, is one that should never be forgotten. It certainly hasn't been by the 20 people who shared their experiences with Ferguson et al. (2008).

Is it any surprise that when people with intellectual and developmental disabilities finally had a voice in the disability movement, the themes that resonate are self-advocacy and self-determination? Walter Feist died almost one year to the day after his move from Fairview. For him, it was too little, too late.

FROM MENTAL RETARDATION TO INTELLECTUAL DISABILITY

The first chapter of this book provides a comprehensive look at the ways in which intellectual disability is now understood and conceptualized. The shift from the use of the term *mental retardation* to the term *intellectual disability* during this era reflects more than just a change in names, however. All prior terms referring to the construct, including *mental retardation, mental deficiency,* and *mental subnormality,* as discussed in previous chapters, attempted to provide a descriptive label or name for an underlying construct that shared several theoretical assumptions. The first such assumption was that the disability resided within the person. As noted previously, to *have* "mental retardation" was to *be* defective. The locus of that defect was the mind.

Perhaps the most obvious indicator that the construct underlying the terms *mental deficiency, mental subnormality,* and *mental retardation* referred to "defects of mind that resulted in impaired mental performance characterized by mental slowness," was the eventual agreement on the term *mental retardation* to name the underlying construct. The noun *retardation* refers to the act of retarding. *Retard* is a verb meaning "to slow down or delay." In fact, the earliest use of the term *retarded* or *retardation* in reference to a person's performance was in Leonard Ayres's (1909) classic text *Laggards in Our Schools: A Study of Retardation and Elimination in City School Systems,* which was published in 1909, and did not use the term to refer to a form of feeblemindedness at all. *Laggards* was a study of dropout and graduation rates in urban school districts. Students who failed to progress from one grade to the next were referred to as "laggards" or as "retarded"; yet the term *retarded* referred only to the fact that they were delayed with regard to their progress through the grades, and not to any internal defect or feeblemindedness. Only later did the term *retarded* shift from referring to the event or circumstance of not progressing from one grade to the next to referring to the student or person who was mentally slow and not progressing.

Mental retardation was a term meaning, literally, "mental slowness," and it was used to name an underlying construct or idea in which defects of the mind resulted in performance limitations characterized by mental slowness. Among other reasons to change the name of the construct, one that should be pointed out is that a term emphasizing the cognitive impairment as simply "mental slowness" does not, of course, capture the complexity of the impact of neural impairments on cognition and intellectual functioning. Mental slowness may be a manifestation of the neural impairment on cognition and intellectual functioning for people with intellectual disability, but it hardly is the only such manifestation and perhaps not the most significant such manifestation.

When, in 1992, the American Association on Mental Retardation's Terminology and Classification committee adopted a "functional" model of mental retardation which proposed that the disability was manifested as a state of functioning that existed within the fit between the person's capacities and limitations and the context in which the person functions, it was recognizing that intellectual disability involves limitations in human functioning. What was, however, dramatically different with the construct that underlies the term *intellectual disability* when compared with the construct underlying the term *mental retardation* was with regard to where the "disability" resided; the former (mental retardation) viewed the disability as a defect within the person, while the latter (intellectual disability) views the disability as the fit between the person's capacities (and implied in that is limited capacity as a function of neural impairment) and the context in which the person is to function. The term *mental retardation* referred to a "condition" internal to the person (e.g., slowness of mind); intellectual disability refers to a state of functioning, not a condition. The 1992 committee did not change the name of the construct, but changing the underlying understanding of the construct led inevitably to the change in name.

As described in Chapter 1, present understandings of intellectual disability are framed within understandings of disability as related to typical functioning; the term *disability* is an umbrella term for limitations in functioning. Intellectual disability, thus, is first a *disability,* as understood as a disability manifesting as limitations in intellectual functioning. Intellectual functioning is defined in the American Association on Intellectual and Developmental Disabilities (AAIDD) 2010 manual (Schalock et al., 2010) as referring to a general mental ability that includes reasoning, planning, solving problems, thinking abstractly, comprehending complex ideas, learning quickly, and learning from experience.

At the core of the construct is that intellectual disability manifests as limitations in intellectual functioning, evidenced by a poor "fit" between a person's capacities and the context in which the person must function. Capacity is the ability to perform a task, in this case, a mental, cognitive, or intellectual task. Because intellectual disability manifests as limitations in intellectual functioning, evidenced by a poor fit between a person's capacity and the context, the "disability" is not seen as residing within the person. This does not imply, however, that by ensuring, through environmental supports or through instruction, a better fit between the person's capacity and the context, an underlying body-function impairment (e.g., central nervous system [CNS] impairment) is in any way fixed. It simply recognizes that intellectual disability is not defined by the CNS impairment but instead by the person's functioning (e.g., the fit between the person's capacity and the context). Intellectual disability refers to limitations to intellectual functioning manifesting in activity limitations and participation restrictions *across all life activity and human functioning domains.* In fact, the ongoing need for extraordinary supports across multiple life domains may be an effective way to differentiate intellectual disability from other cognitive disabilities, where support needs are more focused or narrow.

What is more important, though, is that these new ways of conceptualizing disability, and intellectual disability, in the context of person–environment fit or engagement models of human functioning, emphasize that successful human functioning results from the engagement between capacity—emphasizing personal strengths—and the context, emphasizing supports defined as strategies, resources, and activities that enhance human functioning. This model presumes that limitations in personal strengths can be at least partially offset by supports, and that poor functioning may result from of lack of supports or limited opportunities for participation.

IN PURSUIT OF LIBERTY, EQUALITY, AND COMMUNITY

The civil rights movements of the previous decades culminated, in the period from 1980 onward, in a modern era of civil protections for people with disabilities. H.R. Turnbull and Turnbull (2000) argued that the civil rights movements on behalf of African Americans, particularly *Brown v. Board of Education* (1954), resulted in two complementary, interdependent, interactive, and concurrent rights movements: access to a free and appropriate public education that resulted from the *PARC v. Commonwealth* lawsuit, discussed in Chapter 8, and resulting in the passage of what is now called the Individuals with Disabilities Education Act (IDEA), and access to the community, brought about by the deinstitutionalization movement.

Within the disability movement, the principles of individualism and liberty created a new class of "rights bearers," including people with intellectual disability. This resulted in an explosion of disability legislation, with cases under IDEA, Section 504 of the Rehabilitation Act, the Developmental Disabilities Assistance and Bill of Rights Act, and, with its 1990 passage, the Americans with Disabilities Act (H.R. Turnbull & Turnbull, 2000, pp. 411–412). These civil protections argued that people with disabilities should not only be treated equally but, in fact, be treated "more equally" (p. 412). Historically, people with disabilities had been the victims of a great deal of discrimination; as five justices of the Supreme Court noted in the Cleburne decision, the history of treatment of people with intellectual disability was "grotesque" (H.R. Turnbull & Turnbull, 2000, p. 412).

The rub, of course, is in the implementation of such protections. Laws and civil protections have changed; attitudes and beliefs about people with intellectual disability and what they can do are more intractable. Shapiro (1993) noted the post–ADA case in which the owner of a private zoo in New Jersey denied entry to the zoo to children with Down syndrome because they "scared the chimpanzees." Such examples of blatant discrimination may be the exception, but there are other, everyday examples of ongoing attitudinal barriers to full equality. Perhaps no area illustrates this better than issues of human sexuality and intellectual disability. As children and youth with intellectual disability mature through childhood into adolescence and adulthood, they face the same challenges pertaining to their emerging self, their sexuality, and the establishment and maintenance of relationships and friendships with which all adolescents struggle. Unfortunately, many of these issues are only addressed if and when they become problems for the adolescent or adult, or others in his or her life.

Schwier (1994) noted an example of a couple with intellectual disability who, when "caught" kissing and holding hands at the sheltered workshop, were separated and threatened with punishment.

It is likely that the lives of that couple were so circumscribed by the systems that controlled where they lived and worked, and so devoid of meaningful opportunities to share personal private time, that to address the appropriateness or inappropriateness of their kissing and hand holding at "work" (a sheltered workshop) is to miss the forest for the trees. Contrast that scenario with the following, also from Schwier's book:

> *Allen*:   We are newlyweds. The weddin' was okay. Everybody said they really enjoy it. My brother came. I met Nadine back in '77 cause I move here. In 1960, I was in institute for ten years in Oregon. A girl I know there induced me to Nadine. I thought she was really nice. Couple year before we get married, we know each other.
>
> *Nadine*: I think he cute when I see him. I don wanna tell nobody how old I am. I was a baby when my family just drop me off at institution. My dress was all white and had a belt on it. I had white flowers. My bridesmaid was my friend.
>
> *Allen*:   We talk about our own baby, but we don't have enough money. We need to talk to a doctor and see if we would be possible to do operation so Nadine could have a baby. It's a big responsibility. I like lots of things about Nadine. We can do things together when we're married. We don't hold hands very much like some people. Sometimes if I go somewhere, she want to go with me and if she go somewhere, she want me to go with her. (pp. 77–81)

The couples interviewed in Schwier's book (some married, some dating, some with children, some without children) speak about the same concerns, joys, benefits, and challenges that all people face in starting and maintaining a relationship. Yet people with intellectual disability face unique challenges, beginning with getting a marriage license. Most states have revoked eugenic-era marriage restriction legislation (or such legislation is long-dormant and no longer applied), but most states have a requirement for informed consent and "coherence" that may be difficult for a person with impaired cognition to circumvent. Parental and professional worries about potential exploitation contribute to these barriers; people with intellectual and developmental disabilities are particularly vulnerable to sexual abuse, but the reality is that sexual abuse and sexual assault of people with intellectual disability are often committed by paid service providers and occur in disability service systems (Sobsey & Doe, 1991).

There are, of course, examples of the hurdles people with intellectual disability face in achieving equal rights. The 2006 case in which the use of a "growth attenuation intervention" was used to stop the growth of a 6-year-old girl—called Ashley, in the media—who could not sit up, walk, use language; who received nutrition through a gastrostomy tube inserted into her stomach; and who had some degree of intellectual disability is only one of such examples (R. Turnbull, Wehmeyer, Turnbull, & Stowe, 2006). The "intervention" consisted of high doses of estrogen, a hysterectomy, and breast tissue removal. The parents and medical staff intended to reduce the chance that the girl would be placed out of her parents' home by making it easier for her parents to care for her at home (Gunther & Diekema, 2006).

That the physicians and parents involved in this case felt it was acceptable to perform such invasive procedures to ease the burden of care says enough about how far there is to go before true equity is achieved. That the article was published in a peer-reviewed professional journal speaks to an even higher level of concern, beyond just the judgment of an individual physician or parent, but under the sanction of a profession. Ironically, perhaps, at the heart of tragedies such as that propagated on Ashley, is a misguided sense of quality of life issues for people with intellectual and developmental disabilities.

Throughout the United States and much of the world, the 1980s was a time of the quality revolution and opportunity development. Legislatively, the U.S. Congress focused on quality and opportunities through passage of Section 1619 of the Social Security Amendments (PL 95-265), which addressed work disincentives with the Social Security Disability Insurance and Supplemental Security Income programs, the Civil Rights of Institutionalized Persons Act (CRIPA, PL 95-402), and the Assistive Technology Act (PL 100-407). Advocacy was also advanced during this decade through the founding of Disabled Peoples' International and the United Nations proclaiming 1981 as the International Year of Disabled Persons. Quality of life, in the eyes of the profession, has become a sensitizing notion to guide the provision of services and supports—a framework, as it were, under which to organize the system that emphasizes key values found in this era in the disability movement: well-being, self-determination, inclusion, and so forth.

From the atrocities of withholding treatment to infants with Down syndrome committed by physicians in the 1970s, to the growth attenuation travesty in 2006, others—often, but not always, physicians and medical personnel (certainly not all, or maybe even the majority, of physicians and medical personnel)—impose their limited expectations for what people with more severe intellectual and physical impairments can impair in making treatment (or lack thereof) decisions on "quality of life" judgments. One flaw in the "old" quality of life formula is that it made scientific that which is basically ethical, theological, or policy related. The history discussed in prior chapters in this text warns to be cautious about such formulations.

Another flaw is that the formula assumes a static condition, namely, that neither the person's natural endowment nor the contributions by home and society will change. Here, too, history proves that endowment and contributions do change, largely because technology, practices, culture, and policies change. Predicting quality of life is problematic, especially for a person who is not at the end of life's course and for the person's family (R. Turnbull et al., 2006, p. 351).

Yet another example of the long road ahead pertaining to equality is in the area of organ transplantation. In January 2012, yet another person with intellectual disability, a young girl, was denied a transplant (kidney) because of the presence of intellectual disability. Sandra Jensen, a woman with Down syndrome who was active in the California Self-Advocacy movement, was, in 1995, denied a heart–lung transplant on the basis of her intellectual disability. For the first time, advocates, within in and outside of the medical community and including self-advocates, rallied and, ultimately, Sandra Jensen became the first person with intellectual disability to receive a dual transplant, receiving a new heart and lung. Today, most states have passed laws that prohibit discrimination in organ donation and organ transplantations, but as illustrated in 2012, old opinions about quality and worth of life die hard.

The past three decades have been times of great progress in civil protections, but to some degree the codification of such protections make even more egregious the frequent and recurring violations of basic human rights. For many people, progress is simply too slow. In the story of Allen and Nadine, related by Schwier (1994), Nadine suffered a brain aneurysm and died one year after her marriage to Allen. One wonders if they had not had to battle societal prohibitions about relationships and sexuality for people with intellectual disability whether they would have married earlier and enjoyed more time together (they met in 1977 but were not married until 1991).

VOICES OF THE PAST: EMPLOYEES OF AN INSTITUTION REMEMBER

This text has focused on the lived experiences and voices of people with intellectual disability. Adding to the narrative has been the voices and roles of parents and family members, as well as professionals. One group of people whose voices have not been heard, however, are those people who work in daily direct support roles with people with intellectual disability. The narratives about horrific abuses in institutions often depict workers as uncaring, cruel, and controlling. Certainly, some were, and most could be if pushed far enough. Most people who worked in such support roles, however, were not ogres; they were simply caring people who were trying their best in difficult circumstances.

In their effort to account for the history of the Fairview Training Center in Oregon, Ferguson et al. (2008) interviewed direct support personnel and revealed a much more complex picture. For one thing, people who work in institutions also live as part of the world and culture that, over time, shifts in its judgment about people with intellectual disability and bring those same ideas to their work as part of their own enculturation. The myths of people with intellectual disability as "eternal children" or as a "social menace" still abound in mass media and public discourse. Literature and entertainment are rife with portrayals of disability as threatening, pitiful, inspirational, and burdensome. It is inevitable that stereotypes would influence the perspectives of people who worked in the institutions that were, for so long, deemed by society as appropriate places to house people with disabilities. These institutional workers were as isolated and confined as the residents they served. Their views of the institutions and people who lived there were also shaped by their views of themselves and the work they did daily. The research found viewpoints of staff that were simplistic and nuanced, oblivious and critical, resentful and proud. The stories these people told are part of the history of institutions that must also be told and remembered.

If living at Fairview was about trying to find yourself in a sea of people, then working there was also about scale and numbers. In the 1960s, Fairview was at its largest, with about 3,000 residents. By 1978 that number had declined to 1,500. In the mid 1980s there was an ebb and flow to the resident and staffing ratios as placements declined. There was increased movement from Fairview to the community, and staffing increased as a result of federal concerns for safety and rights. In 1987, when discussions and plans to finally close Fairview were gaining depth and prominence, the number of residents reached 600. Even as residents moved out, new staff was hired, with the total number nearly doubling in the 1980s.

The employee experience of entering, living, working at, and leaving Fairview was quite different from the experience of being a resident. While residents experienced a formally administered round of life, staff—especially when speaking of the early days—described a sense of community and family. In contrast to what most residents told us, life at Fairview for staff—at least through the 1960s and most of the 1970s—was very much one of family and community. Many people who came to work at Fairview stayed for many years, some rising through the ranks to become administrators of one kind or another, including superintendent. Quite a few staff lived on grounds—a practice that extended back to Fairview's beginning in 1907. One former employee talked about hiring people who said they needed a temporary job to work in the "shop": "I'm between jobs. I'm just gonna work here until I can find something decent to do. Invariably every one of them that I hired stayed until they retired" (Ferguson et al., 2008, p. 61).

> The staff originally lived in the upstairs with the clients living downstairs. And then as Fairview become quite a bit bigger, the staff lived in the "apartments" as it was called . . . and the doctors lived up on the hill in the houses there. (Ferguson et al., 2008, p. 62)

Two people interviewed remembered living at Fairview as children because their parents worked there—"we lived in those houses [because] my parents were both physicians and so we lived up on the hill." In fact, whole families lived and worked at Fairview often for their whole working lives.

> Like the guy that was directing [the] housekeeping department—his brother worked in the laundry, his wife worked in food service, his father had worked in support services here, his son worked in direct care. (Ferguson et al., 2008, p. 62)

One person who remembered growing up at Fairview—first when she lived in one of the "houses on the hill" and later when she would accompany her mother to work at the hospital—described the staff sense of "family" at Fairview this way:

> It was considered way out in the country, there was very little built around it at that time. And it was truly its own community. Uh, the grounds were farmed. We had people that were far more able there at that time, and quite a few more people, too, and so the people that lived there, if they were able, helped care for some that were less able and they worked the grounds as farmers. We had cattle and there was a small dairy farm, and hogs and large fields of wheat growing and these were all farmed. (Ferguson et al., 2008, p. 62)

Another former employee also talked about the laundry and the greenhouses "where they used to grow the flowers and give them to the offices and cottages" to which his wife, also a former employee added, "I think they took some of the laundry [from] the penitentiary too. . . . They had a chicken farm where we had our own chickens. There was a garden for our own produce. It was just like any farm except on a large scale" (Ferguson et al., 2008, p. 62).

In many ways, Fairview was nearly self-sufficient in these early days and served as a resource for other nearby state facilities like the penitentiary, the Oregon State Hospital, the tuberculosis hospital and Hillcrest School (for girls between 12 and 21 years old). Even the Fairview physical plant "supplied the steam and warmth to all the buildings at Fairview, plus Hillcrest" (Ferguson et al., 2008, p. 63). The hospital, in particular, served not only Fairview but also some of the other state-operated facilities. As one former employee remembered, "Oh, we had a great hospital. When I first went to work there we took care of the ladies from the penitentiary when they were pregnant and had their babies. We delivered the babies there at the hospital" (Ferguson et al., 2008, p. 63). Hillcrest was another nearby facility that sent its residents to the Fairview Infirmary. It was

> very practical because we had x-ray and lab services and so they could come in and do that and get some of their emergency suturing and that type of thing there and it was very practical although we stopped doing that towards the end. (Ferguson et al., 2008, p. 63)

The hospital provided health care for the residents and the on–grounds staff as well, so that when "you burnt your finger you could see the doctor" (Ferguson et al., 2008, p. 63).

> There were two operating rooms and they did all of their own sterilization of supplies and packaging of instruments and had an amazing collection of that. And we actually took care of all of our own "codes" [emergency incidents] until I think 1985, because I certainly got in on a few of those. We didn't call 911. We just took care of it. (Ferguson et al., 2008, p. 63)

Of course, supplies were not the only things being sterilized: "They took care of whatever surgery was required in their patients. Appendectomies, laparotomies for taking out ovaries of young girls . . . but then they did a lot of surgery to prevent pregnancy" (Ferguson et al., 2008, p. 63).

Having many people in one place, however, created other kinds of problems and needs. Feeding some 3,000 people a day, for example, was a major undertaking. Of course, the gardens and animals provided a lot of the basic food, but preparing and serving food at that scale might have resulted in the institutional cuisine some of the residents remembered. One of the former employees described the

> two dining rooms. An upper dining room where the employees [ate] and the residents, or patients as they were called at one time, were fed at the lower level dining room and everybody ate family style. (Ferguson et al., 2008, p. 63–64)

One of the residents interviewed reported that when she worked in the dining room she got to eat the employees' food, but when she didn't work in the dining room she ate the patients' food and it was "the terriblest chicken and terriblest gravy that I ever ate. It was powdered potatoes . . . and the pudding tasted so terrible it made me throw up" (Ferguson et al., 2008, p. 64). This same resident also reported the "tin trays and tin plates and all this tin silverware. Then after they remodeled Fairview, they had plastic bowls and plastic cups and plastic dishes and trays" (Ferguson et al., 2008, p. 64). A former employee remembered food being delivered to the cottages with nonambulatory residents in "Aladdin trays." Clearly, there was no fine china, or even ordinary plates and glassware in the food service at Fairview as one of the last administrators described when comparing life at Fairview to life in the community for one former resident:

> We have a lady who was living in her own apartment—had a little bedroom, a little bathroom and a separate closet area that was basically what she had at Fairview. Because of how it worked at Fairview with people in and out . . . a lack of privacy she

couldn't have her things out and she was always competing with everybody in these apartments for attention . . . because that's what fit in that world. You go into her place now and you see china. . . . It is sorta like she is finally in a situation outside of Fairview where she is actually allowed to be a woman. Got to have all her stuff out. We never had china at Fairview. Not unless you were really stupid cause it would be gone in no time and it might well be a Frisbee at you. Out where she is living right now, she's got a beautiful place. (Ferguson et al., 2008, p. 64)

The sheer scale of the numbers of people living together also led another former employee to research. As a doctor, he had a strong interest in epidemics and how to manage them in large groups of people. His research initially found that "out of 3,000 patients roughly 750 of them were being currently treated for active tuberculosis or had old healed tuberculosis" (Ferguson et al., 2008, p. 64). He went on to isolate those individuals who had been "newly infected. . . at the hospital or transferring them to the TB hospital" (Ferguson et al., 2008, p. 64) and gradually eliminated TB at Fairview. His work testing the livestock and finding evidence of live TB virus led eventually to destruction of the herd, even though later they discovered that the positive test was really a result of bacteria in the soil. The chickens were next and the combination of suspected TB and other fiscal forces that were questioning the feasibility of maintaining the livestock part of the Cottage Farm led to dismantling this part of Fairview's operation. For one former employee this decision was shortsighted since "they didn't look at the positive parts of these farms where it could be something for the 'kids' to do. They enjoyed every minute of it that they could get out in the orchard and dairy and work" (Ferguson et al., 2008, p. 65).

Fairview was also, according to a former doctor interviewed, "a hotbed of epidemic hepatitis," and later he explored managing "two drawn out epidemics of meningococcal disease involving a total of 18 resident cases. For unknown reasons, this problem was largely centered in Snell Cottage . . . 18 resident cases and, as I recall, there was something like 5 deaths" (Ferguson et al., 2008, p. 65). While infections can happen in any setting, whenever people are congregated together, these viruses can spread quickly. In Fairview the risks that such infections would become epidemics that could result in resident death were much greater.

Staff remembered the residents as part of "the Fairview family." Children of staff visited their parents at work and as one long-time employee remembered,

it was a family when we worked there. We played with the kids like they were our own . . . we had a lot of fun. They enjoyed coming down to the shop. They didn't necessarily do anything except what they actually could do, but they were treated like part of the family and they appreciated that. (Ferguson et al., 2008, p. 65)

Staff talked about taking the "kids home for weekends and they would rake leaves and eat with us and just be part of our family." Residents were "kids" to staff for many years. "I say 'kids' because that's what we called them at that time. It didn't matter what their age was, they were kids to us and they were our kids." There were nearly 3,000 "kids" at Fairview in the 1960s, ranging in age from babies to Larry Peters, who "was the oldest Down Syndrome gentleman in Oregon. He got to be 81" (Ferguson et al., 2008, p. 65).

Fairview was its own community, largely isolated—even hidden—from the rest of Salem, with one particular exception. Nearly everyone interviewed remembered the Fourth of July parade tradition. During other holidays, some residents would go home to their own families and many staff would take time off to be with more extended family members, but the Fourth of July "was a big deal." Here are two accounts.

> Fairview was accepted by the community positively at that time because we had a parade every 4th of July. A competition of who could put out the best float and it was really something that the kids looked forward to because they got a 4th of July picnic and then we used to fundraise donations from the community every year, [we had] fireworks on the field there and we had a regular traffic jam. (Ferguson et al., 2008, p. 66)
>
> Many people would come to the 4th of July parades at Fairview and there would be cars parked all up and down Strong Road to see . . . and a lot of community people would be in the parade. It was very much an involvement [with the community]. The folks that owned old antique cars would come, the 4H people would come with their horses. Each cottage . . . would have their own float and these were very elaborate . . . and very creative. (Ferguson et al., 2008, p. 66)

Another former employee remembered the mother of one of the direct care staff making "costumes like birds" for the residents to wear. "It was very exciting and then in the evening when it got dark they'd set off fireworks" (Ferguson et al., 2008, p. 66). At least until a grass fire ended that part of the celebration. As time passed to the 1970s and 1980s, the larger community stopped attending the Fourth of July parade, but it continued up until Fairview closed.

Another, somewhat smaller, link with the community came from the early 1960s, when an influx of funding allowed the building of a new multipurpose building that included a gym and swimming pool that was sometimes open to the larger community. Despite these exceptions, however, Fairview largely remained its own separate community. This relative isolation began to change in the mid-1970s.

In the mid 1970s, according to one person interviewed, "Fairview fell on a cycle of trouble." Efforts to improve matters first led to a new superintendent and administratively dividing "the campus into three smaller institutions . . . and on top of this were some fundamental services . . . food services, the plant, laundry and all that sort of thing" (Ferguson et al., 2008, p. 66–67). Staff that had been living in the newly renovated houses on the hill was required by administration to pay a market-based rent or move off campus. As staff moved, some of the former staff residences were refitted as group-home training sites, as a new commitment to prepare residents for community living began. One of the first of these instances was as a result of a change in the definition of what was then termed *mental retardation* by the American Association on Mental Deficiency (now AAIDD). This change resulted in some individuals no longer qualifying to reside at Fairview. The administration made the decision to comply with the new definition to whatever extent possible. "It may mean that we won't be releasing them immediately, but they will be on a plan for release and there were not all that many actually. There were about 35 that were considered inappropriate placements" (Ferguson et al., 2008, p. 67).

As some individuals began to leave Fairview, however, the state decided to close Columbia Park, one of the other two institutions for people with intellectual disabilities, and transfer them to Fairview. Staff worked hard to minimize "transfer trauma" for the new residents. Indeed, the merger went so smoothly that discussion began about closing the other facility in eastern Oregon. So even as some residents left for community options, the population at Fairview continued to grow.

As Ferguson et al. (2008) described, by the 1970s a new era of thinking about individuals with developmental disabilities was emerging, as has been described in Chapter 8. Public acceptance, and funding, began to grow for children with disabilities to live with their families and attend their neighborhood schools rather than being removed and isolated from families and community life. The 1990, *Oregon Long Range Plan for Developmental Disability Services* (Agosta, Keating, Deane, Ashbaugh, & Bradley, 1990) observed that

> prior to the advent of community services in the late 1960s and early 1970s, for many individuals with disabilities, there was no real resource outside their own families except for Fairview. (p. 5)

During the 1970s and early 1980s, however, fewer children, youth, and adults were placed at Fairview as community options began to grow. Things were changing, as one woman somewhat wistfully recalled, returning to work at Fairview in the early 1980s after living on the grounds as a young child:

> Coming back and working there—but I'd been there all along really. Every time I went and visited my mother I'd go along with her on call and see people. But when I first lived at Fairview, it seemed more of a home. There were less restrictions as far as federal guidelines and people seemed to relate a little more naturally. There weren't a lot of guidelines on how to relate to people and so I'm sure there were some things that happened that weren't necessarily that good. (Ferguson et al., 2008, p. 68)

Lack of guidance, even if it did permit people to "relate a little more naturally," also provided staff with the freedom to do "things that happened that weren't necessarily that good" (Ferguson et al., 2008, p. 68). There were episodic efforts to curb inappropriate staff treatment of residents. For example, a former administrator reported the following:

> One day I walked around and picked up all the physical restraints around campus. It wasn't a phase down job. It's gonna end. And how do I know it's gonna end? 'Cause I knew everybody out there. Every manager out there is gonna keep his one strap back, because of a time when you just have to have it. And those times when you just have to have it occur more often . . . at night or on the weekend with a shortage of staff . . . I made them a bad promise, which is if they are needed we'll return 'em selectively. Once they were gone, they never wanted them back. (Ferguson et al., 2008, p. 68)

About 15 years later, another administrator reported something quite similar, but with a different outcome. By this time chemical restraints were more of an issue than physical ones.

> One of the things we decided to do was get rid, entirely, except for pure health and safety stuff, every restraint in every way. So we'd go out and train people on how to deal with issues that they ran into with people living there that weren't power struggles. It didn't work. Still had people using timeout rooms and all that stuff just as much as they did

before and the only way that this was really going to work was to make it inconvenient, difficult for staff. So it went from you could go and lock somebody in the timeout room and then go do your own thing to you would have to take the person to the timeout room and stand outside the door the whole time to make sure they were safe and then you had to go through a process of recording how much you did this . . . That reduced it substantially, but it didn't get rid of it.

We did a similar kind of thing around psychotropics. None of this you can just walk in and, "you seem hyper today so I'm going to give you a shot of thorazine." A huge documentation, you had to have expanded Individual Diagnostic Team meetings every time you did that kind of thing and after it happened a certain number of times, even another group of people had to meet all together. We just about "meetinged" that one to death. It became such a hassle, especially for the physicians who were ordering it to deal with it, plus we brought in other psychiatrists with a more modern drug orientation. (Ferguson et al., 2008, p. 69)

In May 1983, the U.S. Attorney General notified Oregon's governor and the Superintendent of Fairview that the U.S. Department of Justice (DOJ) was initiating an investigation of alleged unlawful conditions at Fairview based on CRIPA. Their concerns included a belief that residents were being subjected to deplorable conditions, were being deprived of basic civil rights under the constitution and were denied an appropriate education under the Education for all Handicapped Children Act (PL 94-142, now IDEA).

In 1985, advocates from the Association for Retarded Citizens——Oregon (now The Arc of Oregon), the Oregon Advocacy Center, and several families of Fairview residents prepared litigation against the State over Fairview's conditions. By 1986, they had filed a civil rights lawsuit through the DOJ, claiming that Fairview was failing to provide adequate training, medical care, and education for residents; failing to protect residents from health and safety hazards and failing to provide enough sufficiently trained staff members for its residents. At about the same time, the Health Care Financing Administration (HCFA) conducted a two-week investigative site visit at Fairview. The federal team found that the center was incapable of providing even minimal care—describing deficiencies in a 96 page document—and decertified the institution in April 1987. The decertification blocked the flow of federal Medicaid funds, which amounted to 60% of Fairview's budget. Eight million dollars were withheld for 14 weeks until the state approved new services. Fairview was recertified after the state agreed to make improvements by June 30, 1989. In the same period, new 1986 Medicaid regulations required better staffing ratios, and the buildings and grounds had to meet new accessibility standards. In the words of one employee: "It was a hectic time" (Ferguson et al., 2008, p. 70).

Not surprisingly, the actions of the DOJ "had a real impact on the staff . . . didn't do much for morale" (Ferguson et al., 2008, p. 70). One former employee reported that "what did help improve morale at that time was figuring out ways to beat them at their own game and we had some scandalous schemes worked out!" (Ferguson et al., 2008, p. 63). Federal inspectors and others involved would often make visits on evenings and weekends when they had reason to believe that cottages would be short staffed. Staff soon organized a call-ahead warning system so that key administrators were called when inspectors arrived on grounds, while staff "stalled" until they could arrive. As inspectors traveled from cottage to cottage, this "early warning system" would activate to call ahead to where they were going next. Staff struggled to understand the changes, referring to the time when "the government started taking over with their heavy hand" (Ferguson et al., 2008, p. 70). This employee went on to describe the following:

> A friend of mine was in charge of a cottage for years and years before the government got interested, but all of a sudden it was reported that she was abusive to the kids. . . . It got to the point that if someone was going to dive out a window and you had to reach out and grab them and hold them tight enough to prevent them from [falling], you were in deep doo doo because you created a blue spot on their arm. There's not too much defense against that especially if they are going to be hardnosed about their rules and regulations. (Ferguson et al., 2008, p. 70)

Staff reported that "one thing that was hard on Fairview was the publicity that we got in the papers. People would read about us, but they wouldn't come out and see what was actually going on . . . All the public knew was that they were getting beat on out there. Abused" (Ferguson et al., 2008, pp. 70–71).

Some staff came to see the purpose of the scrutiny as seeking "to destroy Fairview" and lines became drawn between the advocates for downsizing, or even closure of the institution, and the defenders who believed that the goal

> was not to destroy it and not to close it down—I opposed it then and I oppose it now— but to make it better and to have it serve its proper role and it's my opinion that to create a very strong community program you needed a very good backup system and in this case [it] was Fairview. (Ferguson et al., 2008, p. 71)

After Governor Neal Goldschmidt toured the institution with the HCFA regulators, he said he was appalled by the living conditions and promised reforms.

> It has long been deeply held belief in this state that society has an obligation to help those who are least able to help themselves. We will not shirk that obligation. We will reaffirm the promise John Kennedy made to those with developmental disabilities more than two decades ago, that although they may have been the victims of fate they shall not be the victims of neglect. (Ferguson et al., 2008, p. 71)

As a result of HCFA actions, the Oregon legislature spent more than $30 million to fix multiple problems and regain federal funds. "We knew what the citations were" so the administration sought to respond. Many of the citations had to do with lack of staffing and this led to a situation where "you didn't have enough staff to maximize the freedom of the people who lived there by providing them with training because there just wasn't enough." Consequently, staff was doubled over a short period of time in 1987—resulting in more than two staff members per resident. By the end of 1987, new admissions were halted and the population began to drop substantially with the placement of more than 200 residents into community group homes throughout Oregon. Some people voiced the opinion that part of the strategy of those wishing to downsize or close Fairview was to raise the costs:

> The way you get rid of the institution is you jack the price up so much that anybody in their right mind would say it's too expensive. When you do that primarily through

staff—if doubling the staff is good, [then] triple. . . . at the same time presenting data showing the huge waiting lists and [funding] was all being eaten up by this one archaic facility called Fairview. (Ferguson et al., 2008, p. 72)

Adding a lot of new staff created some problems as well because in order to hire a large number of people quickly, you cannot demand much in the way of training or experience. As one former employee reported, "the interview goes something like, 'Do you walk? Do you talk? Do you breathe? You're hired for direct care" (Ferguson et al., 2008, p. 72). For employees already at Fairview, the culture began to change immediately with the new staff:

Many of the people who worked there—their parents had worked there before them and their children worked there after them and we were insular. Many people had gone to work there right out of high school and that was the only job they'd known and when we got the federal mandates . . . we ended up hiring so many more staff. In some ways it was very good because there was more staff, and Lord knows there was enough work, but it also brought in a lot of people that had never been around that environment and they had to be taught a lot of things that the rest of us had grown up seeing and knowing. (Ferguson et al., 2008, p. 72)

Fairview became "an absolutely impossible place to work" according to one former employee who "just marvel[ed] at the steadfastness and 'sticktotiveness' and the affection which was what held the employees there" (Ferguson et al., 2008, p. 72).

Despite the immense amount of funding and new staff pouring into the institution, within 16 months HCFA again threatened decertification and withholding of federal funds, even though the deficits had been reduced to a 10-page list. Oregon Human Resources administrators speculated that HCFA was taking into consideration the pending DOJ lawsuit that was scheduled to go to trial in October 1988. One employee spoke of it in terms of being constantly under attack: "There was always incoming. And the positive part of that was that it really pulled people together" (Ferguson et al., 2008, p. 72).

Prior to these events in the late 1980s "there wasn't really a focus to do a lot of treatment" at Fairview, but "after 1987, once the dust sort of settled from adding all those staff and firing a whole bunch of people who didn't cut it . . . there got to be some stability" (Ferguson et al., 2008, p. 7). During this period, the longtime employees sought a strategy that might preserve Fairview. The strategy that emerged focused on the question: "Would they close an organization that is building something?" and Project Possible was born. The plan was as follows:

We were talking about a facility where parents could go visit their children quasi-privately . . . it took us 3 years to raise the money. Donkey softball games. The staff was developing things. There was a weight loss contest and we had all the typical running events. But the theory was if we're building something like that and [it] is successful, doesn't that show stability. (Ferguson et al., 2008, p. 72)

Project Possible eventually resulted in a new building called the Possible Building. The project helped to focus staff and rebuild morale, but in the end, as one former employee reflected,

> I think the legislature let us build that as kind of a joke. They couldn't see where it could possibly happen and I think according to the architects in those days it would run close to $300,000. We raised the funds and we built it. It was [all] volunteer help except for the raising of the beams where we had to get equipment to do that. (Ferguson et al., 2008, p. 73)

In the end, however, the pending lawsuits, continued threats to federal funding, and the expense of keeping a small population housed in a large and declining facility created the perfect storm for permanent closure. The financial problems created by decertification and the pending lawsuits also brought professionals, advocates, and family members together for future planning for both Fairview and community services. A centerpiece of the *Oregon Long Range Plan for Developmental Disability Services* (Agosta et al., 1990) was to move 300 Fairview residents into newly developed community programs

In December 1988, HCFA agreed to a comprehensive plan of reduction and improvement. The agreement was signed on December 21, 1988, by the entire Oregon congressional delegation and by February 1989, the state had settled the DOJ lawsuit through a consent decree. In September 1990, Oregon's long-range plan for individuals with disabilities, described in the Interim Report to the Emergency Board, stated that the population would be reduced to 800 by 1989 and 500 in the following years. In the end, it simply became too expensive to simulate a real work environment and provide a decent quality of life in an old institution—the cost of serving a single resident had grown from $60,000 to more than $212,000 per year.

In 1996, the state developed a long-term plan for developmental disabilities services that phased out the institution by the year 2000. As the state steadily reduced Fairview's population, the number of group homes expanded dramatically. In 1985 there were 86 community homes for 900 individuals; by 2000 there were 533 community homes for more than 2,780 individuals.

The process of closing Fairview was difficult. As one former administrator reflected,

> it is going to be painful for everybody. Even people that think it is the very best thing that can happen. It is still going to be painful for them to deal with all the change and to figure out some way in the whole process of getting the outcome they want and still treating everybody well. (Ferguson et al., 2008, p. 74)

The process was further complicated by the fact that many years at Fairview had not really prepared residents for living in the community. "All the treatment programs were oriented to [creating] the best institutional person you could" (Ferguson et al., 2008, p. 74).

> You could look like hell and eat at Fairview, but you couldn't go into a restaurant that way. You could walk all over campus without learning how to cross streets. There were all kinds of behaviors that were okay at Fairview that weren't okay in the community and no where had anyone tried to build a concerted placement process for everyone at Fairview. They tried using smaller houses to get people used to it, but I don't think that really did anything. (Ferguson et al., 2008, p. 74)

Another issue was maintaining enough staff to provide the needed services and supports to residents as both residents and staff left. The plan was to make sure that everybody with the most intensive needs left first because there was too much risk . . . for people who were medically fragile . . . and without proper care some of those people would die . . . if Fairview didn't place them before doctors and nurses and physical therapists left, they would die first. . . . And people with behavioral issues that weren't going into state-operated homes were next and then people with behavioral issues that were going into state-operated homes were last. That way we could have a solid core of already hired employees. (Ferguson et al., 2008, p. 75)

There was a commitment to moving residents back to their home communities near family members. Reconnecting residents with families proved to be very difficult, however. Some families were told decades earlier not to visit their relatives in Fairview because it was bad for them. Many family ties were cut in this way, and reconnecting families became a major goal of the closure effort.

I had a number of people who contacted folks who had never—they had either gotten a message from relatives—a gentleman up in Portland whose sister—they and their mother came to visit very early on when he was little—and clearly told by a nurse, you really upset him when you come. You really should not come again. I don't want you to come back here again. It is really disturbing him. All he does is start to hurt himself when you come. He's just a vegetable anyway, was the term and so they never came and the sister's assumption all these years, was that he's just a vegetable and he wouldn't know. (Ferguson et al., 2008, p. 75)

SEPARATE IS NEVER EQUAL

On November 29, 1975, President Gerald Ford signed into law the Education for All Handicapped Children Act (PL 94–142). Fully implemented in 1978, PL 94–142 not only opened the doors to public schools for children who had, to that point, been denied such access, it also created thousands of new jobs for teachers interested in working in the field of special education. The passage of this act was, as noted in Chapter 8, a crowning achievement of the parent movement, but the implementation and growth of opportunities for students with intellectual disability to learn alongside their nondisabled peers is really a story of the 1980s and onward. Although the act was to be fully implemented by states by 1978 (Weintraub, Abeson, Ballard, & LaVor, 1976), in practice, many students with intellectual disability, particularly students with more extensive support needs, were still being educated outside of the public school system through the 1980s.

In November 2010, the U.S. Department of Education celebrated the 35th anniversary of what is now known as IDEA. President Barack Obama's statement on this occasion emphasized what is often forgotten about IDEA; that it is first and foremost a landmark civil rights act. "In America," President Obama stated, "we believe that every child, regardless of class, color, creed, or ability, deserves access to a world-class education" (White House, 2010; see Figure 9.4).

In recognition of this milestone, the U.S. Department of Education released a video titled, aptly, *Celebrating 35 Years of IDEA*. At the end of the video, the narrator stated that "It's an American idea: Today's child will be tomorrow's citizen. Education shapes our expression of liberty, and separate—well, that has never been equal."[3]

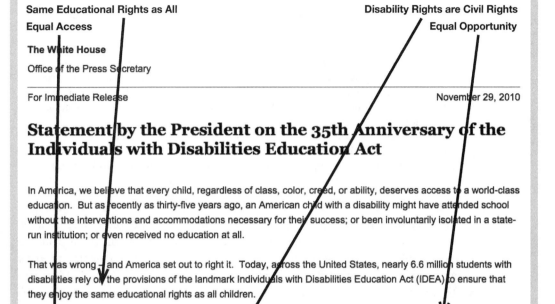

Figure 9.4. Excerpt from statement from President Obama on the 35th anniversary of IDEA.
(From Office of the Press Secretary, The White House [2010, November 29]. *Statement by the president on the 35th anniversary of the Individuals with Disabilities Education Act* [Press release]. Retrieved from http://www.whitehouse.gov/the-press-office/2010/11/29/statement-president-35th-anniversary-individuals-with-disabilities-educa).

Separate has never been equal. It is a lesson we should have learned by now. The advances in educational opportunities and progress in achieving meaningful outcomes for students with disabilities in the course of the last three decades as a result of IDEA has been, by any accounting, exceptional, and yet despite the progress of the past few decades with regard to both the pedagogy for and importance of educating students with intellectual disability in the general education classroom, there still exists support for, or perhaps resignation to, the option of segregated, self-contained settings as viable placement options for students with intellectual and other severe disabilities. In fact, there is data to suggest that there has been regression in placement practices, with fewer students with severe disabilities now being educated over the first decade of the 21st century (Jackson, Ryndak, & Wehmeyer, 2009).

The history of special education begins, of course, before the passage of PL 94-142. A number of federal policy initiatives pertaining to the education of students with disabilities paved the way for the passage of that law. Programmatically, the field of special education was heavily influenced by the emergence and expansion, in the 1960s, of behaviorism as a clinical approach to treating people with mental retardation. Writing about that era and its influence on special education practice for students with intellectual disability, Doug Guess, an early pioneer in the education of students with the most extensive support needs, noted the following:

> Thus, evolving over the next decade [e.g., 1970s] was a major commitment by professionals in higher education to the research and application of instructional procedures and approaches identified with the field of applied behavior analysis, extending to all areas of exceptionality and, eventually, the education of nondis-abled students.
>
> It is difficult to separate out the behaviorally derived instructional practices in the 1970s from other social and educational changes that affected in a significant way the lives of persons with severe cognitive and multiple disabilities. (Guess, 2000, p. 92)

The other social and educational changes Guess mentions were, indeed, significant. To a large extent, the field of special education had only one "model" upon which to build a system: the model of homogeneous grouping still so in evidence in the country's residential services in the mid-1970s. Schools implemented the new federal requirements using the only structure that made sense as long as disability was understood to equate to personal defect and deficit: separate schools, separate classrooms, and separate curriculum. By the early 1980s, however, there was a growing discontent with segregated education emerging from the major parent groups as well as organizations like the American Association for the Education of the Severely and Profoundly Handicapped (AAESPH), later called The Association for Persons with Severe Handicaps and now just TASH, which was established in the mid-1970s. The AAESPH began publishing a professional journal, *AAESPH Review,* that published research pertaining to the education of students with extensive support needs, and quickly became a force in advocating for the inclusion of students with severe disabilities in the general education setting—first schools, then classrooms.

In the 1980s, a growing concern emerged about the excessive use of aversive procedures to reduce "unwanted" behavior among people with disabilities, especially people with severe disabilities who were in public school and other community settings. Up to this point, the use of punishers to reduce behavior was an accepted practice. Most textbooks included instruction on how to use punishment procedures in applied settings, along with the related overcorrection and time-out procedures. Guess (2000) identified some of the aversive procedures reported in the published literature to reduce unwanted behavior or to punish incorrect responses in learning tasks, including electric shock; slaps to hands and thighs; ice on cheeks, chin, under chin; gums/teeth brushed with antiseptics; forced body movements; white noise at 95 dB; forced exercise; contingent tickling; hair pulling; ammonia capsule under nose; pinching; water squirted in face; lemon juice squirted in mouth; and physical restraint (Guess, 2000, p. 97).

As scholarship provided evidence of the ineffectiveness of such punitive actions to reduce or eliminate unwanted behavior, parent groups, like The Arc, and professional associations such as TASH and AAIDD, advocated for the cessation of their use. Such practices could, really only occur when children were segregated; the social acceptability of such practices was very low. As the residential supports system increasingly emphasized community inclusion, and as, through application of the normalization principles and the community imperative (discussed in Chapter 8), community increasingly became the normative standard for supporting people with intellectual disability, a similar push for inclusion emerged focused on schooling. Through the 1980s and into the 1990s, the twin imperatives to eliminate aversive practices and to promote student inclusion resulted in the development of approaches, like positive behavior supports, that embraced the person–environment fit models of disability and emphasized changes to the context in which students lived or learned that reduced the need for problem behaviors and implemented positive strategies to increase successful functioning.

The inclusion movement began with efforts simply to get students with intellectual and severe disabilities into classes with their nondisabled peers, establishing the basic tenet that students with disabilities should be educated in their neighborhood schools with their same-age peers. Progress in including students with intellectual disability has been slow, with the use of separate classrooms and separate settings still widely prevalent. Schools seem never to have resolved a perceived conflict between including students with extensive support needs with their nondisabled peers and providing appropriate instruction, particularly when such instruction might need to occur in ecologically valid, nonschool settings. To a degree, these issues were trumped in the early years of the 20th century, when the passage of sweeping federal school reform efforts threatened to marginalize students with disabilities even further. The alignment of language in the 2004 reauthorization of IDEA with that school reform legislation, requiring that all students receiving special education be involved with and progress in the general education classroom, created a context that further challenged educational practice. On the positive side, students with intellectual disability were, for the first time in years (if ever) receiving instruction on core academic content areas such as math, science, and reading. On the other hand, concerns with high-stakes testing and the minimization of the focus on "other educational needs," which include life skills and "functional" content, became common (Wehmeyer, 2011). A.P. Turnbull, Turnbull, Wehmeyer, and Shogren (2013) argued that this has ushered in a third generation of the inclusion movement in which the focus is on what students learn, and not principally on where students learn; but that research is clear that the "place" where students with severe disabilities can acquire the academic and social skills they need to succeed is in the general education classroom.

Progress in inclusion in schools is painfully slow. Federal school reform efforts are invigorating a renewed focus on teaching students with intellectual disability critical skills such as reading or math; yet research shows that few students with intellectual disability are actually receiving their instruction on core content areas in general education classrooms and, when they do, few of the needed accommodations and modifications to the context and to instruction are in place (Wehmeyer, 2011). It is clear, however, that students with intellectual disability can succeed in the general education curriculum when they are provided with the supports and instruction they need. Ryndak and Alper (1996) provided a compelling example of the impact of inclusive education for students with intellectual disability. These authors described a student, named Maureen, labeled as having "moderate mental retardation" (still trainable, in the jargon of far too many educators) who had received her education from the age of 5 to 15 in self-contained classrooms for students with intellectual disability. At the end of her final year in a segregated setting, the interdisciplinary team planning her education described Maureen with functional levels consistent with moderate mental retardation. Her individualized education program objectives from that year included improving phonics and comprehension skills to the second-grade level, reading and writing dollar amounts, and solving three- and four-digit addition and subtraction problems. When she entered an inclusive seventh-grade class, her social behaviors improved almost immediately. Within the first year, Maureen was completing age-appropriate work with some adaptation, including excelling on age-appropriate math tasks involving the Pythagorean Theorem and simple algebra. Maureen was not simply "mislabeled," because she continued to need accommodations and supports for a wide array of academic and other outcomes. When Maureen graduated from high school with her nondisabled peers five years later, she and her family made plans for her to be included in a college setting and live in the dormitory.

Since Maureen graduated, there has emerged a network of two- and four-year colleges and universities providing supports for people with intellectual disability to engage in postsecondary education. Blumberg, Hutchins, Daley, and Petroff (2012) tell the story of one young man whose postsecondary education opportunity at the Career and Community Studies (CCS) program at the College of New Jersey propelled him to a better future:

> My name is Phillip Hutchins and I am 27 years old. I was born with Cerebral Palsy. I currently live in Milford New Jersey with my loving parents. I just graduated from the College of New Jersey after completing the Career and Community Studies Program. As I tell my story you will know what college did for me.
>
> In my mind, self-determination has to start with you believing in yourself. You have to set your own goals and you have to be the one that wants to achieve the goal you set for yourself. When I was a little boy, my parents tried to tell me that I had to do things to help me get better from the Cerebral Palsy. I did not want to do them at all. Then one day the light went on for me. I was going to graduate high school and because of that I made a goal for myself. That goal was that I wanted to walk without my walker to get my diploma. That is where self-determination kicked in for me because I knew for me to reach my goal I had to be the one that wanted to work hard and it could not be my parents telling me to do, it had to be me. The best thing is I worked hard and I did walk without my walker to get my diploma.
>
> The reason I mention that story first is because that determination helped me when I started college. My first goal in college was to do well in the classroom. I knew if I did, it would help me with my dream job. In my four years of college I believe I achieved that goal. Being in college has motivated me to do even more with my life.
>
> In college I decided to make my career path a two-part career and being in college has helped me with both parts. The first job that I want is to be a motivational speaker because I want to go around the world and tell people that as long as they believe in themselves they will achieve any goal they want.
>
> College helped me with both parts of my career path. For motivational speaking, I made business cards and brochures to hand out. They helped me make letters to send out to schools, and helped me set up speaking engagements. My goal when I am not speaking is to work in an office setting and the way college helped me is they put me in an office every semester as an internship. I worked at the TCNJ Admissions Office on campus for a whole year. I also worked at the Special Olympics office for one summer. I worked at the Cancer Society office for one semester. The last job I had was at the NJ State Disability Services office that I just ended.

After all the internships I have had the best advice I can give you so you can get a job and keep it is you need to speak up when you need something. The big thing is in any job you get you need to meet a few co-workers that you can trust.

A big part of the CCS program was the mentors we had in the program. They were a big help to me when it came to the classroom work because they would meet me in the labs and help me with all my homework that needed to get done. They were also a big help to me when it came to my public speaking career because they were the ones that helped me get everything done for my speaking career.

I want to leave you with a few final thoughts. I know college may not be for everyone, but if you decide to go to college it can help you in so many ways with your career path. The last thing I want to leave you with is that if you remember early in this article I said that my parents were the once [sic] that had to push me to do the best I can and now that I have achieved a lot of goals in my life I have them to thank. The reason I say this is because if there is someone in your life that loves you and they are trying to give you advice to reach your goals that you want in life just know they are doing it out of love. Again though remember that the number one way that you will reach any goal you want in life is if you believe in yourself first. (pp. 18–19)

THE PROMISE OF TECHNOLOGY

Technology use has been an important part of the lives of many people with intellectual disability since the 1980s. Assistive technologies, in the form of assistive and augmentative communication devices, mobility devices, or devices to promote greater independence, have been seen by people with disabilities and their supporters alike as critical to bridging the gap to successful functioning. In a 2004 Harris Survey sponsored by the National Organization on Disability, Americans with disabilities who used some form of assistive technology were asked how their lives would be affected if they did not have the special equipment or device they were using. Respondents were clear that they rely on technology to ensure the basic foundations for a life of quality—more than a third indicated they would not be able to live independently or care for themselves at home; a quarter said they would not be able to get around their communities, and so forth.

Yet despite the promise of technology to support a better life, research continues to show that people with intellectual disability have limited access to such technology. With the emergence of electronic and information technologies, such as smartphones and tablet PCs, the digital divide becomes an even larger barrier to people living richer, fuller lives (Tanis et al., 2012). Technology development company AbleLink Technologies has designed and developed technology solutions for people with intellectual disability since the mid-1990s, and the impact of such technology is evident in the stories of people provided such supports (pseudonyms used):

Andy had never said, "I love you" to his mom. One day, he was sending e-mails in the dining room and his support person overheard him signing off from his e-mail by saying, into a recorder that would attach his recorded message and send it: "I love you, Mom." Within 24 hours, his mother called the support person in tears to express just how much that sentiment from him touched her. She continued to talk about how much his communication skills had improved over the short time since he had begun e-mailing with her. (e-mail from D. Davies, sent to the authors, June 16, 2012.)

Similarly, another person's support staff person related:

When we started using the AbleLink Endeavor tablet [a cognitively accessible desktop application for tablet PCs], we thought Heidi would never touch it. But AbleLink had pre-loaded Heidi's desktop with Rod Stewart videos (her favorite). She is enamored with the tablet and uses it more than anyone else in the house. Recently Heidi and her team began to explore how we could help her fulfill her dream of living in an apartment program. When I asked Heidi what I thought she would need to be successful in an apartment program, she waved the AbleLink tablet around and said, "this!" The wonderful news is that Heidi will be moving into an apartment that is equipped with the Endeavor technology in May. She is beyond overjoyed, and her direct support team is confident she will be successful and happy in her new home. (e-mail from D. Davies, sent to the authors, June 16, 2012)

REAL JOBS FOR REAL PAY

Like education, the landscape for employment for people with intellectual disability has both changed dramatically in the past decades and remained frustratingly the same. The 1950s and 1960s saw the rapid growth of sheltered workshops across the country, and placement in a sheltered workshop was felt by most people of the time to be the most logical and desirable outcome for people with intellectual disability. Indeed, it was surprising that people with intellectual disability were seen as being able to work at all. The idea that people would progress from the sheltered workshop to meaningful employment in their communities never really came to fruition. In the mid-1980s, model demonstration projects examining a new "place-and-train" model of employment (as opposed to the pretraining and placement model exemplified by sheltered workshops) developed the concepts that undergird supported employment (Kiernan, 2000). There are a myriad of examples of people with intellectual disability working, alongside their nondisabled peers, in community-based competitive jobs. Wehman (2011) related one such story recently:

> Nicki is a 21-year-old student with moderate intellectual disabilities who lives with her family. She has limited expressive language and communicates primarily through her body language and willingness to participate in activities. Nicki participated in a community-based vocational education program and then received supported employment services to assist her with gaining and maintaining a job. As a result, she has worked part-time at a small college dining center as a food preparation assistant for more than 1 year while still in school. Her job duties include making salads and preparing potatoes for baking. She also assists her co-workers with cleaning the work station by taking dirty pans to the sink area. Notably, her job was created by negotiating specific duties from a food preparation worker's job description. Nicki works approximately 25 hours a week and every other Saturday as part of her school curriculum and earns $8.25 per hour. Transportation is provided to and from work by the school during the week and by her parents on the weekends. Nicki is supported at work by her co-workers, managers, assistive technology (AT), and her job coach. (p. 145)

At the same time that the practices making supported employment possible were being developed and implemented, the U.S. Department of Education, Office of Special Education Programs began focusing on the importance of preparing students with disabilities for the transition from school to work, and eventually to independent living, postsecondary education, and other desired adult outcomes, resulting eventually in the inclusion (in the 1992 amendments to IDEA) of a set of mandates with regard to transition services provision. Supported employment models matured and expanded and innovative models such as self-employment and customized employment developed even further ways that people with intellectual disability could work in real jobs, for real pay.

Yet in the same issue of the *Journal of Vocational Rehabilitation,* in which Wehman relates Nicki's story, Rogan and Mank (2011) point out that employment rates for people with disabilities, in general, have not grown over the past several decades, that the growth trend of supported employment has actually declined in the past decade, and that there is an upswing in the growth of sheltered workshops and segregated day programs.

INTELLECTUAL DISABILITY IN THE 21ST CENTURY

Gunnar Dybwad had as much impact on the field of intellectual disability in the latter half of the 20th century as almost anyone. An early executive director of the National Association for Retarded Children, he was central to persuading leaders of the Pennsylvania chapter to sue the state, and he played a meaningful role in Supreme Court decisions affecting access to schools and to community for people with intellectual disability. Dybwad passed away in 2001 at the age of 92, and his last published work, written with the support of our colleague, Hank Bersani, was the final chapter in a book celebrating The Arc's 50th anniversary. Titled "Mental Retardation in the 21st Century," it seems apropos to reprint Dybwad's (2000) final written words as the penultimate observation on intellectual disability in this book.

> I would like to present some thoughts from the viewpoint of an 89-year-old with 64 years of experience in the fields of human services and disability. Thus, I have a vivid memory of conditions that to most readers will only be historical facts that they have read. I saw firsthand the dismal conditions in the overcrowded institutions that originated in good intentions, to give asylum and protection, and quickly became warehouses to offer society protection from the so-called "mental defectives." I saw in the late 1930s overcrowding with all its dire consequences. In Letchworth Village, considered to be one of the 'better' New York State institutions at that time, I found a dormitory with 100 beds and 125 children in those beds. Then came World War II with the consequent manpower problems and the postwar period with its radical economic and social changes.
>
> I also vividly remember something else that rose out of the postwar period. Parents of children with intellectual limitations spontaneously came together and organized locally throughout the country, what became, in 1950, the National Association for Retarded Children (NARC). The strong voice of this new group was soon heard in Congress and statehouses across the nation, effectively challenging the prevailing perceptions of 'mental deficiency,' and demanding radical changes to meet the needs of the children, especially in education.
>
> These efforts of the parent movement were eminently successful. Empowered by the disclosure that President Kennedy's family had a member with mental retardation, parents grew stronger in their advocacy for their family members.
>
> Today, advocacy organizations across the globe advocate for and with people with intellectual impairments in uniform agreement of the importance of community inclusion for all. Today, there are revisionist historians who seek to minimize the horror of the Nazi Holocaust, or even to deny its existence. We are confronted with our own holocaust in the area of intellectual disability. Parent associations, like The Arc, were

successful in developing special education opportunities and, to a lesser extent, community services for adults with intellectual impairments.

However, and I think significantly, the parents' success in developing community services such as in sheltered workshops, recreation, and home care did not extend to the institutional field. To the contrary, during the very years of progress in the community, the large state institutions deteriorated to a truly unbelievable level of overcrowding, unsanitary conditions, and physical and sexual abuse (not infrequently committed by the staff, newly hired without any relevant training). This not only resembled concentration camp conditions, but there was a striking similarity to a much discussed aspect of the Holocaust, although every one of these state institutions had a considerable medical, psychological, educational, and social work staff who could not help but see, hear, and indeed smell what went on. Although practically everyone belonged to a professional organization with strong ethical standards, with one or two exceptions, no one felt impelled to protest that blatant abuse either directly or through a professional organization. These were sad days—days we must not forget. It was not until a group of lawyers found parents willing to act as plaintiffs in class action suits that the public became aware of what had been going on for years. Detailed accounts of these atrocities and inhumane conditions were preserved in literally thousands of pages of sworn testimony by expert witnesses from their often extensive visits to the facilities, but conveniently filed away in steel cabinets.

At the 1996 Congress of the International Association for the Scientific Study of Intellectual Disabilities, I suggested in a plenary session that the time had come for professionals to confess as well as profess, to acknowledge their responsibility for the past horrors of institutional management, and their responsibility toward those who have been (and too often still are) confined to those institutions. Acknowledgement of that must be a part of our planning for the 21st century.

The actual Holocaust story is kept alive because of a strong belief that this is necessary to prevent a repetition in years to come. Likewise, the institutional horrors must be kept alive by eyewitnesses, as it is in Burton Blatt's trailblazing *Christmas in Purgatory*, which he published at great risk to his professional reputation. It must not be forgotten, it cannot be erased from our professional history.

A SELF-MADE MAN

It was the best of times, it was the worst of times, it was the age of wisdom, it was the age of foolishness, it was the epoch of belief, it was the epoch of incredulity, it was the season of Light, it was the season of Darkness, it was the spring of hope, it was the winter of despair, we had everything before us, we had nothing before us, we were all going direct to Heaven, we were all going direct the other way—in short, the period was so far like the present period, that some of its noisiest authorities insisted on its being received, for good or for evil, in the superlative degree of comparison only. (Dickens, 1859, p. 1)

Dickens could have been writing about the lives of people with intellectual disability in 2012. Great promise and ongoing disappointment; the spring of hope, the winter of despair. As of August 2012, as this final chapter was being written, the state of Texas executed Marvin Wilson, a man widely agreed to have intellectual disability, despite vociferous protestations from advocacy organizations. On the same day, papers reported that Amelia Rivera, who earlier in the year had been denied a kidney transplant because of her intellectual disability, underwent a successful transplant. Later that week, Banner Health, one of the nation's largest nonprofit healthcare systems in the United States, agreed to pay $255,000 in penalties for firing a man with intellectual disability without providing adequate job accommodations. Two days later, the state of California joined as the latest state to eliminate the term *mental retardation* from its state statutes.

Gunnar Dybwad's assertion that the atrocities of the past must not be forgotten form, in large measure, the intent of this text. In making that case, the final word must, rightfully, go to someone who lived within the systems that were created for people with intellectual disability and who, despite such oppressive and repressive conditions, triumphed. There are many people who could, and maybe should, have that final word. Turning back, however, to Raymond Gagne

Figure 9.5. Ray Gagne. (Image from author's personal collection.)

(see Figure 9.5), whose autobiography, titled *A Self-Made Man,* recounted the experiences of living with the label of intellectual disability during the last half of the 20th century. As was recounted in Chapter 7, Ray Gagne became a leader in the self-advocacy movement, founding a self-advocacy organization in Massachusetts, serving on the board of directors for The Arc of the United States, chairing that association's national self-advocacy committee and even lecturing on self-advocacy before a room full of distinguished professionals at Harvard University.

Ray Gagne closed his autobiographical account with the following paragraph:

> I wrote this story to let people know what it was like growing up in an institution from the 1950s through the 1970s. The total lack of power in making decisions about my life made me angry, and I was treated as an outcast. The staff's abuse, neglect, and insensitivity kept me from being educated and learning the other basic skills that many children learn from caring adults. When I got into the real world, I wasn't sure what my role was. Nobody ever talked to me or taught me how to be successful. I learned to survive mostly on my own and with the help of a few good people.
>
> I feel that what happened to me should never happen again. (Gagne, 1994, p. 334)

CONCLUSION

The modern era has brought about dramatic changes in the lives of people with intellectual disability. Not only has the way people are referred to changed, but also the way that intellectual disability is understood. It is now widely agreed that the places in which people with intellectual and developmental disabilities should live, learn, work, and play are the same places accessed by the rest of the public. There is much yet to be done, certainly, but there is every reason to believe that this vision of inclusion for people with intellectual disability is not just a wish, but is attainable if we commit ourselves to doing so.

NOTES

1. There is more than a little irony here, of course. The official, traditional term for residents leaving institutions such as Fairview without permission (i.e., running away) was *elopement*.

2. Pseudonyms are used to protect respondents' privacy.

3. See http://www.youtube.com/watch?v=DUn6luZQaXE.

REFERENCES

Agosta, J., Keating, T., Deane, K., Ashbaugh, J., & Bradley, V. (1990). *Oregon long range plan for developmental disability services: Commitment to community.* Salem: Oregon Mental Health and Developmental Disability Services Division.

Ayres, L.P. (1909). *Laggards in our schools: A study of retardation and elimination in city school systems.* New York: New York Charities Publication Committee.

Blumberg, R., Hutchins, P., Daley, R., & Petroff, J.G. (2012). Getting to work: How a college program promotes career development and self-determination. *Research to Practice in Self-Determination, 2,* 17–19.

Brown v. Board of Educ., 347 U.S. 483 (1954).

Dickens, C. (1859). *A tale of two cities.* New York, NY: Dover Publications.

Dybwad, G. (1996). Setting the stage historically. In G. Dybwad & H. Bersani Jr. (Eds.), *New voices: Self-advocacy by people with disabilities* (pp. 1–17). Cambridge, MA: Brookline Books.

Dybwad, G. (2000). Mental retardation in the 21st century. In M.L. Wehmeyer & J. Patton (Eds.), *Mental retardation in the 21st century* (pp. 431–433). Austin, TX: PRO-ED.

Edwards, J. (1982). *We are people first: Our handicaps are secondary.* Portland, OR: Ednick.

Ferguson, P.M., Ferguson, D.L., & Brodsky, M.N. (2008). *"Away from the public gaze": A history of the Fairview Training Center and the institutionalization of people with developmental disabilities in Oregon, 1908–2000.* Monmouth: Teaching Research Institute, Western Oregon University.

Gagne, R. (1994). A self-made man. In V.J. Bradley, J.W. Ashbaugh, & B.C. Blaney (Eds.), *Creating individual supports for people with developmental disabilities* (pp. 327–334). Baltimore, MD: Paul H. Brookes Publishing, Co.

Goffman, I. (1961). *Asylums.* New York, NY: Doubleday.

Guess, D. (2000). Serving persons with severe and profound disabilities: A work in progress. In M. Wehmeyer & J. Patton (Eds.), *Mental retardation in the 21st century.* Austin, TX: PRO-ED.

Gunther, D., & Diekema, D. (2006). Attenuating growth in children with profound developmental delay: A new approach to an old dilemma. *Archives of Pediatric and Adolescent Medicine, 160,* 1013–1017.

Gustafson, A. (2000, February 25). Last two residents leave sprawling facility. *Salem Stateman Journal,* p. 1A.

Gustafson, A. (2000, March 13). Brothers go without therapy. *Salem Statesman Journal,* p. 6A.

Hunsberger, S. (2000, February 18). Fairview resident moves on. *Salem Statesman Journal,* p. 1A.

Jackson, L., Ryndak, D., & Wehmeyer, M. (2010). The dynamic relationship between context, curriculum, and student learning: A case for inclusive education as a research-based practice. *Research and Practice in Severe Disabilities, 34*(1), 175–195.

Kiernan, W.E. (2000). Where we are now: Perspectives on employment of persons with mental retardation. In M.L. Wehmeyer & J. Patton (Eds.), *Mental retardation in the 21st century* (pp. 151–164). Austin, TX: PRO-ED.

Lakin, K.C., Larson, S.A., Salmi, P., & Webster, A. (2010). *Residential services for persons with developmental disabilities: Statues and trends through 2009.* Minneapolis: University of Minnesota, Research and Training Center on Community Living, Institute on Community Integration.

Nirje, B. (1969). The normalization principle and its human management implications. In R.B. Kugel & W. Wolfensberger (Eds.), *Changing patterns in residential services for the mentally retarded* (pp. 179–195). Washington, DC: President's Committee on Mental Retardation.

Research and Training Center on Community Living. (2005). Status of institutional closure efforts in 2005. *Research Policy Brief, 16*(1), 1–8.

Rogan, P., & Mank, D. (2011). Looking back, moving ahead: A commentary on supported employment. *Journal of Vocational Rehabilitation, 35,* 185–187.

Ryndak, D.L., & Alper, S. (1996). *Curriculum content for students with moderate and severe disabilities in inclusive settings.* Boston, MA: Allyn and Bacon.

Shapiro, J.P. (1993). *No pity: People with disabilities forging a new civil rights movement.* New York, NY: Times Books.

Shipley, S. (2000, March 16). Career change. *Salem Statesman Journal,* p. 6A.

Schalock, R., Borthwick-Duffy, S., Bradley, V., Buntinx, W., Coulter, D., Craig, E., . . . Yeager, M. (2010). *Intellectual disability: Definition, classification, and systems of support* (11th ed.). Washington, DC: American Association on Intellectual and Developmental Disabilities.

Schoultz, B., & Ward, N. (1996). Self-advocates becoming empowered: The birth of a national organization in the U.S. In G. Dybwad & H. Bersani Jr. (Eds.), *New voices: Self-advocacy by people with disabilities* (pp. 216–235). Cambridge, MA: Brookline Books.

Schwier, K.M. (1994). *Couples with intellectual disabilities talk about living and loving.* Rockville, MD: Woodbine House.

Sobsey, D., & Doe, T. (1991). Patterns of sexual abuse and assault. *Sexuality and Disability, 9*(3), 243–259.

Tanis, E.S., Palmer, S., Wehmeyer, M.L., Davies, D., Stock, S., Lobb, K., . . . Bishop, B. (2012). Self-report computer-based survey of technology use by people with intellectual and developmental disabilities. *Intellectual and Developmental Disabilities, 50*(1), 53–68.

Turnbull, A.P., Turnbull, H.R., Wehmeyer, M.L., & Shogren, K.A. (2013). *Exceptional lives: Special education in today's society* (7th ed.). Columbus, OH: Merrill/Prentice-Hall.

Turnbull, H.R., & Turnbull, A.P. (2000). Newly in pursuit of an old philosophy: Rebalancing liberty, equality, and community. In M.L. Wehmeyer & J. Patton (Eds.), *Mental retardation in the 21st century* (pp. 413–430). Austin, TX: PRO-ED.

Turnbull, R., Wehmeyer, M., Turnbull, A., & Stowe, M. (2006). Growth attenuation and due process: A response to Gunther and Diekema. *Research and Practice for Persons with Severe Disabilities, 31*(4), 348–351.

Walz, T. (1998). *The unlikely celebrity: Bill Sackter's triumph over disability.* Carbondale, IL: Southern Illinois University Press.

Ward, N., & Schoultz, B. (1996). People first of Nebraska. In G. Dybwad & H. Bersani Jr. (Eds.), *New voices: Self-advocacy by people with disabilities* (pp. 203–215). Cambridge, MA: Brookline Books.

Wehman, P.H. (2011). Employment for persons with disabilities: Where are we now and where do we need to go? *Journal of Vocational Rehabilitation, 35,* 145–151.

Wehmeyer, M.L. (2011). Assessment and intervention in self-determination. In T.E. Scruggs & M.A. Mastropieri (Eds.), *Assessment and Intervention: Advances in learning and behavioral disabilities* (Vol. 24, pp. 213–249). London, United Kingdom: Emerald Publishing.

Wehmeyer, M.L., & Berkobien, R. (1996). The legacy of self-advocacy: People with cognitive disabilities as leaders in their community. In G. Dybwad & H. Bersani Jr. (Eds.), *New voices: Self-advocacy by people with disabilities* (pp. 245–257). Cambridge, MA: Brookline Books.

Wehmeyer, M.L., Bersani, H., & Gagne, R. (2000). Riding the third wave: Self-determination and self-advocacy in the 21st century. In M.L. Wehmeyer & J.R. Patton (Eds.), *Mental retardation in the 21st century* (pp. 315–333). Austin, TX: PRO-ED.

Weintraub, F.J., Abeson, A., Ballard, J., & LaVor, M.L. (1976). *Public policy and the education of exceptional children.* Reston, VA: Council for Exceptional Children.

White House. (2010). *Statement by the President on the 35th anniversary of the Individuals with Disabilities Education Act.* Washington DC: Government Printing Office.

Index